Personal Counseling Office
Penn State Erie, The Behrend College
4701 College Drive
Erie, PA 16563

Helping
Clients
Forgive

Helping Clients Forgive

An Empirical Guide for Resolving Anger and Restoring Hope

Robert D. Enright and
Richard P. Fitzgibbons

American Psychological Association
Washington, DC

Fifth Printing April 2006
Sixth Printing March 2007
Seventh Printing September 2008
Eighth Printing March 2010
Ninth Printing November 2011

Published by
American Psychological Association
750 First Street, NE
Washington, DC 20002

Copies may be ordered from
APA Order Department
P.O. Box 92984
Washington, DC 20090-2984

In the U.K., Europe, Africa, and the Middle East, copies may be ordered from
American Psychological Association
3 Henrietta Street
Covent Garden, London
WC2E 8LU England

Typeset in Goudy by World Composition Services, Inc., Sterling, VA

Printer: United Book Press, Inc., Baltimore, MD
Cover Designer: Naylor Design, Washington, DC
Technical/Production Editor: Jennifer Powers

The opinions and statements published are the responsibility of the authors, and such opinions and statements do not necessarily represent the policies of the APA.

Library of Congress Cataloging-in-Publication Data

Enright, Robert D.
    Helping clients forgive : an empirical guide for resolving anger and restoring hope / Robert D. Enright, Richard P. Fitzgibbons.
       p. cm.
    Includes bibliographical references.
    ISBN 1-55798-689-4 (alk. paper)
    1. Forgiveness. 2. Psychotherapy. I. Fitzgibbons, Richard P. II. Title.

RC489.F67 .E57 2000
616.89′14—dc21

00-026160

British Library Cataloguing-in-Publication Data
A CIP record is available from the British Library.

Printed in the United States of America

To
our wives, Nancy and Adele;
our children, Shawn and Kevin; Lily Maria;
and our parents, Margaret and the late William; Margaret and John.

CONTENTS

PART III: PHILOSOPHICAL FOUNDATIONS AND
EMPIRICAL INVESTIGATIONS

EXHIBITS, TABLES, AND FIGURES

PREFACE

People who forgive someone who has hurt them can greatly improve their emotional health. Dr. Robert Enright's research has shown that people who forgive can decrease anger, anxiety, and depression and increase self-esteem and hopefulness following a forgiveness intervention. Dr. Richard Fitzgibbons's clinical observations of patients in treatment support these findings.

Our collaboration began with a telephone call in 1994. Dr. Enright called Dr. Fitzgibbons, inviting him to the National Conference on Forgiveness, the first held at an American university.

After a slight pause, Dr. Fitzgibbons queried, "A forgiveness conference? I thought that academics basically were ignoring forgiveness."

"Well, yes, we are and to a considerable degree, but here at the University of Wisconsin–Madison we've been scientifically studying the topic since 1985," replied Dr. Enright.

"I've been using forgiveness in therapy since 1976. I'd be delighted to attend, and I'm looking forward to meeting you."

At that conference in 1995, clinicians and academics in areas as diverse as social work, psychology, psychiatry, philosophy, sociology, law, and criminal justice spent 3 days together discussing and debating the fine points of forgiveness. We all saw the need to extend and deepen our dialogue, given the paucity of published works on the topic. It was there that the seeds of this book were sown. Dr. Fitzgibbons and Dr. Enright agreed to begin gathering data toward the eventual publication of a book for clinicians.

There were several reasons why we started with a book on psychotherapy rather than on another theme that emerged from the conference. First, forgiveness, as it seemed to us, has a vital role to play in all of the helping professions. If forgiveness works by diminishing the resentment and anger associated with anxiety, depressive, and other diagnosable emotional disorders, then forgiveness may be important in people's emotional healing from events and relationships that cause considerable suffering even if these individuals do not have a psychiatric disorder per se.

Second, this idea linking forgiveness to healthy emotional regulation was, at the time, more of a hypothesis or speculation than a statement with support from both scientific observation and published case studies. We wanted to see for ourselves whether this conjecture had merit. We decided to approach the idea in two ways, through scientific test and detailed clinical observation. Over the years since that conference, we have collected the data and the case studies that support the idea. We thought it necessary, then, to share these observations with other helping professionals.

Third, we surmised that if our hypothesis were correct and if we could amass the necessary data and observations, then forgiveness might become a major player in the helping professions. For that to happen, we must enter into dialogue and debate with many in the helping professions to refine and strengthen the ideas that connect forgiveness with emotional health. This book, in part, was written to begin that dialogue. We do not claim to have the answers yet. We certainly have come a long way since that initial telephone call. It is now time to share what we know with others and to be open to refinement, correction, and the building of new knowledge about forgiveness. Clients and patients will be the beneficiaries.

As readers will learn, we use a "scientist–practitioner" approach throughout the book. The scientist and academic will need a deep, rigorous explication of the construct of forgiveness and thorough details on our scientific methods. We assume that the scientist's understanding will be enhanced by learning the practical clinical material. The practitioner will need detailed case studies and examples to successfully apply within clinical practice the principles outlined here. We assume that the clinician will develop a more complete understanding from the scientific presentations in the book. We will have more to say about this dual scientific and clinical approach in the "Plan of the Book" section in the Introduction.

We wish to thank a host of people who have contributed to this volume. We are indebted to the Human Development Study Group at the University of Wisconsin–Madison. These graduate students, professors, and interested people in the community formed a think tank in 1985 that has been at the creative center of the ideas and models described here. We thank Margaret and Nancy Enright and Mary Jane Tadeo for their editorial assistance. We are indebted to the staff at Comprehensive Counseling Services outside Philadelphia, especially Carolyn DeFer, Vinetta Madafarri, and Dr. Fitzgibbons's psychologist associate Peter Rudegair. We are grateful to the John Templeton Foundation for a grant supporting this work.

We are indebted to Margaret Schlegel and Mary Lynn Skutley at APA Books. Margaret provided much insight and impressively detailed notes to help us revise this book. Mary Lynn saw the importance of this work years before the academic community took interest. We are indebted to Mary Lynn for her vision. Dr. Paul Coleman, Dr. Kevin Murrell, and an anonymous reviewer provided encouraging, challenging feedback for which we are grateful. Peggy McMahon provided a literary eye to our efforts. To Barb Lienau, who typed the various drafts, we say thanks. We are particularly indebted to our spouses, Nancy Enright and Adele Fitzgibbons, for providing love, wisdom, insight, patience, and support throughout the entire project.

Helping Clients Forgive

INTRODUCTION: WHY LEARN ABOUT FORGIVENESS AND FORGIVENESS THERAPY?

Imagine therapist Paul Coleman's surprise. He had just completed 40 sessions with a warring couple, who approached him with the proposition of starting over. Their interest in wiping the slate clean and beginning therapy again was based on a small comment that Dr. Coleman made at the 40th session. "You should try to forgive one another" was his advice. The husband and wife let him know that this one word, *forgiveness*, spoken almost without thought at a session's end, made all the difference in their marriage. In thinking back over the session, the therapist did not even remember making that remark. In fact, his usual ideas about forgiveness fell into such categories as "move on with your lives" or "let go of the resentment." Rarely did he even use the word *forgiveness*. Yet, that day Dr. Coleman subconsciously used it, transforming the couple's lives and, self-admittedly, rejuvenating his clinical practice (Coleman, 1998).

Powerful stuff, this forgiveness concept is. Those working to forgive, with therapists who have taken the time to understand its nuances, seem to be helped substantially. Case studies and therapist observations both suggest that forgiveness of deep offenses from other people can be psychologically healing in many ways (see, e.g., Bristol & McGinnis, 1982; Fitzgibbons, 1986; Hootman & Perkins, 1982; Hope, 1987; Weil & Winter, 1994; Wolter, 1989). If clients see the benefit of forgiving, as Dr. Coleman's couple did, and if clients begin to hear more about this topic, then undoubtedly therapists will be asked, with increasing frequency, to help them work with forgiveness in therapy.

There is at present no book, based on empirical research, describing the process of forgiveness that will help therapists assist their clients to forgive. This book is intended to fill that void.

Of course, forgiveness will not solve all client problems. Forgiveness has a specific task: to help people overcome resentment, bitterness, and even hatred toward people who have treated them unfairly and at times cruelly. In other words, forgiveness is a specialist in quelling that kind of anger that debilitates the injured or wounded individual. Excessive anger is not always noted by therapists as a concomitant to the common psychiatric disorders. Our research work at the University of Wisconsin–Madison and our clinical work in Philadelphia have accumulated substantial evidence on the effectiveness of forgiveness as a tool for resolving excessive anger in a variety of contexts and disorders. Our work has been publicized on television, on radio broadcasts in the United States and Canada, in national magazines and professional journals, and at conferences and workshops. People are learning more about this topic and are requesting it in therapy. Therefore, it is essential that professionals have access to research on the effectiveness of forgiveness, a clear outline of how to use forgiveness in a therapeutic setting, what forgiveness can and cannot accomplish, suggested areas in which the use of forgiveness may be effective, and how forgiveness can be used to prevent or reduce excessive anger, thereby assisting in the treatment of many disorders in children, teenagers, and adults.

This book is directed to psychologists, psychiatrists, social workers, health care workers, counselors, hospice team members, employee assistance personnel, members of the clergy, marriage and family counselors, educators, and those in the criminal justice system—indeed to anyone who works with individuals who may be suffering from excessive anger and thus desire to explore new ways to resolve their resentment. Without the kind of careful explanation of forgiveness that we intend to provide here, a strong possibility is that misunderstanding and misuses may arise that could discredit a very promising therapeutic approach. By laying out in a formal fashion the empirical evidence, the philosophical underpinnings, and the methods for using forgiveness for specific clinical problems, this book will serve as a guide for all of those who wish to use, study, or research forgiveness with clients.

We understand that many of the clinicians reading this book have full caseloads, without a great deal of time to read all that they might wish. We urge clinicians to take the time to study forgiveness and forgiveness therapy for four reasons. First, forgiveness has been shown to be effective in reducing clients' anger, anxiety, and depression while increasing their sense of hope and self-esteem. Details of these findings will be presented in chapter 6. Second, many clients come to therapy because they have experienced considerable injustice from others, sometimes over years. Forgiveness is one of the direct routes to dealing with the angers born out of injustice in a way that is constructive and healing. Third, the principles of forgiveness therapy are not particularly difficult to master. Yes, clinicians will be challenged to understand forgiveness from an interdisciplinary perspective, including philosophy, psychology, and psychiatry, but none of the concepts are so foreign that one will be left scratching his or her head in frustration. People have been thinking and talking about forgiveness for thousands of years. This is no new concept with so many buzzwords that one must learn a new language. Fourth, clients and patients themselves, as we shall see in the opening example in chapter 1, are now asking for help in forgiving. A truly ethical approach is to aid the client in ways that he or she wants and needs. Knowing forgiveness therapy well is a sign of respect for those whom we serve.

We can almost hear some clinicians saying, "But I was schooled in certain models of therapy, not in forgiveness therapy. Will I have to change my theoretical orientation for this?" Our answer is, no, the vast majority will not have to alter their orientation, because forgiveness therapy can take place within a wide variety of orientations. For example, psychodynamically oriented therapists will still trace a client's presenting problem to past events. They still will focus on clients' insight gained about how they and others were treated in these past encounters. Therapists will be in the familiar territory of examining the client's emotions of shame, anger, and disappointment with people, usually in the family of origin, through the analysis of transference. They will add the active approach of forgiveness to this familiar process.

Cognitive–behavioral therapists still will examine and try to alter current reinforcers, set up a series of tasks that disrupt maladaptive cognitions or behaviors, and work on changing cognitive schema. In fact, forgiveness therapy offers explicit approaches for altering thoughts about the past events and people who have been unfair to the client. Rather than changing what they do, therapists will be given added material, shown to be scientifically effective, to help the person deal with hurts or traumatic experiences.

Family and systems therapists will continue to examine communication patterns that lead to anger and frustrations in the home, office, or other environments in which people's interactions affect the well-being of others. Not only will therapists be asking the participants for insight, but also will have active, helpful approaches for diminishing the anger that can grow into disrespect, hatred, fantasies of revenge, and even violence.

Every clinician has worked with clients who seem "stuck" in anger or who have anger management problems. Sometimes the best approaches just do not go far enough to reduce and even eliminate that anger and so restore emotional and relational well-being. Forgiveness offers a way to augment existing approaches, especially with those clients or patients mired in anger. Those who are skeptical of this, when all else fails, may want to try forgiveness therapy. After a while, forgiveness therapy may be at the top of the list as a new client, couple, or family comes for help.

WHAT IS FORGIVENESS THERAPY?

Forgiveness therapy is a way for both client and therapist to examine those situations in which the client was or is treated unfairly for the express purpose of helping the person to understand the offender, to learn to slowly let go of anger with this person and, over time, to make a moral response of goodness toward the offender or offenders. This process may require many months or even years.

Forgiveness therapy does not ignore the client and his or her needs. On the contrary, the paradox is that as the client or patient takes the light of scrutiny off of self and places it in a moral way on the offenders in his or her life, it is the client who is healed. As readers will see, our emphasis on a "moral" response is vital for understanding forgiveness therapy. There is nothing new about forgiveness therapy if it reduces simply to "moving on" or "adjusting." There is much new about it when the therapist challenges the client or patient to "have compassion" and "do no harm" regarding a person with whom the client is angry and frustrated.

Forgiveness therapy provides the therapist with an innovative and practical way to help clients learn to resolve their anger without hurting others or themselves. Through the process of working at forgiving and compassionately understanding offenders, clients will become freed from the negative or toxic effects of their own justifiable anger. The mental health field to date has relied primarily on the expression of anger as a method of dealing with this powerful emotion or on the use of medication. We are providing a psychotherapeutic approach to help the children, teenagers, and adults honestly face their anger and let go of it in a healthy and effective manner.

Many clients continue in the denial of their anger because they fear that if this powerful emotion emerges into consciousness they will not be able to control it. Others rely excessively on the expression of anger for coping with this emotion and can suffer numerous negative consequences from doing so. Forgiveness provides a new and effective way to diminish anger other than through expression, but it does not preclude the appropriate expression of anger.

Please bear with us on these points; they will become clear as one reads further in this book.

FORGIVENESS AS PROCESS

Because forgiveness sometimes unfolds slowly, forgiveness therapy cannot be rushed. People need time to uncover anger, especially that anger that has dwelt with the person for years. Even a decision to forgive takes time, because the client must first understand exactly what forgiveness is and willingly choose it as an option. The work of forgiveness in therapy involves seeing the offender in new ways and allowing feelings of empathy to emerge. Even allowing for a period of suffering on the client's part is an aspect of forgiveness therapy, as will be shown. As the person grows, he or she will have questions about the meaning of the suffering that he or she endured. The person will need time to incorporate the issue of forgiveness into a newly emerging identity. Forgiveness is about transformation of people more than it is about certain therapeutic techniques.

The therapist will have to be aware of the client's or patient's religious beliefs because forgiveness is embedded in many religious traditions, including Jewish, Christian, Islamic, Buddhist, and Hindu. People take what the philosopher Yandell (1998) called the *cosmic perspective*, in which the client sees an offender in a broad, spiritual context. Clients who begin to forgive may ask such questions as: "Is the person loved by God?" "Where will that person go when he or she dies?" "Is the person capable of being transformed and showing genuine goodness?" The therapist's task, it seems to us, is to be open to the client's exploration of the situation in light of his or her belief system. A therapist, of course, will avoid imposing his or her own views here. Viktor Frankl (1959), a well-respected therapist in his own right, urged therapists not to ignore this dimension of their clients. In fact, a Gallup poll found that more than 80% of Americans believe that they cannot forgive "deeply from the heart without God's help" (Poloma & Gallup, 1991, p. 91). These are challenging ideas, but ones that can be sensitively and competently addressed with a respectful attitude toward the client.

LEARNING ABOUT FORGIVENESS THERAPY

We are confident that motivated readers will be able to efficiently and effectively learn how to do forgiveness therapy well. The process model that we present is deliberately not tied to any particular tradition; this, to us, is a major strength. The model is straightforward in the basic ways to use it, and it does have empirical and clinical support backing it. We do have aspects of the psychodynamic and the cognitive and social cognitive as part of the model, but it can be adapted to any approach with a little thought, experimentation, and creativity. Because forgiveness therapy and our model are relatively new, therapists can enter into the exciting process of innovation and discovery along with us.

PLAN OF THE BOOK

This book is for a variety of people: It is for clinicians working directly with clients and patients; it is for academics who are teaching and learning about the clinical process; it is for scientists who wish to study, validate, and extend what we present here. We are well aware that the needs of these three somewhat diverse groups are not the same. Clinicians sometimes want to "cut to the chase," reading the practical material first. Academics, on the other hand, often want to step back and examine the assumptions, constructs, and model. Scientists want precise information so that replication and extension are possible. We provide information for all of the above professionals.

We have divided the book into three parts. In Part 1, we provide the background necessary for understanding forgiveness therapy and the construct of forgiveness itself. We begin with a brief discussion of forgiveness therapy, then move deeper into what forgiveness is and is not. All of this is necessary if the reader is to understand the construct before applying it in practice, in the classroom, or in the laboratory. Chapter 4 concerns ways in which people develop in their understanding about forgiveness. We discuss the clinical implications of this developmental model. Chapter 5 in particular presents our process model used in forgiveness therapy and so should be carefully read by all. We point out in places in which certain information may be more for the academic than the clinician, especially where we go into considerable philosophical or scientific depth. Chapter 6, the scientific validation of our model, is one example. Certainly, all clinicians are welcome to come along on the philosophical and scientific ride, but if a reader is busy and seeks "gist," we will point out those sections that may be skimmed for now.

Part 2 of the book concerns helping therapists in both the identification and resolution of excessive anger in their clients through forgiveness therapy in depressive, anxiety, and substance abuse disorders; childhood and adolescent disorders; marital and family therapy; eating, personality, bipolar, and impulse disorders; and Tourette's syndrome. Excessive anger is more prevalent in these disorders than is currently recognized and regularly interferes with treatment. We review the scientific literature on anger in each disorder. Then we present case study descriptions demonstrating how unjust treatment leads to anger and how the psychotherapeutic uses of forgiveness can diminish this anger and related emotional symptoms. When a client forgives, not only does anger decrease, but so do other psychological symptoms such as depression and anxiety. Forgiveness appears to be effective in stabilizing the mood in a variety of disorders.

We are not claiming that forgiveness alone will solve all psychological problems. On the contrary, forgiveness can be part of an overall treatment plan in many cases. Yet, our concern is that the issues of anger, born out of unfairness, and its reduction through forgiveness are not being given sufficient attention in current clinical practice and most research. One research team concurs regarding the problem of anger: "Anger is a common but unrecognized problem among patients with psychiatric disorders" (Mammen, Shear, Greeno, Wheeler, & Hughes, 1997, p. 105; see also Snaith & Taylor, 1985). If our ideas have merit—that forgiveness can reduce and even resolve significant amounts of anger and related emotions in people manifesting a variety of diagnoses—then we will be providing clinicians with an important procedure to help clients and patients. Let us reiterate that our ideas are a beginning, not a definitive ending. The field of forgiveness therapy is in its early stage of development. We are open to feedback and change as we progress in our knowledge.

Part 3 goes into more depth on the philosophical foundations and empirical investigations of forgiveness for the academic reader and the clinician who seeks more information. We urge all to read chapter 15, because one can never have enough information on the construct of forgiveness itself, especially given that social scientists and practitioners have, until recently, discussed this topic so rarely. There are a number of skeptics now writing about forgiveness. Readers may wish to see what their arguments are against the practice of forgiveness in chapter 16. We end Part 3 with an examination of three empirical approaches to forgiveness: our social cognitive model, other researchers' interventions, and measures of forgiveness. As readers will see, not all forgiveness interventions work, nor do researchers agree on what constitutes effective forgiveness therapy. If you wish to screen clients for the degree of forgiveness that they exhibit toward another person, you will want to examine the measures described and critiqued in chapter 19. We end with a look to the future in the Epilogue.

One concept in particular that needs clarification is the words *client* and *patient*. In consulting many helping professionals, we realize that some use the term *client* whereas others use *patient*. Psychologists tend to favor the former word, and some psychiatrists favor the latter. Because we are writing this book for all helping professionals—psychologists, psychiatrists, and others—we will not be able to settle on only one word throughout the book. Our compromise is to sometimes use the word *client* and at other times the word *patient*. We ask tolerance from those professionals whenever we use the word that they do not prefer.

FORGIVENESS: THE MISSING LINK

Forgiveness may be one of those issues that is missing in the healing process of many clients. So often clients come to therapy because they have been treated unfairly by others. There is no professional protocol other than forgiveness therapy, to our knowledge, that offers a systematic approach for dealing with the injustice and working through the anger toward emotional health.

We have seen people who are so mired in anger that they did not have the energy to find a good job. Forgiveness freed them not only to seek employment but also to move out of the city in which they lived to take advantage of a better offer. We have witnessed people who have been estranged from family members for years find their way back to positive and meaningful relationships. We have seen people who labeled themselves as "crazy" realize that they have a legitimate complaint against an offending person. Forgiveness gave them the courage to face the injustice, recognize the emotional pain, let go of their debilitating resentment, and cast off their self-defeating label for themselves. The cases presented in the book will give readers myriad insights into what forgiveness can do.

As we delve into the world of forgiveness therapy, that new and exciting world with much potential, we hope that readers will share their creativity, experience, and wisdom with us. This is a work in progress, one that should grow and deepen for many decades. Let this be a team effort in which interested people begin to cooperate in the development of new knowledge in this area.

I

FORGIVENESS AS A KEY TO HEALING IN PSYCHOTHERAPY

1

FORGIVENESS IN PSYCHOTHERAPY: AN OVERVIEW

Every month, a group of counselors, clinical psychologists, social workers, and pastoral counselors meet for mutual support and to explore the latest trends in services to clients. At the most recent meeting, Dr. Loretto, a counselor in private practice, presented a particularly difficult case involving Sally, age 43, married 20 years, and the mother of four children. Her presenting problem was distress over conflict in her marriage. For the past 3 years she and her husband James have separated several times but have managed to reconcile each time. The reconciliations were tentative and unstable because trust was not yet established. Each was guarded, waiting for the next "blowup."

"Sally is stuck in anger," Dr. Loretto explained. "She is fuming, and I can't seem to move her toward greater trust or even acceptance about what has happened. James refuses to attend therapy sessions, which is further dividing them. I've tried relaxation techniques with her and other stress reduction procedures, but they help only so much. Any suggestions?"

"Perhaps she needs to reinterpret what has happened in the marriage. Is it possible to work with her on how the conflicts may be making her a stronger person?" Dr. Marks suggested.

"I suppose I could try it, but you know, each fight they have seems to erode the relationship and her confidence a little bit more."

"I wonder if you should have her simply confront her anger. Is she aware of how angry she is?" asked Rev. Botham, the pastoral counselor.

"No, I doubt she is aware of the depth of it," Dr. Loretto clarified, "but I could be opening a hornet's nest here. Insight is fine, but in this case, what do we do with the anger once it comes to the surface? She is fragile right now. Her recourse may be to make a permanent break with James. I'd hate to see such a break right now under these circumstances."

"You've been working with her for a while," said Rev. Botham, "so she probably is motivated to stay in the marriage."

Dr. Lawrence, the clinical psychologist, thumbed through a file folder looking for a particular journal article. "Here, perhaps we should read this." He put a copy of Freedman and Enright's (1996) article on the table. "This is a study of emotional compromise in incest survivors and how forgiveness therapy helped them recover. If Sally is deeply angry, forgiveness may help."

After they all had a chance to briefly skim the article, Dr. Lorreto remarked, "It would be a way of offering her something constructive to do with her anger once she admits to it, I suppose, but I am unfamiliar with the process." The group nodded their agreement. They were intrigued but unsure how to begin.

Dr. Loretto took the lead. He suggested that those who were interested make a commitment to study forgiveness for the next several months, bringing in case material that seemed particularly relevant for the group to discuss. Dr. Loretto met separately with several of the group members while he intensively studied the approach, reading key articles and discussing with other clinicians the role of forgiveness in their clinical practice.

Months later, Dr. Loretto reported, "Sally has been attempting to forgive James for a while now. I'm finding that forgiveness does make her more positive and hopeful about herself and her relationship with James. What I find most fascinating is how forgiveness has led her to explore other meaningful relationships in her life. As it is turning out, she and her father interacted very similarly to the way she and James relate. She is particularly angry with the way her dad would be demanding and uncommunicative with her. When James does this, it really pushes her button. As I have worked with Sally on forgiving her father, she has begun to be more objective about the marriage and more understanding of the patterns in her marriage. For example, she began to see that James didn't know how to handle all of her intensity coming his way, and so he became verbally aggressive. She dug in her heels, just like she did when she was younger with her father. Sally's forgiving her father has helped her be more mature and less reactive in her relationship with James. They still have a long way to go, but forgiveness is giving both she and James hope that was not there before."

APPLYING FORGIVENESS IN CLINICAL PRACTICE

Ten years ago, it was rare for clients to come to therapy deliberately seeking help with forgiveness issues. More recently, this is changing as people read about or see on television stories of forgiveness and reconciliation. Yet, the majority of clients still do not suggest forgiveness as an approach to anger reduction and healing. Therapists may have to take an active role here.

Forgiveness therapy may not be compatible with forms of therapy that claim to be silent about right and wrong, justice and mercy. In other words, forgiveness therapy may not be congruent with forms of therapy that claim to be value free. To practice forgiveness therapy, the therapist must be able to help the client determine that certain behaviors are wrong and unfair and to help the client determine that other behaviors, such as mercy, can under certain circumstances be right and good. Therapists must be comfortable dealing with these moral issues to practice this form of therapy.

Starting With Anger

A key feature of forgiveness therapy is understanding, confronting, and reducing or even eliminating anger. Anger is an internal state that includes both feelings and thoughts and an external state when expressed verbally and behaviorally. When angry, a person experiences physiological arousal and related emotional pain to unfair treatment or frustration. Thoughts include an awareness of the injustice or frustration (which is usually associated with feelings of sadness) and a plan to respond (which is often associated with a sense of pleasure). A person can be angry without awareness, but awareness of the problem that is causing the anger is essential to recovery. The kind of anger at the center of forgiveness therapy is characterized by seven points:

1. The anger is focused on another person or other people.
2. The anger is intense, at least in the short term.
3. The anger sometimes leads to a learned pattern of annoyance, irritation, and acrimony with others who may not be the source of the anger.
4. The anger can be extreme in its passivity or its overt hostility.
5. The anger is sometimes regressive, appropriate for those much younger.
6. The anger abides.
7. The anger is based on a real injustice and hurt, not some fanciful occurrence irrationally perceived.

Forgiveness is an antidote to this kind of anger in a number of clinical disorders. The significant prevalence of excessive anger in clinical disorders is presented in Part 2 from the published literature, especially from more recent research studies. The uncovering of this intense anger will surprise many therapists, just as the uncovering of anger amazes most patients in their therapy. In the seven clinical chapters of Part 2, our model for the use of forgiveness in psychotherapy is demonstrated in numerous clinical cases.

Our hope is that the uncovering of resentment and of thoughts for revenge will be given more attention by therapists in the treatment of all disorders. Initially, there may be some obstacles for the therapist in using this approach. Some may feel uncomfortable dealing with anger, or there may be a need for a client to deny anger in certain relationships. We hope to strengthen the confidence of therapists by demonstrating methods for the utilization of the powerful therapeutic approach of forgiveness for the resolution of conscious and unconscious anger that is influencing psychological symptoms and interfering with treatment and recovery. This is essential because patients have strong defenses against their anger, and the uncovering of their resentment can be challenging and demanding.

There is at present no consensus in the mental health field about the nature, role, and treatment of anger in depressive and other disorders. For example, the cognitive–behavioral school has rarely addressed the role of anger in the treatment of depression. Once anger has been uncovered, many therapists have tended to rely on the expression of anger as the primary method for dealing with this emotion, especially when associated with depressive disorders. Previously, psychoanalytical theory held that depression was anger turned inward and, therefore, patients were encouraged to express their anger as an important aspect of their treatment. As anger was expressed, depressive symptoms were believed to abate. However, many patients with severe depression felt too weak to proceed in this manner, whereas others failed to experience improvement in their depressive symptoms after giving vent to their anger from different life stages. In some people, the depression intensified, and others found the advice unhelpful.

We hope that, after reading this book, therapists who make decisions about treating anger in their patients will consider the use of forgiveness. We believe that such a decision will provide enormous benefit to clients and patients and will enhance the effectiveness and satisfaction of the therapist. So far, the research studies on forgiveness have demonstrated numerous benefits to patients, including a lessening of depressive symptoms, diminished anxiety, increased hope, improved self-esteem, and a decreased preoccupation with offenders. In addition, the benefits observed in almost 25 years of clinical use include improved stability of mood, less impulsive behaviors, and improved ability to control angry feelings with less overreaction or misdirection of anger. Other results include improved marital and family relationships and decreased obsessional thinking and compulsive behaviors.

The major focus in the clinical chapters will be on the work phase of forgiveness. Throughout this phase, various types of forgiveness exercises are used with patients to resolve anger from different life stages at both the conscious and unconscious level. These exercises are often written down for the patient so that they can work on them at home between sessions. Also, the patient may be encouraged to practice using forgiveness with an offender during the session. Each time forgiveness is used for a particular hurt or disappointment, it seems to remove certain amounts of anger. As the anger is resolved, patients experience relief; however, they are informed that therapy will take some time depending on the degree of pain and anger present. Often patients do not truly feel like forgiving but do so cognitively in the hope that it will help with the healing of their disorders.

In the treatment of depressive disorders, we demonstrate through the use of a variety of clinical cases how the removal of anger associated with sadness from various life stages by forgiveness facilitates the healing of depression. We also present how forgiveness assists in the treatment and recovery from a variety of other disorders. Numerous aspects involving the use of forgiveness in the treatment of the excessive anger in these disorders are described and areas of resistance and conflict are discussed, even those that involve the therapist. The complete mechanism by which forgiveness affects healing is not fully understood and warrants much further research. Nevertheless, it has been shown to be an effective psychotherapeutic approach for clients and patients.

Journaling and Forgiveness

Clinicians may find it useful to have clients keep a journal of their progress in forgiveness therapy. Because this form of therapy includes some teaching and learning, the person will have a chance to reflect on such issues as the meaning of forgiveness, who hurt him or her, the depth of anger and how this alters with time, his or her perceptions of the offender and how these change, as well as other aspects of the forgiveness process. We have begun using this in our scientific interventions. Although we have no data yet on the merits of journal keeping, initial indications are that these exercises help the client or patient stay focused and organized. It seems to be an excellent way to gauge progress and is of benefit when the person feels a need to revisit an issue months later. For example, a client may feel that he or she has already worked through anger at an offender, only to awaken early in the morning months later, deeply angry all over again. Reviewing what he or she wrote in the past can serve as a bridge to confronting this issue once again, perhaps aiding the person's moving through it more quickly and efficiently because of earlier insights. We have more to say about journal keeping in chapter 5.

THE PHASE MODEL OF FORGIVENESS

The phase model of forgiveness, our primary model for forgiveness therapy, has been scientifically tested and found to be quite helpful to clients. We discuss the scientific details in chapter 6. We describe four phases that form a developmental progression, with numerous individual differences within them. Not everyone goes through the processes in the same way or at the same speed. Within each phase there are a series of units most people seem to pass through, the details of which are presented in chapter 5. For now, we give a brief overview of the four phases: uncovering, decision, work, and deepening.

Uncovering Phase

This first phase describes the client's insight about whether the injustice and subsequent injury have compromised his or her life. This can be an emotionally painful time. Yet, if the client or patient concludes that he or she is suffering emotionally because of another's injustice, this can serve as a motivator to change. The emotional pain can be a motivator to think about and to try forgiveness.

Decision Phase

This is a time for the client to think about what forgiveness is and is not (not unlike the information we cover in chapters 2 and 3, but in less detail and without the technical language). A decision to forgive is a cognitive process, not one in which forgiveness is completed. The client must distinguish a commitment to forgive and all that is involved in the process. Otherwise, on committing to forgive, the client may conclude that most of the work is over. On the contrary, it is only beginning.

Work Phase

Here the person begins to understand that the offending person is more than the offense (or offenses) committed. The one forgiving may begin to experience some compassion toward the person. The focus shifts from self, in which most of the attention was centered in the Uncovering Phase, to the offending person. In this phase forgiveness therapy begins to look different from traditional modes of therapy.

The client starts with insight, with cognitive exercises because, as Fitzgibbons (1986) realized, it is often easier to understand an offender than it is to feel empathy or compassion for him or her. At this point the person thinks of forgiving the offender even though he or she may not feel like forgiving. Following cognitive decisions to forgive and insight, emotional transformations toward the offender may emerge. In our view, this tandem of thinking anew about an offender and then feeling anew is part of a developmental sequence. As the level of anger diminishes, people have more understanding and compassion and truly feel like forgiving. First cognition, then affect seems to be the typical sequence. The key is that the client is seeing the offender in new ways and may become ready to respond in new ways.

Deepening Phase

Insights about an offender often stimulate other thoughts: Have I needed others' forgiveness in the past? What was it like for me when I was forgiven? Is there any sense in all of the pain I endured? Am I motivated to interact in new ways with the offender and with people in general? The answers may lead to a recycling through the other phases, this time in a deeper, more insightful way. Figure 1.1 is a visual illustration of this cycling. Forgiving is a moving target. As people learn to forgive, they may choose to appropriate that learning toward even deeper forgiveness. Later, they may begin to generalize the learning to new situations and people.

Developmental Nature of the Phases

We consider the phases to be developmental in that the first, the Uncovering Phase, precedes the emergence of the others. The Decision

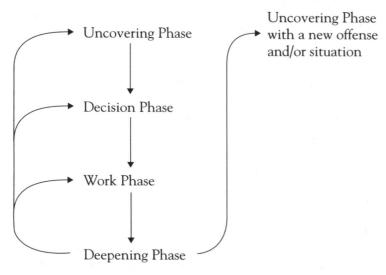

Figure 1.1. Phases of Forgiving

Phase usually precedes the Work and Deepening Phases. This is not a rigid, stepwise model in that people must start with Uncovering and proceed in order to the end. It is possible, for example, for someone to feel empathy for an offender (in the Work Phase) which sparks an interest in exploring the details of the injustice and subsequent emotional hurt in the Uncovering Phase.

Timelines

There are no set expectations about when a person will forgive. Of course, this is in conflict with some managed care programs that set a certain number of sessions for the therapy. We cannot pretend to have a solution to this problem. In fact, forgiveness therapy may add to this problem because in most cases, it does take time. Therapists must be ready to invest in the lives of those seeking forgiveness therapy.

A CASE EXAMPLE

Miriam, age 40 and married, entered therapy after experiencing a panic attack at work. When first seen, she was depressed and anxious. She attributed her emotional pain to the recent recollection of a troubling childhood and adolescent memories with her angry father. She reacted by talking to her father and by seeking support from her husband and mother. She had been sad and angry for several weeks prior to her panic attack as a result of her father's denial and her mother's lack of understanding.

Forgiveness was explained to Miriam as a therapeutic intervention that would help her to both understand and to assist in resolving her emotional pain with her father. She realized that her father had himself struggled with a difficult family background and that he had never deliberately wanted to hurt her. She made a decision to work at forgiving him with the hope that this would help in the healing of her anger, anxiety and depression. At this time she was told that forgiving her father would not interfere with her ability to be honest with him and that it would not lead to her being vulnerable to him.

At the end of the first session she was given a cognitive forgiveness exercise written on a note pad, which stated

1. Imagine yourself as a girl and teenager telling your father how he hurt you.
2. Then think "I want to try to understand and to forgive him."

She attempted this work of forgiveness during her therapy sessions and continued at home on a regular basis. She was asked to spend several minutes twice daily in this cognitive forgiveness activity. It was also recommended for use during those times when she was experiencing significant emotional pain. At the follow-up sessions the daily forgiveness exercises were reviewed, and any difficulties were discussed.

Other major conflicts became apparent during a session with her husband Luis, in which he expressed anger toward Miriam. He claimed that she had been misdirecting anger and mistrust meant for her father at him for many years. He related, "You try to portray me to others as an angry man, when the problem is really your father—not me."

Miriam admitted that at times she may have overreacted toward him. Yet, for the first time in therapy she related many examples of Luis's angry, controlling, and insensitive behaviors toward her. She stated, "Luis, you have a terrible temper and have hurt me much more than my father did." After the uncovering of this marital anger, Luis could hardly control his rage, screamed at her, threatened to end their marriage, and walked out of the session. Miriam, in tears, disclosed a long history of emotionally abusive behaviors by Luis.

The focus of therapy then shifted to the marital sadness, fear, and anger. Miriam recognized that Luis's angry behaviors were the result of his modeling after his own father, who had been verbally and physically abusive to his wife (Luis's mother), and reminded her of her father's actions when she was young. The use of forgiveness with Luis was explained to Miriam as a psychotherapeutic process that would help her with her marital conflicts and would help her become stronger with Luis. Because she had begun to experience relief from using forgiveness with her childhood hurts with her father, she was willing to begin the work of forgiveness with Luis also.

After the therapist took the history of Luis's family, Miriam was again given a written cognitive forgiveness prescription, which stated

1. Daily, think "I want to try to understand and to forgive Luis for the hurts of the past."
2. Consider thinking "Luis does not trust people because of how he was hurt as a boy due to the emotional absence of his mother and the anger of his father."

She used this forgiveness activity twice daily for several moments, but also needed to use it many times during the day when she felt highly anxious or depressed and when under stress from Luis's behavior. Miriam found it much easier to forgive her father for the hurts of her childhood than Luis for his ongoing insensitive treatment. She would often call her therapist between sessions for support in dealing with her newly recognized anger and with Luis's resentment and mistrust.

Miriam felt relief in using this forgiveness activity. She was able to continue to work for many months on this because she had always been sensitive to an emotionally wounded little boy inside Luis for whom she felt very sorry. His father's emotional abuse of Luis's mother had resulted in a disabling depressive illness in her life that limited her ability to give to Luis. His father also had hurt Luis because of his temper. The understanding of his childhood pain and its impact on his difficulty in trusting her helped Miriam continue the work of forgiveness. She became stronger as she grew in her ability to uncover and release her anger with Luis.

The Work Phase of forgiveness was challenging because Luis was threatened by her therapy. As Miriam's health improved she began to set firm limits on Luis's behaviors, and he sensed that he was losing control over her. Eventually, despite the therapist's attempts to keep him engaged, he refused to participate in therapy. Then Miriam completed an anger checklist on Luis, identifying his active and passive–aggressive angry behaviors, which she gave to him in an attempt to uncover his anger. Subsequently, forgiveness prescriptions were sent home to Luis from the therapist, which stated

1. Consider thinking of understanding and forgiving your father for all the ways in which he hurt you and your mother by his temper.
2. Consider daily thinking "I don't want to be as angry as my father or be controlled by him."

Miriam continued to identify Luis's anger and mistrust and how these emotions influenced his behaviors and to grow in assertiveness with him. She was clear about what she would and would not tolerate. She began to discuss with him regularly that he was repeating his father's emotionally abusive behaviors and suggested that he work at forgiving his father. Gradually, as Luis saw Miriam doing the work of forgiveness with her own parents, he began to talk less defensively about his own anger. Eventually, he returned to the conjoint sessions.

Miriam's anxiety and depressive symptoms diminished, in part as a result of resolving her anger with her husband and with her family of origin. Miriam's and Luis's relationship improved significantly as he began the work of forgiving his father. Later in this book we describe in greater detail the psychotherapeutic uses of forgiveness in the treatment of anxiety and depressive disorders and in marital therapy.

THE MEANING OF FORGIVENESS

Let us begin with two central ideas about what constitutes forgiveness—morality and transformation—and then present our formal definition.

Morality

Forgiveness is centered in morality, which in its simplest form is concerned with the quest for the good. When people seek the good, they do so in relation to others. Thus, morality has an interpersonal sense about it. It is not a self-satisfying, hedonistic pursuit. To be moral does not imply that one must use certain language forms or behaviors to qualify as a moral person, but it does imply that the focus is on relationships and other people, with good intentions toward them.[1]

Two aspects of human goodness that are connected with forgiveness are justice and mercy, ancient forms of morality that at times seem to be in conflict with one another. The *lex talionis* (eye for an eye) of Hebrew society is contrasted with love of neighbor. We have the image of Christ taking the whip to the money changers in the temple and then lovingly going to the cross on behalf of those same merchants. In Islam, Allah is seen as both just (which includes punishing) and forgiving (which implies mercy). The philosopher Gouldner (1973) contrasted reciprocity (giving back in proportion to what is given) and beneficence (giving something for nothing) as principles in tension within society.

Justice precedes mercy when someone forgives. A person who forgives has been treated unfairly (unjustly) by another person or group of people. Forgiveness is the merciful response to this injustice. In other words, the one who forgives has a clear sense of right and wrong, concludes that the other acted wrongly, and offers mercy. Forgiveness is centered in the forgiver's genuine desire for good toward the one who unfairly hurt him or her.[2] When a person is merciful, he or she gives a person good things that he or she does not deserve and refrains from a punishing stance that may be deserved.

Justice not only precedes but also can co-exist with forgiveness. It is possible for a wronged person to choose forgiveness and justice at the same time. For example, a person from whom someone stole $20 could forgive the thief and ask for the money back.

Transformation

Whether one examines the idea of forgiveness within the ancient religious traditions or modern philosophical or social scientific fields, forgive-

---

[1] We are not implying that one ignores goodness toward the self. On the contrary, when morality is centered in relationships, the self is included. An exception is in the case of altruism, in which one gives up rights to help others.
[2] This is in contrast to the *appearance* of being good for one's own gain.

ness implies transformation. By this we mean a qualitative alteration in a number of areas: (a) The forgiver changes previous responses toward the offender, (b) the forgiver's emotional state may change for the better, and (c) relationships may improve. Forgiveness is a developmental variable that shifts perspectives, feelings, attitudes, behaviors, and interactions. To transform in this case is to begin moving in a new direction—from judgmental to understanding, from resentful to loving, from anxious to relaxed, from conflicted to cooperative.

The Definition of Forgiveness

It is important at this point to introduce more formally our definition of forgiveness, a definition we draw on in the remainder of the book. The definition forms the basis for our process model of forgiveness therapy. Our intent is to generate a definition that is "water tight," not easily sunk by outside arguments or examples. If a critic is able to give legitimate examples, falling within the purview of our definition, that clearly describe a phenomenon other than forgiveness, then we must revise or completely change the definition.

Following North's (1987) ideas, we define *forgiving* as follows:

> People, upon rationally determining that they have been unfairly treated, forgive when they willfully abandon resentment and related responses (to which they have a right), and endeavor to respond to the wrongdoer based on the moral principle of beneficence, which may include compassion, unconditional worth, generosity, and moral love (to which the wrongdoer, by nature of the hurtful act or acts, has no right).

We elaborate on the varied aspects of this definition in the next chapter and defend it in a philosophical way in chapter 15. In chapter 3, we continue with themes of definition by reviewing what forgiveness is not. Those academics wishing to know our views in-depth and our defense of those views should take the time to read chapters 2, 3, and 15 in sequence.

Although clinical work rarely involves giving patients definitions, it is critical for therapists to be ad hoc educators as a patient struggles to understand how forgiveness (or the lack thereof) may be important to those struggles. Therapists must be prepared to aid a client's understanding about forgiveness, correct misperceptions, and help him or her deepen understanding as the therapy progresses.

For example, Phyllis was hesitant to enter into forgiveness therapy at first because she equated the acts of forgiveness and reconciliation. She came from an abusive home in which her mother was physically cruel to the children, beating and neglecting them for the slightest infractions of family rules. Phyllis's husband Branden showed a similar pattern in their marriage, physically abusing her whenever he became intoxicated. Phyllis's initial fears were that, if she forgave, then she would have to automatically go back into that relationship with him. When she realized that forgiveness was her own internal response to Branden and his abusive actions, not a decision to trust him or some blind reconciliation, she was more willing to give it a try.

Knowing what forgiveness is not should help a therapist decide whether a client is misunderstanding forgiveness or whether he or she simply is not interested in this approach. Common misperceptions include, as with Phyllis, a confusion of forgiveness and reconciliation. Other misunderstandings are the equating of forgiveness with forgetting, condoning and excusing, and even moral weakness. Chapter 3 discusses the many ideas in contemporary society that supposedly stand for forgiveness but are far from its genuine meaning. Readers can gain even further insight into misunderstandings of forgiveness in chapter 16, in which we discuss skeptics' ideas that criticize the practice of forgiveness. Therapists who do not have a firm grasp of these other ideas as well as a deep understanding of forgiveness may unintentionally lead the client down a path, in the name of forgiveness, that has nothing to do with that concept.

SOME CAUTIONARY NOTES

It is important to note at the outset that forgiveness therapy has its own stumbling blocks that clinicians should reflect on. Consider seven cautions:

1. Clinician enthusiasm for the concept of forgiveness does not mean that the client will share that view. Forgiveness always is a choice, one the client is free to try or to reject. There should never be subtle pressure on the client to forgive. At the same time, however, some clients blanch at the idea of forgiveness at first but then change their minds. The person's first pronouncement about forgiveness is not necessarily the last. Therapists should be open to transformation in the client.

2. Even if the client should willingly choose to try to forgive, he or she may have a change of heart weeks later. The work of forgiveness, as in any work that opens old wounds, can sometimes increase anger, sadness, or anxiety in the short run. If the client needs to back away from the issues temporarily or even permanently, this, again, is the client's choice. In our experience, it is rare for a person to understand forgiveness, make a decision to try it, and then to quit. Even so, alternative approaches must be available under these circumstances.

3. Family pressures toward forgiveness sometimes exist and make the patient miserable. If a patient is asking for forgiveness therapy because family members think it is a good idea, take the time to discern whether the patient also shares that view. Being pressured into forgiveness, especially in a family context, can lead to scapegoating as the person refuses to consider it.

4. Be aware of whether anyone in the family is using forgiveness as a "weapon." It is not uncommon, especially if those other family members misunderstand forgiveness, to try manipulating the client into a hasty reconciliation. "Sure, you talk the talk of forgiveness, but then you don't give me a second chance." Try to ascertain a client's level of guilt under such circumstances. Others' misunderstanding about forgiveness may have to be clarified within therapy.

5. Some family members or friends may be adamantly opposed to the idea of forgiveness. One person once related to us that as she became interested in forgiveness in the context of incest, her friends began to joke about forming a "revenge group" as a more viable alternative. Even though she knew that they were joking, she felt a definite ambivalence about going forward with treatment. Under such circumstances, it may be best to go over again what exactly the patient will be doing in the therapy. We say this because the vast majority of criticisms against forgiveness stem from a misunderstanding of just what forgiveness is.

6. Despite the best instruction and patience, some clients may continue to significantly misunderstand what forgiveness is and is not. In an age of relativism in which anyone is free to define terms as they wish, it is difficult to carry on a rational conversation if both sides have radically different definitions of anything of importance. If, despite best efforts, a patient continues to insist that forgiveness is a form of reconciliation that would be dangerous for him or her, then the clinician may have to try another form of therapy or refer the patient to another therapist. This is a rare occurrence, but it can happen.

7. Clinicians may encounter significant opposition from other therapists who think that forgiveness is inappropriate within the therapeutic context. Although this attitude was far more likely to be seen in the 1970s and 1980s, it still may be encountered today. If so, a therapist should try to engage the skeptic in dialogue about just what is inappropriate or dangerous about introducing forgiveness into therapy and about the limitations of the current approaches to treating

anger. In our experience, there are two reasons for this kind of skeptical attitude: (a) The therapist has an unresolved and deep hurt from his or her past. Professionals who deny injustice or who let resentment fester, almost as a way of life, are often opposed to forgiveness. Their unresolved pain should not limit examining this potentially helpful form of therapy. (b) The therapist misunderstands what is meant by forgiveness. Taking the time to clarify the term can work wonders in the dialogue with skeptical but open-minded professionals.

With these cautions in mind, let us continue exploring forgiveness within psychotherapy, starting with a clarification of our definition.

2

DEEPENING THE UNDERSTANDING
OF FORGIVENESS

If forgiveness therapy is to be successful, therapists must study and master the meaning of forgiveness. We cannot overemphasize how important this is. Keeping an accurate definition will enhance the client's knowledge about this topic. In our experience, the vast majority of people entering this form of therapy have misunderstandings about the concept, despite using the word frequently ("Forgive my being late" or "Forgive me for saying this, but . . ."). One component of forgiveness therapy is education. Therapists can aid a client's understanding about forgiveness, correct misperceptions, and deepen his or her understanding as the therapy progresses.

In chapter 1 we introduced our definition of *forgiving*, which is presented again here, with important clarifications of each of our terms:

> People, upon rationally determining that they have been unfairly treated, forgive when they willfully abandon resentment and related responses (to which they have a right), and endeavor to respond to the wrongdoer based on the moral principle of beneficence, which may include compassion, unconditional worth, generosity, and moral love (to which the wrongdoer, by nature of the hurtful act or acts, has no right).

By the words *rationally determining*, we mean that the person does not rush to a hasty judgment of the offender, the forgiver is free of mental defect whereby he or she does not distort reality, and the forgiver sees that the other has done moral wrong. When we say *willfully abandon*, we mean that the person is actively engaging in changing the response of resentment. Forgiveness is not a passive activity but one filled at times with struggles and ambivalence. We are not implying by the word *willingly* that all of this is accomplished by decision and conscious processes. In our experience, a person who decides to abandon resentment in early morning is not quickly finished with the task by midday. The internal struggle can last for months or even years.

By the words *responses* and *respond*, we mean the feelings, thoughts, and behaviors that accompany resentment (on the one hand) and beneficence (on the other hand). When abandoning resentment, a person is likely to show fewer[1] (a) negative emotions ranging on a continuum from annoyance (on the "lighter" side of negative emotions) to hatred (on the "heavier" side of negative emotions); (b) negative thoughts ranging from judging the person as inadequate (on one end) to evil incarnate (on the other); and (c) negative behaviors ranging from ignoring or being "cool" to serious revenge-seeking. When exercising beneficence, a person is likely to show more[2] (a) positive emotions such as slightly liking the person (on the lighter side) to selfless love (on the other end of this spectrum)—there are a number of moral emotions that could be part of forgiveness: compassion, caring, and concern, for example; (b) positive thoughts from wishing the person well to considerations of unconditional worth (not because of the other's immoral actions but because he or she is a person and all people are worthy of respect); and (c) positive behaviors from making eye contact or smiling to taking an active interest in the other's welfare.

Next, we define the moral principle of beneficence and its related expressions. *Beneficence* is a genuine sense of goodness in which people "aid others without thought of what they have done or can do for them" (Gouldner, 1973, p. 266).[3] It is an umbrella term for more concrete principles such as charity or hospitality (Gouldner, 1973). Of course, this principle will not address the moral issue of forgiveness until the beneficence is expressed in a limited and specific context of injustice.

Compassion is a moral emotion in which the person suffers along with the injurer (on the moral emotions, see Sherman, 1990). This does not

---

[1] The word "fewer" here might imply two patterns: 1) a lessening of these qualities in the same person across time; 2) the forgiver showing fewer of these qualities than people who have been equally wronged but have not forgiven.

[2] As in the case with the word "fewer," "more" here connotes these patterns: 1) an increase in the forgiver across time; 2) the forgiver possessing more of these qualities than people who have been equally wronged but have not forgiven.

[3] By "genuine" we mean that the forgiver does not have an ulterior motive such as gain for self exclusively in the "forgiving." The goodness is an end in and of itself.

necessarily imply that, for example, as Harry forgives Mary, he feels sorry for her because she feels so much regret for what she did. On the contrary, some offenders never acknowledge wrongdoing even to themselves. Compassion here implies that Harry has a sympathetic feeling toward Mary because she is a vulnerable human being, despite her unjust act or her subsequent response to that act.

Unconditional worth is the insight that the offender is a person. Being a person confers on him or her a sense of importance, not because of what was done, but in spite of it. The forgiver sees that no matter what another does, he or she is still of worth, worthy of respect because of personhood. In other words, the offense is not the primary defining characteristic of the one who did wrong (on unconditional worth and respect for an offender, see Enright and the Human Development Study Group, 1994; Holmgren, 1993, 1997).

Generosity involves giving to the offender more than he or she deserves, again because the offender is seen as a worthwhile person. In the context of forgiveness, generosity has a sense of mercy to it because of the offender's injustice.

Moral love extends generosity and beneficence by investing in the other person's well-being. Aristotle (see McKeon, 1947) distinguished four forms of love: (a) *storge*, or feelings of mutual affection; (b) *philia*, or a brotherly friendship; (c) *eros*, or romantic attraction; and (d) *agape*, or a moral love characterized by concern and respect, not necessarily because of others' positive deeds toward the one who is loving (see also C. S. Lewis, 1960; Outka, 1972). Throughout the centuries, *agape* has taken different meanings. For Aristotle, people love in a moral sense those who are part of the *polis*, part of civilized society, because they, like the one showing *agape*, are capable of mutual respect and affection. Early Christianity, in contrast, began to see *agape* as a lavish outpouring of unconditional love by God, in the person of Christ, for all people in need of redemption. As one is forgiven, he or she is directed to forgive (see John's gospel, chapter 15, as one example). The mutuality in the *polis* was replaced by servanthood in which the one who loves may give more than the one loved, but this imbalance of giving and receiving is immaterial to the one showing *agape*. Modern philosophers, including North (1987), equate this love with a "softened heart" toward one who is undeserving. Therapists will find that significant amounts of anger need to be resolved in therapy before the client experiences benevolence, compassion, and moral love. Therapists should not convey the expectation that clients should experience compassion or love early in forgiveness therapy. The movement toward such benevolence requires difficult and often lengthy work in therapy.

There are two paradoxes embedded in the definition:

1. One gives up what one has a right to (in this case, resentment and related responses).
2. One gives to another that which is not necessarily deserved (in this case, the thoughts, feelings, and behavior that characterize the moral principle of beneficence).

In our experience, clients who are new to forgiveness therapy are likely to ignore any of the following: the requirement that they carefully examine the other person's wrongdoing before acting, the interplay of abandoning resentments and offering beneficence, and the fact that forgiveness is paradoxical. Confusions can easily develop despite a client's good intentions to forgive.

REFINEMENTS IN OUR DEFINITION BASED ON PSYCHOLOGY

We present 14 ideas below, all from a psychological perspective, that qualify or deepen the definition.

Forgiveness Is a Continuum

Forgiveness is not an "all-or-none" phenomenon. Each time a person forgives, a certain amount of anger may be removed from a hurt. In other words, there are degrees of forgiveness from slight to complete (see Nelson, 1992). If we were to give 100 people a forgiveness test with a range of scores, then people will vary along a bell-shaped curve from high to low. Another interpretation is that if we were to give, for example, Jill the same forgiveness test over a 1-year span, she may show a trend toward improvement in the scores if forgiveness therapy is successful.

Using Principles Compared With Being Aware of Principles

A forgiver is not necessarily aware of the moral principle that is being expressed. For example, a person may begin to show moral love to another without saying "I am now deciding to exercise the principle of moral love." The forgiver makes a decision to be kinder, but the precise form of internal or external language need not altogether pinpoint the principle.[4] The exer-

---

[4] We agree with Kohlberg (1969) that it may be more developmentally advanced for a person to articulate the principle being considered, but this is not necessary to forgive.

cise of the moral principle of unconditional worth is similar. A forgiver may begin, in a vague sense, seeing the other as worthy of respect regardless of what he or she does. Nonetheless, that forgiver may not be consciously aware of or articulate a rule through language that states "I will endeavor to see the person as worthwhile regardless of the circumstances. I will define the person by his or her intrinsic qualities, not by behaviors."

Forgiveness Is Unstable or Stable

Scores on a forgiveness test also can vary from stable to unstable. Jill may show considerable stability on the lower end of the scale on repeated testings as she seethes for months over what her friend Sue did. As Jill begins to forgive, she may vacillate between a higher and a lower score, again for months, before settling into a stable pattern, this time at the upper end of the scale.

Forgiveness Is Superficial or Deep

Jill also could vary in a more subtle form of forgiveness—from surface to deep. On the one hand, she may get a high score on a forgiveness test but may not understand the principles involved in her decision. On the other hand, she may score low because the betrayal is fresh and the hurt deep, but she still understands where she is moving: toward greater beneficence, compassion, unconditional worth, and moral love toward Sue. Of course, it is possible to observe synchrony between the "low–high" and "surface–deep" dimensions: She may score high on a scale and understand well why she is scoring high; she may score low and be unreflective about this.

The surface-to-deep dimension can be realized in each of the psychological categories of affect, cognition, and behavior. The above example centers on cognition, or the awareness of moral principles. In the affective category, a person may have slight compassion or deep, stable, and lasting compassion. In the behavioral realm, the expression of generosity and moral love can be self-protective and guarded or altruistic.

Another dimension of depth on which forgiveness can vary is the motivational. We find that many people begin therapy with the intent to rid themselves of unwanted emotions such as anxiety or abiding anger and to break the emotional control of those who have hurt them. This is admirable and shows the tenacity to improve psychologically. Because forgiveness is centered on the psychological well-being initially of the offended and later on the offender, the motivation for engaging in forgiveness usually shifts from self to other, from surface to a deeper need to respond morally toward the offender.

Forgiveness Is Developmental

Forgiveness develops. There is a tendency to start in confusion and hurt as one realizes what happened. This is followed by sorting out what happened, deciding to forgive, and moving into the struggle to abandon resentment and respond with goodness toward the offender. This development cannot be rushed and is different for each client.

Forgiveness Is Person-Centered

Forgiving is between people, not between people and inanimate objects such as tornadoes or floods (Kolnai, 1973–1974; Lambert, 1985; Murphy, 1982; Smedes, 1984). We say this because of the moral quality of forgiveness. How can one be beneficent to a flood? Certainly people seek forgiveness from God and report that God forgives them, but our focus is on the human-to-human form of forgiveness.

The Quality of the Wrong May Vary

The wrong experienced by the forgiver might be physical, psychological, emotional, or moral harm (Kolnai, 1973–1974; Murphy, 1982; Murphy & Hampton, 1988; Smedes, 1984). In some cases, the harm may be a combination of any or all of these (Eastin, 1988).

The Depth of the Wrong May Vary

In an earlier publication (Enright & the Human Development Study Group, 1991), we said that forgiveness usually takes place in the context of deep hurt. We now disagree, because our experience leads us to conclude that even the slight but annoying hurts of everyday life may result in anger and then lead us to forgive those responsible. It also is our experience that forgiving the deeper hurts has more profound implications for our well-being.

The Wrong Is Objective, Not Subjective

The wrong is objective, not merely perceived or imagined. This ties into our definition that forgiveness takes place in a context of rational determination. Some claim that forgiveness is primarily a perceptual activity because everything outside of our perceptions is neutral (see Kahrhoff, 1988). If this is so, then why do all with healthy nerve endings in their hands feel pain when pressing a hand to a hot stove?

The Quality of the Forgiveness May Be Dependent on Various Factors

The quality of forgiveness may vary with such issues as the severity of the original offense, the prior relationship, and the offender's subsequent reactions (see Newman, 1987). It also may vary with the forgiver's understanding and prior practice of forgiveness.

The Expression of Forgiveness Will Vary by Culture and Religion

There is no one specific way to express forgiveness to another, although certain cultures have rituals that are specific and idiosyncratic (see, e.g., Loewen, 1970a, 1970b). Yom Kippur, as one example of a Jewish forgiveness ritual, and the Catholic and Episcopal sacraments of penance, as examples of Christian forms, illustrate the varied expressions that forgiveness can take. Therapists may have to take some time to get acquainted with a given client's cultural and religious textures of forgiveness.

The Expression of Forgiveness May Be Cognitive, Emotional, or Spiritual

Fitzgibbons (1986, 1998) observed in clinical practice that people sometimes begin the process by internally (cognitively) stating that they forgive. There is conviction and determination to continue forgiving, but there are no feelings of forgiveness, no compassion or love toward the injurer. Eventually, some people grow in understanding the offender, then in compassion, and only then feel like forgiving. Fitzgibbons (1986) described this as emotional forgiveness. Others, who are profoundly hurt by another, cannot bring themselves to even utter internally that they forgive, despite the desire to do so. In such cases, the clients turn to God, asking for help in forgiving. Still others alternate among and eventually unite cognitive, emotional, and spiritual forgiveness toward an offender.

Who Is Offended and Offender Is Not Always Clear

Forgiveness is not necessarily clear-cut in that there is one offended and one offending person. At times, Harry and Mary will both offend the other. There are several other rational permutations: a person forgiving a group such as a family, a family forgiving one person, and groups forgiving other groups (see Shriver, 1995).

The Quality of Forgiveness Is Not Always Clear

Forgiveness, from a psychological perspective, seems like a skill, a coping strategy, and a commitment. For example, forgiveness seems like a *skill* because the person must practice and take time to learn. There is a cumulative effect in which ability eventually may improve and be maintained.

Forgiveness seems like a *coping strategy* as well. The person who forgives focuses on survival and improvement under difficult circumstances. When exercised, a coping strategy leads to improved psychological functioning, as usually happens with forgiveness (see chapter 6). At times forgiveness seems like a *commitment* (to another's welfare). There are both a certain dedication and conscious choice involved in forgiving.

Although forgiveness may have qualities in common with a skill, coping strategy, and commitment, it also has the qualities of a moral virtue. Thus, if we isolate, say, the concept of skill and insist that it alone captures the true meaning of forgiveness, we are likely to distort its meaning. Jill, in her anger at Sue, could learn the skill of tennis and use it as a catharsis as she bangs a strong forehand down the line, but she is not taking a moral stance here. Because a skill is amoral, it could never capture the richness of forgiveness apart from a moral virtue or a way of living one's life in a good or beneficial way. Because the idea of forgiveness as a moral virtue is both complex and subtle in its philosophical detail, we reserve the discussion of forgiveness as a virtue until chapter 15.

3

WHAT FORGIVENESS IS NOT

Knowing what constitutes forgiveness was our first step. We now must explore the myriad concepts and expressions that people too often confuse with forgiveness. One job of clinicians is to ascertain which of the incomplete or incorrect ideas below clients or patients are entertaining about forgiveness before proceeding more deeply with the therapy. As we present a concept that is confused with forgiveness, we ask: What features does the concept share with the definition of forgiveness? How does the idea differ from the genuine construct of forgiveness?

We do not want this discussion merely to be the statement of our opinion, which will be countered in the future by others' opinions. Little will be accomplished if we say "Condonation is not the same as forgiveness," and another writer says "We believe condonation to be a synonym of forgiveness." Our basic approach to settling opinion is as follows. We first generate legitimate examples of the concept currently under scrutiny, such as condonation. Then we show how the example takes the construct of interest far afield of forgiveness. In other words, some concepts can appear to be very much like forgiveness if certain narrow examples explicating that concept are used. Yet, to qualify as a synonym, no reasonable example of the concept can be used that places the concept outside the meaning of forgiveness.

We realize that some readers will not want all of our detail in trying to settle opinion on these issues. In such a case, readers may wish to skip our *arguments*, focusing instead on each *misperception* until they understand what that misperception is. As an overview, we present a checklist of 20

37

misperceptions (see Exhibit 3.1). The checklist may be a convenient summary for clients and will help quickly identify the client's particular misperceptions. Therapists may then wish to read those sections of the text for greater insight, which may aid the client's understanding and clarity.

We divide the discussion into three sections. The first section speaks to distinctions that have arisen primarily but not exclusively within philosophy as authors debate the fine points of forgiveness. The second section addresses those instances in which a person has an accurate, although incomplete, view of forgiveness. An author may take a slice of forgiveness but forget to take the entire pie in explaining what forgiveness is. If one describes an airplane as having wings, instrument panel, rudder, and landing

EXHIBIT 3.1
Checklist for Ideas Regarding What Forgiveness Is Not

Philosophers' Distinctions Between Forgiveness and Related Concepts
- ✔ Pardon, legal mercy, leniency (a merciful judge is not the one hurt)
- ✔ Condoning and excusing (putting up with an offense or letting it go)
- ✔ Reconciliation (two people coming together again)
- ✔ Conciliation (to appease, placate an offender)
- ✔ Justification (believing what the person did was fair)
- ✔ Forgetting (ceasing to remember the offense, possibly leaving one vulnerable to the offense again)
- ✔ Becoming disappointed (one can be disappointed without being unjustly treated by another)
- ✔ Balancing scales (getting back something in kind, punishing the offender)
- ✔ Self-centering (forgiving only for one's own benefit, focusing on oneself, and not the offender)

Reductionistic Thinking That May Be Accurate but Incomplete
- ✔ Letting time heal the wound (passive rather than active)
- ✔ Abandoning resentment (one can abandon resentment but have a cool, detached attitude toward the offender)
- ✔ Possessing positive feelings (one can have positive feelings toward people who have not been unfair)
- ✔ Saying "I forgive you" (one can forgive without using specific words)
- ✔ Making a decision to forgive (decisions to forgive are part of but not all that is encompassed in the definition: i.e., one who decides to go to college does not receive a degree until work is accomplished)

Common Colloquialisms Confused With Forgiveness
- ✔ "Forgiveness is a quick fix" (forgiveness can be a struggle that takes time)
- ✔ "I've accepted what happened" (one can accept an *event* while rejecting a *person* involved in the event)
- ✔ "I accept what happened knowing that God will punish him or her" (this could be cloaked revenge)
- ✔ "I have moved on" (One can "move on" while rejecting a person)
- ✔ "I have the satisfaction of not letting the person get to me" (this may be cloaked revenge)
- ✔ "I like to let the person know how much he or she owes me" (this may be a form of cloaked revenge)

---

gear but forgets to mention anything about an engine, one has not accurately described the airplane, despite the inclusion of many accurate aspects of it. The third section turns to common colloquialisms used to describe forgiveness that nonetheless distort its meaning.

At the chapter's end, readers should have a clearer idea of what forgiveness is by examining what it is not. Being aware of a client's precise areas of misunderstanding should aid in leading him or her into ever more accurate views of the concept.

PHILOSOPHERS' DISTINCTIONS AMONG RELATED CONCEPTS

Within the last three decades of the 20th century, philosophy delved more deeply than any other discipline into the meaning of forgiveness. Philosophers made important strides in distinguishing forgiveness from a number of related ideas. Without this scholarship, the concept of forgiveness would remain superficial. Even the best dictionaries compare forgiving with pardoning, reconciling, and excusing (see, e.g., *Webster's New Collegiate Dictionary*, 1979). Clients or patients who consult the dictionary for added meaning to their already established ideas about forgiveness may compound error.

Pardon, Legal Mercy, and Leniency

There has been a consensus within philosophy for many years that forgiving and pardoning differ (Downie, 1965; Enright & the Human Development Study Group, 1991; Hunter, 1978; Kolnai, 1973–1974; Lauritzen, 1987; Murphy, 1982; Murphy & Hampton, 1988; Roberts, 1971; Smart, 1968; Twambley, 1976). Both are within the realm of mercy, and so both give to an offending person undeserved social or moral good. Pardon, however, is played out in the public arena of jurisprudence, whereas forgiveness is played out in the private realm of personal injury and injustice. Pardon involves a judge presiding over a case in which charges are brought against a defendant. In deciding to reduce or even eliminate a deserved sentence, the judge never should be the one personally wronged by the defendant. In other words, there are objective checks and balances intended to dissuade biased people from passing judgment on the offender. Forgiveness, in contrast, belongs to the offended, one who does have subjective hurts and swirling ambivalence toward the offender. Forgiveness is not an official act in reducing a deserved sentence, but a personal choice of mercy by the one hurt.

Pardon and forgiveness do not have to coexist. Can we not imagine instances in which an injured party forgives someone who does not receive legal mercy from the state? Can we not imagine the reverse: The state pardons a criminal while the victim seethes over the decision? Finally, can we not imagine instances in which a person forgives without there being any possibility of legal pardon? Not all forgivable offenses are legal offenses. Insensitivity, rudeness, and betrayal of certain trusts are not crimes legislated by the state.

Some may argue that pardon is not always in the legal realm. For example, a parent may be punishing a child by telling her that she must stay in her room for an hour. As the parent then reduces the punishment to only a half hour, the parent is pardoning the child. Even in this private expression of pardon, the example is not one of forgiveness. The parent may pardon the child but still be harboring resentment. In this example, there is pardon but no forgiveness. Conversely, the parent may be reducing resentment and increasing a sense of compassion for the child as she remains in her room. This is a case of forgiveness being used without pardon.

Pardon always involves issues of punishment and leniency, whereas forgiveness does not. Is it not possible to forgive without punishment being involved at all? What if someone decides to forgive his father, deceased for the past two decades? It would seem odd to say that the forgiver is commuting punishment, pardoning, or being lenient with his father (see O'Shaughnessy, 1967).

If a client confuses forgiving and pardoning, he or she may be hesitant to explore forgiveness within therapy. After all, the client may believe that the offender is being let off the hook. We must recall that the definition of forgiveness does not include dropping legal charges or turning away from demands for fairness and civility on the offender's part.

Condoning and Excusing

When a person condones, he or she recognizes a moral infraction in the other person but puts up with it because of the pressure of circumstances (Kolnai, 1973–1974). For example, an employee, Jennifer, condones her supervisor's rude behavior to keep her job. She refrains from retaliation; she keeps quiet about her discontent even though upset. A forgiver, too, recognizes the injustice, as the condoner does, but does so for decidedly moral reasons. Jennifer, in condoning, may view her boss as a snake; in forgiving, she actively strives to see him as a human being worthy of respect, not because of his actions but in spite of them. Condonation can leave a person with smoldering resentment; one who forgives seeks to end the resentment for moral reasons.

If a client confuses condonation and forgiveness, the therapist must take steps to correct the misperception. Otherwise the therapist unwittingly may be deepening the client's resentment as he or she silently puts up with unfairness in the name of "forgiveness." His or her clinical symptoms may worsen rather than ameliorate.

To excuse is to conclude that the problem is not worth an argument (Kolnai, 1973–1974). Unlike condonation, a person who excuses does not necessarily see a moral infraction on the offender's part. If a person is just learning a particular skill, such as a child learning to set the table for meals, we can excuse, rather than forgive or condone, if he or she drops a glass or fails to place the fork in the right spot.

Clinicians should take care to distinguish instances needing excusing and those needing forgiving. Therapists will encounter cases, for example, in which a person may wish to forgive a parent for not being perfect when the client was growing up. Because no one can reach perfection, there is nothing to forgive. The client, instead, may need to examine his or her own expectations of the parent. Perhaps those expectations were and continue to be too high. Forgiveness should take place only in the context of genuine, not imagined, unfairness. A person who is disappointed with someone else is not necessarily a candidate for forgiveness therapy until it is established that a moral wrong was committed. Certainly the therapist can address the client's disappointment but then avoid issues of forgiveness when there is no unfairness.

Reconciliation

Forgiveness and reconciliation are sometimes equated (Hargrave, 1994; Lauritzen, 1987). Both are concerned with welcoming a person who may have acted unfairly. Yet, there are differences. Forgiveness is one person's individual choice to abandon resentment and to adopt friendlier attitudes toward a wrongdoer. Because forgiveness is a free choice on the part of the one wronged, it can be unconditional regardless of what the offender does. Reconciliation always involves at least two people—the offender and the offended. Reconciliation, when there has been a serious moral breech, should be conditional on the offender's willingness and ability to change the offensive ways.[1] Reconciliation is dependent mainly on the ability of the individuals involved to reestablish trust, that is, a sense of safety in their relationship. We say this because hasty "reconciliation" with a physically abusing partner could be life threatening. Whenever an offended person wishes, he or she can commence forgiving. Whenever that same person wishes reconciliation, he or she must await the negotiation, the discussion, and the cooperation of the other party.

---

[1] If both have offended each other, then both may have to change certain behaviors to reestablish the relationship.

Forgiveness is an internal process; reconciliation is an overt, behavioral process of two or more people working out an existing difficulty. Forgiveness must not be contingent on the offender's willingness to reconcile. Otherwise, the offended person is trapped in unforgiveness until the injurer decides to make amends and change. Is this not giving extraordinary power to one who already has behaved badly? Forgiveness is a necessary condition for genuine reconciliation, but a willingness to reconcile on the offender's part is not a necessary condition for forgiveness.

In our many discussions with people about these ideas, some claim that reconciliation is the ideal that should be connected with forgiveness. Writers such as Augsburger (1981) agree.[2] Under many circumstances, and certainly when the offense is minor, reconciling is a moral good following forgiving. This link between forgiving and reconciling has a long history. One goal of forgiveness within the Hebrew and Christian traditions is to effect reconciliation with neighbor or God. Yet, even in these traditions, forgiving and reconciling are not automatically equated. For example, consider Paul's words in his letter to the Romans (5:8): "But God showed his love for us in that while we were yet sinners Christ died for us" [Revised Standard Version]. The unconditional act of forgiving love did not lead to all people being automatically reconciled to God. For example, elsewhere in this same letter Paul wrote (1:18) "For the wrath of God is revealed from heaven against all ungodliness and wickedness of men who by their wickedness suppress the truth." The goal in the Hebrew and Christian traditions is reconciliation when forgiveness is offered. The goal of reconciliation following forgiveness is not always reached.

The ideal goal is not always reconciliation when one person forgives another. We already discussed the example of a physically abusing spouse. There are other examples: a partner who is continually unfaithful despite many attempts to reconcile by the other partner; a chronic gambler who continually absconds with the family's funds; a supervisor who will not pay a fair wage despite concerted effort on the worker's part. The examples are many.

This distinction between forgiving and reconciling is delicate and should be approached with great care because the distinction (or lack thereof) can be distorted. For example, one of us was greeted by a beaming friend who said, "Thank you for pointing out the distinction between forgiving and reconciling. I've been looking for an excuse to dump my husband and when I realized I could forgive without reconciling, I immediately started divorce proceedings as I forgave." The distinction between the two concepts became this person's excuse to leave her husband. Her use of the word

---

[2] See Augsburger (1981, p. 28) in particular.

immediately suggests a lack of deep thought before she acted. Our making the distinction should not be interpreted by anyone that there is no relation between forgiveness and reconciliation. This is just as incorrect as assuming that the two must be inextricably linked regardless of circumstances.

Clinicians need to assess those cases in which a client or patient is returning to a dangerous relationship because he or she thinks that the two must be united regardless of circumstance. Therapists need to assess those rarer cases in which a person now is quitting a relationship that is important to him or her because he or she thinks that forgiving and reconciling should not be unified regardless of circumstance.

Conciliation

Some say that part of the definition of forgiving is the act of conciliation (see, e.g., McCullough, Worthington, & Rachal, 1997). Although there is an aspect of this word that is moral (for instance, its archaic meaning is linked with genuine reconciliation), there are too many nuances in which it suggests something that is amoral or even immoral. For example, conciliation can mean to appease, to gain someone's favor through pleasing acts. Cannot a person gain favor through insincerity or condonation? Conciliation also has the meaning of placation. As Satir (1988) pointed out, one who is continually self-condemning to gain another's favor is placating, a state connected with psychopathology in her family therapy work.

If conflated with forgiveness, the act of conciliation can be dangerous as clients deny their own rights in the name of placation. It also can be dangerous because some may unwillingly try to win over another—conciliate—for Machiavellian advantage. Whenever a word that does not have an unambiguous moral meaning is equated with forgiveness, there is likely to be mischief perpetrated on the meaning and activity of forgiveness.

Justification

A client who believes that the other person somehow was justified in the action may pose two problems. First, forgiveness would be inappropriate if it is true that the other was justified. Suppose, for example, that an adolescent, who was formerly angry with his parents because they denied him access to the family car for a month, now believes that the discipline was justified because his driving habits were becoming a bit lax. Because there is no moral infraction by the parents, forgiveness is not the correct response here. On the other hand, suppose another client was denied the opportunity to date as a condition for payment of college tuition because the parents said that he "just wasn't ready," even when he reached the age of 25. If this client sees the parents as justified, he may need to rethink what it means to act in a way that is justified. He may be wrong in his initial assessment.

Clinicians must distinguish genuine conclusions of justification from false or distorted forms. Otherwise therapists may proceed with a forgiveness therapy that is unwarranted or withhold the therapy that is warranted.

Forgetting

How often have we heard the words "forgive and forget"? Perhaps forgiving and forgetting are joined in people's minds because, when we forgive and forget, we try to "put the past behind us," as the colloquialism goes. Yet, the two concepts are different (Kolnai, 1973–1974; Smedes, 1984). When we forgive, we tend to remember in new ways. Rather than seeing the offender as evil incarnate, we see a vulnerable, fallible person. We do not cease to remember what happened. People carry memories of past, painful situations with them for many years. A person may not remember the precise feeling of pain in her broken wrist, sustained as a child, but she certainly will be able to recall quickly the event itself.

There are at least two complications in therapy when a client confuses forgiving and forgetting. First, some clients will be anxious that, in forgetting the past, the injustices against them will continue because they forgave. After all, if people forget who hurt them and why, then they again are vulnerable. Some clients who hold these beliefs will not be receptive to forgiveness therapy, and this is their prerogative. Others, on realizing that they have never forgotten past traumatic events, may come to realize that forgiveness does not impart a kind of moral amnesia. These clients eventually may choose forgiveness therapy.

A second complication arises in those clients who are anxious that, on forgiving, they might not forget, a state that is highly desirable to them. In other words, some clients desperately want to forget the traumas against them and, if forgiveness will not accomplish this forgetting, they have no interest in the therapy. The therapist might reassure the client that loss of memory is not the real goal, but the reduction in clinical symptoms of depression, anxiety, and the lack of hope and possibly a stronger relationship. Forgiving, whereas it may not eliminate memory of past events, may (without absolute assurance) reduce clinical symptoms.

Becoming Less Disappointed

People become disappointed for many reasons, not always in the context of being treated unfairly by others, where forgiveness continually resides. As a person forgives, he or she may or may not become less disappointed with the wrongdoer. For example, Alice thought she had an amicable relationship with her husband Seth, until he abandoned her and their three children. As Alice forgave him, she remained disappointed with Seth's lack of commitment as she relinquished resentment and began feeling more compassion and empathy for him. Because injustices sometimes remain as people forgive, the disappointment about the situation remains.

If a person believes that forgiving and lessening disappointment are equivalent, then that person may distort forgiveness. For example, if Mike is disappointed that his right hand is now arthritic, should he be encouraged to forgive his hand? If Sally considers the peeling paint on the west side of her house to be unsightly, might she forgive her house? If Sunny hates cloudy days, might she forgive the gray skies of winter?[3] Can we see how forgiveness unravels when we do not hold to proper, accurate definitions of the concept? Disappointment may accompany resentments when we are treated unfairly, but because disappointments also emerge in contexts other than unfairness, we cannot treat the two as synonymous. If we do, then we take forgiveness out of the moral realm, distorting its essence.

Balancing Scales

Flanigan (1992) asserted that part of forgiveness is balancing the scales with the offending party before forgiveness is complete. By this she meant that the wronged party must somehow get back what was taken or punish the other in some way before moving on. For example, if the ex-husband gets the Porsche in the divorce settlement, the ex-wife, who coveted that car, will not forgive until she gets a car of similar value. In another example, a wife who reconciles with her husband may withhold sexual intimacy with him for a specified period of time because of his extramarital affair.[4]

Flanigan (1992) made room for this concept because the women she interviewed for her book claimed that they engaged in this practice of scale-balancing as they forgave. Perhaps in their ambivalence they were blending some justice-seeking and a pinch of revenge into the forgiveness process.[5] We must be careful when we incorporate new aspects into the definition of forgiveness because interviewees say it is so. Oftentimes, those interviewed in social scientific research have not reflected on the concept of interest for months or years before responding. Accepting people's spontaneous ideas as true (which they have not pondered) is a potential distortion for any definition. If the researcher confines the interviewee's data only to a descrip-

---

[3]Certainly a therapist may proceed with therapy when a person is disappointed, but forgiveness therapy is not recommended when the disappointment is not centered on moral issues regarding other people.

[4]This view is not shared by any other writer on forgiveness to our knowledge.

[5]Flanigan's (1992) participants were describing what they called "unforgivable" situations. Thus, they may have been ambivalent.

tion of what the people think forgiveness is, then there is no problem. To take the next step and now incorporate the findings into the definition of forgiveness is giving too much credence to spontaneous pronouncements.

Scale-balancing is not within the realm of mercy. It may be within the realm of justice, if tempered and appropriate, but we can imagine people seeking revenge in the name of scale-balancing disguised as forgiveness. It is important to ascertain whether a client is equating forgiveness with scale-balancing. Leaving the details of scale-balancing to an angry person is potentially dangerous and destructive to self and important relationships. We are aware of a man who tried this following his wife's affair. As his form of scale-balancing, he asked that she report to him on her daily activities for a period of several months. The wife complied and now a year later their largest area of conflict is her resentment over the scale-balancing incident and his guilt for being so demanding at the time when he was so angry. We must remember that a judge is never the offended party in a court of law, at least in part, because the state knows that the angry one will not always serve true justice. Anger can distort how people view both justice and forgiveness.

Self-Centering

Self-centering is one of the most serious misunderstandings of forgiveness because it distorts not only the meaning but also the entire course of forgiveness therapy. Some come to forgiveness therapy with the initial motivation to help the self overcome emotional trauma. This is not dishonorable. As we know, many seek help because of emotional disruption. Yet, the essence of forgiveness must be distinguished from initial motivation. Even if a client initiates forgiveness therapy to help himself or herself, this does not mean that forgiveness is centered solely on the self. On the contrary, by definition, when one forgives, he or she lets go of resentment and focuses on the other person's humanity and ultimately offers compassion to that person.

REDUCTIONISTIC VIEWS OF FORGIVING

In the previous section, most concepts discussed had one detail in common: They did not contain within their meanings the moral element that defines forgiveness (the concept of pardon is an exception). In this section, most of the concepts will have this in common: They are part of the definition of forgiveness but lack completeness. As in the previous section, a client who believes that forgiveness is reduced to a particular element within the definition is distorting the meaning of forgiveness, making therapy difficult.

Letting Time Heal the Wound

Part of forgiveness is the reduction of resentments and other negative emotions toward another. This usually takes time. Yet, forgiveness must not be confused with the passive waiting for time to heal the wound (Kolnai, 1973–1974). Forgiveness is an active struggle to reduce the resentments. It takes work and can be difficult. If a client believes that forgiveness therapy is primarily a waiting game, then he or she will be missing the point. Sometimes it is the client's resistance to feeling emotional pain (inevitably involved in forgiveness therapy) that makes him or her adopt a passive approach. Our experience leads us to conclude that time by itself does not necessarily reduce clinical symptoms when the person has been deeply hurt by others' unfairness. For example, a middle-aged man made a stealthy trip across state lines to place a pipe bomb under the car of his wife's paramour. The affair was 16 years ago. His hate did not diminish; it grew over time.

Abandoning Resentment

The philosopher McGary (1989) argued that forgiveness is nothing more than reducing resentment toward an offender. Unlike the above ideas, he does not view the reduction as passive and time dependent. His definition of forgiving is consistent with the first of our two-part definition covered in the previous chapter. Yet, McGary argued against adding the second part to the definition—that of a more compassionate and empathic stance toward the person. What is intriguing about his argument is that he manages in a certain way to keep forgiveness within the moral realm as he takes the concept away from a sympathetic focus on the offender.

McGary's (1989) argument goes something like this. As a person gives up resentment, he or she can be motivated by the desire to be rid of negative emotions and by the desire to improve his or her relationships with people other than the offender. McGary is aware of the psychological defense of displacement in which an angry person kicks the cat or yells at the children. Forgiving as he defined it, is moral because the children and cat have more peaceful environs as the person forgives.

What is missing from the definition is anything approaching a moral sense toward the offender. A client may cease resentment but then have a cool detachment toward the offender. Giving up resentment by itself is not necessarily moral, especially if it is not done on behalf of the offender for his or her good. For example, Alice may cease resenting Seth because she concludes that he is not worth the trouble. She may see him as morally unredeemable and incorrigible. Is she forgiving Seth as she judges him this way?

Is it not possible for someone to commit a horrendously immoral act in the name of reducing resentment? For example, what if Sam, so resentful of Reggie stealing his car, murders him, thus reducing resentment? Sam may even be kinder to the kids and the cat, but has he acted morally? Is it not absurd to conclude that Sam has forgiven Reggie as he lays the flowers at his grave? Unless forgiveness is centered in the moral realm, a realm that makes room for the forgiven, the meaning of forgiveness may be distorted beyond recognition. Clients who have the characteristics of McGary's forgiver actually may be hiding deep anger from themselves.

Possessing Positive Feelings Toward Others

McGary (1989) reduced the meaning of forgiveness by choosing only the first of the two-part definition. Others take only the second part, associating forgiving with compassion, love, and empathy only. For example, Casarjian (1992) suggested a "forgiveness exercise" in which one practices feeling love as one passes strangers on the street.[6] Seeing aspects of peace in others makes one more peaceful. We have no qualms with the practice of seeing goodness in others. Yet, if those others have not wronged us, we cannot be forgiving them. We must remember that forgiveness is not something other than what it is. The exercises Casarjian recommended may make people feel more connected, they may reduce alienation, but they do not deal specifically with forgiveness. Again, our using examples that fit the concept of interest, but not forgiveness, may be in order. As we look with love at a new baby in our arms or at a puppy scampering on the floor, are we forgiving them? What offense have they committed that warrants forgiveness? All feelings and acts of love are not forgiveness. Otherwise, clients or patients may erroneously take the easy but wrong roads, as they love only those who love them (or at least do not hate them). Forgiveness asks us to love those who may not love us and who may have wronged us.

Saying "I Forgive You"

Although language can symbolize forgiveness, it cannot be a substitute for it. Even if a person uses the seemingly correct words, he or she might be masking resentment. The sincerity of the words matters. Furthermore,

---

[6]Casarjian (1992) did associate forgiving with the other's injustice elsewhere in her book.

because forgiveness is mostly an internal response, it has a wide variety of verbal and behavioral expressions, including the possibility of saying nothing about forgiveness. If the forgiver believes that his verbal proclamation will do more harm than good, then he may refrain from using the words. We all know of situations in which someone happily expresses forgiveness, only to be met with the blank stare of the recipient who mutters, "For what? What did I ever do to you?"

Making a Decision to Forgive

Some claim that forgiving is a decision rather than a process. Worthington and DiBlasio (1990) described the use of a forgiveness session within psychotherapy in which couples ask for forgiveness for specific acts (such as condemning the other in public). Only when ready does the offended one make the decision to forgive. There is much preparation before the couple enters the session, at which time each seeks the other's forgiveness for as many as five offenses.

Is a single session sufficient to sort out the complexities of 10 acts of seeking forgiveness and 10 acts of receiving forgiveness? If the partners had done much work prior to the session so that it is a kind of wrap-up, then we have more confidence. If the seeking and receiving are for relatively minor offenses, then we have more confidence.

Are decisions ever sufficient to define any moral quality? For example, suppose Harriet decides "I will be more merciful to the poor by working in a soup kitchen." Her decision is part of a moral process. She now must contact the administrator of the kitchen, show up for work, and dip the ladle into the broth. It would seem odd if Harriet felt that the moral requirements in attending to the poor were somehow realized upon her decision to be merciful. If on another occasion she decides "I will forgive my mother," Harriet now must work on reducing resentment and increasing friendlier attitudes. The decision itself does not fulfill all the requirements of the moral process. Harriet must now act accordingly.

In defense of certain aspects of this approach, we see that the authors acknowledge the necessity of more time when a partner is hesitant to extend forgiveness. This seems reasonable because the acts of abandoning resentment and increasing mercy need time to develop and cannot be forced, merely willed into existence, or ordered about by one's thought processes. In our view, the definition of forgiveness necessitates that we in the helping professions consider forgiveness to be an unfolding process, one that does not run smoothly, filled with starts and stops, only eventually culminating in reduced anger and more compassion. A decision to forgive is only a part of this process.

COMMON COLLOQUIALISMS CONFUSED WITH FORGIVING

In this section, we consider those expressions that we frequently hear from clients or patients who are describing their attempts to forgive. Again, we compare the statements with the definition to see their validity.

"Forgiveness Is a Quick Fix"

Some enter forgiveness therapy with the mistaken notion that forgiveness is a quick, easy way to solve their problems. Perhaps this is what Prager (1997) was arguing against in his essay "The Sin of Forgiveness." He referred to the notion of "dumbing down" forgiveness in criticizing those who would have people forgive with little thought, with little effort, and with little time involved. Certainly, it is not the case that all instances of forgiveness are like being locked in the gym with only the 200-pound weights to work with. Sometimes it is quick, almost effortless, and painless, but when people are deeply hurt they rarely find a quick, pain-free solution.

If a client sees forgiveness as the effortless answer to all of life's problems, then he or she is starting with false expectations. Reviewing the process of forgiveness with him or her (see chapter 5) may lead to a more accurate view of what will come.

"I've Accepted What Happened"

Forgiveness is a form of acceptance, but not all forms of acceptance constitute forgiveness. If a client accepts what happened but does not accept the offender as a human being worthy of respect, he or she is not forgiving. Some people make peace with the past but not with the people of the past. This is the client's prerogative, but he or she will be distorting the situation if he or she equates this with forgiveness.

"I Accept What Happened Knowing That God Will Punish Him or Her"

Sometimes people let others do the punishing. Yet, nowhere in the definition of interpersonal forgiveness is punishment mentioned. If a client takes this attitude, perhaps he or she is focusing more on justice than on forgiveness. Of course, the two can be a tandem, but this form of justice-seeking is no substitute for genuine forgiveness.

"I Have Moved On"

One might "move on" without ever having accepted the situation. By not looking back, the person does not allow himself or herself the opportunity to feel bitter. There are many ways to move on. Some ways include the one who hurt us (reconciliation), some involve a softened heart, hoping the other will change (forgiveness), whereas others entail running as fast and furiously as possible away from the person (which can be, but is not always, a form of denial). If the moving on is devoid of moral considerations of the other, it is unlikely that forgiveness is playing a part. Forgiveness is the client's choice exclusively, yet if he or she wants to forgive and confuses it with an amoral form of moving on, the therapist may need to instruct a bit more on the meaning of forgiveness.

"I Have the Satisfaction of Not Letting the Person Get to Me"

Sometimes a person will "forgive" so that the other will be bewildered as they play out a tit-for-tat game of subtle revenge. Forgiveness that is displayed as a way to seek and maintain advantage over another is a form of pseudoforgiveness (Augsburger, 1981).

"I Like to Let the Person Know How Much He/She Owes Me"

Forgiveness does involve a certain amount of forgetting, not because the offended fails to remember, but because he or she refuses to continually bring up the subject to the offender. Because the offense no longer is the defining aspect to whom the offender is, the offended one usually does not broach the situation, especially when they reconcile. As in the above example, this expression is a form of cloaked revenge.

THE MAZE OF FORGIVENESS

Just because clients or patients use the word *forgiveness* does not mean that they understand its meaning. Too often in society the word is used casually: "Please forgive me for being 10 minutes late." As we have seen, *forgiveness* is used in place of many other words, such as *excusing*, distorting the intended meaning. Clients come to therapy with misperceptions; each may have a different meaning of forgiveness, unaware of any error in his or her thinking. Therapists will have to take the time to introduce proper meanings, allow for periods of confusion in a client's thinking, and discuss nuances in definition before proceeding too deeply into forgiveness therapy. Please be aware that as the therapist corrects one misperception, the person may fall into yet another error. Being an educator is part of the therapist's job.

As already stated, Exhibit 3.1 is a checklist of the various misperceptions described in this chapter. Therapists may wish to keep it accessible each time they begin work with a new client or patient.

4

THE SOCIAL–COGNITIVE
DEVELOPMENT OF FORGIVENESS

A person's understanding of forgiveness involves more than we presented in the previous two chapters. Another element concerns people's social–cognitive developmental level of reasoning about forgiveness. Since the 1980s we have asked people to think about forgiveness, the conditions under which they would forgive, and their meaning of forgiveness itself.

Our research suggests that people vary in their level of cognitive complexity in their perceptions of forgiveness. This will be, of course, of interest to developmental researchers, but it is relevant to practitioners as well for three reasons. First, a client whose perception of forgiveness is rather primitive may need a different therapeutic approach to one whose perception is more advanced. Being able to make these differentiations with clients is an important initial task for the practitioner.

Second, clinicians should find the client's perception of forgiveness useful for diagnosing his or her current level and helping him or her to advance to the next level. Therapists can then assist the person if he or she needs a more subtle or complex understanding of forgiveness. Third, the model is also useful when clients believe that they have forgiven someone but still feel stuck in anger or in a strained relationship with the offender. In these cases, the model may help the practitioner explain to the client what deeper levels of forgiveness may be needed to heal both the person and the relationship. Scientists may want a discussion of our scientific studies, through which we validate the developmental sequence. Five studies are discussed in chapter 17.

We present the basic six levels of forgiveness reasoning, together with clinical examples of how people may use these levels in therapy. We conclude with an overarching theory to try to explain how people develop toward understanding the unconditional, loving nature of forgiveness.

DEVELOPING UNDERSTANDING ABOUT FORGIVENESS

Our initial efforts to study the social–cognitive development of forgiveness were led by the questions: Do people think that certain conditions must apply before they forgive? For example, might some believe that the offending person must apologize before forgiveness is offered? Is there a statistically reliable progression that describes the way that people develop in their understanding of these conditions? We thought that these were important questions because the imposition of conditions can constrain the person's perceived freedom to forgive. For example, suppose a client believes that the injuring person must apologize before forgiving. If the offender refuses to acknowledge wrongdoing and refuses to apologize, then the client is unlikely to forgive. The specific conditions held to be important for a given client may become a stumbling block for him or her.

We speculated, and research described in chapter 17 supported, a social–cognitive developmental progression as outlined in Exhibit 4.1. The progression moves from the simple to the more complex, from a lesser to a greater inclusion of a variety of people who are affected by the forgiveness decision, and from conditional to unconditional conceptions of forgiveness.

In contrast to Kohlberg's (1969) somewhat rigid view of stages as invariant and universal, we see the progression in forgiveness as more "messy," in that people might regress or skip levels. We doubt the progression is universal if we eventually find differences across cultures regarding people's understanding of forgiveness. Nonetheless, if certain cultures have a generally similar understanding of forgiveness as in the United States (where the initial validation studies occurred), then we would expect general parallelism in the developmental progression across the cultures.

We have been and remain ambivalent about just what kind of progression this is. In our initial publication we referred to it as a *stage sequence*, aligning ourselves with the Piagetian and Kohlbergian traditions of describing changes across time in people's understanding of justice. Our ambivalence began to show, however, as we referred to the sequence as *styles of forgiveness* in a subsequent publication (Enright, Gassin, & Wu, 1992) and then as *soft stages* (Enright & the Human Development Study Group, 1994). "Styles," in our view, were somewhat analogous to a soft-stage model, following Rest (1986) in justice reasoning. Rest saw the justice stages as flexible, in which stage regression is possible, and people reason on a variety of stages at the

EXHIBIT 4.1
Styles of Forgiveness Reasoning About the Condition Under Which a Person Will Forgive

Style 1	*Revengeful forgiveness.* "I can forgive someone who wrongs me only if I can punish him or her to a similar degree to my own pain."
Style 2	*Restitutional or compensational forgiveness.* "If I get back what was taken away from me, then I can forgive." Or, "if I feel guilty about withholding forgiveness, then I can forgive to relieve my guilt."
Style 3	*Expectational forgiveness.* "I can forgive if others put pressure on me to forgive. It is easier to forgive when other people expect it."
Style 4	*Lawful expectational forgiveness.* "I forgive when my religion demands it." Note that this is not Style 2 in which forgiveness is to relieve one's own guilt about withholding forgiveness.
Style 5	*Forgiveness as social harmony.* "I forgive when it restores harmony or good relations in society." Forgiveness decreases friction and outright conflict in society. Note that forgiveness is a way to control society; it is a way of maintaining peaceful relations.
Style 6	*Forgiveness as love.* "I forgive unconditionally because it promotes a true sense of love. Because I must truly care for each person, a hurtful act on his or her part does not alter that sense of love." This kind of relationship keeps open the possibility of reconciliation and closes the door on revenge. Note that forgiveness is no longer dependent on a social context, as in Style 5. The forgiver does not control the other by forgiving; he or she releases the other.

same time. In even later publications, we began to use the word *pattern* rather than *style* or *soft stage* to further distance ourselves from the stage models of justice.

The study of forgiveness is too new to commit to one view of stages, especially aligning ourselves with traditions that take bold but perhaps rigid stands on invariance, regression, and universality. We are aware of the exploratory nature of our initial investigations. As is always the case, when researchers use a cross-sectional design rather than multiple longitudinal designs, we are observing cohort differences that may or may not be robust developmental differences. For example, as we compare fourth graders' responses, which we categorize into styles, with seventh graders' responses, also categorized into styles, the differences not only may be explained by age but also by cultural or familial experiences that have differed for each cohort.

With these cautions in mind, let us describe the basic sequence of people's understanding of the conditions under which they would or would not forgive (see Exhibit 4.1). We use the word *styles* to distinguish the various levels. Style 1, *revengeful forgiveness*, describes a thought form in which forgiveness is conflated with getting even with someone. The merciful quality of forgiveness is lost on the one who reasons in this way. We hear young children say "I'll forgive you if you let me sock you on the arm like you did to me." The two are evening the score and moving on, but they do not seem to be forgiving and receiving forgiveness.

When a person first learns that his or her spouse has been unfaithful, a common immediate fantasy is that if they have an affair too, that will even the score and they can go on from there. Some impulsive individuals may even act out this fantasy, whereas most pass on to the next level.

It seems obvious that an adult who clings to this immature and distorted view of forgiveness will have much difficulty in interpersonal relations. The need to get even can escalate conflict to hate-filled proportions. When children engage in this form of "forgiveness," we suspect, they are simply moving on, putting a minor offense behind them as they become friends again.

Clinicians should be careful in a diagnosis of this level in adults for two reasons. First, a patient may at first appear to be on this level but is only "letting off steam" for a while. The therapist should be able to sense this with the passage of time as the patient settles down to do the therapeutic work and talks less angrily about the situation and more respectfully about the offender. The person actually may be on a higher level of reasoning. Second, and in contrast, a client's need to get even may be disguising an aggressive revenge motive, all out of proportion to the original offense. In this case, a therapist might misdiagnose by underestimating the serious nature of the problem. The person, in other words, does not have only an immature thought form but also violent behavioral impulses requiring much more than a forgiveness intervention.

Style 2, *restitutional* or *compensational forgiveness*, does not present as severe a solution to forgiveness as does Style 1. Here, the forgiver wants what was taken. For example, a child who steals another's pen is forgiven when the pen is returned. The child does not seek the pound of flesh that characterizes Style 1. Style 2 is more reciprocal and less punishment oriented than Style 1. At times, the compensation is internal. A child who feels guilty for feeling resentful toward a friend may "forgive" to feel better. In our interventions with adults who have been abusively hurt by others, this style sometimes constitutes their initial motivation to forgive. Yet, this is more of a survival mechanism, and their motivations often change over time as they work through their feelings about the offense and the offender.

In the case of a person whose partner was unfaithful, this client would require a sincere apology from the partner. The client would not deem it necessary to have an affair before reconciling, as in the previous style. The compensation in this case would be the partner's renewed affection. The client may not think it necessary to take the first step in eliciting affection from the partner.

Adults who reason this way can become stuck in their anger if no restitution is forthcoming. In the case of a partner's abandonment, in which the two do not communicate, the client may want to wait, delaying the work of forgiveness, because restitution is not yet realized. Under these circumstances, it may be helpful if the clinician turns the attention away from the partner's restitution, which will not occur, and focus instead on the benefits that the client may realize in forgiving. He or she will benefit from a diminishment of anger but should also be aware that this is part of a moral response.

Style 3, *expectational forgiveness*, is more cognitively complex than Styles 1 or 2 in that the reasoner takes a group perspective, considering peer group or family counsel on whether or not to forgive. In Styles 1 and 2, the decision to forgive was centered within the dyad, within the context of the relationship between the injurer and the injured. Now, in expectational forgiveness, the reasoner seriously considers the condition of pressure from peers or family as a motivation to forgive. Of course, this may be positive or negative depending on the quality of the advice and whether or not the injured person truly wants to forgive.

Consider two examples with adolescents. Jim felt that he should forgive his friend Marcus after the latter stole the lock to his gym locker. His anger was preventing him from taking the first step. Their mutual friends urged Jim to forgive, which was the impetus to begin the process. Because of the peer influence, Jim forgave and found some emotional relief. Yet, because the peer pressure was so strong it seemed to dominate all other considerations, including the justice requirements of the situation. In other words, he never asked for his lock back or for monetary compensation so he could buy another one. In this case, the positive outcome (emotional relief and a tentatively restored relationship) was mixed with a negative outcome (a relationship that was now a bit strained, as Marcus did not understand the seriousness of what he did).

In a second example of expectational forgiveness, consider the case of Martha and Jasmine. Jasmine began spreading rumors about Martha's boyfriend David, so that the relationship between Martha and David became strained. Martha, fuming over what happened, was not ready to forgive, but their peer group strongly suggested that she do so. Following this suggestion, Martha attempted forgiveness, but it was more of the pseudo variety, ambivalent and filled with a sense of Martha's own superiority. Her rush to forgiveness short-circuited the anger process for her. As a result, true forgiveness was not realized, and the rift deepened.

Now consider examples with adults. A man, who felt his brother purposefully took the limelight away from him, decided not to include this brother in his wedding party. His family, however, prevailed on him to forgive his brother, who they say merely acted out of insecurity. They asked the husband-to-be to rise above the situation and "do the right thing." The man complied, but he ignored the brother during the ceremony and events leading up to it.

In the case of the spousal affair, clinicians should be aware of residual anger remaining in the client who primarily reasons with expectational forgiveness. If family or friends pressure the person to "forgive," he or she may say forgiveness is occurring and even believe that it is occurring. Yet, the internal transformation that constitutes forgiveness probably is not happening. Those who give into peer or family pressure without being convinced that forgiveness is a good idea often bottle their anger but deny this.

In such cases, clinicians may need to discuss the apparent discrepancy between what the client is saying and feeling about forgiveness. Until the client understands and acknowledges this discrepancy, forgiveness therapy may move slowly because of the client's psychological defenses that are denying anger and rationalizing about the benefits of forgiveness.

Therapists should realize that adults can have vestiges of this style of reasoning. If a therapist too enthusiastically advocates for forgiveness therapy, a client who reasons to some degree on this level may forge ahead without deep understanding and with much ambivalence. Forgiveness is a choice that cannot be rushed. Mild influence by peers or family can be positive, but as we have seen, it should not override other issues.

Style 4, *lawful expectational forgiveness*, concerns a sense of obligation to forgive. If a person is a member of an organization that encourages forgiveness, this can serve as motivation for a person to forgive. Some Christian denominations, for example, hold that forgiveness is an obligation. The forgiver on Style 4 is aware of the institution's beliefs and requirements. Rather than relying only on a peer group's or family's counsel, he or she seeks the counsel of an entire organization. Some of the religious organizations have been considering these issues for over a thousand years.

Our suggestion for any therapist who has a client reasoning on this level is to see the subtlety behind the dictate to forgive. Too often those who do not share the beliefs of the client or the client's organization quickly conclude that the advice must be bad because it is obligatory. There is a distinction between *grim obligation*, in which the client does not understand the dictate but forges ahead nonetheless, and *wise obligation*, in which the client understands and appreciates the moral principle underlying the call to forgive. For example, Martin Luther King, Jr., in writing the book *Strength to Love* (King, 1963), called for forgiveness, in part, because of the insights he gleaned from his own Christian beliefs. His call to forgiveness had a sense of obligation to it but is based on a clear understanding of the principle of moral love.

We suggest that the clinician work with a client to see the moral issue that may be hidden behind the law. Why does the religious group want him or her to forgive? What moral principle is being exercised as one forgives? Is this principle good? Is it good for the offended, for the offender, for the family, and for the religious community? Why does the client say this? In this way, distinctions can be made between those organizations that have a grim obligation to forgive and those that have a wise obligation because the exercise of that obligation is based on principles of mercy and love. If the person does not see the principle behind the law, perhaps it is best to first help the client understand and evaluate the principle before moving ahead. Otherwise, grim obligation may occur, complicating the client's sense of anger, which already may be high because of the offense requiring the exercise of forgiveness.

For example, Mary considers herself to be a particularly religious person. She is the head of several influential committees at her church and is viewed as an excellent role model. When her husband Jason admitted to a 6-month affair, Mary's immediate response was to verbally proclaim her forgiveness. In therapy, Mary reiterated her forgiveness, which struck the clinician as unusual because it seemed to happen so quickly. After a few sessions, both the clinician and Mary began to realize that Mary's forgiveness was offered more to please her pastor at church and not to truly offer a loving, moral response to Jason. Her anger, she realized, remained. In fact, she eventually talked of forgiving herself first for falling into the trap of living out the expectation that she must be a perfect role model. Over time, her faith deepened as she understood more clearly the spirit behind her pastor's suggestion that she should consider forgiving Jason.

Not all reasoning on this level involves religion. We know of a group of moral philosophers, for example, who hold one another to high moral standards. This society of scholars believes that moral principles serve as a lawful guide to behavior. If forgiveness is morally good, then it should be practiced. Of course, when someone is initially hurt, deep anger can temporarily overshadow the principle, making forgiveness difficult in the short run.

Style 5, *forgiveness as social harmony*, is the first level on which the person sees forgiveness as a moral principle. By this we mean that the person has thought through the relevance of forgiveness and has decided that it should form the basis of resolving interpersonal conflicts in a variety of situations. This form of reasoning differs from all preceding it because all the others have an *external motivation*, such as getting even, compensation, and various forms of peer or family pressure. Style 5 has more of an *internal motivation*: Forgiveness is good in and of itself. The one important exception to this sense of internal motivation is this: The person, although believing in forgiveness for its own sake, also believes that forgiveness is worthwhile because of the good it may produce in families, groups, and societies. This view does not suggest that the person will forgive only if it leads to restored relationships, but it does imply that if the person forgives over and over without any noticeable, positive results, then he or she may grow discouraged with forgiveness.

The patient reasoning on this level, who is trying to forgive the partner's affair, may be easier to work with in the short run because he or she understands and appreciates forgiveness. On the other hand, the person will be approaching forgiveness with a certain pragmatic expectation: Forgiveness is good, and if it is good, it should produce good results in the relationship, given enough patience and perseverance. Be aware of the patient's possibly growing frustration if the partner does not cooperate. In fact, he or she may become increasingly frustrated with forgiveness and more angry with the partner if forgiveness does not bear fruit. Under these circumstances, the therapist might want to review with the client what is good about forgiveness and point out that the goodness does not always lead to the desired result in relationships. This may focus the person on the intrinsic goodness of forgiveness and make the amelioration of anger possible.

Style 6, *forgiveness as love*, is founded on the moral principle that forgiveness is, in fact, intrinsically valuable because it allows for the expression of moral love regardless of circumstances. Here the person is less interested in the good outcomes and is more interested in goodness itself. This may not seem practical in therapy, but it is. The forgiver on this level is no longer dependent on others' responses. Others, as we know, can disappoint us. The person is able to confidently go ahead with forgiveness, knowing that this itself is a good thing to do. Even if the other person should reject the overture, the client will rightly believe that he or she has offered something worthwhile. The person so reasoning is likely to persevere with forgiveness and reap the benefits of reduced anger, anxiety, and even psychological depression.

For example, Martina, in her 40s with a husband and two children, entered therapy because she was physically abused by her mother when she was a child. For these many years, she harbored deep resentment toward her mother that was affecting her relationship with her husband and children. She was able to acknowledge and grieve the losses that such abuse caused her. Yet, in making an attempt to understand her mother's own upbringing, nothing emerged for her to explain the abuse. Her mother, now in her 60s, did not want to discuss the past. Martina decided nonetheless to forgive her because she earnestly wanted to heal their relationship, which grew even more distant with time. She forgave out of love. Martina did not have encouragement from her husband, who considered the abuse to be barbaric. Her friends also were opposed to forgiveness. Even the promised outcome of restored harmony was not immediately forthcoming because of her mother's rigid stance in denying the past. The unconditional forgiveness opened the door of healing for Martina.

Because this form of reasoning is so important, let us spend a moment in the next section reflecting of the underlying cognitive patterns that make Style 6 possible.

A COGNITIVE THEORY OF UNCONDITIONAL FORGIVENESS

In our view, and based on the developmental findings, understanding forgiveness as a moral and unconditional act is a more accurate and more advanced view than putting conditional constraints on forgiveness. Readers who reexamine the styles in Exhibit 4.1 may note that every developmental level except Style 6 actually is a cognitive distortion of the essential meaning of forgiveness. Style 1 confuses forgiveness with revenge, Style 2 confuses it with restitution or compensation, Styles 3 and 4 confuse it with obligation rather than a loving response to another, and Style 5 confuses it with an outcome-based reinforcement system rather than a moral principle as an end in and of itself.

Without some sense of Style 6, a client may commence forgiveness therapy with errors in understanding the basic ideas underlying that therapy. How can the therapist help the client deepen his or her understanding of forgiveness, thus possibly creating a more successful experience for the client?

A key to the client's cognitive development in matters of forgiveness may be in Exhibit 4.2 (based on Enright & the Human Development Study Group, 1994). The theory is derived from Piaget's notion of the concept of *identity*, which is centered on the understanding of equality. Piaget (1952) first explicated identity as a component of concrete operations, but he did not apply it to the social realm. In identity, $A + 0 = A$, in that an element (0) is added to A but does not alter A. In the nonsocial realm, Piaget spread seven pennies in a row and then did the same with a row of seven candies, with each candy under one of the pennies in the row above. When he spread out the candies (but did not add to their number), leaving the pennies closer together, children understood that there was no addition to the number of candies despite the appearance that their numbers had increased. The principle of identity, in other words, was operating for the children. No increase in number means that the two rows of pennies and candy retain the same number of objects despite the appearance that one row now may have more.

EXHIBIT 4.2
Cognitive Operations and Insights That May Underlie a
Forgiveness Response

Identity model	Abstract identity→ (Abstract application of "If $A + 0 = A$, then 0 does not alter A")	Unconditionality → (Social forces, behavior, or internal transformations do not alter worth as a human being)	Inherent equality→ ("Regardless of how you treat me, we are both of worth")	Forgiveness (Charity in the face of injustice)

In the social realm, identity may make possible people's understanding of the concept of *unconditionality*. Social unconditionality is the important insight that a person is the same despite a change in appearance or behavior. The beardless man who now has a full beard is the same man. The neighbor who breaks her leg is the same neighbor despite hobbling around on crutches. On a broader scale, a person who understands the concept of unconditionality is capable of reasoning that a person retains his or her membership in the human community despite a change in health, socioeconomic status, or even morals.

The insights of unconditionality may make possible the moral principle of *inherent equality*—we are all equal as human beings regardless of how we treat others. We may dislike a person's behavior, but if we understand inherent equality, we should understand that alterations in surface appearances, in moral behaviors or moral reasoning, do not alter a basic truth that that person is a human being. If all human beings are worthy of respect because they are persons, then it follows that that person is worthy of respect, not because of what he or she did but because he or she holds a special place of personhood (see Holmgren's, 1993, philosophical analysis that complements this cognitive developmental analysis).

The insight of inherent equality makes genuine forgiveness possible because the forgiver looks beyond the particular offense and judges a person on the basis of his or her personhood, not primarily on the deservingness of the person's actions. Identity as a cognitive operation clarifies how it is possible for a deeply emotionally injured person to try forgiving the perpetrator. Nothing added to (or subtracted from) the person's sense of worth alters that worth. The other is worthwhile regardless of actions. Identity further clarifies why a forgiver does not demand mutual respect. Whether the offender respects the forgiver or not, the forgiver understands that the other is a person and that people are worthy of respect. Of course, all who understand identity, unconditionality, and inherent equality must remain rational about the other's trustworthiness. Being a person worthy of respect does not mean that he or she is unconditionally worthy of trust.

The gist of understanding forgiveness is for the client to understand that the offender is his or her equal in terms of inherent worth. Being equal morally, the offender is worthy of love, unconditionally expressed. In turn, a forgiver who has been deeply and continually abused should begin thinking of himself or herself in terms of Piagetian identity: Regardless of how little love the offended received from the offender or anyone else, the offended, too, is a person and because of this is worthy of unconditional respect and moral love. The point is for the client to see the unconditional respect due both the offender and oneself (again, see Holmgren, 1993, for a philosophical analysis of forgiving as an act of self-respect).

It is important to keep in mind that even if a client has the capacity to understand unconditionality and inherent equality, he or she will not automatically practice and appreciate forgiveness. In other words, identity and all that it implies may be a necessary but not a sufficient condition for forgiveness. For example, one who understands unconditionality may focus only on oneself, seeing the self as worthy of respect, but then fail to understand an offender in similar ways. As another example, a person may understand all of the ideas in Exhibit 4.2 but then express mercy through an advocacy for legal pardon, but not forgiveness. Cognitive insight alone, in other words, is not the driving force behind forgiveness. One must be motivated to forgive, one must know the pathway to forgive, and one must practice forgiveness if he or she is to be a successful forgiver.

Yet, cognitive insights can support attempts to forgive. We have three suggestions for therapists hoping to deepen a client's insight into the concepts of Exhibit 4.2. First, it seems reasonable to assume that identity develops from the concrete to the abstract. Helping a client see that altered physical appearance in a person does not alter the essence of that person is a developmental precursor to the more abstract forms of identity. We suggest that therapists begin apart from the client's relationship with an offender and start in more neutral territory. Has a loved one changed physically because of an accident or the aging process? The therapist could discuss whether the person's essence—his or her personality or belief system—was altered. The point is to give the client the practice of identity and unconditionality in a context that is not threatening. Second, the therapist could challenge the client's thinking patterns. On which aspects of an offender is the client focusing most heavily? An inability to forgive or disinterest in forgiving often is the result of the client paying much more attention to the other's behaviors than anything else. In many cases, the client is concentrating on the offender's specific behaviors of offense and defining the offender exclusively in those terms. Aiding the client in expanding his or her perceptions of the offender may foster a sense of inherent equality. One suggestion that has been helpful, especially as a result of unfair treatment in marital and family relationships, is to attempt to identify the positive personality traits in the offender and to review them regularly.

Third, and based on the findings of Girard and Mullet (1997), many clients are capable of glimpses into the insights of unconditionality and inherent equality, even if briefly. Just because clients prefer to think of forgiveness in terms of apology and repentance does not mean that they cannot understand a person in terms of identity, looking beyond apologies to the essence of the person. After all, Piagetian identity is a concrete operational development, emerging in childhood. In our view, it is not that the ideas of Exhibit 4.2 are so abstract and developmentally advanced that adolescent and adult clients are incapable of the insights. A lack of practice, in all likelihood, is a cause of their absence in clients more than any other reason.

Perhaps we need to rethink our role as therapist. Forgiveness therapy challenges us to be not only an advocate, a sympathetic listener who offers unconditional positive regard, but also an educator who helps the client understand as clearly as possible the difficult concept of forgiveness before moving further into the healing process. We are now ready to present the model that we use in therapy to help clients forgive.

5

THE PROCESS MODEL OF
FORGIVENESS THERAPY

George, a 42-year-old executive, came to therapy because of discomfort with generalized anxiety. He had difficulty sleeping and frequently was irritated at home, especially with his wife Bernice, and he tended to have little patience with the couple's four children. His productivity at work was falling off, based on his midyear evaluation. He felt a lack of enthusiasm for his current career, despite years of climbing the corporate ladder.

In therapy, George began to realize that he was furious with his supervisors and coworkers because he was overlooked three times within the past several years for promotions that he had expected. He began to resent those who jumped ahead of him in advancement, and he was baffled by his bosses' passivity toward him. His work-related anger affected his whole life.

In chapter 1, we outlined our phase model of the forgiveness process. In this chapter we look at these phases more closely and in terms of the units that are typical of each phase. We outline some of the concrete exercises that we have found to be useful in each phase. Although the phases are not invariant and although not every client will work through every unit in the forgiveness process, for purposes of illustration, we follow George through each phase to show the concrete kinds of work the units in this process would entail, including the relevant forgiveness exercises for the client. In the chapters in Part 2, we examine forgiveness therapy as it has been applied to specific clinical problems.

In 1985, a group at the University of Wisconsin–Madison began to meet every Friday morning to discuss the question, How do people forgive?

At the time, a body of literature was just emerging on the use of forgiveness in therapy. For example, Smedes (1984) had only recently published his seminal work for the general public. That book now has become a modern classic and has helped many people hurt by injustice. Linn and Linn (1978) also published an influential book, basing their model of forgiveness on Kübler-Ross's stages of death and dying. Beyond that, the published literature contained case studies of forgiveness within therapy (Hunter, 1978) and reflections from a psychiatrist (Kaufman, 1984) and a counselor (Close, 1970). Fitzgibbons's (1986) treatise was a year away, and Hope's (1987) essay was 2 years from publication. From religious perspectives, there were works by Augsburger (1970, 1988), Calian (1981), and Donnelly (1982). Finally, two important dissertations (Droll, 1984/1985; Trainer, 1981/1984) added to our discussions. As yet, there were no published scientific works devoted to forgiveness.

Our goal then as now was to be as accurate as possible in formulating how people go about forgiving. We wanted to avoid the trap of reductionism in which theorists commit to a few processes or one major mechanism in describing forgiveness. After years of study, we built the model described below. Denton and Martin (1998) asked over 100 clinical social workers their opinion about the way forgiveness therapy usually proceeds. The social workers' descriptions approximated and supported the process model as we describe it.

Our approach is more prescriptive than descriptive in that we wanted a model that would work in helping unjustly treated people to forgive, if they chose. In taking our ideas to hundreds of people for informal discussions, we revised and refined until we were satisfied that we had captured the essence of the forgiveness process. We then put the model to the scientific test, assessing validity of the model for effecting forgiveness and psychological improvement in those going through our programs. We continue to discuss the model, listen to hundreds of people each year, and make subtle refinements.

THE PHASE MODEL OF FORGIVENESS THERAPY

The phase model provides a useful cognitive map for practitioners to track the progress of forgiveness therapy. As we have emphasized, the phases and particularly the units within the phases are not invariant for every client or clinical problem. Nonetheless, therapists should keep them in mind as they work with clients. The units, for example, can be particularly useful for the clinician to personally review when a client in therapy seems "stuck." By reviewing the phases and units, the therapist may discover the process that needs to be addressed so that therapy can proceed. The therapeutic goals for each of the four phases are briefly described in Table 5.1.

The specific units within each phase are described in Exhibit 5.1. The units show wide differences in the time that people spend in each, in the sequence of units, and in the ease or difficulty that they experience in working through each unit.

There is no way to predict how long it will take a person to forgive. In the Uncovering Phase, for example, some people spend 2 months or more confronting and working through their anger. Others have already moved past their anger at the time of their first therapy meeting. The inability to predict how long a person will need to forgive makes it difficult, as mentioned in chapter 1, to comply with some managed care companies' expectations that the practitioner estimate a certain number of sessions for the therapy. In fact, an awareness of the depth of the work needed to fully complete the forgiveness process may cause practitioners to doubt whether they can work with clients on forgiveness in the limited number of sessions that may be allocated by their health care plan.

We remain optimistic, however, that the creative practitioner will find ways to integrate the work of forgiveness within these time constraints, much as they do other work in therapy. One positive aspect of forgiveness therapy is that it can use journaling and homework exercises between sessions that can accelerate progress. The practitioner working with clients with limited sessions may want to space these sessions with homework assignments carefully planned to make the maximal use of the sessions. Another positive aspect of the work is that it can be done in a group format, allowing clients to move forward more quickly when they are able to not only work on forgiveness in their own lives but also witness the process in the lives of others.

TABLE 5.1
Goals of the Phases of Forgiveness

Phase	Goal
Uncovering	Client gains insight into whether and how the injustice and subsequent injury have compromised his or her life.
Decision	Client gains an accurate understanding of the nature of forgiveness and makes a decision to commit to forgiving on the basis of this understanding.
Work	Client gains a cognitive understanding of the offender and begins to view the offender in a new light, resulting in positive change in affect about the offender, about the self, and about the relationship.
Deepening	Client finds increasing meaning in the suffering, feels more connected with others, and experiences decreased negative affect and, at times, renewed purpose in life.

EXHIBIT 5.1
The Phases and Units of Forgiving and the Issues Involved

UNCOVERING PHASE

1. Examination of psychological defenses and the issues involved (Kiel, 1986)
2. Confrontation of anger; the point is to release, not harbor, the anger (Trainer, 1981/1984)
3. Admittance of shame, when this is appropriate (Patton, 1985)
4. Awareness of depleted emotional energy (Droll, 1984/1985)
5. Awareness of cognitive rehearsal of the offense (Droll, 1984/1985)
6. Insight that the injured party may be comparing self with the injurer (Kiel, 1986)
7. Realization that oneself may be permanently and adversely changed by the injury (Close, 1970)
8. Insight into a possibly altered "just world" view (Flanigan, 1987)

DECISION PHASE

9. A change of heart/conversion/new insights that old resolution strategies are not working (North, 1987)
10. Willingness to consider forgiveness as an option (Enright, Freedman, & Rique, 1998)
11. Commitment to forgive the offender (Neblett, 1974)

WORK PHASE

12. Reframing, through role-taking, who the wrongdoer is by viewing him or her in context (M. Smith, 1981)
13. Empathy and compassion toward the offender (Cunningham, 1985; Droll, 1984/1985)
14. Bearing/accepting the pain (Bergin, 1988)
15. Giving a moral gift to the offender (North, 1987)

DEEPENING PHASE

16. Finding meaning for self and others in the suffering and in the forgiveness process (Frankl, 1959)
17. Realization that self has needed others' forgiveness in the past (Cunningham, 1985)
18. Insight that one is not alone (universality, support) (Enright et al., 1998)
19. Realization that self may have a new purpose in life because of the injury (Enright et al., 1998)
20. Awareness of decreased negative affect and, perhaps, increased positive affect, if this begins to emerge, toward the injurer; awareness of internal, emotional release (Smedes, 1984)

Note. This exhibit is an extension of Enright and the Human Development Study Group (1991). The references at the end of each unit here are prototypical examples or discussions of that unit.

Units Within the Uncovering Phase

The primary goal of the Uncovering Phase is for clients to have a much better understanding about how the original unfairness and their reaction to it have affected their psychological health. This involves acknowledging and working through a number of levels of pain. At the end of this phase, the layers of pain that the client may have explored include anger, shame, depleted energy, cognitive rehearsal, comparison between offender and self, possible permanent injury, and altered worldview. Each person will differ in the number of layers that they must work through and the intensity with which each is experienced.

We outline eight units in the Uncovering Phase, all of which concern initial emotional reactions to the injustice and the complications that arise when anger abides (see Exhibit 5.1) and also journaling and homework exercises.

Examining Psychological Defenses and Issues Involved

Let us first distinguish between a client or patient who chooses to explore forgiveness within therapy and one who is assigned to a particular therapist. Both may show wide differences in their readiness to forgive. In the former case, a client who willingly seeks forgiveness therapy may have read a book or talked with another client. Already there is a sense that forgiveness may be worthwhile. Already there is insight that another has offended. The second patient, on the other hand, may never have considered forgiveness. In fact, he or she may be in denial about the offense or the amount of emotional turmoil that he or she is experiencing.

Before forgiveness therapy will be successful, the client or patient must accurately conclude "I have been wronged, it hurts, and I wish to do something about this." Because forgiveness, from a philosophical standpoint, is supererogatory, it is always the offended one's choice whether or not to forgive. This, of course, is compatible with the ethics of therapy in which a person is free to reject any form of therapy. Some people will not progress past Unit 1. Some will not want even to explore the issues involved in Unit 1.

Our discussion is predicated on the assumption that the person is willing to examine the varied facets of this unit. First, the issue of psychological defenses must be confronted. Is the client using a particular defense to avoid the real issue? Denial, particularly the denial of anger, is a common defense seen initially in therapy. Repression will mask at least temporarily the actual issue at hand. For example, Mary, age 32 and sexually abused by her father, came to therapy because of general nonspecified anxiety. She was fearful most of the day for most days. She had repressed the childhood trauma. Slowly, as therapy progressed, she began to remember some of the abuse. Her initial strategy in therapy was to examine the anxiety itself, apart from any specific life events that may have led her to a learned pattern of anxious thoughts and behavior. In fact, she denied that she was angry.

Mark, on the other hand, came to therapy because of his boiling temper. He tended to displace his disappointments and hurts onto his wife and children. He, too, was the product of child abuse years before. Mark's displacement of anger onto his family allowed the therapist to begin with a fundamentally important issue: Mark, in fact, is quite angry. This eventually led him to the wisdom that he actually was most angry with his mother. Displacement gave way to insight. Mary's psychological defense was more complicated than Mark's. The emotions that she was symbolically showing (anxiety and a denial of anger) were not as directly related to the injustice as Mark's emotions (anger in both cases). Our point is this: Certain patterns of psychological defense will make the exploration of injustice against the client more or less difficult than when other defenses are manifest. Later in this chapter, we discuss defenses again, and we raise specific questions to ask clients that focus on psychological defenses and anger.

We recommend that the therapist discuss the concrete issues of injustice that may be contributing to symbolic or masked expressions of anger. Of course, this can take much time to unfold, especially when denial and repression are rigidly and deeply held. Yet, the feelings of discomfort that may have precipitated therapy are motivation to do this kind of exploring. The more concretely the client or patient explores the issues of injustice, the better.[1]

There may be more than one incident that surfaces. Mark's example showed that he felt offended by his wife and his mother. Even though his anger toward his mother was responsible, in part, for his anger toward his wife, he may need to forgive both. Also, his wife may need to forgive him because of his pattern of displacing anger onto her and the children. An important point to remember is this: The initial person whom the client targets for forgiveness therapy may not be the one who is most hurtful to that client. The initial person targeted may actually be someone on whom the client displaced his or her anger because of other incidents with other people.

George's problem, as shown at the beginning of the chapter, concerned a lack of promotion and raise in the company at which he worked for 14 years. He watched as three younger colleagues climbed the ladder ahead of him, despite his strong job evaluations by superiors. "At first, I just kind of stood back and observed all of this with a stunned disbelief. The bosses said nothing to me . . . no encouragement, no explanation . . . no nothing. I figured the situation would soon change, but it didn't. I wasn't angry at first, just kind of numb."

Once the client acknowledges that he or she was treated unfairly, it is important to examine rationally the degree to which this is the case. Recall that forgiveness takes place in the context of rationally determining that unfairness occurred. The therapist must distinguish, for example, cases

---

[1] The therapist must be careful not to manufacture issues of injustice for the client. Not all presenting problems require forgiveness therapy.

of borderline personality disorder in which the injustice is manufactured by the client. The therapist must distinguish cases in which the claim of injustice is actually a defense of displacement.

Again, keeping the client or patient focused on concrete incidents is best: What happened? When did this happen? How often did it happen? Who was unfair? Why do you say that he or she was unfair? As the client understands what happened and when, there is a better chance that he or she will be accurate in the assessment of unfairness. Hunter (1978) made the important statement that a therapist will have a clinical sense when the client is engaging in false forgiveness; there is a certain insincere quality about the person that even those untrained in therapy can spot.

The major issues in Unit 1 are to (a) assess whether certain defenses are preventing the client from rationally examining what happened and (b) help him or her understand what did happen and who was unfair. The chapters in Part 2 of this book illustrate the different ways that a therapist can achieve these objectives.

Confronting Anger

Once the psychological defenses begin to break down, there is a tendency for the person to become angry or more angry than before. The anger can linger for months or even years. An important point of forgiveness therapy is to acknowledge this anger, allow for its expression (within reasonable limits), and set as a goal the diminution of this emotion toward the offender. If the client or patient believes that it is wrong to acknowledge or express anger, this unit will proceed slowly.

For George, his anger came out at home: "Bernice [his wife] noticed that I was more agitated and temperamental than usual. I'm usually not someone who goes home and kicks the cat or anything like that, so I had to take a personal inventory. I was pretty surprised when I looked inside and saw all this anger wanting to boil over at my bosses." For Louise, her anger came out on the highway. For the first time she began to understand what was meant by the phrase "road rage."

Admitting Shame

Patton (1985) was the first to see the link between being unjustly treated and the development of shame. Shame is the sense of public scrutiny and concomitant embarrassment. Of course, not all clients have experienced the kind of unfairness that precipitates shame, but many do. Examples of unfairness that seem to lead to this sense of public display include incest, as people whisper about what happened to the victim; divorce or abandonment, as the client must adjust to a new social status; and being fired from a job on which the client worked diligently.

What therapist and client must realize about shame is that it is an added layer to the pain already experienced by the client. The anger, or some other symbolically expressed emotion, resulting from injustice constitutes a first layer of pain. Shame constitutes a second. The additive nature of anger and shame deepens a client's discomfort.

Because shame contains an element of embarrassment, the therapist must proceed carefully and slowly, especially if the anger lingers. On the one hand, the client may be hesitant to discuss this complication of the injustice. On the other hand, the added pain experienced may motivate the client to explore this area. Therapists should realize that at this juncture new people to forgive may emerge for the client as he or she sees the insensitivity of those who may be talking about or subtly condemning the client because of the original unfairness experienced. (A neighbor, for example, may ask "What did you do to get fired? Bosses don't dismiss people for no reason.") Whether the therapist should continue forgiveness therapy with the original target person or temporarily switch to one who caused or continues to cause shame is idiosyncratic to this therapeutic situation.

George recalls feeling shame at work: "Here I am with seniority, but a low paycheck, seniority but inferior status. I was embarrassed." It took him several sessions to admit this. Many patients also feel guilty as a result of discovering the depth of their previously denied anger.

Being Aware of Depleted Emotional Energy

When a person is attaching great amounts of emotional energy toward a particular person or event, he or she can become emotionally drained. In fact, this emotional emptiness sometimes is the impetus for the patient's seeking therapy in the first place. To aid the patient's insight that the anger and related emotions are depleting his or her energy, we sometimes ask a question similar to the following: Suppose you have 10 elements of energy to get through the day. Think about the person and situation we have been discussing. How many energy elements do you expend on that person and event each day—1 element, 4 elements, 7 elements? How many elements are left for all of the other struggles of the day?

Many people realize that they are spending an inordinate amount of time dealing with the incident. Sometimes the incident happened 20 years ago, yet energy is depleted at a rapid rate even now. Such insights add a third layer of pain as George realized, "I was exhausted by what happened. If productivity is such a big deal for the company, then why were they leaving me to stew in my own juices? It definitely began to affect my work. I didn't realize it at the time, but eventually I discovered that I was not only angry, but also sad by the whole thing."

Being Aware of Cognitive Rehearsal

When people have serious problems to solve but are having a difficult time reaching a solution, they at times fall into a pattern of dwelling on the situation. Therapists sometimes refer to this as "obsessional thinking" or "preoccupation" with the offender. The person may be watching television and miss the plot because the hurtful person was on his or her mind. The offended person can be traveling in the car for miles, paying only minimal attention to the art of driving because the unjust person is on his or her mind. Dreaming about the person and waking up and beginning the day musing about the person are not uncommon when the hurt is deep and the problem unsolved.

A complicating factor is the unconscious nature of the cognitive rehearsal. Most people are unaware at the time that they, again, are pondering the offending person. Therapists sometimes ask the client or patient to keep a journal for 1 week in which he or she enters a record whenever the offender is the object of thought. In this way, therapist and client can pinpoint when the cognitive rehearsal is at its most intense and how often it happens. The exercise usually is a revelation to the client, who was unaware of how often he or she reflected on the one who did wrong.

These kinds of insights, although valuable, also add a fourth layer of pain for clients: realizing that the person they may be trying to put out of their life is very much entwined in that life. George recalls, "I sometimes would be carrying on a conversation with one of my children when I realized that I had missed the last several minutes of what she was saying to me. She'd talk and I'd be nodding my head and saying 'yes, uh-huh,' but I wasn't really listening. I had my mind on work."

Comparing Self and Offender

At this point in the therapeutic process, the patient already has four layers of pain, not because of the therapy but because of the hurtful incident and the patient's subsequent reactions to it. A fifth layer is added when the patient begins to compare his or her unfortunate state (or at least a perception of misfortune) and the more fortunate state of the offender (again, this is usually a perception if not a reality). David Kiel's (1986) insights are classic: He was gunned down in his store and paralyzed by a robber. In the months of rehabilitation that followed, Kiel became bitter and then depressed as he envisioned the robber walking around free and on two strong legs while Kiel languished in the wheelchair. The contrast was emotionally devastating until he learned to forgive.

The patient does not always experience this fifth layer of pain. This unit, therefore, is not always a part of therapy. Only if the patient brings up such a comparison is it appropriate to discuss it, in our opinion. A vulnerable client is open to many suggestions, including the one that he or she is even more miserable than is actually the case.

For George, he began to compare himself with the younger colleagues: "As vacation time approached, one of the 'youngsters' as I called them was talking about taking his family skiing to Colorado. He was not the least bit concerned about the expense. I thought to myself, 'I can't afford that and he takes it so lightly.' It hurt." It is difficult to face the pain of envy that can emerge here.

Facing Permanent Change

Forgiveness therapy can proceed slowly for a number of reasons, one of which is the hesitance to admit that one's life has been inextricably changed. Denial of this fact is not dishonorable, especially when the client needs more time to adjust to what happened. At some point, however, the client must face the fact that the unfairness has changed his or her life. This adds the sixth layer of pain. Kiel (1986) again is a classic example. At first he could not admit to the paralysis. His anger was more masked than overt, not allowing him to confront the unfairness or to mourn his loss. Facing the reality freed him to do both. If a client sees a solution to the pain, and forgiveness is one such solution, breaking the pattern of denial is easier.

Close (1970) offered another example. One incest survivor with whom he worked did not want to admit to herself that she no longer was a virgin. This presented a serious block to therapy until she acknowledged this change, mourned it, and moved toward forgiveness. Of course, permanent change befalls only those with particularly arduous injustices. Many will not experience this sixth layer of pain.

Having an Altered "Just World" View

Flanigan's (1987, 1992) insights are important here. Her clinical experience taught her that clients, especially victims of traumatic injustice, alter their basic philosophy of how the world works. Before the traumatic event, the client may have thought that the world was safe and that people usually try to act fairly. Following the trauma, all of this can change at least temporarily. They see the world as cruel and unsafe and people as self-interested. Our own interviews with scores of people support this finding. When adults break up with a partner, a common pronouncement is "No man (or woman) can be trusted."

As in the case of cognitive rehearsal, people often drift into these new ideas unconsciously. Only when their worldview is held up to examination do they see the extent to which their view has changed. To aid clients in their insight, we sometimes ask them to consider how they saw the world before the unfairness and how they see it now. The conclusions can add a seventh layer of pain as they see a more pessimistic philosophy of life that has replaced a more optimistic, if more naïve, philosophy.

"The glass seemed half-empty most of the time for me," George said. "I was becoming cynical, which was very unusual for me because, to this point in my life, I tended to be positive. Bernice noticed it and brought it to my attention. I realized that I'd better do something about the job situation before I infected the whole family."

It is important that the client and therapist realize a solution is forthcoming—forgiveness. Otherwise, the insights are serving only the purpose of letting the client know how miserable he or she is. Insight alone will not solve the problem created by injustice.

At the end of the Uncovering Phase, clients should have a much better understanding about how the original unfairness and their reaction to it have affected their own psychological health. The seven layers of pain that are now known to the client or patient are

1. anger
2. shame
3. depleted energy
4. cognitive rehearsal
5. comparison between offender and oneself
6. the possibility of permanent injury
7. a more pessimistic philosophy of life.

Each person will have a different pattern of these seven layers, varying in number and intensity for each.

Using Journaling or Homework Exercises

Therapists might consider asking patients, early in the Uncovering Phase, to write their story in which one person treated them unfairly. What happened? What was the context in which the unfairness occurred? Why is it unfair?

Specific questions can focus on the psychological defenses and anger (Units 1 and 2) with the questions Are you angry? Have you been using a defense mechanism to deal with the hurtful event? Does your defense mechanism actually hurt you? Are others adversely affected by what you do? Details of therapeutic journaling and more ideas on homework questions to pose to clients across the process of forgiveness can be found in Enright (in press).

For the unit on admittance of shame (Unit 3), the therapist might ask Do you have shame? What is the cause of the shame? Is your pride getting in the way of accurate perceptions, or are you accurately perceiving others' views of you? Therapists should feel free to be innovative in the questions and suggestions for when the client might work on these questions.

When the client is ready to focus on energy depletion (Unit 4), he or she might reflect in writing on the questions we presented earlier: Suppose that you have 10 points of energy each day to help you do all that you must do. How many of those points of energy, would you say, are used in "stewing" about the person you are considering forgiving? Are you tired of being tired?

For the cognitive rehearsal unit (Unit 5), an exercise for journal writing might include this: In your journal, please reflect on the comparisons that you may be making between you and the one you wish to forgive. State one of his or her advantages and one of your disadvantages. Then challenge the perception to see if this is true. You might want to continue this pattern until you are able to see how you compare yourself with him or her. A similar pattern can be suggested for the unit on permanent change (Unit 7). Have the client write down any perceptions of permanent change and then challenge that perception to assess its validity.

An exercise that compares and contrasts the patient's worldview before and after the hurtful event may prove useful (Unit 8). Before the incident, what was your view of people in general? Are people basically good? What is good in life? What is your purpose in life? Why is there suffering in the world, and how is it eased? Then have the person reflect on his or her current responses and how they have changed across time.

Finally, the person should be challenged to review the written responses for each unit. What is the person's level of anger and emotional pain resulting from the other person's unfair treatment? The answers usually serve as a strong motivation to continue with forgiveness therapy.

Units Within the Decision Phase

As we said earlier, emotional pain can be a great motivator to seek help and to change. The knowledge gained in the Uncovering Phase can serve as the motivator to continue. The gist of the Decision Phase is in the person's own decision to choose forgiveness.

Developing Insight That Previous Coping Strategies Are Ineffective

The units of the Uncovering Phase act in a tandem with this unit as the person judges whether he or she is coping well. The seven layers of pain aid in this judgment. At this point, many people conclude that they must change their way of responding to the injustice. Using the descriptive words of philosophy, North (1987), referred to this unit as a "change of heart." In other words, the person begins to move away from the quest for revenge. If the old strategies are not working, especially expressive anger, what are the alternatives?

As people ask such a question targeted toward the one who hurt them, they slowly may begin to challenge the pessimistic philosophies that crept into their worldview and sense of identity (Unit 8 in Exhibit 5.1). If the emotional pain continues and if the pessimistic philosophy is part of this pain, then the philosophy itself may be challenged. At this point, clients sometimes enter a search for new ways of relating not only to the offender but also to people in general. Some fall back to ways of viewing the world that were effective for them as children or as adults prior to the injustice. If the older way of interpreting the world included much idealism, this way is embraced with a greater subtlety and maturity than before. Sometimes the person develops entirely new ways of seeing and interpreting the world, including what Yandell (1998) called "cosmic perspectives," including metaphysical or religious beliefs, especially those that make a place for forgiveness and responses other than resentment and revenge.

Our main point is this: As a client, who has been living with resentment for a long time, begins to question that resentment, the therapist should be ready for more general questioning and searching by the client, not unlike what Frankl (1959) observed in his patients who struggled with the meaning of suffering and pain in their lives following the Holocaust.

Being Willing to Consider Forgiveness as an Option

Before a person forgives, he or she should be given ample opportunity to learn about what forgiveness is and is not. In fact, such knowledge is essential if forgiveness therapy is to proceed well. He or she should be given sufficient opportunity to choose or reject forgiveness as an option. As we know, there are many alternatives available to a patient who rejects the idea of forgiveness.

For those who willingly choose to explore forgiveness, we recommend that they be introduced to the following:

- The definition of forgiveness that includes the abandonment of resentment (to which they have a right) and adopting friendlier attitudes (to which the offender may not have a right)
- The paradoxes inherent in the definition
- The distinctions between forgiveness and condoning or excusing, forgetting, and reconciling.
- The concern that to forgive is to make the forgiver a "doormat."
- The interplay between forgiveness and justice-seeking.

All concerns should be discussed in an atmosphere of open-minded dialogue.

George was not sure that forgiveness was appropriate for him because he equated forgiveness with a kind of weakness. He thought he should simply "take it like a man." When he understood that forgiveness does not equate to weakness and that he still could learn to "take it" as he forgave, he was more open to the possibility.

Committing to Forgive the Offender

A commitment to forgive, as shown in chapter 3, is not the same as forgiveness. In our view, this is a developmental step in which only a small slice of forgiveness is considered: refraining from revenge-seeking or thoughts of revenge, if these are occurring in the client. Here we focus on the first half of our definition, that of abandoning resentment and its complications.

Many people, without realizing it, seek revenge from those who offend them. Failure to return a telephone call, speaking ill of the person to others, even besmirching a deceased person's name are examples. In this unit, we ask for a commitment from the person not to condemn the other or to take subtle revenge. Of course, we must distinguish between discussing the offender in a therapy session or in a conversation with a friend and condemnation. The two are different. We would not want to create the false and unhelpful belief that the person can no longer discuss what happened.

Fitzgibbons (1986) observed over a decade ago that people tend to first forgive in a cognitive sense before they move toward affective forgiveness. This unit is intended to appropriate this observation. A commitment to forgive is a decision, a cognitive act. It can occur even if the client is still angry and resentful. All this unit asks of the client is that he or she make a conscious commitment not to act on the resentment. It is an important step because the person now realizes that he or she has a certain control over what happened and how to respond.

If people resist in the commitment, perhaps they do not understand just what constitutes forgiveness (Unit 10) or are yet so angry (Unit 2) that they have not progressed from the Uncovering Phase. George had some difficulty here because there were so many people to forgive. Where should he start, with the supervisors who passed him by or with the younger coworkers who showed no sympathy for him? He decided to forgive the younger workers first, starting with Sally, the latest to advance up the ladder. He then would turn his forgiveness toward the other coworkers and then to the bosses.

Using Journaling or Homework Exercises

We find it helpful for clients to write down the previous solutions they may have attempted in dealing with the unfair situation. On a 1-to-10 scale, the client rates the effectiveness of each solution, with 1 representing a *very ineffective* solution and 10 representing a *very effective* one. If a client sees that solutions without forgiveness are ineffective, then he or she may be motivated to try forgiving the offender.

Those willing to consider forgiveness as an option might write down the definition of forgiveness and reflect on the advantages and disadvantages of trying it. The writing might form the basis of a discussion between therapist and client, as he or she considers forgiveness.

Finally, have the person consider the statement: Do no harm to the one who hurt you. How can you act on this statement? How have you done harm, even in a subtle way, to him or her? How can you reverse this trend?

Units Within the Work Phase

When a patient progresses to this phase, he or she is entering into the deep process of forgiveness. The work ahead is difficult but can pay dividends for emotional relief and possibly even reestablished relationships.

Reframing

To reframe is to rethink a situation or to see it with a fresh perspective. This is a cognitive exercise preceding an affective exercise, again based on the observation that cognitive insight usually comes before positive affective responses toward an offender. We ask a series of questions to challenge the person's view of the offender. The point of all questions is to help the patient see a person who is, in fact, a human being and not evil incarnate. As examples, consider the following questions that we pose:

- *What was it like for the offender as he or she was growing up?* Not all clients have the luxury of knowing the offender's history, but in many cases the one who offends is well known (Subkoviak et al., 1995). The client is not asked such a question to condone what happened ("Oh, now I see. My Uncle Charlie had such a poor upbringing that he just couldn't help himself when he bilked me out of my life's savings."). Instead, he or she is asked to reframe who the offender is, perhaps someone who is vulnerable, scared, or confused. Uncle Charlie might be seen as one whose background led him to fear desperately that he would be one day poverty-stricken and unable to provide for himself, leading him to behave in a greedy manner.
- *What was it like for the offender at the time of the offense that you are considering?* Again, the question is not meant to foster condonation, but understanding.
- *Can you see him or her as a member of the human community?* We are not asking whether the person sees the offender as husband, wife, employer, or any specific designation. We are

asking whether the patient sees him or her as a human being. It may be important to distinguish forgiveness and reconciliation at this point if the patient grows uncomfortable with the image of rejoining a person who is seen as untrustworthy.

In our experience, people who have not forgiven sometimes espouse a modern version of the flat-earth theory. They would like to grab the offender by the nape of the neck; march the offender to the farthest reaches of the realm; and drop the offender, listening as he or she picks up speed in the fall. Our third question above is meant to challenge the person's view in that the offender, regardless of what he or she did, is a human being. If all humans have inherent worth (Enright & the Human Development Study Group, 1994), if all humans are worthy of respect (Holmgren, 1993), then the client or patient is challenged to rethink whom the offender actually is.

At this point, we would like to introduce other angles to reframing, none of which we have included in the research outlined in the next chapter. The philosopher Yandell (1998) in directly considering our approach with clients suggested the following fascinating additions to our procedure:

- *Reframe toward oneself.* Is it possible that the client may have contributed to the offender's objectionable behavior? As an example, suppose that Daphne is offended that Darwin yelled at her in front of all the office workers today as she asked him to do extra work. Our usual form of reframing would ask Daphne to see whether Darwin was having a bad day (let us suppose that he was coming down with the flu). To reframe toward oneself in this situation, Daphne must ask herself whether she should have known or inquired about Darwin's state of health that morning before asking for more work.

  We must be careful with this form of reframing. For example, an incest survivor must not conclude that she in any way encouraged or contributed to the sexual abuse. Sometimes people are cruel without any prompting at all. A case of spousal abuse is similar. Even if the battered spouse showed disrespect or insincerity, there is no psychological or moral theory that remotely suggests physical violence as an option in this circumstance. The behavior is wrong regardless of what the other did. We must be careful that clients do not blame themselves for another's moral failure. Yandell's (1998) point is that sometimes a client does contribute to another's behavior. Knowing this may accelerate forgiveness.

- *Reframe the relationship.* Daphne may do well to assess how she and Darwin have gotten along these past 3 years when they worked together. If their interactions are typically civil and respectful, she may see him in a new light. Past actions of respect are no excuse to condone present uncivil behavior, but the history between them may soften her judgment against him.

- *Reframe the cosmic perspective.* This extends our question "Can you see him or her as a member of the human community?" Yandell (1998) suggested that people with particular religious worldviews ask questions consonant with that view. For example, any of the monotheistic traditions might lead a person to ask: Is he or she is a child of God? Might he or she be granted salvation? Will I see him or her in heaven some day? Is he or she loved by God to the same extent that I am loved? Yandell suggested that such questioning adds information. The more information a forgiver has, the deeper he or she may forgive. We like this critique and intend to pursue these issues in future scientific studies.

George had no idea of Sally's upbringing, and so he began his reframing when she was promoted: "I realized that she was nervous about the possibility of not being promoted. She used to talk of the 'glass ceiling' in which women look up and want to advance up to the next higher level, but it remains inaccessible. I think she was so nervous about being trapped in the lower position that she did not focus on anyone else, at least temporarily, but herself, which is understandable to me now. Society created an expectation in her that she would not get ahead. It made her fight harder. I began to see her as a fighter; I mean this in a positive sense. Her silence at my plight was not a judgment about me. It expressed her own deep concerns about the way the corporate world seems to work. Yes, she could have been more sympathetic, but I understand."

Showing Empathy and Compassion

Following the cognitive exercises of reframing, the client examines the emergence of empathy and the moral emotion of compassion. We find that it is difficult for some clients to "step inside the other's shoes" because that client does not feel safe around the offender. Empathy is one of the developmental characteristics of forgiveness. It cannot be engineered or simply willed into existence. Its emergence takes time, sometimes a great deal of time. Therapy, in other words, can support its emergence but cannot force it.

A clue that a person may be ready to step inside the other's shoes is gleaned from the success of reframing. Does the client seem to understand who the other is, without distortion? Distortions can take two forms: One is overdeprecation, whereas the other is overadulation. In both cases the client fails to distinguish the person and his or her actions. In overdeprecation, the client judges the person's worth in light of the hurtful acts. In overadulation, the client equates the person's acts with his or her worthiness, concluding that the acts must be fine if the person is of value.

If the client is condemnatory about the person rather than his or her acts, then reframing has not progressed sufficiently yet. Continuing with the reframing exercises is warranted here. If he or she shows placation toward the harmful acts, then perhaps the client is failing to distinguish forgiveness and reconciliation. Reintroducing the definition of forgiveness, including what it is and is not, may be in order.

Empathy, in other words, is not some automatic step devoid of complication or even danger. The therapist needs to provide guidance to a client who empathizes with a perpetual abuser but then does not assess the abuser's trustworthiness. Empathy can work on the side of forgiveness, but it also can work on the side of enmeshment and enabling. This is why reductionism must be avoided in our forgiveness models. Empathy, as part of a total program including the understanding of forgiveness, reconciliation, and reframing, can be an aid to psychological improvement. Isolated from these other features of forgiveness therapy, it can work against the client's best interests.

Only when the client is ready should the therapist proceed to the exercise of stepping inside the offender's shoes. If reframing was successful, the client is likely to get a sense of the offender's confusion, fear, or vulnerability. Empathy need not occur in large doses or for extended periods at first. It is sufficient if the client for a moment can get a quick sense of the other's vulnerability. For particularly offensive injustices, the client should continue to distinguish forgiving and reconciling. Where there is no danger, especially when the relationship has been on solid ground, this exercise can proceed more quickly and for longer duration.

Empathy is morally neutral. As one steps inside another's shoes, the one who empathizes can use this new information for good or ill. Compassion, however, is one of the moral emotions because its goal is the other's good. To have compassion is to come alongside another person and be willing to help, to suffer along with him or her. As repeated from chapter 2, one aspect of forgiveness is to reach out, within reason, to the offender. Compassion is the fuel that makes this possible. Again, therapists do not want to create a situation for a patient in which he or she misunderstands forgiveness or reconciliation, yet rushes to compassion. See the quality of a moral virtue, of which forgiveness is one, in chapter 15. The virtues are expressed within a mean, within an average, avoiding extremes. Compassion must be understood in this context.

Compassion can be the beginning of the person's release from the thickening of hatred that has a way of building and frothing as the years pass. It is one of those emotions that is incompatible with the destructive emotions of bitterness, hatred, and revenge-seeking. When a person is feeling compassion toward the offender, it is unlikely that he or she will feel these other destructive emotions. Compassion, in other words, can be a buffer, a protector against the emotions that lead to the various layers of pain discussed in the Uncovering Phase.

Compassion emerges in a way we do not yet fully understand. It remains one of those mysteries of forgiveness therapy. We see it unfold even though we provide no particular techniques to ensure its growth. It is conceivable that as the person studies the definition of forgiveness, engages in reframing, and tries to empathize, compassion develops. More study is needed on this point.

George recalls "When I saw that Sally was *still* nervous after her promotion, I began to feel for her. The promotion did not lead to greater confidence in her. She once was talking and said something about how we all advance to the level of our own incompetence. She was very concerned about making it on that new level. She is a more vulnerable person than I had thought. I guess we all carry our own unique burdens. It was easier to forgive her at this point, although I can still get angry."

Bearing the Pain

The Israeli psychiatrist Morton Kaufman (1984, p. 186) was the first to link forgiveness with the courageous act of "the readiness to bear pain" caused by the offense. He did not mean that the patient permanently must accept the debilitating emotions of anxiety and depression, but instead implied that the patient begins to mature as a person by accepting what happened. Allen Bergin's (1988) ideas are similar. He refered to the importance of absorbing the pain passed down through the generations within a family. Families seem to have a characteristic pattern of hurting the members in certain ways. If one person in a given generation takes the courageous step of bearing up under the pain, of absorbing the pain, then the intergenerational transmission of that pattern of hurtful interactions (what Bergin called "the pain") may cease.

It may take time for a person to understand or accept the ideas expressed here. Clients who resist the idea do so for a variety of reasons. First, there may be a misunderstanding about what is meant by "bearing" or "absorbing" the pain. The therapist may need to point out that this is a transitional step, one that passes away as the person quietly begins to live with the hurt caused by the injustice. In other words, on bearing the pain the client makes it possible for that pain to cease. Second, the person may erroneously conclude that he or she cannot seek fairness now. This, too, is not accurate because the forgiver can seek justice as he or she forgives, as we have discussed before. What we are suggesting is this: The hurtful event happened; it is part of one's historical record; it cannot be reversed; the person is capable of bearing the pain caused by this historical event while seeking a fair solution in the present. Yet, if the client truly understands the subtlety of "bearing the pain," he or she may seek justice in ways different from when he or she is angry and upset at the offender. Third, he or she may not be developmentally ready for this step, which requires, in Kaufman's (1984) words, "courage." The person may be still developing a sense of the other through reframing or may be struggling with empathy and compassion.

As Kaufman (1984) reported in his case study, and as we have observed, patients who begin to quietly bear the pain realize that they are stronger than they had thought. One incest survivor reported that on bearing or absorbing the pain she considered herself not a victim but a survivor. Our unit of bearing the pain is not a passive step. It involves waiting, but with the expectation that the suffering will pass as forgiveness deepens.

For George, bearing up under the pain of not being promoted meant that his family was healthier: "I forgave for Bernice and the kids. I was coming home in a better frame of mind. I had more energy to play with the children after supper. I even was able to carry on a conversation with the children without spacing out in the middle."

Giving a Moral Gift

Forgiveness, being a moral virtue, is expressive. It does not occur only within the one who forgives. The goodness is expressed to others. As we saw in chapter 1, beneficence toward the offender is part of the definition of forgiveness. Yet, there are an infinite number of ways to demonstrate beneficence: with a smile, expressions of concern, a friendly note, or even an altruistic concern for the other's welfare. Beneficence, being supererogatory, cannot be forced or rushed or even expected. Some people are so hurt by another person that the thought of beneficence is caustic. At times the therapist and client must be content with the diminution of resentment.

At other times, the expression of beneficence completes both the process of forgiveness and psychological healing. In Freedman and Enright's (1996) study, for example, some of the incest survivors, near the end of the intervention, reached out to their fathers (or father figures) in new and unexpected ways. One visited her dad's grave for the first time. Another began to revive the memory of her father, talking positively to her children about their grandfather, which was a gift to the children, who now have a connection to their past, absent before this. Another visited her father in the hospital and helped with his care. When he died, she reported her thankfulness for having forgiven, otherwise both the struggle and confusion of forgiveness and mourning would have intertwined.

George reported, "At first I was resistant to helping Sally or any of the others with their work when they needed assistance, but as I began to forgive, I found myself helping whenever I was needed. I could help with a genuine motive of wanting to aid them. It felt good."

Using Journaling or Homework Exercises

We recommend that the therapist ask the patient to deepen his or her story of the other person in the journal. Add specific detail regarding these issues: What was life like for the person when growing up? What was life like for the person at the time of the offense? What has the relationship with the person been like in a broader sense than the offense itself? What is the person like when you see his or her true humanity by taking a global perspective? What is the person like when you take the cosmic perspective, seeing him or her in a spiritual, religious sense (if such a perspective is part of his or her worldview). Then, ask the patient to reread all of the above journal entries and ask: How has your view of the person changed as a result of answering these questions?

For the affective transformations of empathy and compassion, have the client write down his or her feelings toward the offender as the client experiences those emotions at the moment. Are there any signs of positive emotions, even if they slip quickly by? Has the anger been lessening?

Next, the therapist might want to ask the patient to write in the journal what it means, in this case, to accept the pain that the offender imposed. How difficult is it to accept the pain? Again, the patient could rate the difficulty on a scale from 1 (*very difficult*) to 10 (*very easy*). The patient's worldview may prove helpful, because certain religious traditions give examples and provide role models for bearing the pain.

Finally, the therapist might consider encouraging the client to reflect in writing on the kind of gift appropriate to give the offender. Is it appropriate to send a note, help with a chore, prepare a nice dinner? Evaluate each idea; the client must feel comfortable with the final idea.

Units Within the Deepening Phase

The Deepening Phase in particular is the one in which the units can appear earlier, in other phases. It is important, therefore, that the therapist be cognizant of the units as they spontaneously emerge for the client.

Finding Meaning

We are indebted to the work of Viktor Frankl (1959) for his exposition on meaning for the client who has suffered. Frankl believed that the heart of healing was in finding a rational meaning, a narrative that made sense to the one suffering. Forgiveness, of course, is in such a context of suffering when the injustice is profoundly unfair and the hurt deep. People will vary greatly in their narratives of meaning in suffering depending on their worldview. If the client's worldview makes room for suffering, sees it as an inevitable part of the world, and even sees benefit in it, then the client is likely to make substantial progress with this unit. Frankl, being an existential psychologist, allowed for considerable freedom and creativity when the client was seeking meaning.

George recalls, "This chance to work on forgiveness had made me a more patient husband and father. I think I am gaining in maturity and tranquility. Without the adversity, I doubt this would have happened. The family has gained." See Reed (1998), Reed et al. (1999), and Frankl (1969) for more information on finding meaning in suffering.

We have the following suggestions for those therapists who will cultivate meaning from the client's suffering:

- Does the client's worldview include a way out of suffering, or is suffering only to be borne without relief in this world? If there is a way out, explore what that is. If there is no way out of suffering, explore whether the client is exaggerating the worldview, giving it a pessimistic spin.
- Is the suffering something that benefits others? If so, try to find out who those others are.
- What good usually comes from suffering, according to the worldview?
- How can one find relief for self and others while suffering, according to the worldview?
- Is suffering a reality of this world, or is it caused primarily by one's own perceptions? If the worldview states that suffering is one's own making, be careful of self-blame, guilt, and depression if the suffering does not clear. Be careful that the client does not passively accept what happened without recourse to justice. After all, if the client sees himself or herself as the primary problem, then why work for change in the world?
- Does the narrative make sense in light of forgiveness, and does the narrative seem to help ease the client's psychological symptoms?

Having Needed Others' Forgiveness

At times, people who are hurt by another think that it is wrong to forgive. At these times it may be helpful to ask the person if he or she has ever wronged others. Was forgiveness extended? How did that feel? What were the consequences of receiving forgiveness? Answers to these kinds of questions can motivate a person to forgive. Taking Yandell's (1998) ideas about reframing into this context, the person might examine his or her forgiveness from another person, or a group such as a family, or God. The person's worldview may expand or limit this exploration.

We place this unit into the Deepening Phase because many people are so intent on their own situation that the questioning becomes a distraction. At the end of the forgiveness process, however, some people begin to generalize their forgiving to others, even considering the reverse cases of receiving forgiveness. All of these examinations deepen understanding of forgiveness and can serve as a motivator to continue forgiving. When a person is ambivalent about whether to forgive, asking questions like the ones here early in therapy may aid in the decision.

Knowing That One Is Not Alone

Sometimes the pains of injustice can make us feel isolated and alone. As the person forgives, he or she may see that others are there to help. This tends to make the exploration easier and the motivation stronger. As with the unit above, a therapist may wish to explore the issue of support earlier in therapy if the person is feeling particularly isolated. Directly seeking such support may be necessary to continue. Finding a confidant who will discuss the issues is helpful. Again, depending on one's worldview, having recourse to divine help may be important, as we saw in Poloma and Gallup's (1991) research in our introduction. Having recourse to support earlier rather than later in therapy may be important. On the other hand, some may wish to explore the entire sequence of forgiveness units before recycling through on a deeper level.

Realizing a New Purpose

As a person masters forgiveness, he or she sometimes wishes to give back to others what he or she has learned. Quite a few of the incest survivors in Freedman and Enright's (1996) study expressed an interest in counseling other incest survivors. This unit oftentimes is focused on people not involved in the original offense. It is a generalization, not of forgiveness, but of beneficence in a context other than one's own need to forgive. It is a giving back to the community when one's life is beginning to become more settled. The new sense of purpose may develop long after therapy is over. Yet, the therapist should be open to this kind of transformation because the seeds of it may be sown within therapy. In essence, this is an action-oriented dimension of therapy involving new goals related to what was learned in therapy.

George decided to do his best at work, regardless of the consequences. His goal was to be a respectful colleague, one who tries hard and does his best. He also decided that if the situation of nonpromotion continues, then he will apply to other companies. He has the energy to do this and he would, in all likelihood, get excellent letters of recommendation because of his newly found maturity at work.

Being Aware of Affective Transformation

In chapter 1, we discussed forgiveness as being transformational. At therapy's end, many patients or clients may, if they have had enough time to explore and struggle with the varied units that constitute the forgiveness process, realize that their sense of well-being is developing. As resentments diminish and as a sense of beneficence grows, lower levels of anxiety or depression and higher levels of hope and self-esteem may emerge. As George remembers, "I think what I got most out of all this is a greater sense of humility. I don't have to always have my own way. This has definitely quieted me inside. Sure, I can still have my bad days, but for the most part, I am more emotionally steady than before I went through all of this." Of course, such outcomes can and should be scientifically tested. That is our task for the next chapter, to examine the scientific tests of this model.

Using Journaling or Homework Exercises

Each question in the "Finding Meaning" section of this phase could form the basis of journal writing and reflection. A key question is: What have you learned as a result of the suffering that you have endured?

To help the person realize his or her need to be forgiven, the therapist might ask the patient to reflect on this question: Can you recall a specific incident (not necessarily involving the one who hurt you) in which you hoped to be forgiven? What was it like to be on the receiving end of the gift? How might these insights aid your forgiving?

Does the person have a confidant with whom he or she can discuss the journal entries? If not, he or she may wish to write down potential people here. If he or she has the support, this may be a good time to reflect on the quality of that support and how the companion has aided forgiveness.

As the person grows in forgiveness, ask him or her to reflect in writing on any new purpose in life that may be emerging. These insights could be discussed in therapy. Finally, it is helpful for the person to write about the new sense of well-being that is developing. A good way to assess progress is for the client to reread the early journal entries concerning anger and contrast them with the changes occurring now.

6

EMPIRICAL VALIDATION OF THE PROCESS MODEL OF FORGIVENESS

This chapter provides considerable scientific detail for the academics, who may not only want to understand the details of the science but also wish to critique what we did, how we did it, and what we report finding. It is also for the clinicians, whose skepticism about forgiveness in therapy leaves him or her questioning the validity of our approach.

For those busy clinicians who do not wish this level of detail, we recommend that they skim the details of each study and read the "Results and Discussion" sections of each, along with the "General Discussion" near the chapter's end.

The research team at the University of Wisconsin–Madison published four papers detailing the use of the process model in interventions with elderly people (Hebl & Enright, 1993), late adolescents hurt by parents (Al-Mabuk, Enright, & Cardis, 1995), incest survivors (Freedman & Enright, 1996), and men hurt by the abortion decision of their partner (Coyle & Enright, 1997). In each case we used the process model as it was developed at the time. In the early formation, that model consisted of 17 units, whereas the later version had 20. In all cases the modifications were modest. For example, Unit 15, giving a moral gift to the offender, was implicit in the earlier version. We decided to make this more explicit when we realized a drift within the psychological community toward deemphasizing forgiveness as a moral construct. Units 16 (finding meaning) and 19 (finding new purpose) were added as the research team observed participants struggling to make sense of what happened. As with Unit 15, these processes were implicit and became explicit in the interventions.

We begin with the first empirically based intervention ever published on the topic of forgiveness, Hebl and Enright (1993). That it was done in the 1990s rather than the 1950s is testimony to how new the exploration of this topic is within psychology.

FORGIVENESS WITH ELDERLY WOMEN

Hebl and Enright (1993) tested the process model with 24 elderly women. The mean age was 74.5 years; all were at least 65. Women in particular were chosen to enhance homogeneity of the groups because of the abundance in this age group. Letters of invitation were mailed to 204 potential participants. The following conditions had to be met for a person to be included in the study: The person has a specific person in mind to forgive, the participant felt emotionally hurt by what happened, and she is not going through a mourning process. The last was included because the dynamics of forgiveness are quite different from mourning, and we did not want the two to overlap, possibly complicating our observations and findings.

Of the 24 chosen, 37% were married and 63% were widowed or divorced. The screening survey revealed that 21% were dealing with what they perceived to be family injustice, 50% with friendship conflicts, 12.5% with in-law problems, and 16.5% with other interpersonal unfairness requiring forgiveness.

Instruments and Testing Procedures

Three instruments were administered in a group format at pretest: self-esteem, depression, and anxiety. These together with two forgiveness instruments were given at posttest. We decided not to give the forgiveness assessments at pretest so that the control group was not exposed to the purpose of the study. Otherwise, the control group might focus on forgiveness during their discussions. The test administrator was unaware of the research hypotheses.

Standard instruments were given at pretest: the Coopersmith Self-Esteem Inventory (Coopersmith, 1981), the Beck Depression Inventory (Beck, Ward, Mendelson, Mock, & Erbaugh, 1961), and the Spielberger State–Trait Anxiety Inventory (Spielberger, Gorsuch, Lushene, Vagg, & Jacobs, 1983).

The Psychological Profile of Forgiveness Scale (PPFS) was the measure chosen to assess the degree to which the person forgave a particular person for a specific injustice. The PPFS was the precursor to the Enright Forgiveness

Inventory (EFI) now in use (see chapter 19). Enright and seven graduate students developed the inventory by generating five items in each of six categories: the degree of negative affect felt toward the offender, the degree of positive affect felt, the degree of negative cognition, the degree of positive cognition, the degree of negative behavior, and the degree of positive behavior demonstrated toward him or her. If the offender was deceased or if the two were not interacting, the participant considered the behavioral items in terms of how he or she would respond were the offender present. (See exhibit 19.1 in chapter 19 for examples of items)

The participant considered the degree to which he or she agreed or disagreed with a given item on a 4-point Likert scale (the EFI is on a 6-point Likert scale). The 30-item scale has a range of scores from 30 to 120, with a high score representing high forgiveness. In this study, Cronbach's alpha of internal consistency reliability was .97.

The second forgiveness instrument, the Willingness to Forgive Scale, presents 15 hypothetical scenarios (e.g., suppose someone steals your car). The participant is presented with 10 multiple-choice responses and is asked to consider how she in all likelihood would respond if, in fact, someone stole her car. Examples are "get even," "just forget it," "talk with a counselor or friend," "forgive," and others. The participant is given 1 point every time she advocates for forgiveness in choosing a likely response to the difficulty. The instrument, rather than assessing degree of forgiveness toward a particular person (as in the PPFS), measures a person's readiness to forgive in general.

Intervention Procedures

The 24 participants were randomly assigned to either an experimental group that received forgiveness therapy or to a control group that received traditional support group therapy. Each group met for 1 hour once per week for 8 weeks. The same male therapist led both groups. He had many years of counseling experience and had spent several years studying forgiveness before the study. We wanted to control for the competence of the therapist across studies and equalize the participants' perceptions of the group leader. All sessions were audiotaped and were rated by two experienced therapists for his accuracy in following the treatment manual or procedure. The raters, unaware of the hypotheses, stated that the therapist had high accuracy in fulfilling the intent of each program.

The Forgiveness Sessions

The procedures of the process model were written in manual form and used as a guide by the therapist. The participants were not given the manual but a written outline detailing the session for the following week. The form of each session was as follows: the first half-hour was spent summarizing the main points for that day; about 5 minutes then was taken for reflection on questions pertaining to the particular unit under consideration; the 12 participants were randomly divided into two smaller groups for more in-depth consideration of how the unit pertains to oneself; this was followed by a general discussion by the entire group.

Session 1 concerned accurate understanding of what forgiveness is and is not, including information on pseudoforgiveness. The psychological defenses that can keep a person from a forgiveness response also were discussed. Session 2 focused on anger. The person was asked to reflect on the depth and intensity of hurt at this time. Session 3 targeted the complications that can befall a person who lives with an abiding sense of deep anger. For Session 4, the participants considered committing to forgiveness as a way of dealing with the injustice and concomitant anger and complications.

The work of forgiveness, in the form of reframing, empathy, and compassion, comprised Session 5. The participants were challenged to step inside the offender's shoes and see, if possible, a vulnerable person. In Session 6, the group leader asked people to reflect on those times that she needed others' forgiveness. This was done to increase a sense of how important forgiveness can be for the one who receives it. It also served to let the participants realize that they themselves are not perfect but are prone to error and injustice toward others. Session 7 concerned the issue of bearing the pain. It was pointed out that bearing the pain stops displacements that can victimize others. Bearing of pain can be a gift to the one who offended and to those who are vulnerable around us. At the final session, the participants reflected on the entire path of forgiveness, including the remaining units not yet discussed.

The control group met weekly in a support group to discuss other issues relevant to elderly people, such as health care, but forgiveness was not part of those discussions.

Results and Discussion

A 2 × 2 (experimental and control groups, pretest to posttest) analysis of variance was used to analyze the dependent measures of self-esteem, anxiety, and depression. Significant differences were found for the main effect of time (pretest to posttest) for trait anxiety and depression. In other words, both groups seemed to benefit from their own intervention. At pretest, both groups were about at 42 on trait anxiety, higher than average. At posttest, they averaged about 33, within the normal range. Even though the experimental and control groups did not differ from one another in trait anxiety, the averages at posttest were quite different from a clinical perspective ($M = 25.77$ for the forgiveness group and $M = 40$ for the support group). In depression, the groups went from an average of about 10–11 to about 7, clinically nondepressed in both cases but showing improvement within the normal range.

The forgiveness variables were analyzed with one-tailed t tests at posttest. The overall PPFS showed statistical significance favoring the forgiveness therapy. Of the six subscales, four were significant favoring the experimental group: absence of negative affect, absence of negative cognition, presence of positive affect, and presence of positive behavior. For the Willingness to Forgive Scale, the experimental group had higher forgiveness scores compared with the control group with a two-sample test of proportions. This suggests that those in forgiveness therapy were more willing than those in the control group to choose forgiveness as a general problem-solving strategy when faced with hypothetical situations of unfairness.

It appears that both groups were effective in bringing about a change in the participants' emotional situations of anxiety and depression. Of course, it is possible that time alone is responsible, but the fact that the changes were realized in trait anxiety and depression suggests otherwise. These two variables are not easily influenced by the passage of time in such a systematic way with 24 people. Surely some may show a spontaneous amelioration of symptoms after 8 weeks, but for the entire sample to show trends toward improvement seems unlikely without the interventions. We should recall Wampold et al.'s (1997) findings that all good interventions are capable of showing positive results. This does not detract from either one, but shows that the pathway to emotional healing can be varied.

This study was the first to show that it is possible to effect change in forgiveness through deliberate intervention. Two patterns emerged, one dealing with the degree of forgiveness offered to a specific offender and the other with a general tendency to consider forgiveness when injustices arise.

It is important to examine effects in other studies that use a different leader because the particular leader here may be so effective that he is primarily responsible for the positive forgiveness effects. Observing the outcomes with different populations also is in order to generalize the findings. The next study was done, in part, to address these scientific issues.

FORGIVENESS WITH COLLEGE STUDENTS HURT BY PARENTS

Al-Mabuk, Enright, and Cardis (1995) reported two studies done with college students who experienced parental love deprivation. By deprivation, we mean that the student perceived at least one of the parents to be emotionally distant for a period of years as the student grew up. Study 1 differs from all other studies reported here because it was a test of the first part of the process model only, up to the Decision Phase. We wanted to see whether exposure to the entire model, which we observed in Study 2, was any more effective than coming to a decision to forgive. Recall that some researchers make the claim that forgiveness is primarily a decision. If this is so, then Study 1 should be as effective, or nearly as effective, as Study 2.

Study 1: Forgiveness as Decision Making

Forty-eight college students (37 women and 11 men) from a midwestern university served as participants. Average age was 20, and average year in school was the junior year. Seventy-eight students were initially screened for parental love deprivation. Only those scoring at least one standard deviation above the mean on that measure were eligible for the intervention. Of the 24 forgiveness group participants, 15 reported such deprivation from the father, 8 from the mother, and one from both. In the control group, 18 reported deprivation from the father and 6 from the mother.

Instruments

The screening device consisted of 22 questions toward mother and father, answered separately and counterbalanced across participants. Examples of questions are as follows: While growing up, I often felt my mother (father) was busy doing her own thing; I received many hugs and kisses from my mother (father); I felt resentful toward my father (mother) for saying cruel things to or about me. Each item was rated on a 5-point Likert scale with a high score representing high parental love deprivation, with a range between 22 and 110. As a further check on parent–child difficulties, we asked each participant whether he or she retained resentment and to list about four specific incidents of parental love deprivation while growing up. These specifics had to be listed for a student to be eligible for the intervention.

As in Hebl and Enright's (1993) study, the following scales were given: the PPFS (Cronbach's α = .92), the Willingness to Forgive Scale, the State–Trait Anxiety Inventory, and the Beck Depression Inventory.

Other instruments included the Hope Scale, a 30-item Likert-type 1-to-5 scale for each item (range is 30–150, with a high score representing high optimism toward the future), the Coopersmith Self-Esteem Scale (Coopersmith, 1981), and an Attitude Toward Mother/Father Scale, consisting of 25 items each for mother and father assessing the current relationship ("I dislike my mother" or "I really enjoy my father"). The 5-point Likert format, from 0 to 4, has a range of scores from 0 (*harmony in the relationship*) to 100 (*high conflict*).

Testing Procedures

All of the assessments were in a group format. The screening measure was given at pretest only. Four were administered at pretests and posttests: Willingness to Forgive, Attitude Toward Mother/Father, Hope, and Anxiety. Three were given at posttest only: Psychological Profile of Forgiveness, Depression, and Self-Esteem. All scales were counterbalanced.

Intervention Procedures

A randomized experimental and control group design stratified by gender was selected. The forgiveness group had 19 women and 5 men; the control group had 18 women and 6 men. The same male therapist, trained for several years in counseling and educated in the literature on forgiveness, led all group sessions for both groups. Both experimental and control groups met for four 1-hour sessions, two sessions per week for 2 weeks. Both used a workshop format. The general pattern was this: a half hour of didactic instruction, 10 minutes of self-reflection, then about 20 minutes of group instruction.

Forgiveness Sessions

A written manual was prepared as a guide for the group leader but was not shared with the participants. Session 1 was intended to introduce the participants to the definition of forgiveness, including what it is not, and to the meaning of parental love deprivation. The various complications to unfairness were discussed and reflected on. These included denial, repression and other defenses, anger, shame, cathexis, and cognitive rehearsal. The participants were challenged to consider their current worldviews. Were these beliefs about how the world works mostly positive, mostly negative, or stereotypical? To what extent did the difficulties with parents contribute to the existing worldview?

Session 2 began with a review, followed by a challenge to begin resolving the interpersonal hurt. Each participant was asked to reflect on his or her current strategy for resolving the difficulty. Forgiveness as a way to deal with the problem was presented, including the ways that forgiveness can ameliorate anger and its complications. The session ended with each student listing the costs and benefits of both forgiveness and his or her current problem-solving strategy.

Session 3 introduced the ideas surrounding a "change of heart" (Unit 9 of the process model). This included the various obstacles and supports to a forgiveness response. Some of these variables may include cultural conditioning, family and peer support, philosophical and religious beliefs, and the type of problem and depth of suffering experienced. Each person was asked to gauge the degree of his or her readiness to begin forgiving.

Session 4 concerned the commitment to forgive. After a review of the first three sessions, the group facilitator challenged those ready to forgive to examine the implications of abandoning resentment and related responses. It was pointed out that forgiveness is a genuine act of mercy toward the parent or parents, which may include positive affect as it eventually emerges. Forgiveness can include the seeking of a new relationship, to the extent that one can trust the other. Reframing (Unit 12) was briefly mentioned as an aid to the decision to forgive. At the end, all of the participants were given a contract to sign, only if they chose, committing to forgive the parents. These contracts were given privately and remained private.

Control Procedure

The control group engaged in a human relations program intended to enhance communication and interaction skills in general. Issues of leadership (Session 1), two-way communication (Session 2), self-discovery (Session 3), and person perception (Session 4) were included.

Results and Discussion

For those scales given at pretest and posttest (Attitude Toward Mother/ Father, Hope, Anxiety, and Willingness to Forgive), change scores were calculated and t tests used to assess differences between the groups. Hope and Willingness to Forgive were statistically significant, favoring the forgiveness group. After the intervention, the experimental group was more optimistic about the future and considered forgiveness as an option in dealing with hypothetical injustices more than did the control group. It is obvious that genuine forgiveness toward the parent was not accomplished, given the statistical equivalence of the two groups on the Attitude Toward Mother/ Father Scale. For example, the experimental group began the study with a mean of 37.5 on this variable toward the father; at posttest the mean was 32.5. Given that harmony is realized around a score of zero, there was room to grow here.

This sense that forgiveness was not accomplished toward the parent was further supported in examining the posttest-only measure, the PPFS, which was not significantly different across the groups. This was found despite the fact that 23 of the 24 experimental respondents signed the contract at Session 4 committing to forgive the parent. Neither depression nor self-esteem, given at posttest only, showed group differences that were significant.

It seems that there is a distinction between committing to forgive a parent and actually forgiving. The task here was to see whether a workshop focused on the commitment to forgive could, in fact, induce that commitment. This occurred. We further were interested in the extent to which the commitment would foster actual forgiveness, which it did not, and psychological improvement, which it did only for a sense of hope toward the future, but not in the clinically relevant areas of depression, anxiety, and self-esteem. What might happen with the forgiveness variable and the clinical indicators if we put parentally love-deprived college students through a regimen including the entire process model? Study 2 was commenced to answer this question.

Study 2: Examining the Full Model

Forty-five college students (29 women and 16 men) from a midwestern university different from Study 1 were the participants. Average age and years in school were similar to Study 1. These were chosen, similar to the Study 1 criteria, from an initial pool of 331 students. Of the 24 experimental participants, 12 reported love deprivation from the father, 7 from the mother, and 5 from both. Of the 21 control group respondents, 12 reported love deprivation from the father, 6 from the mother, and 3 from both.

Instruments and Testing Procedures

All measures from Study 1 were retained here (Cronbach's α = .94 for the PPFS). All except for self-esteem and depression (which were given at posttest only) were given at both pretests and posttests. As in Study 1, testing was in a group format, and all scales were counterbalanced.

Forgiveness Sessions

Again, a manual representing a description of the units of the process model was prepared and used only by the group facilitator, who was the same male therapist as in Study 1. The number of workshop sessions was extended from four to six to accommodate the greater amount of forgiveness material that now would be presented.

Sessions 1–4 were similar to Study 1, with the exception that Session 4 had more in-depth coverage of reframing. The students were asked to "step inside the parents' shoes" and examine the target parent's experiences while the parent was growing up and while striving to provide for a family as an adult. The intent was to see the parent as a vulnerable person who is imperfect, not someone who is so perfect that he or she should be held to standards above most others.

Session 5 concerned the affective exercises of empathy and compassion toward the parent. These are not easily induced and cannot be rushed. Our intent was to have the student be aware that such affective transformations are possible and to be aware of them as they emerged when reframing who the parent is.

The themes of empathy and compassion served as a bridge in Session 6 to the more abstract notion of bearing or absorbing the pain. The students reflected on the fact that they cannot rewrite the past because it, in fact, did happen. Instead, the students were encouraged to reflect on the meaning of "absorbing the pain," not to internalize such unwanted emotions as anxiety and depression, but to bear up under the pain so that others do not needlessly suffer because of the student's own distress. It was clarified that the student can become a conduit for good in the family now and in the future, following Bergin's (1988) ideas. The student's own occasional failings with other people served as a motivator to continue examining forgiveness. The session ended with the exploration of the student's affective state and whether forgiveness might be emerging for him or her. Because forgiveness is a process that may unfold slowly, the students were instructed that more time and effort may be necessary for complete forgiveness.

Control Procedure

As in Study 1, the control participants engaged in a human relations workshop.

Results and Discussion

All but one of the measures (state anxiety) administered at both testing sessions showed significant change score, t-test differences between the experimental and control groups, favoring those who participated in the forgiveness sessions. The PPFS went up from a mean of 81 at pretest to a mean of 101.5 at posttest within the experimental group. Recall that the highest possible score is 120. In contrast, the control group went from a mean of 82.2 to 86.6. (The subscales of the PPFS were not analyzed.) On trait anxiety, those participating in the forgiveness workshop went from an average of 46.1 (above the expected norms) to 34.8 (which is considered normal). Hope, willingness to forgive in hypothetical situations, and attitudes toward the parents improved. As an example of gains, recall in Study 1 that attitude toward the father mean was in the 32-to-37 range for the experimental group. Here in Study 2, the pretest mean for the experimental group was 36.7 and fell to 18.4 (with zero representing perfect harmony).

On the posttest only measures, self-esteem was statistically higher for the experimental than for the control group. Psychological depression showed no posttest group difference because both groups were nondepressed. A floor effect prevented a valid observation of this variable. We again gave participants the contracts to sign at the final session, this time giving the contracts to the control group as well. As in Study 1, 23 of 24 experimental participants privately signed the contract. In the control group, only 10 of 21 signed it.

The results here are encouraging because of the broad-based nature of the findings. The experimental group not only improved in two dimensions of forgiveness, but also improved in trait anxiety, self-esteem, hope, and attitude toward the parents. It appears that the full process model is effective in reversing the deleterious effects of parental love deprivation in late adolescence, whereas a focus only on a part of that model concerned with commitment to forgiveness is not.

Our research program to this point still did not include follow-up information. Wash-out effects that plague so much intervention work may play a part in forgiveness as well. The next study addresses this issue.

FORGIVENESS WITH ADULT INCEST SURVIVORS

Freedman and Enright (1996) tested the process model with 12 female incest survivors from the Midwest. All reported having been sexually abused as children. Mean age was 36 years with a range between 24 and 52 years. Fifty percent reported abuse from their biological father, 8% from a step-father, 16% from a brother, 12% from a grandfather, and 8% from an uncle. Average educational level was 15 years, and all participants were White. Three of the participants were married, 5 were single, and 4 were divorced. The average age of onset of abuse was 6.3 years, and the average duration of abuse was slightly less than 6 years. Sexual contact included the following: 42% experienced intercourse, 17% fondling and oral-genital contact, and 42% fondling only.

Instruments

A screening interview and a crisis symptom checklist were given to all potential participants. Those who met the criteria of being sexually abused, involving contact, with a male relative and who had not experienced abuse over the past 2 years were eligible for the study. Also, participants had to show clinical symptoms on the screening interview, the checklist, and pretest measures.

The following scales were given at pretest, posttest, and follow-up: the PPFS (Cronbach's α = .92 in this study), State–Trait Anxiety Inventory, Beck Depression Inventory, Coopersmith Self-Esteem Inventory, and the Hope scale. In addition, a self-report forgiveness measure devised for this study was given. Three definitions of forgiveness were presented to partici-pants after the intervention began and at periodic intervals during the intervention. The word *forgiveness* was not used in the definitions. Partici-pants were then asked to answer five questions about their feelings toward the offender. This assessment was done to gauge the extent to which the participant had completed the forgiveness process toward the perpetrator. If a respondent reported that she agreed with the statements specifically regarding her offender and if the rationale behind her decision appeared valid, then she was judged to have genuinely forgiven and the intervention terminated at that point. We did this because the intervention was criterion-referenced without a set time limit for each participant.

Testing Procedures

Because we had a relatively small sample size, we wanted to reduce the standard error of measurement as much as possible for each scale. To do this, we actually had each participant at pretest fill out each scale three times at 2-week intervals. In other words, the PPFS, for example, was given on Monday, then 2 weeks later was readministered, then 2 weeks later again was readministered. This occurred for each dependent measure. An average of the three assessments at pretest constituted the pretest score for any given measure. The same procedure held at posttest. The only exception to the three assessment procedure occurred at the follow-up for the original experimental group. Because the intervention had been over for more than a year for this group, it was difficult to ask them to fill out questionnaires over a 6-week period. Thus, they completed all follow-up assessments only once. At every assessment period, the scales were presented in random order.

Intervention Procedures

A randomized experimental and control group design was used. Each participant was matched with another on age and pattern of abuse. The members of a given pair were then randomly assigned to condition. The intervention was individual with a female intervener who had experience working with sexual abuse victims and who had extensive training in the psychology of forgiveness. We also used a crossover design in which an original control group participant began the intervention after her counterpart experimental participant completed it. The experimental participants met with the intervener for an individual 1-hour session once per week. The control group was a waitlist condition in which the participants were free to seek therapy as they wished throughout the waiting period.

The experimental participants were each given a manual detailing the forgiveness process with examples pertinent to sexual abuse. Each participant worked through the material at her own pace. The range of time was 10–16 months with an average of 14 months per participant.

Experimental sessions were randomly audiotaped with the participants' permission and were rated by graduated students regarding the accuracy in which the session matched the intention as outlined in the manual. Independent judges agreed 88% of the time that the content on the audio-tapes (30 in all) matched the stated intentions in the manual.

The Forgiveness Sessions

Participants, given a copy of the manual, were instructed to read the material in the order presented. The manual formed the basis for the 1-hour discussions each week. There was one written unit in the manual for each unit of the process model as outlined in chapter 5. Because we have made modest refinements on the model since this research, only 17 of the 20 units were represented in the manual, which is available from Robert D. Enright on request.

Results and Discussion

Data were analyzed in four separate comparisons. In the first, the dependent measures were converted to change scores from *pretest to posttest* and compared through *t*-tests between the experimental and control groups. Statistical significance was found on all measures favoring the experimental group except for self-esteem. Within the PPFS, the overall scale was statistically significant as well as the following subscales: significant increases in the positive affect and cognition subscales and significant decreases in the negative thoughts and behavior subscales all favoring the experimental group. The subscale change patterns do not match exactly those in Hebl and Enright (1993), in which positive affect and behavior and negative affect and cognition showed change. The only subscale not to show improvement across the two studies is in positive behavior. Perhaps there are trust issues that need to be worked out before participants are ready to show generosity toward a person who has deeply and unfairly hurt them.

For the overall PPFS, the experimental group went from a mean of 60.5 (which is quite low compared with the pretest M = 81 in Al-Mabuk, Enright, & Cardis, 1995) to 85.6 at posttest (the Al-Mabuk et al. posttest M = 101.5). The discrepancy in the averages across the two studies is not surprising, given the profound betrayal that is incest.

A key to psychological healing may not be just how high one scores on the forgiveness scale, but how much improvement was realized. In both the Al-Mabuk et al. (1995) and Freedman and Enright (1996) studies, the experimental group gained on the average about 20 to 25 points on the forgiveness scale from pretest to posttest. Of course, along with the 20-point gain there may be a certain level of score that must be reached before the participants benefit psychologically (such as in the 80–90 range, for example), but this cannot be determined with the data available.

What is interesting is that participants do not have to score exceptionally high on the forgiveness scale to realize considerable psychological improvement in hope, anxiety, and depression. Even though the participants in Freedman and Enright (1996) scored at *posttest* where the participants in Al-Mabuk et al. (1995) scored at *pretest* on forgiveness, this was associated with considerable psychological improvement. As examples of the considerable psychological improvement within the experimental group, their trait anxiety mean fell from 53.3 (above published norms) at pretest to 35.2 (average level of anxiety as determined by published norms) at posttest. In depression, the experimental group went from 18.2 at pretest (moderately depressed) to 6.8 (nondepressed) at posttest.

For the second set of comparisons, the change in the control group between pretest and the first posttest was compared with the change in this same group from the first posttest (before they started the intervention) to the second posttest (after they had the intervention). All five dependent measures showed statistical significance, indicating that the control-group-turned-experimental benefited from the intervention. There were increases in forgiveness (of about 23 points), hope, and self-esteem and decreases in anxiety (from above published norms to normal levels) and depression (to nondepressed levels). For the PPFS, subscale changes were similar to those experienced within the original experimental group.

The third set of comparisons involved change between the original experimental group and the control-group-turned-experimental after both had the intervention. No differences were expected if both interventions were equally effective, and no differences were found. For the final set of comparisons, we compared the change from pretest to follow-up for the original experimental group with the change from the first posttest (when the control-group-turned-experimental began the program) to the second posttest (once they completed the program). We did this to assess whether the original experimental group maintained its gains on the dependent measures. There was a 14-month gap between their completion of the program and the follow-up. We found no difference between the two groups, which indicates that the original experimental group maintained its pattern of improved psychological health. They remained nondepressed ($M = 5.5$) with average levels of anxiety ($M = 34.7$ for trait anxiety at follow-up). Their forgiveness scores improved to 91.1.

Beyond the statistical results, individual participants made positive comments about their experience in forgiving their perpetrator. Most felt that forgiving the sexual abuser helped in areas other than the incest, such as with their own families now and at work.

FORGIVENESS WITH MEN HURT BY THE ABORTION DECISION OF THEIR PARTNER

Coyle and Enright (1997) tested a forgiveness intervention with 10 men who reported that they were emotionally hurt by the abortion decision of their partner. Their ages ranged from 21 to 43 years with a mean of 28.3 years. All were from the Midwest, and all were single at the start of the study. Eight were White, 1 was Pakistani, and 1 was biracial (White and African American). Six identified themselves as Christian, 1 as Muslim, and 3 as agnostic. The average length of time since the abortion was 6 years (range = 6 months to 22 years). Eight were ambivalent or against the abortion at the time of the procedure, whereas 1 initially supported it and another was not informed until later. All who contacted us and were eligible participated in and completed the study.

Instruments

An initial screening interview was given to assess whether the man could identify one person other than himself whom he blamed for the abortion. He also had to exhibit psychological difficulty with the abortion experience. Also given were the Spielberger State Anxiety Inventory (not the trait component), the State Anger Inventory (not the trait component; Spielberger, Jacobs, Russell, & Crane, 1983), the short form of the Perinatal Grief Scale to assess his grief over the loss (Potvin, Lasker, & Toedter, 1989), and the EFI; Subkoviak et al., 1992, 1995). The EFI evolved from the PPFS expanded to 60 items but retaining the subscale structure. Details of the scale are in chapter 19. Items were rated on a 6-point Likert scale with a range of scores from 60 to 360 (with a high score representing high forgiveness).

Testing Procedure

Following Freedman and Enright (1996), participants were given three rounds of pretests at 1-week intervals (2 weeks in Freedman and Enright). All instruments were given in random order. A total score for any given instrument was derived by adding the three scores at pretest and taking an average. The same procedure was followed at the first posttest and the follow-up.

Intervention Procedures

The participants were randomly assigned to the forgiveness treatment or a no-contact control group. The experimental group began a 12-week intervention following the pretests. They met individually with the intervener once per week for about 90 minutes. After the posttests were given, the control group began the forgiveness intervention. The female intervener had extensive experience in clinical settings (master of science in psychiatric nursing).

The Forgiveness Sessions

A written manual was prepared as a guide for the intervener. As in all other research programs described here, the manual and intervention were based on the process model. The features of the process model were interwoven with issues of anger, helplessness, guilt, relationships, and grief. Each problem was addressed individually, and then forgiveness was offered as a healthy solution to the problem.

Session 1 began with a discussion of what forgiveness is and is not. The subsequent sessions focused on the five problem areas related to forgiveness.

Consider the sessions on helplessness as an example. Many of the participants reported a sense of helplessness over their partner's abortion decision. Discussions and venting of anger led to most acknowledging a sense of resentment. Forgiveness as an alternative to deep, abiding resentment was explored. Forgiveness was presented as a choice that will not leave the participant helpless. Bearing the pain is an active step to combat helplessness that may aid forgiveness. The intervener pointed out the incompatibility between the courageous act of forgiveness and the passive approach of helplessness. Genuine forgiveness was contrasted with pseudoforgiveness.

Throughout the sessions, the intervener asked about the participant's developing ideas about forgiveness to evaluate progress and to determine whether to continue with a particular theme or to move on. The final session focused exclusively on forgiveness, with a review of the basic processes.

Results and Discussion

As in Freedman and Enright (1996), four sets of comparisons were made. The first compared the *t*-test gain scores from pretest to posttest between the two groups. As expected, all dependent measures (forgiveness, state anxiety and anger, and grief) showed statistically significant differences favoring the forgiveness treatment group. That group went from a mean of 196 on the forgiveness inventory to 251, a gain of 55 points. Only on the positive behavior subscale were no differences found. Their anxiety went from an average of 57.66 (above published norms) to 38.33 (normal levels).

The second set of statistical comparisons involved the gain for the control group from pretest to posttest compared with that same group's gain from Posttest 1 to Posttest 2, after they had the forgiveness intervention.

All dependent measures except for anger showed statistically significant gains favoring the group once the participants were exposed to the forgiveness intervention. There was partial support for the hypothesis regarding anger. As with the original forgiveness therapy group, the control-group-turned-experimental gained in forgiveness (86 points of improvement on the EFI) and reduced clinically in anxiety (from 57 to 32.8) and in reported grief.

When comparing the original experimental group after intervention with the control-group-turned-experimental after it had the intervention, no statistically significant differences were found with the gain score t-tests. This suggests that both groups changed in a similar way on the dependent variables after intervention. Finally, we compared the gain from pretest to follow-up (the second posttest) for the original experimental group with the gain from the first posttest to the second posttest for the control-group-turned-experimental (after they had the intervention). This was done to assess whether the original experimental group maintained their gains after 12 weeks away from the program. The findings revealed no differences between the two groups, supporting the notion that the original group maintained its pattern of improved psychological health.

It is interesting to note that these men came into the program with considerable emotional discomfort. Their anxiety mean scores (57) at pretest were higher than the incest survivors' means (about 50) at their pretest. As in Freedman and Enright's (1996) study, the average forgiveness scores after intervention showed that the participants were not near the ceiling of the measure (which is 360, and the averages were in the 250 range). Again, this points to the idea that amount of gain may be more important to psychological health than complete forgiveness. Of course, it is possible that clients may have to pass a certain threshold on the EFI before the gains on this scale pay dividends emotionally. Finally, the behavioral dimensions were the ones least likely to change. This may be because none of the participants remained with the partner who made the abortion decision. Had they actually reconciled with their partners, the results may have been different.

GENERAL DISCUSSION

Taken together, these four studies speak well to the scientific validity and therapeutic utility of forgiveness interventions. Forgiveness therapy can be successful with men and women from young adulthood to old age. Presenting problems can vary widely from parental love deprivation to incest to nonconsensual abortion decisions. A variety of interveners produced the results, which suggests that the results are not caused by the abilities of one or two particularly skilled individuals.

Whether forgiveness therapy produces results superior to traditional approaches is not yet clear. That forgiveness can take its place alongside well-established techniques such as support group therapy is important, especially given the long history of support groups and the relatively short history of forgiveness within therapy. We were surprised at the strong results revealed in the study with incest survivors. No published research on incest with other approaches has demonstrated such deep and long-lasting effects for women suffering the emotional effects of sexual abuse. Perhaps forgiveness will be shown to be more effective than traditional approaches for certain kinds of problems. We suspect that deep trauma born of injustice will be particularly affected by forgiveness therapy. This, of course, is speculation requiring more scientific investigation.

At the least, forgiveness therapy is a challenge to the traditional approaches to emotional healing because of its underlying assumptions. Consider seven assumptions of forgiveness therapy. First, the intention of forgiveness therapy is not to shine the light on oneself, but on the other person who was unfair. Insights into one's own emotional and cognitive states are springboards for looking at the offender. Rarely does therapy operate this way. Forgiveness therapy operates from the assumption that one's own emotional states are not the primary problem. Injustice is. Adverse emotional states can arise secondarily from a lack of resolution of the injustice.

Second, although the presenting emotional difficulties such as heightened anger, anxiety, and depression and lowered self-esteem may be direct responses to life's difficulties, this is not always the case. More primary emotions may be resentment and even bitterness when one has been treated unfairly. The more secondary emotional difficulties may be responses that develop as a person abides with the resentment over weeks, months, or years. It is these secondary emotions, when experienced at high levels, that seem to motivate a person to enter therapy. If this is true for a particular client, then the job of forgiveness therapy is not to address the secondary difficulties first, unless they are at critical levels, but instead to address the more primary emotions of resentment and related feelings. As the resentments are replaced by compassion and related emotions signifying beneficence, then the potentially harmful secondary emotions such as anxiety, depression, and excessive anger should change for the better. In fact, the forgiveness interventions reviewed here suggest this sequence of restored psychological health.

A caveat on this second assumption of forgiveness therapy is that therapists following a more traditional script may misjudge on which emotions to concentrate full effort. If an adolescent who has a history of being treated unjustly, for example, comes to therapy with symptoms of anxiety, inability to concentrate, and excessive energy, it may be a mistake to recommend psychopharmacological intervention without a concomitant focus on underlying resentment and bitterness pointed toward the injustice. The medication may alleviate the presenting symptoms but not allow for a full examination of the injustices that precipitated the resentments in the first place. As the medication masks symptoms, therapist and parent may conclude that the child is on the road to recovery. Although this indeed may be true, the patient may have to revisit the issues of unfairness years later once he or she is no longer taking the medication. We certainly are not calling for a moratorium on the psychopharmacological approach. We are challenging those who rely on it, however, to consider which presenting emotions are primary and which secondary.

Third, not all cries of injustice are accurate. A person exhibiting a strong sense of vanity, for example, will see unfairness at every turn. Under such circumstances, forgiveness therapy would be unwarranted because it would feed the vanity, reinforcing the person's faulty belief that unfairness has occurred whenever he or she does not attain all that is wanted. The therapist must distinguish genuine unfairness from its pseudoinjustice counterpart.

Fourth, forgiveness therapy is explicitly moral. Therapists who maintain a decidedly neutral stance about morals will be challenged by this. One cannot forgive apart from a moral stance of mercy and beneficence toward an offending person. The therapist must be ready not only to help the client focus on the offender but also to do so with the language of morality—fairness and unfairness, mercy, even love.

Fifth, there is an explicit educative form to the therapy. One does not wait for the client to somehow discover forgiveness and then mysteriously to embrace the idea. We say this for at least two reasons. If you will recall, the Willingness to Forgive Scale, used in Al-Mabuk et al. (1995), produced few responses at pretest, suggesting that forgiveness is not a central idea in people's consciousness. If the therapist waited for the client to "discover" forgiveness, we suspect that the third-party payments would run out long before the insight developed. Second, in our experience, many clients who come to forgiveness therapy have distorted views of what constitutes forgiveness. It is confused with condonation, excusing, forgetting, reconciling, pardoning, being weak, circumventing justice, and other misperceptions. People need to be educated about what forgiveness is and is not if accuracy is to prevail in therapy.

Sixth, forgiveness therapy seeks to alter a person's internal script about who one is. An unjustly treated person need not retain the potentially harmful identity of "victim." Although therapists who use forgiveness should clearly acknowledge a person's victimization, forgiveness offers a way out of that identity. Not only can such therapy help a person shift focus from victim to survivor, but it can also lay aside eventually even this moniker. In other words, forgiveness therapy is not about acceptance per se, but is about transformation in the form of how one views oneself and how one views and responds to one's offender.

Finally, not only is forgiveness therapy about dealing with specific psychological reactions to unfairness, but it also is about generalizing and deepening the learning that takes place in therapy to one's everyday interactions. Our experience with the incest survivors in Freedman and Enright (1996) is that they wished to appropriate the learning, gained while focusing on their fathers, now toward their husbands, children, supervisors, coworkers, and others. The technique of forgiving gave way to a new sense of one's own personhood.

INTRODUCTORY REMARKS ABOUT
THE CLINICAL CHAPTERS

As we move now into the chapters focusing on clinical disorders, let us reflect on three points as brought out earlier. First, not everyone will understand forgiveness in the same way. As we have seen, one dimension on which forgiveness can be analyzed is a cognitive–developmental continuum. Some people will have less complex and others more complex reasoning. We chose only those cases in which there was sufficient understanding to make forgiveness therapy worthwhile.

Second, people will vary, on initial interview, in the progress that they have made in forgiving. Some are in denial of their anger, others seek help because of the debilitating consequences of their anger. We have tried to select case studies in which people, as they commence therapy, are near the beginning of the process model. We want to illustrate how anger, an early point in the process, is transformed through insight and the developing emotions of empathy, compassion, and related developments.

Third, people will vary in the degree both to which they have forgiven another and to which they are willing to forgive. In our case studies, we present an ending point in each case more to show that the patient has improved than to suggest that he or she never again will revisit the issues surrounding the particular person who was unfair. Forgiveness usually does not end when the therapy sessions end.

All cases selected have certain common features: (a) There is an injustice toward the patient that has resulted in emotional, behavioral, and relational difficulty for that person, and (b) each person sees the injustice and willingly chooses to practice forgiveness. Of course, not all clients or patients choose to forgive; we respect that prerogative. (c) Each person has spent sufficient time in therapy so that success is likely. Not all cases are successful, but from our experience the majority of those who do the work of forgiveness and take sufficient time to forgive have observable reduction in distressing psychological symptoms.

With these caveats in mind, let us turn to the clinical literature and case studies in Part 2 for a variety of psychological disorders.

II

APPLYING FORGIVENESS WITHIN SPECIFIC DISORDERS AND POPULATIONS

7

FORGIVENESS IN DEPRESSIVE DISORDERS

Myrna, age 30 and single, sought treatment for depressive symptoms that she believed were the result of painful feelings of loneliness in her life. She had hoped that she would find a man whom she could trust because she wanted to marry and have a family. Aware of anger toward those who had hurt her in the recent past, Myrna was surprised at the amount of anger toward other men in her life that was uncovered during therapy.

In this chapter we describe the use of forgiveness in the treatment of Myrna's depressive disorder, as well as the role of her anger and mistrust in her relationship with the therapist. We also present the role of anger in depressive disorders, an overview of the four phases of forgiveness therapy, and the uses of forgiveness therapy in clinical cases of various depressive disorders. The limitations of forgiveness are also discussed.

From our clinical experience, identification and treatment of anger in patients with depression is an essential aspect of treatment facilitating recovery and protecting against relapse. The degree of anger in the patient with depression should be evaluated by an adequate history and the use of objective and subjective anger measures. Many patients with depression are able to identify significant amounts of unresolved anger that were denied over an extended period of time. When used in association with other therapeutic modalities, including psychopharmacology, cognitive and behavioral therapy, or marital and family therapy, the psychotherapeutic use of forgiveness can resolve the anger associated with depressive disorders (Fitzgibbons, 1986). Forgiveness has been shown to reduce depressive symptoms in one study of women who had been sexually abused (Freedman & Enright, 1996) and has been recommended in the treatment of depression (Fitzgibbons, 1986).

ROLE OF ANGER IN DEPRESSIVE DISORDERS

Numerous studies have shown that anger and hostility are common among patients with depressive disorders (Fava, 1998; Fava & Rosenbaum, 1997; Fava et al., 1993, 1996, 1997; Gould et al., 1996; Morand, Thomas, Bungener, Ferreri, & Jouvent, 1998). As far back as 30 years, Overall (see Overall, Hollister, Johnson, & Pennington, 1966) identified a hostile mistrustful subtype of patients with depression who exhibited high overt hostility, agitation, suspicion, anxiety, somatic concern, tension, and guilt. These symptoms appeared with second greatest frequency among depressed patients with an overall prevalence rate of 34% (Overall, Goldstein, & Brauzer, 1971). In another study of depressed patients (Baker, Dorzab, Winokur, & Cadoret, 1971), 60% reported increased irritability. Snaith and Taylor (1985) reported moderate to severe irritability in 36% of depressed inpatients. Depressed patients reported significantly greater levels of anger and hostility than nondepressed control patients (Fava, Kellner, Munari, Pavan, & Pesarin, 1982; Riley, Treiber, & Woods, 1989), with no significant relationship between anger expression measures and severity of depression (Riley et al., 1989). As Fava and Rosenbaum (1997) observed, these findings clearly challenge the psychodynamic hypothesis of a reciprocal relationship between depression and anger. Also, Montfort (1995) suggested that many irritable, elderly patients are often misdiagnosed with personality disorders, when in fact they are experiencing hostile depression.

The *Diagnostic and Statistical Manual of Mental Disorders* (4th ed., *DSM–IV*; American Psychiatric Association, 1994) description of major depressive disorder includes irritable mood as one of the core symptoms of this form of unipolar depression in children and adolescents. In one study of children and teenagers with major depression, irritability was reported in 83% of the participants (Ryan et al., 1987). In another study of adolescents with depression, oppositional defiant disorder was comorbid in 73% of those with severe major depression and in 47% of those with mild major depression (Biederman, Faraone, Mick, & Lelon, 1995). In addition, conduct disorder has been documented in 20–30% of depressed adolescents (Biederman et al., 1995; Kovacs, Gatsonis, Paulauskas, & Richards, 1988). Angold and Costello (1993) reported in their review of recent studies high rates of conduct and oppositional defiant disorder (21–83%) in adolescents with major depression.

Comorbid antisocial behavior, the most extreme manifestation of excessive anger in children, has been reported to be an associated feature of major depression in pediatric patients (Geller, Chestnut, Miller, Price, & Yates, 1985) and has predicted the persistence of depressive symptoms in 9-year-old boys (McGee & Williams, 1988). Excessive anger has been shown to be associated with suicidality in adolescents. Simonds, McMahon, and Armstrong (1991) found that young suicide attempters were more hostile than were community control adolescents. Apter, Bleich, Plutchik, Mendelsohn, and Tyano (1988) reported that in a group of adolescent psychiatric inpatients, those with conduct disorder had more suicidal feelings than those with major depression. Hawton, Osborn, O'Grady, and Cole (1982) reported that 50% of adolescents with a history of antisocial behavior who took overdoses repeated an overdose within a year, a much higher repetition rate than that of adolescents who overdosed without an antisocial history. A significant correlation was found between measures of suicidal behavior, aggressive behavior, and impulsivity in a study of 118 inpatient adolescents (Horesh, Gothelf, Ofek, Weizman, & Apter, 1999). In another study of adolescent inpatients, aggression was found to be as important as depression in some kinds of suicidal behaviors (Apter et al., 1995).

Adolescents with a history of a previous overdose or who repeated self-harm differed from nonrepeaters in having higher scores for depression, hopelessness, and trait anger (Hawton, Kingsbury, Steinhardt, & Fagg, 1999). In already highly anxious and depressed suicidal adolescent inpatients, a trend toward increased aggression was noted among multiple suicide attempters on all parameters evaluated (Stein, Apter, Ratzoni, Har-Even, & Avidan, 1998). On the basis of this study, Stein et al. recommended that the treatment of youngsters with a history of suicide attempts must include the evaluation and management of aggressive impulses, as well as depressive features.

Fava, Anderson, and Rosenbaum (1990) first reported a series of cases in which patients with depression presented anger attacks. Patients were classified as having anger attacks if they exhibited the following criteria: (a) irritability during the previous 6 months, (b) overreaction to minor annoyances, (c) occurrence of at least one anger attack during the previous month, and (d) experience during one of the attacks of at least four of the following: tachycardia, hot flashes, chest tightness, paresthesia, dizziness, shortness of breath, swearing, trembling, panic, feeling out of control, feeling a desire to attack others, physical or verbal abuse, and throwing or destroying objects (Fava et al., 1991). Because treatment of these anger attacks with Prozac produced marked improvement in behavior, it was hypothesized that the attacks were variants of major depressive disorder (Fava et al., 1990). Also, depressed patients with anger attacks were significantly more likely to meet criteria for borderline, histrionic, narcissistic, and antisocial personality disorders compared with depressed patients without anger attacks (Fava, Rosenbaum, et al., 1993).

Two single-site studies on 127 and 164 outpatients with major depression revealed anger attacks in 44% and 39% of depressed patients, respectively (Fava et al., 1993, 1996). A multicentered study of depressed outpatients found that anger attacks were present in 38% of 94 patients with major depression and 28% of the 74 patients with dysthymia, with an overall rate of anger attacks of 34% (Fava et al., 1997).

In another study of anger attacks at two sites, 67% of patients with depression met the criteria for anger attacks (Gould et al., 1996). Also, patients with anger attacks were significantly more depressed than were patients without such attacks. Patients with depressive disorders had twice the prevalence of anger attacks than did those with anxiety disorders. In this study, a patient who scored at the 75th percentile on the Beck Depression Inventory (BDI; a score of 22) was 3.2 times more likely to have anger attacks than a patient who scored at the 25th percentile (a score of 8). Anger attacks were related to the level of depressed mood as measured by the BDI. In a French study of 103 depressed patients, the prevalence of anger attacks was 46% during a 1-month period (Morand et al., 1998).

Anger is associated with treatment nonadherence in patients with depression (Pugh, 1983). Weissman, Fox, and Klerman (1973) found that 43% of depressed patients demonstrating angry affect in an interview failed to start outpatient treatment after discharge from the hospital.

RELATIONSHIP BETWEEN DEPRESSION AND ANGER

The temporal relationship between depression and anger is not clear. Gould et al. (1996) questioned whether depression might be secondary to the social and interpersonal consequences of anger attacks. In our clinical work, we have come to the view that anger develops soon after neglectful treatment or unjust hurt and is closely associated with sadness from the injury. Individuals can deny their anger, express it, and forgive (Fitzgibbons, 1986). Riley et al. (1989) found that patients with depression have a tendency to suppress rather than express their anger. However, results from a study of depressed children showed that they were less able to control their anger in a thoughtful, nonimpulsive manner compared with nondepressed children (Kashani, Dahlmeier, Borduin, Soltys, & Reid, 1995). Anger can easily encapsulate sadness within the unconscious and interfere with the healing of this sadness from childhood, adolescence, and adulthood. If the anger is resolved through a forgiveness process, it can facilitate the healing of the associated sadness.

OVERVIEW OF THE FOUR PHASES OF FORGIVENESS IN PATIENTS WITH DEPRESSION

Uncovering Anger and Hurts

When the history of a patient with depression is taken, major emotional hurts and anger associated with them are identified in significant relationships from childhood into adult life. Most people can readily admit conflicts in adult relationships, but often they have little insight into the role of disappointments from their family of origin that may have provided the basis for their depression. This is particularly true of conflicts in the father relationship because the denial of anger in childhood and adolescence is strongest in that relationship, in our clinical experience. Also, because as Mammen et al.'s research (1999) has demonstrated, those with and without anger attacks often appear similar in sessions, inquiring about the presence of anger attacks is important in the Uncovering Phase.

At the beginning of treatment, the work of uncovering is facilitated through the use of a valid subjective measure of anger that rates both active and passive–aggressive forms. In addition, at times a family member is asked to complete an anger checklist that evaluates the patient's active and passive–aggressive anger. Such measures assist the therapist in helping the patient understand both the depth of anger and the primary method of expression. When the results are presented, many people with depressive disorders are surprised to discover the high level of anger indicated. At this point, regular discussion about the masking of anger at different life stages can be initiated. The three basic mechanisms for dealing with anger—denial, expression, and forgiveness—need to be reviewed. Predominant misunderstandings that may need clarification are that anger is an emotion that can be resolved only through expression, that it is experienced only in extreme degrees, and that the absence of blatant manifestations precludes the presence of anger.

Therapists can encounter considerable resistance when they tell patients that the patients have a problem with anger but fail to give them a safe and effective method for its resolution. These patients fear their anger or feel guilty about it and, in the absence of a reliable method for removing it, simply deny its presence. By teaching patients how to resolve anger within themselves, therapists are more likely to help clients put an end to their denial.

Next, cognitive forgiveness can be assigned at this stage on the basis of the person's depressive symptoms and history. Now the patient may be asked to think of the possibility that he or she wants to try forgiving an individual believed to have hurt the patient. Making a decision for forgiveness is a first step. At the onset, there may be little conscious awareness of the depth of the hurt and the subsequent sadness and anger that were present in the relationship. Cognitive forgiveness exercises, however, are a powerful method for bringing forth unconscious emotional pain in those with depressive illness, and initially their effectiveness may depend largely on the degree of trust in the therapist. Some patients with depression are aware of disappointment and anger with an emotionally distant spouse, but they have limited awareness of unresolved sadness and anger with an emotionally distant parent. When they use cognitive forgiveness exercises, they begin to discover the anger that they have denied and, as a result, may begin to feel some relief from its burden and accompanying sadness.

Another strategy that can be used in uncovering anger is to present to clients the possibility that failure to deal honestly with anger and hurts from different life stages may interfere with their recovery from depression. If significant resistance occurs in uncovering anger, the therapist can relate how others have overcome this hurdle; the power of story is not to be underestimated because it allows a person to step back and make important connections.

To the surprise of many, various degrees of active and passive–aggressive anger associated with depression are uncovered at this stage, and violent fantasies and impulses as well as anger attacks may become evident.

Decision Phase

The major factor influencing a client's decision to begin the work of forgiveness is the knowledge that it will help with the resolution of the depressive illness. Many decide to forgive their offenders with great reluctance, and they may state that they do not really feel like forgiving them at all. We usually inform these patients that as they grow to understand their offenders and their life struggles, eventually they will feel like forgiving. The distinction between cognitive and emotive forgiveness is important because many people believe that they are unable to begin the work of forgiveness until they really feel like forgiving the offender.

Another factor that strengthens those in therapy in the pursual of the hard work of forgiveness is the relief clients experience from emotional and mental pain as they begin to forgive. Some, however, lose their motivation to continue the process of forgiveness because they want to experience, own, and discuss at length their anger regarding the offender before they are willing to let it go. By relating successful case histories of patients with depression who have used forgiveness in their treatment, therapists can help patients become more willing to make a decision on forgiveness.

When working with clients who have experienced severe betrayal pain leading to depressive illness, therapists may need to omit the word *forgive* because it may imply that those who have caused the injury will never be held accountable for their behavior; such misunderstandings of forgiveness sometimes take time to overcome. These clients are advised to state that they desire to let go of their hostile feelings and thoughts for revenge. When that step has been taken, they can comfortably move into the Work Phase of letting go of their anger.

Another helpful factor influencing the decision to forgive is the realization of the damage that can be done to the self by holding onto strong anger. The damage can include failure to overcome emotional pain, misdirection of anger toward people who do not deserve it, the excessive expression of anger in relationships, the development of physical illnesses, or continued emotional control by the offender. Therapists need to be prepared to make these negative consequences known to clients. At the same time, therapists should be able to communicate to clients the benefits of forgiveness when recommending the decision to forgive. These include

- freedom from the emotional pain of the past
- greater stability of mood
- improved ability to express anger appropriately as the degree of denied anger diminishes
- diminished guilt arising from unconscious anger
- decreased anxiety
- the courage to be vulnerable
- decreased fear of angry impulses or thoughts
- improved loving relationships.

Many will decide for forgiveness only after reassurance that they do not have to become vulnerable toward the offender and that forgiveness does not preclude expressing anger or pursuing justice. (See chapter 3 for what forgiveness is not.) The resolution of anger with an offender and the investment of trust toward that person are two related but different processes. One can forgive and, at the same time, not trust someone who has inflicted hurt.

For some people, the decision to forgive occurs only after significant pressures are applied by others in their lives. Spouses, other family members, and partners may threaten to separate or even end a relationship unless the individual makes a commitment to resolve the anger associated with depression. Depressed patients of this type have been described by Overall et al. (1966) as mistrustful and hostile. Because of their difficulty in trusting, these clients are usually limited in their ability to try to make a decision to forgive, and they also have an impaired capacity to trust the therapist initially. They regularly use anger as a defense against their mistrust and fear of betrayal. Once a difficulty in trusting has been uncovered, the origins of the conflict must be identified. When clients learn that they may well be controlled by the offenders for the rest of their lives if they do not let go of their anger, many finally decide to work at forgiveness with clenched fists and white knuckles.

With the hostile, mistrustful, depressed patient who misdirects anger regularly, it may be necessary at times to refuse to continue the therapy unless a commitment is made to try to let go of resentment. The inappropriate expression of anger may be directed toward the therapist, but the person in treatment must come to the realization that such anger does not benefit anyone and simply delays the resolution of the depression.

Individuals who use anger as a defense against feelings of sadness and inadequacy are often reluctant to decide to forgive. We find that their self-esteem needs to be strengthened before such a decision can be made, especially in the case of young men. In the final analysis, many people work at forgiveness in the hope that it will help in the healing of their depressive illness.

Work Phase

Forgiveness is possible through a process of attempting to understand the early emotional development of the offenders. Over time, through a detailed history-taking, it becomes clearer that the behavior of many individuals can be attributed to their emotional scars. The process of forgiveness opens up one's ability to understand that significant others have loved as much as they were capable of loving and that the pain was not necessarily inflicted deliberately. As this understanding grows, anger diminishes.

In the Work Phase of forgiveness, we recommend that the patient consider wanting to forgive another for certain patterns of behavior without dwelling excessively on a particularly traumatic memory. The patient is advised to spend several minutes twice daily forgiving an offender. The patient is regularly given a written note or "prescription" that states that the patient think about understanding and forgiving the offending persons discussed during that session. This forgiveness exercise also is used during the session and is helpful in evaluating the patient's ability to engage in the work of forgiveness and in examining difficulties and resistances.

The patient may spend longer than several minutes daily working on forgiving depending on a number of factors including degree of emotional pain present and whether the hurts are ongoing. Forgiveness is also recommended during times when strong feelings of sadness are present. If strong feelings of anger emerge, the patient is encouraged to spend time each day forgiving the offender and working toward understanding and forgiving others from the past who have caused similar hurt. The daily work of forgiveness in patients with depression usually goes on for many months and in some for years.

Regarding hurts from the past, a forgiveness exercise may be assigned in a relationship in which the person has little or no conscious awareness of the presence of anger. For example, if indicated by the history, the patient may be asked to understand and to think of forgiving a parent for not meeting certain emotional needs. In trying to understand the childhood and adolescence of an emotionally distant or irritable father, a patient usually comes to realize that the father himself struggled with similar difficulties when he was young and that he had, in fact, unconsciously modeled after his own father (the patient's grandfather). This understanding enhances the ability to forgive the parent. Nevertheless, such patients may spend weeks or months thinking of themselves as children and teenagers trying to understand and forgive a parent for specific disappointments. This process rarely entails going to others and informing them that one is working at forgiving them.

Clients may decide that they want to try to understand and to forgive anyone in the past who has influenced their adult feelings of sadness and anger. These patients might be asked to reflect on the following thought: "Dad or Mom, I want to try to understand and forgive you for all the ways you disappointed me when I was young."

We refer to this as a *past forgiveness exercise*, and we use it regularly in the treatment of depressive illness. Clients are regularly given a written statement that asks them to try to understand specific conflicts in the offender's life and to think of forgiving an offender from the past. At follow-up sessions, the forgiveness exercises relating to both past and present relationships are reviewed in a manner similar to the way in which cognitive exercises are examined after being assigned (Beck, 1976) and difficulties or resistances are discussed.

Many clients with depression find themselves developing a conscious awareness of the need for forgiveness in daily living as a way to gain control over intense angry feelings. Those with anger attacks report that the regular use of forgiveness diminishes the intensity and frequency of those attacks. Other benefits that clients report are relief from emotional pain, a greater stability in their mood, the ability to seek and give forgiveness, and renewed energy that comes as the need to control angry impulses and thoughts diminishes.

For most people, forgiveness begins as a cognitive or intellectual process in which there is no true feeling of forgiveness and many have difficulty believing that they are really forgiving (cognitive forgiveness). As their understanding grows of their offenders (especially those from their childhood and adolescent years), they will experience more compassion, and feelings of forgiveness may follow (emotional forgiveness). The process moves slowly, but meanwhile cognitive forgiveness can be effective.

At times there is great value in reenacting painful life events in the session by asking clients to try to express aloud their disappointments, anger, and desire to forgive offenders. Often clients are highly resistant to this exercise if it does not end with a method for dealing with anger other than simply expressing it. These psychodrama techniques are helpful when denial is very strong, when anger is expressed primarily in a passive–aggressive fashion, or when there is excessive displacement of the anger onto significant others.

We have seen that clients with depression blame those closest to them for their symptoms. This is especially the case when there has been childhood emotional trauma with parents. These clients can be helped by the suggestion that they are, in part, misdirecting their anger and by clarifying how anger can be masked and then later misdirected. If these clients are willing to use past forgiveness exercises with a parent, they often come to realize the sadness and anger that was experienced early in life and denied.

If the client is forgiving a particular individual and the anger is not decreasing, this may point to either a misplacement of the anger or an unconscious association with someone else from the past who hurt the depressed person in a similar way. The therapist may then ask the patient to think of the childhood and adolescent years and to reflect for a few minutes in the session as to whether this may be occurring.

For those depressed clients with anger attacks or very intense anger, the resolution of resentment can be facilitated by a process that begins with the physical expression of anger in a manner in which others will not be hurt. In this process the client does not visualize the offender as a target of the anger. This is followed immediately by cognitive forgiveness exercises aimed at letting go of the desire for revenge. Relief from intense anger also may be experienced if the person imagines the verbal expression of hostile feelings against the offender and then attempts to give up the desire for revenge.

At times, the participation of the offender in treatment can be of value in the resolution of the patient's resentment and depressive symptoms. Some parents have detailed their childhood experiences and marital stresses to their adult child and have asked for understanding and forgiveness for the times when they hurt or neglected the patient. Such bold steps have often included promises to improve the relationship in the future. Some clients will not be open to accept these apologies and promises and, in fact, might use the apology to emotionally hurt a parent. This can be prevented by the therapist evaluating the openness of the client to understand, to receive the apology, and to forgive the parent through role playing the parent in a session. The therapist can then determine at what point in time it is appropriate to bring a parent into the therapy.

In some instances, the therapist might consider playing the role of the offender and suggest that the client consider the possible reasons for what appeared to be insensitive behavior. By role playing, the patient may be asked to picture a younger self and to listen and respond to the therapist as understanding and forgiveness are sought for hurts that influenced the development of depressive symptoms. The use of antidepressants can be helpful in diminishing the level and expression of anger, but they do not resolve the basic conflicts that give rise to the anger.

A number of obstacles are encountered in the use of forgiveness in the treatment of depression. These include the following:

- the lack of parental modeling for this process
- role models who regularly overreacted in anger
- powerful denial of resentment from family of origin
- overwhelming impulses for revenge
- inability of loved ones to admit that they were wrong
- difficulty in growing to trust others
- narcissism
- significant others who continue to disappoint regularly
- a compulsive need to control.

In the case presentations a number of interventions will be described that address these obstacles including other role models in their lives or in history or literature and growth in trust. Because anger is used to defend against feelings of fear, especially the fear of betrayal, many individuals are not able to move ahead with the forgiveness process until their basic ability to trust is enhanced or until they feel more hopeful. Misperceptions that arise are (a) the belief that forgiveness occurs quickly and that there is no need to spend time working on it, (b) the belief that a one-time cognitive decision to let go of anger resolves all anger from past or present hurts, (c) the belief that forgiving precludes healthy assertiveness, or (d) the belief that the process holds more benefit for the one forgiven than for the forgiver.

Some people hold onto their anger because it may make them feel alive. Others believe that it gives them a feeling of power or that it may form a bond of intense passion with a former loved one and cover a feeling of emptiness. Revenge, too, is sometimes seen as a sign of strength and intelligence, whereas forgiveness may represent weakness. (See chapter 16 for a rebuttal to forgiveness as weakness.) Anger, it is believed, gives offenders the attention that they want and projects a strong image (Novaco, 1976). There are clients, too, who have no real desire to be healthy or who derive benefit from self-pity or playing the sick role. Finally, some individuals are aware that as they forgive they will be led into the reality of disappointments in relationships. Therefore, they will not forgive until they develop loving and trusting relationships that they believe will ease the pain that may arise with forgiveness.

Although forgiveness diminishes the level of anger in clients with depression, it does not fully heal the sadness from different life hurts. However, most clients who work on forgiving experience emotional relief as they are able to overcome their angry feelings and then discover a lessening in the intensity of their depressive symptoms.

Deepening Phase and the Limitations of Forgiveness

In the Deepening Phase, clients have become familiar with the benefits of forgiveness and use it more often when they feel sad or irritable. Absorbing the pain that brought about the sadness and anger can be a slow and arduous process. For many who sustained a major loss or betrayal at a particular life stage, significant love and appreciation can strengthen them and enable them to accept the pain from the past.

Over time, many are able to let go of past hurts and accept them by recalling that parents and other family members loved as much as they were capable of loving given their life conflicts. However, a harsh reality may be that some patients were betrayed so deeply that they may never be able to fully absorb their pain. This response to forgiveness is found frequently in those who were abandoned by loved ones. Some betrayals can be broken down into smaller hurts that can slowly lead to forgiveness with absorption of the pain.

There are a number of life experiences in which the process of forgiveness is particularly arduous and lengthy. These include, in addition to abandonment by loved ones, parental abuse; rape or incest; loss of a career; prolonged insensitivity by a loved one; economic injustice; and a legacy of mistrust, hatred, or narcissism that has been passed from generation to generation.

In the Deepening Phase with those clients who are depressed and also mistrustful and hostile, therapeutic efforts to build their trust can help in the diminishment of their anger, because this anger is often a defense against their fears of betrayal. Their therapy continues to use forgiveness against offenders from different life stages but incorporates cognitive decisions to try to trust people of proven reliability. The slow development of deeper trust in the therapist facilitates this process.

In this phase, clients are often relieved from the burden and weight of their inner resentment. The resolution of anger helps stabilize their mood and protects them from a recurrence of their illness. We now present four case studies that illustrate the use of forgiveness within depressive disorders.

DEPRESSION IN A VICTIM OF SEXUAL ABUSE

Our first case study, about Nicole, is from Freedman and Enright (1996).[1] In her 14 months of work, Nicole slowly began to see forgiveness as a beneficial response, freely offered, to her father. What follows is an adaptation of Freedman and Enright's article, describing this client's experience.

Nicole, age 51 and divorced, was sexually abused by her father as a child. The abuse consisting of her father's fondling and rubbing himself against her body. Nicole's family did not believe her when she reported the abuse at age 6, nor were they supportive. She did not receive any therapy or outside help at that time. Nicole's father, however, also stopped all forms of affection and attention toward her. According to Nicole, until age 25, everything she did centered on getting love from her father. At the first interview, Nicole said that she had experienced anxiety, panic attacks, depression, and low self-esteem for most of her life. Nicole felt resentment toward her father and said that she had not forgiven him, but she was curious about the idea. Before coming to us, Nicole was in psychotherapy for 8 years (about once or twice a week) and participated in an incest survivor's group. She also experienced serious physical health problems, such as cancer, and stated that "the medical procedures I went through were an easier experience than the betrayal by my father."

Although Nicole went home on holidays (her parents lived 90 minutes from her), she saw her father as infrequently as possible. She never stayed overnight, talked primarily to her mother, and rarely enjoyed the visits. She described the relationship with her father as "very superficial" and that, on occasion, he was verbally abusive.

The first part of the forgiveness process for Nicole was recognizing how she had been using the defense mechanism of displacement. She would frequently act out the feelings that she had toward her father while she was with other men. Realizing her unexpressed anger toward her father helped Nicole understand and express her feelings more directly. Nicole used writing as one way to express the anger.

---

[1] This case study is from "Forgiveness as an Intervention Goal With Incest Survivors," by S. R. Freedman and R. D. Enright, 1996, *Journal of Consulting and Clinical Psychology, 64*, pp. 983–992. Copyright 1996 by the American Psychological Association.

During the intervention, Nicole was able to work through her feelings of guilt for the way that her body responded to her father's physical touch and for many of the things that she did as a result of the abuse. Nicole believed that she was responsible for the abuse continuing because she remembered enjoying some of her father's touches. When Nicole realized that her body was responding in a normal way to physical touch, she was better able to recognize that she was not in any way responsible for the abuse. She also felt guilty for sexually experimenting with other children, a not uncommon reaction for people sexually abused as children (Browne & Finkelhor, 1986; Finkelhor, 1984; Friedrich, 1993). She worked on accepting her behavior and viewing it in context as the result of another's abuse and her own confusion. Gradually, Nicole was able to forgive herself for the hurts that she may have inflicted on other children.

Nicole frequently compared her life with her father's life, and she felt that there was a real injustice in the fact that she was suffering more intensely than him. During the sessions, Nicole was able to identify the positive aspects of her personality that developed as a result of the abuse. Her sensitivity and compassion toward others was one example. Her suffering allowed her to be compassionate toward others in her present life who experienced painful relationships, hardships, and other major disappointments. Discussing the idea that life is unfair helped Nicole understand that many people are hurt through no fault of their own and that she had no control over some aspects of her life.

When she realized that even after all these years she still felt anxious, depressed, insecure, and dissatisfied with her relationships, Nicole was willing to make a commitment to forgive her father. At first, her decision to forgive was primarily a self-interested activity; she forgave to feel better. As Enright, Gassin, Longinovic, and Loudon (1994) explained, most people consider the idea of forgiveness when they are experiencing emotional pain so hurtful that they must do something to bring about change. She was able to recognize positive qualities about her father and view him as more than just an abuser. For example, Nicole remembered her father teaching her to drive; also, he told her that she was smart and encouraged her to go to college. Nicole gathered information from her aunt (her father's sister) about his childhood. She realized that her father had a very unhappy childhood and that his own family had many problems. Nicole learned that her father was severely abused as a child. She began to place her father's behavior as an adult in the context of his childhood upbringing. She remembered that when she met her father's parents she had not liked her grandmother and was very leery of her grandfather. Nicole began to feel sorry for her father because of his difficult childhood. She could now give her father credit for two decisions he had made: to stop drinking and not to beat his children.

Through reframing, Nicole was able to demonstrate behaviorally the compassion and empathy that she felt for her father. At Christmas, she was able to give him a hug and was also able to send him a birthday card and gift, knowing that he would be appreciative. Nicole realized that the sadness she felt was probably felt by her father. Her positive behavior toward him illustrated that she was able to accept and absorb the pain rather than pass it on to him or to others. At this point, Nicole felt that she had forgiven her father intellectually but not emotionally. Two letters she received from her father and the catalyst of her intellectual forgiveness moved Nicole into emotional forgiveness. She stated that "the letters showed me the very sweet and caring side of my dad, his vulnerability." Nicole went to her parents for Easter and "had an exceptionally good day." She mailed her father a present and stated, "I can now say that I truly feel love for my father. Although I will never stop grieving for the loss of my father, I can now feel positive feelings for my dad and accept what he can give me." By "grieving," Nicole meant that she never had the type of father that she dreamed about and felt sad about this loss.

Nicole's father had a stroke during the end of the intervention and died a few months later. Nicole was able to be there with him, read to him, and feed him. She felt closer to him during that time than she had ever been in the past. When meeting with the interviewer 6 months after the intervention, Nicole said that she had been helped greatly, not only with her father but also with other relationships. She said she coped with her father's death in a way that may not have been possible prior to the intervention. In a following meeting, Nicole stated that learning how to forgive her father made it much easier to relate to and forgive other people when she feels hurt. She had joined a support group that included survivors, perpetrators, and affected parents. Forgiving her father gave Nicole the insight that was necessary to interact in that group with other perpetrators of sexual abuse.

MAJOR DEPRESSIVE EPISODE

Myrna, whom we introduced at the beginning of this chapter, had experienced a number of disappointments in relationships with men that resulted in hopelessness, fears of being hurt again, and periodic intense anger. There was also a history of anger attacks. She related that her hopelessness was influenced by intense hurts as a child and adolescent in her home as a result of regular insensitive treatment by her father and emotionally abusive treatment by her older brother. She was aware that she had intense feelings of anger toward men who had hurt her at work and in dating relationships. She knew that she had developed a great difficulty in trusting men and had a major problem with anger toward them. At the same time, she expressed the hope that some day she would marry and have children.

Myrna was pleased to learn of another method for releasing her anger other than through expressing it. In fact, she felt guilty because she was aware that at times she had overreacted in anger because of her failure to let go of her resentment from past hurts. She had a great deal of insight and was aware that not resolving her anger with men who had hurt her, could cause major problems in a loving relationship in the future. Subsequently, she decided to attempt the work of forgiveness. The greatest challenge to her was that of reframing or truly understanding those who had hurt her, particularly insensitive and crude men in her personal life and work. She related, "If I keep thinking that these guys were troubled, I find it easier to let go of my resentment with them, but it's a struggle."

After Myrna had been working for several months on forgiving hurts in her adult life, the therapist told her that, on the basis of her history and difficulty in trying to control the sessions, she needed to work on uncovering her anger from her childhood with her critical father and abusive older brother. Her initial response was very defensive and she stated, "I'm over all that pain, and there is no reason to go over it." Then I asked if she had ever thought of forgiving her father and her brother, to which she vehemently responded, "No!" Somewhat reluctantly she agreed to think of forgiving her father and brother because she had been experiencing some relief from forgiving for her adult hurts.

Her excellent sense of humor helped her greatly in her struggle with depression, intense anger, and mistrust. Myrna grew in understanding the emotional conflicts in her father and her brother, facilitating her ability to forgive them. Also, she was helped by the change in their behavior toward her. As an adult, each one tried to be kind and supportive and apologized for how they had hurt her when she was younger. She did not feel like forgiving the men she had dated who had hurt her. However, she knew that this was essential if she was going to have a healthy, loving relationship in the future.

In the initial phases of the forgiveness process, Myrna's anger was periodically misdirected at the therapist. Myrna was informed that inappropriate expression of her anger at the therapist did not benefit anyone and simply delayed the resolution of her depressive symptoms. She agreed and committed herself to the work on forgiving and to be more aware of the possibility that she might be misdirecting her resentment.

Myrna was asked to try to think daily that the men who hurt her had their own problems and that she did not want them to control her or limit her happiness. She was asked to read daily a statement that conveyed that she wanted to try to forgive all the men who had betrayed her. At the next session, the daily forgiveness exercises relating to both past and present relationships were reviewed and discussed. At times, Myrna realized how deeply she had been hurt, and temporarily she was unable to continue the forgiveness process. She preferred to experience and discuss the previously denied anger with her father and brother before releasing it.

Myrna had difficulty believing that she was truly forgiving because she did not feel like forgiving the men who had hurt her; however, realizing the benefits, she continued the process. She found that this cognitive exercise of thinking of forgiving decreased her anger and depressive symptoms and improved her ability to try to trust a man again. She came to feel more compassion for those who had hurt her, especially her father and her brother, and developed a greater acceptance of her past hurts.

There were occasions, however, when Myrna tried to forgive a particular man for hurting her, but anger would not diminish. As previously stated, this reaction usually indicates either that there is an unconscious association from the past with someone else who caused similar hurt or that the anger is so deep that it will dissipate only slowly. On reflection, Myrna recalled that there was a man she dated in college who had hurt her deeply, and as she forgave that individual her anger and sadness decreased. The key to Myrna's recovery was her willingness to spend a considerable amount of time on the resolution of her pain and anger through each stage of her life.

Approximately 1 year after her therapy ended, Myrna brought her fiancé into a session because he wanted an evaluation by the therapist to determine if he had any significant conflicts that he needed to address so that they would not interfere with their hope for a good marriage. At that time, they both appeared to be full of good humor and hope, and they demonstrated a great deal of freedom in a loving relationship.

Single people, such as Myrna, who struggle with depressive illness as a result of loneliness and hurts in relationships benefit from working at forgiving those whom they have dated in the past and members of their family of origin. The removal of resentment facilitates the resolution of their depression and protects them from the danger of misdirecting it or causing further personal physical, emotional, or mental harm.

MAJOR RECURRENT DEPRESSION

Those with recurrent depressive illness usually have significant degrees of anger with individuals who hurt them at different life stages. We have seen that the ability to face the anger and forgive offenders often results in the diminishment of the depressive symptoms. In treating recurrent depressive illness, therapists will find that there is great value in asking patients to work regularly at forgiving all those who disappointed them in family life, in important loving relationships, or at work.

Joshua, age 40, married, and father of two children, developed intense anxiety as well as severe depressive symptoms that he attributed to career pressures. His father, too, had suffered from depressive illness. This was Joshua's second major depressive episode.

Initially, Joshua was not aware of his anger with anyone but himself. However, he soon came to realize that he had never faced or tried to resolve powerful feelings of anger toward his father. He deeply resented his father's inability to ever affirm him or communicate his love to him. He felt bitter that his father never pursued professional help for his father's depressive illness. Guilt was experienced almost as soon as he verbalized his feelings of anger, because he was aware that his father had a torturous relationship with his own father (Joshua's grandfather). Joshua was comforted by the knowledge that his anger was justified, primarily because his relationship with his father had resulted in major emotional weaknesses and conflicts in his life.

The cognitive decision to forgive his father also was based on the hope that it might help his recovery from depressive illness, but he had no emotional desire to forgive him. Joshua used past forgiveness exercises in which he tried to imagine telling his father how much his father disappointed him during different stages of his life. That was followed by repeated reflection that Joshua wanted to try to forgive him for past hurts. It was an intense struggle for Joshua and, for a period of time, he experienced increasing symptoms of rage with his father. He even discovered repressed violent impulses against his father that presented clinically as thoughts of harming his children.

Joshua was able to continue the forgiveness process as he grew in compassion and understood the emotional pain that his father had suffered himself as a child and young man toward his own very angry and controlling father. Joshua wept regularly both for his father's pain and for his own. The regular work of daily forgiving his father gave Joshua a sense that the hold of the pain of his past was diminishing in his life. He came to feel freer and less depressed. The awareness that his father had loved him as much as he was able to love comforted and strengthened him. However, the work of forgiveness was arduous, and many times he felt like giving up. Joshua continued because he was determined not to be controlled by his past; he believed that his own father had been damaged by his. Joshua stated, "I have to get rid of this anger and sadness with my father or I will never be healthy."

Some clients with severe depression feel guilty because it takes so long to let go of anger and feel forgiveness. Others experience guilt because they find themselves, at some point, completely unable to give up their anger. Clients also experience guilt as anger emerges with loved ones who have sacrificed for them or struggled with serious family problems, but the guilt diminishes as the anger is legitimized.

In the course of therapy, depressed clients who are married are expected to identify a number of areas in which they are disappointed in important relationships, especially the one with their spouse. They also are expected to work at forgiving those who hurt them in childhood, adolescence, and young adult life including, if indicated by the history, parents, siblings, peers, and employers.

POSTPARTUM DEPRESSION

An irritable mood is a frequent clinical feature in postpartum depression. Snaith and Taylor (1985) found that 74% of a sample of women with postpartum depression had high levels of anger. Pitt (1968) observed that elevated anger was common in women with postpartum depression. Case studies of postpartum anger attacks have been reported (Mammen, Shear, Jennings, & Popper, 1997), and in one study of pregnant and postpartum women, 62% had anger attacks (Mammen, Shear, Greeno, Wheeler, & Hughes, 1997). Women with postpartum onset major depression experience disturbing aggressive obsessional thoughts more frequently compared with women with nonpostpartum major depression (Wisner, Peindl, Gigliotti, & Hanusa, 1999). Also, premenstrual irritability has been shown to be correlated with depression during the pregnancy and in the postpartum period (Sugawara et al., 1997). Another study also demonstrated that high hostility during the pregnancy was correlated with postpartum depression (Hayworth et al., 1980).

Jessica, age 30 and married, had just given birth to her first child. She entered therapy because of symptoms of depression and because of fear concerning powerful impulses she was experiencing that could result in harm to her child. In her confusion and fright, there were times when she believed that her baby was evil and had to be destroyed. Initially, Jessica could not understand why she should develop postpartum depression with such strong anger. She was happily married, enjoyed her work, and had looked forward to the birth of her first child. However, her husband Mike, who was a physician with a keen interest in emotional and mental health, communicated his strong views as to the origins of her depression and violent impulses. He blamed Jessica's mother.

Jessica was the oldest of three children and had grown up in a dysfunctional family. Her father's career demanded constant travel, and he was rarely at home. He died when Jessica was an adolescent. Jessica was never able to please her mother, a very disturbed woman who had been extremely controlling, critical, and demanding all her life. She had tried to prevent Jessica's marriage because she was unable to control her fiancé. Subsequently, she treated him in an extraordinarily rude manner.

Jessica related, "My mother is crazy and probably a manic–depressive." Jessica related that she had grown up in a home in which her mother seemed to derive pleasure from trying to make her feel insecure and fearful. Although she was high spirited and had enjoyed many close friends while growing up, she was always very unhappy in her home. She realized that she had been denying a great deal of anger with her mother for many years because essentially she was her only parent. For Jessica, the most challenging aspect of the healing process was the uncovering of her anger. She stated, "It's very hard and painful for me to admit how angry I have been." As the history prior to the birth of her child was reviewed, Jessica was able to uncover powerful resentment toward her mother, and she identified her as a disruptive force in her life. Finally her mother's lack of acceptance of Mike and her offensive treatment of him depressed and angered her.

Because her mother continued in her attempts to undermine Jessica's relationship with Mike, as a first step in Jessica's treatment, she was asked to keep her mother at a distance until the time when her mother could support the marriage and apologize for her past insensitive behavior. Next, Jessica was given written forgiveness exercises that asked her to think several times daily of trying to forgive her mother for the ways in which she had hurt her as a child, adolescent, and young woman. She was encouraged to use this forgiveness exercise whenever she felt depressed. She decided to work on forgiving her mother when she came to understand that it was the anger toward her mother that she was misdirecting toward her baby. She understood that forgiveness could drain off this abscess of hatred that she harbored toward her mother. As she worked on forgiving her mother, Jessica felt an enormous amount of buried rage against her mother enter her consciousness, and she was grateful that she did not have to deal with her mother during this phase of treatment because of the power of these emotions.

As Jessica continued forgiving her mother, her angry thoughts toward her child decreased significantly. When such painful ideas entered her mind, she would respond to them by thinking that they represented misdirected anger that was really meant for her mother. Then she would say to herself "My mother was a very lonely, troubled woman, and I want to forgive her so that she can no longer control me." After approximately 6 months, the angry impulses toward her child were completely eliminated, and her depressive symptoms were resolved. The forgiveness process with her mother went on for several years.

Other origins of strong anger that are uncovered in treating women with postpartum depression are from hurts and disappointments with spouses, fathers, and significant others.

TOWARD THE FUTURE

As conclusions are published and information is disseminated, there is every hope that therapists themselves will become more open to examine countertransference issues in the treatment of anger associated with mood disorders. The personal journey of the therapist in attempting to resolve anger at different life stages is helpful at various levels. Not least among them will be a greater ability to help their clients recognize and recover from emotional pain and anger.

Forgiveness can play an important role as a therapeutic process to resolve the anger associated with depressive disorders. The treatment of adolescents with a history of severe depressive illness should include the evaluation and management of their anger. The removal of anger can facilitate the resolution of depressive episodes and, in many patients, helps prevent relapses in ways that are not clearly understood. It is hoped that, in the years ahead, research studies will demonstrate the clinical value of the use of forgiveness in mood disorders and clarify its methods of action.

8

FORGIVENESS IN ANXIETY DISORDERS

Andrew, a 35-year-old businessman, sought therapy for the treatment of excessive anxiety, dizziness, and insomnia. His anxiety was always most intense in the morning as a result of dreading to face the work pressures of the day. At the onset of his treatment, Andrew denied any angry feelings. He viewed himself as a strong male who should be capable of handling whatever work pressures came his way. Now, however, he had great difficulty in coping and did not understand what was happening to him.

As with anyone who has never discussed emotional pain with others, Andrew's resistance to facing painful feelings was very strong. Subsequently, the uncovering of Andrew's resentment with his employer because of unreasonable demands took a great deal of time. Even more challenging was his struggle to work at forgiving, on a regular basis, an employer who continued to force extraordinary burdens on him. The treatment of his work-related anxiety and its associated anger was successful, and the case is presented in this chapter. We also describe the role of anger in anxiety disorders, the four phases of forgiveness, and the use of forgiveness in the therapy of generalized anxiety disorder (GAD), panic disorder (PD), social phobia, obsessive–compulsive disorder (OCD), and posttraumatic stress disorder (PTSD).

The psychotherapeutic uses of forgiveness can make a significant contribution to the treatment of GAD, PD, phobias, OCD, PTSD, and adjustment disorders with anxiety. As reviewed in chapter 6, it has been demonstrated that scientifically tested interventions using forgiveness can significantly decrease anxiety. Therapeutic effectiveness is accomplished by removing anger associated with hurts from different life stages that have damaged a person's basic ability to trust or to feel safe. Forgiveness will decrease anxiety directly as a result of the resolution of anger, especially in clients whose anxieties are caused by the fear of their unconscious anger. This is seen particularly in clients with OCD.

As anger from past hurts decreases, past fears and mistrust seem to have less influence over the present. In fact, the healing of anger appears to facilitate a growth in trust. Concurrently, it frees individuals from the negative influence of others who have hurt them.

ANGER IN ANXIETY DISORDERS

Although the *DSM–IV* (American Psychiatric Association, 1994) lists irritability as one of the six symptoms associated with the diagnosis of GAD, the evaluation of anger and hostility in anxiety disorders has received little attention. A number of studies and case reports have documented anger and hostility in patients with PD (Fava, Grandi, et al., 1993; Korn et al., 1992; Starcevic, Uhlenhuth, Kellner, & Pathak, 1993). In one study, patients with PD reported high rates of aggressive ideation and behavior during panic, as well as suicidal ideation (Korn, Plutchik, & van Praag, 1997). Also, defense mechanisms used by patients with PD were consistent with a proposed psychodynamic formulation for PD that emphasizes the patient's difficulty in tolerating angry feelings toward significant others (Busch, Shear, Cooper, Shapiro, & Leon, 1995).

In a two-site study, anger attacks occurred in one third of clients with panic disorders and in 29% of clients with anxiety disorders other than panic (Gould et al., 1996). Snaith and Taylor (1985), using self-report checklist, found irritability in 52% of patients with severe and moderate anxiety. High levels of anger have been reported in patients with PTSD (Chemtob, Novaco, Hamada, Gross, & Smith, 1997; Frueh, Henning, Pellegrin, & Chobot, 1997; Lasko, Gurvits, Kuhne, Orr, & Pitman, 1994), and treatment protocols have been evaluated (Chemtob, Novaco, Hamada, & Gross, 1997; Hertzberg, Feldman, Beckham, Moore, & Davidson, 1998). Given the high levels of anger, Frueh et al. (1997) recommended that clinicians incorporate anger management strategies into treatment plans for patients with PTSD.

Fava et al. (1991) posited that comorbid anger attacks potentiate a poorer treatment outcome response to Axis I anxiety and affective disorders. Also, anger attacks usually are not due to a lack of assertiveness or social skills. Gould et al.'s (1996) study, for example, failed to support the hypothesis that anger attacks are significantly related to the Rathus Assertiveness Schedule (McCormick, Hahn, & Walkey, 1984).

Clinical experience has shown that many clients with anxiety disorders have significant levels of anger. Although anger attacks are an extreme manifestation of anger, many clients with anxiety disorders struggle with lesser degrees of active and passive–aggressive anger. Such anger is often a result of betrayal in childhood, adolescence, or adult life.

Some clients with anxiety disorders feel so fragile in their relationships that they dread admitting or expressing anger. They fear that releasing their resentment might lead to further loss, isolation, and betrayal.

Disappointments, hurts, and betrayal events can lead to the occurrence of sadness, anxiety, and anger. Anger appears to encapsulate both anxiety and sadness and subsequently can interfere with recovery from both anxiety and depressive disorders. Forgiveness removes the anger from this emotional complex, thereby facilitating the healing and resolution of anxiety and sadness. This process is described below.

THE UNCOVERING PHASE

In the first phase of therapy, individuals with anxiety disorders regularly find it difficult to recognize their anger and to make the link between their anxiety and their anger. The failure to identify their anger often results in anxiety that is out of proportion to a situation. Therefore, it can take many sessions to identify specific hurts or stresses in the person's life that have predisposed him or her to an anxiety disorder. Because anger locks into the unconscious at different developmental stages, especially childhood and adolescence, the resentment emerges only when traumatic life events are examined. The initial uncovering of anger rarely is the final word on the true cause of the anger; additional causes will be discovered at a later point in the Work Phase.

On the basis of the client's history of his or her anxiety, cognitive forgiveness is often used to uncover anger during this period. The individual is asked to focus on the desire to understand and to think of forgiving a specific individual or, in fact, anyone who has caused hurt or disappointments that may have resulted in a predisposition toward excessive anxiety and fear. As in the treatment of depressive illness, this exercise can lead to the emergence into consciousness of significant emotional pain from past hurts.

THE DECISION PHASE

As a person begins to understand the connection between anxiety and fear on the one hand and being treated unjustly on the other, his or her motivation to forgive increases. With greater insight into the possible benefits of forgiveness, that motivation can further increase. Sometimes, when a person trusts a therapist who is recommending forgiveness, that client, even though ambivalent, becomes willing to try to forgive an offending person.

THE WORK PHASE

As a matter of routine during the Work Phase, clients are regularly given written assignments that describe who they should forgive and how they should approach the task, that is, either cognitively or emotionally. Those with OCD often demonstrate the greatest resistance during this phase. The defenses surrounding their anger and betrayal pain are powerful, and they dissolve slowly as they face the reality of their hurts. In addition, perfectionistic tendencies can make the work arduous because it involves admitting the depth of the anger that has been denied.

Individuals with PTSD tend to be the most aware of both their anger and who their offenders are. However, they often have the strongest impulse to seek revenge and to strike back at those who have hurt them. In this phase, many individuals want to approach the offender and express their anger while they are working at forgiveness. They need to be cautious of the possibility of losing control of their intense anger and of the limitations of expression in the resolution of anger. Although healthy assertiveness is important, it can have limited value because mere words or behaviors often cannot compensate for the depth of pain and anger from a significant hurt. Also, the expression of anger rarely results in a true sense of justice or in freedom from the desire for revenge.

In contrast to revenge, healthy assertiveness in association with forgiveness is an important aspect of the treatment of those with GAD. Many individuals in treatment develop an excessive sense of responsibility that makes it difficult for them to relax, sleep, and lead healthy lives. In addition to forgiving an offender who has caused tension in their lives, they benefit from taking steps to protect themselves from the unreasonable and damaging demands of others. Assertiveness may be needed with an employer who has unreasonable expectations concerning work hours or with children who demand participation in numerous sports activities to the detriment of a balanced family life. It may also be of benefit with an insensitive or emotionally nonsupportive spouse who has damaged one's ability to feel safe, as well as with demanding people who attempt to make the client feel overly responsible for them or others. Assertiveness is used with forgiveness in these cases so that one will learn to express anger in a healthy way, minimizing the possibility of overreacting.

A number of men with GAD related to their work identify a lack of confidence as an important factor in their vulnerability to excessive anxiety. They discover that a major issue in this conflict is their relationship with their fathers who were either overly critical of them as boys and teenagers or who failed to help them to grow in confidence. Fathers of these boys were also often passive in their dealing with their wives. In this phase of treatment, these men find that forgiving their fathers is difficult, but they feel guilty and conflicted about being angry with them. Fortunately, as their understanding of their fathers' childhood experiences grow, these men are usually able to recognize that their fathers modeled their behavior after their own fathers, and they realize that the hurts were rarely inflicted deliberately. It is easier to forgive someone who did not want to do wrong but nevertheless inflicted unfair hurt.

At this point, the benefits of forgiveness begin to be experienced. Such benefits include a diminished level of anxiety and fear, a decrease in an excessive sense of responsibility, increased self-esteem, improved ability to trust, the ability to lead a more balanced life, and an improved ability to be assertive with insensitive people.

THE DEEPENING PHASE

After resolving significant amounts of anger through forgiveness, most clients with anxiety disorders are able to find meaning in their suffering. Often they become much wiser and more assertive, take better care of themselves in relationships, and usually become more careful about whom they trust. The role of forgiveness within the context of specific anxiety disorders will be presented now through clinical cases.

GENERALIZED ANXIETY DISORDERS

Comorbidity has been shown to be a fundamental characteristic of the course and nature of GAD. The National Comorbidity Study demonstrated that 8 of 10 participants with lifetime GAD also had a comorbid mood disorder during their lifetime (Judd et al., 1998). Unipolar disorders were found to be four times more common in people with this disorder than in people with bipolar disorders. Also, when comorbid mood disorders are present in GAD, a significant increase in associated disability and dysfunction is also found. The clinical use of forgiveness can play an important role in the treatment of both GAD and its comorbidities. The following cases illustrate the value of using forgiveness in treating clients with GAD.

Work Conflicts

A significant factor influencing the development of anxiety disorders today is the marked changes in the workplace with subsequent mistrust and fears. Some people believe that their employer no longer makes a commitment to them regardless of the quality of their work or their years of loyalty. Large numbers of people live daily with the fear of losing their jobs and of not being able to find another good position. Others suffer under unreasonable work demands coupled with a serious insensitivity on the part of their employer to the effects that this pressure has on them and their families.

Andrew, introduced at the beginning of the chapter, was a successful professional who experienced insomnia, light-headedness, and muscular tension as well as periodic severe anxiety before going to work. As the second in charge in his office, Andrew had a demanding career in which he felt overly responsible, and he worried constantly about various work projects. His supervisor Fred was a critical person who never affirmed or complimented him. There were days when Andrew was so overwhelmed by work pressures that he felt like running out of the office. Under these stresses, he was having great difficulty motivating himself to go to work, and he feared for the future if he quit his job.

Initially, Andrew had no conscious awareness of angry feelings. As his insight grew, he soon came to recognize that he had been denying a great deal of anger with Fred, who expected Andrew to do the work of two or three people and to work 60 or 70 hours over a 6-day week. In the uncovering phase, Andrew manifested significant resistance to admitting anger with Fred for the unreasonable demands that he had placed on him. It was suggested to Andrew that he was denying his anger because he rarely honestly faced his emotional pain and because he feared exploding at Fred and subsequently losing his job. He reluctantly agreed to try thinking of forgiving Fred because of his trust in the therapist's advice that this would help his treatment.

The approach used to deal with Andrew's reluctance was to suggest cognitive forgiveness in which he was asked to try to forgive Fred daily for being so critical, demanding, and perfectionistic. When Andrew realized that he had an option for dealing with his anger with Fred other than expressing it, he slowly began to admit that he was denying strong resentment toward his supervisor. He was motivated to resolve this newly discovered anger and, as he continued to forgive, his anxiety diminished. Andrew continued to try to set appropriate limits at the same time he was working on forgiveness.

The Work Phase of forgiveness was difficult for Andrew because he continued to deal with the same problems daily, and he doubted that Fred would change. He did, however, experience symptomatic relief by daily thinking that he wanted to forgive Fred because he recognized that his unconscious anger and resentment had been a constant source of tension. There were days when Andrew found himself so upset with Fred and so drained from his work pressures that he was completely unable to forgive. Andrew related in session, "I am so furious with Fred that I cannot forgive him." The therapist's response was, "Try to think of Fred as a very troubled man and then think, I want to try to forgive him so that he doesn't control me." This suggestion helped with the work of forgiveness, which was proceeding on a cognitive level. However, on some days when Andrew was feeling stronger, he was surprised that he actually felt sorry for his supervisor because he knew that Fred's personal life was miserable.

Andrew's anger diminished gradually over the course of 8 months as he worked to let go of his excessive sense of responsibility and to commit himself to have more balance in his life. Fortunately for Andrew, a change transpired at the office. His supervisor's health could no longer tolerate a 70-hour work week, and Fred had to take a leave of absence. When Fred returned, he could only work part-time. Andrew, then, was appointed director of the office, and he took steps to establish balance in his life and career. In that role he finally felt secure enough to be assertive with Fred, which was of great benefit to him. His determination to provide his associates with a healthier work environment helped him discover some meaning in the suffering that he had endured.

Family Conflicts

Inge, a 34-year-old mother of two children, sought treatment for extreme anxiety, insomnia, and fatigue. She felt overwhelmed by the responsibilities involved in caring for her family and actually feared insanity. The family rarely had meals together, and she and her husband Mike had little quality time with each other because of numerous pressures and demands.

Initially, Inge was unable to recognize the cause of her anxiety. Slowly, she identified a number of significant stresses and then felt angry about them. She was particularly upset by her children's participation in numerous sports, including traveling sports teams, and the excessive importance that Mike placed on such involvement by the children. She became overwhelmed with the demands of practices and games as well as long weekend tournaments. Family dinners, relaxing weekends at home, and time with Mike had become a thing of the past.

Inge recognized that she had been denying how angry she was in her effort to please her husband and her children. She even felt somewhat guilty about her anger, but she eventually came to accept it as being appropriate. As her true feelings emerged, she was able to communicate to Mike that she thought compulsive participation in sports was more important to him than to their children. She insisted that changes had to be made in the family schedule because she was being emotionally harmed by the pressures that she felt from him and their children.

Her decision to forgive her husband and her children for being self-absorbed and insensitive was motivated by a desire to be healthy and by a desire for a better relationship with her family. The work of forgiveness was facilitated by Mike's apology and immediate decision to limit each child to playing only one sport per season and to exclude all participation in traveling sports teams. Regular attempts toward understanding Mike's needs and insecurities that arose from his own lack of success in sports helped her feel more compassionate for him and enabled her to truly feel like forgiving him.

As balance was established in her family life and as she continued to forgive, Inge's anxiety symptoms abated. Later, she was able to help several other friends who felt overwhelmed by similar pressures in their families and was pleased to find meaning in her suffering.

Joy, a 30-year-old single parent, experienced excessive anxiety, irritability, and muscle tension. She was also troubled by periodic episodes of excessive anger, which she did not fully understand and which met the criteria for anger attacks. There was little resistance to uncovering traumatic life experiences and the anger associated with them.

Joy had grown up with a father who was defensive and critical and an older sister Laura who directed anger against her when she was young. She also felt betrayed in a number of valued relationships with men in her life. She recognized that the hurts in the relationships with her father made it difficult to trust men and led her to overreact in relationships.

Joy was motivated to forgive to break the unhealthy pattern in relationships with men and to sever the control of past emotional pain. In reframing, she came to understand that Laura harbored a great deal of resentment toward their father and misdirected it at her. She came to see her father as someone who was unable to control his fears of being betrayed, who used sarcasm and anger to keep others at a distance, and who feared giving himself to anyone.

Joy used past forgiveness exercises during which she pictured herself as a girl and teenager and thought that she wanted to forgive her father and her sister for the ways in which they had hurt her. These forgiveness exercises were initially cognitive in nature. As her understanding of her father's difficult childhood and adolescence with each of his parents grew, she began to feel sorry for him. Eventually, her feelings of empathy helped her truly feel like forgiving him.

The forgiveness exercises with her sister Laura were more difficult because her sister continued to direct anger at Joy that she did not deserve. Joy wanted to honestly discuss with Laura the disappointments in their relationship but was so mistrustful of her that she decided to communicate through writing. Unfortunately, Laura was unable to acknowledge her misdirected anger. In spite of her denial, Joy worked at forgiving Laura on a cognitive level but did not progress to feel like forgiving her, because she was unable to develop empathy for her.

In the sessions, Joy regularly expressed her anger toward her father, sister, and other men who had hurt her and followed this release by stating that she wanted to understand and to forgive them. She recognized that at various times she had misdirected this resentment toward other men she had dated, her mother, her daughter, and coworkers. She came to admit that the betrayal experiences from her family background and from dating relationships had resulted in a need to be in control. These insights enabled her to go to others and ask for their forgiveness.

As Joy's resentment diminished over the next 8 months, she experienced a greater ability to trust in relationships and also felt much calmer. She overreacted less in anger and grew in her ability to let go of the need to control others.

Adult Children of Divorce

Numerous studies have reported difficulty in trusting and anxiety as long-term conflicts in the children, adolescents, and adult children of divorce (Glenn & Kramer, 1987; Guidubaldi, 1988; Hetherington, 1989; Johnston, Kline, & Tschann, 1989; Wallerstein, 1983, 1985; Wallerstein & Blakeslee, 1989, 1996). These anxieties are viewed by Wallerstein (1991) as the universal legacy of divorce, affecting not only the especially vulnerable but all children of divorce. Many have difficulties in trusting (Black & Pedro-Carroll, 1993; Franklin, Janoff-Bulman, & Roberts (1990) and have problems in developing and committing to supportive friendships and loving relationships (Slater & Calhoun, 1988).

Miguel, age 28 and single, sought treatment for anxiety, fatigue, and difficulty in concentration. He had grown up in a dysfunctional family in which both parents were alcoholics. Their relationship was stormy, and life was extremely difficult for the young boy. When he was 10 years old, Miguel's parents were divorced, and he alternated living with each parent; the years that followed were no less painful for him.

Miguel was aware that the instability of his family background resulted in a great deal of inner pain and made it difficult for him to trust. He was fully aware of his strong anger with each of his parents for ways that they had disappointed him throughout his life. He realized that his anxiety and fear were associated with his inner rage toward his parents and resentment toward his siblings, who had serious emotional problems of their own.

His decision to work on forgiveness was based on the hope that it would help him feel better by decreasing his inner rage and his subsequent fears. Miguel used cognitive forgiveness daily and tried to understand each of his parents more, especially their life struggles and hurts, so that he could let go of his resentment with each parent. This work resulted in the emergence of a deep sadness, beginning with his childhood and chaotic family life. He felt profoundly cheated and empty, and at those times, he found himself completely unable to forgive his parents either cognitively or emotionally. He was highly determined to resolve his inner rage, which was draining him and making him anxious. Being a religious person, Miguel began exploring how he could integrate his psychological knowledge about forgiveness with his faith. He began to ask God on a regular basis to help him forgive his parents. As stated in our Introduction, Poloma and Gallup's (1991) research indicates that over 80% of adults in the United States seek God's help when faced with the challenge of forgiveness.

In a number of therapy sessions, painful life experiences were reenacted during which Miguel would try to express disappointment and anger toward each of his parents. Next, he would attempt to verbalize his desire to understand and forgive them. During Miguel's treatment, the therapist played the role of his father and asked him for forgiveness for being insensitive to him; usually Miguel was able to give that forgiveness.

His parents' sobriety over the past few years increased Miguel's respect for them and facilitated the healing of his anger. Miguel did not experience the need to discuss his therapy with his parents. He felt that they were both very fragile people. The more that he understood the weaknesses of his parents from their family backgrounds, the greater his compassion and desire to let go of his resentment. His work of forgiveness went on for 7 years as a result of discovering different levels of anger within himself.

The most difficult aspect of Miguel's treatment was trying to accept the pain of his childhood and his adolescence because he felt that he never had even one parent whom he could trust. Miguel felt that he had been severely neglected, but as he resolved his anger and grew in trust in personal relationships, he developed the confidence that he would no longer be controlled by his childhood pain.

PANIC DISORDERS

Clients with PD often struggle with anger; in one study, a third of those with PD manifested anger attacks regularly (Gould et al., 1996). In a psychodynamic study of PD, patients described themselves as fearful, nervous, or shy as children, and they remembered their parents as angry, frightening, critical, or controlling. They also indicated discomfort with aggression. Stressors associated with frustration and resentment preceded the panic attack. Shear, Cooper, Klerman, Busch, and Shapiro (1993) proposed a model in which inborn neurophysiological irritability predisposes to early fearfulness. In addition, case study findings have reported that some individuals with PD experience spells of anger with aggressive thoughts and behaviors during their panic attack (George, Anderson, Nutt, & Linnoila, 1989).

Clinical experience also indicates that the majority of clients with PD have significant amounts of unresolved anger and have great difficulty in honestly dealing with it. The anger regularly originates from betrayal experiences at different life stages and often interferes with the resolution of panic attacks. With the use of forgiveness in treating PD, it is possible to resolve the betrayal anger and facilitate the recovery process.

The most common events for adults that damage the ability to trust and that predispose individuals to PD include marital infidelity, substance abuse, physical or emotional abuse, job insecurity, severe financial pressure, or excessive responsibility. Childhood factors leading to PD include death or loss of a parent, serious illness, abuse by peers, or poverty. Forgiveness is used in such life events through childhood, adolescence, and adulthood to resolve anger with the offenders.

The anger in panic attacks seen in spouses of alcoholics is difficult to treat when there is a lack of motivation for the offending individuals to commit themselves to a recovery program. These individuals with alcoholism are regularly told that their drinking damages the ability of their spouse to feel safe, thereby predisposing them to panic attacks. Forgiving an alcoholic spouse who continues to offend in the same manner on a regular basis is extremely challenging. However, if the spouse of the alcoholic does not try to resolve the justifiable anger, it will cause additional personal harm. Often the anger in panic attacks only abates after separation from the alcoholic offender, at which time it is not uncommon for that person with PD to seek treatment. For spouses of substance abusers, support groups such as Al-Anon (an adjunct to Alcoholics Anonymous) can be of great help, particularly if a group and sponsor can be found who support the idea of forgiveness in addition to focusing one's energies back to taking care of oneself and not curing the substance abuser.

Equally difficult to resolve is the resentment associated with panic attacks in those who are married to extremely angry and abusive spouses. Also, the hostile feelings and rage in those with PD as a result of sexual abuse in childhood and adolescence can be extremely intense. The feelings of revenge can be overwhelming and at times only respond over time to a cognitive decision to let go of this resentment so that one is not controlled by the past.

Zachary, age 26, single, and a successful professional, entered treatment for symptoms of panic attack. He experienced severe dizziness, sweating, and intense fears. His attacks occurred at work and in his personal life and caused him great distress. After using antianxiety agents, his symptoms diminished. Initially, he was unable to identify any recent stresses that could have produced his extreme anxiety. He enjoyed his career, and although he did not have a special female relationship at the time, he was optimistic about his prospects. Also, he had grown up in a healthy family environment and had close relationships with his parents and his brothers.

Zachary was asked to try to identify anyone who may have hurt him personally or professionally over the past few years. Almost 1 year to date of his panic attack, he recalled that he had been deeply hurt in a relationship. His girlfriend Ana had been regularly insensitive to him, and he discovered that she had been unfaithful. Their 2-year relationship had confused him because at times Ana seemed to enjoy being with him, but at other times she was emotionally distant.

Zachary recognized his deep hurt as well as his fear of being betrayed again in a loving relationship. Although he allowed his anger to emerge, he was unwilling to communicate his resentment to Ana because he felt so vulnerable. His decision to try to forgive her was based on the belief that it would help him move beyond that relationship, decrease his fears, and break any emotional influence she had on his life. In reframing or understanding the offender, he slowly came to see that as the adult child of an angry, alcoholic father, Ana had a great fear of being betrayed in male relationships and that she also had unresolved anger with her father, which she had unconsciously misdirected toward him.

As he worked at daily thinking of forgiving Ana, Zachary stated, "I feel sorry for her. I don't think she will ever be able to have a healthy loving relationship with any man." Not long afterward, he was surprised to receive a call from her. He communicated to her his views of the conflicts from her family background that interfered with their relationship, his anger with her, and his wish to continue to forgive her. Then, however, he declined her suggestion to try to work again on their relationship. He related that he hoped to find a woman with a healthier father relationship because he could not risk further hurt.

While his fears and anger were diminishing, Zachary continued to work at forgiving anyone else who might have hurt him and damaged his trust in his professional life. Then painful memories from 2 years before surfaced from a previous job in which he was verbally abused by his supervisor Lou on a daily basis. He realized that he had denied his anger for numerous reasons, including the fact he was easy going and did not like confrontations with anyone and that he would certainly have lost his job and a great deal of money if he had been assertive in the situation. Zachary came to view Lou as an insecure man who was compulsively driven to insult others to build up his own weak image. This understanding helped him feel some compassion for Lou and facilitated the forgiveness process with him.

Finally, as Zachary tried to think of forgiving anyone from his childhood or adolescence who damaged his ability to trust and feel safe, he recalled that he had been used as a scapegoat regularly by his peers in junior high school because he was not a good athlete. Memories entered his consciousness associated with the fear of leaving his home and being hurt. He decided to forgive his peers and viewed their behavior as the result of adolescent rebelliousness and insecurity and not as a personal attack on him, because they had treated others in a similar manner.

Zachary slowly came to realize that his panic attacks were the result of betrayal experiences in which his trust had been severely damaged in relationships. By understanding and forgiving those who had hurt him, his fears decreased and his ability to feel safe with trustworthy people improved.

Justin, a 33-year-old married father of three, awakened with a racing heart, trembling, and shortness of breath. He was evaluated in an emergency room and informed that he was physically healthy but was experiencing a panic attack. Over the previous year, Justin was under a great deal of stress as a result of beginning a new business that had not yet been successful. He became obsessed with fears of failing financially and had great difficulty in sleeping. Although he knew that he was overreacting, he could not control his fears.

Justin was raised in a stressful home as a result of his father's inability to maintain a stable job because of his alcoholism and explosive temper. The severe financial stress on the family resulted in frequent moves and other hardships. Initially, Justin denied being angry with his father but later stated, "I'm just extremely disappointed with my dad's irresponsible behavior and, yeah, I guess it does make me angry when I think about all the pain he caused our family. I know you're telling me that the reason I have this uncontrollable fear comes from the stresses of my childhood and adolescence; I am angry."

Later he experienced some guilt with his newly discovered anger because he believed that his father had had a terrible childhood himself. Justin's love for his father in spite of his weakness became one of the major motivations for entering into the work of forgiveness. Over a period of 4 to 6 months, as he persistently thought about forgiving his father for all the fears of his childhood, Justin began to experience significant improvement. In this process, Justin tried to view his father as someone who had never felt safe with his own mother and who had subsequent difficulty trusting in relationships. This awareness of the wounded boy inside his father enabled Justin to truly feel like forgiving his father. The understanding of the origin of his fears, the resolution of his resentment with his father for his role in the development of those fears, medication, and cognitive–behavior therapy resulted in the resolution of his catastrophic thinking and fears. Finally,

Justin believed that good could come from his pain. He planned in the future to suggest to his father, who was still an episodic binge drinker, that if he would work on letting go of his own strong resentment toward his deceased mother, it might help him maintain his sobriety.

SOCIAL PHOBIA

Social phobia, more currently described in the literature as social anxiety disorder, has a lifetime prevalence of 13%, and only major depression and alcohol dependence are more prevalent in the United States (Kessler et al., 1994.) The National Comorbidity Study of phobias (Magee, Eaton, Wittchen, McGonagle, & Kessler, 1996) revealed that phobias are common, increasingly prevalent, associated with serious role impairment, and highly comorbid. Thirty-seven percent of participants with lifetime social phobia had comorbid major depression, 39% had substance abuse disorder, and 81% had at least one other lifetime disorder. Also, in one study more than 50% of young adults with anorexia nervosa or bulimia nervosa had comorbid social phobia (Flament & Godard, 1995). The age of onset of social phobias was during the adolescent years. The *DSM–IV* states that the onset also may abruptly follow a stressful or humiliating experience, or it may be insidious (American Psychiatric Association, 1994).

Some clients develop social phobias because of emotional trauma within the family or in other important relationships leading to low self-esteem, patterns of isolation, and difficulties in trusting in relationships. Although anger associated with these traumas is often unconscious, it is usually uncovered in therapy with those who have hurt them. Also, many adolescents and young adults with social phobias drink excessively prior to socializing.

Clients with social phobia benefit greatly from working at understanding and resolving their hostile feelings toward those who have hurt them. Forgiveness can diminish resentment, but it is often a difficult process, especially for those ridiculed or badly betrayed because such individuals may have powerful fantasies of revenge. Continued repression of these fantasies can lead to violent impulses and later to aggressive behaviors in those who once appeared to be quiet and withdrawn.

Rocco, a 26-year-old single professional, came from a stable family and enjoyed good relationships with his parents and his sister. He sought treatment for extreme anxiety and fears associated with socializing with his peers. His fears were so intense that he began to avoid his friends and to isolate himself. Also, fear began to invade his work, and he obsessed about the people he would meet in new work assignments. Finally, he found that he needed to allay his anxieties by drinking before he could go out socially.

Rocco's symptoms developed shortly after ending a 5-year relationship with a girlfriend whom he had hoped to marry. Before the ending of this relationship, Rocco was outgoing and socially at ease, but now he harbored an intense fear of being hurt or betrayed by others. He began to blame his ex-girlfriend Marina for his fears and started to feel powerful resentment toward her. Rocco had been affectionate and devoted to Marina, but he ended the relationship because of her unwillingness to be consistently warm and giving.

When he began to uncover the depths of his anger, he made the decision to forgive Marina as a way to overcome his fears. In the work of understanding and reframing, Rocco was able to recognize that Marina's father manifested narcissistic behavior toward her mother and sister, which resulted in extreme fears of being hurt in a similar manner. "He used Marina's mom," he said, "and then abandoned her when Marina was young. No wonder she grew up feeling afraid that the same thing would happen to her," he pondered. Rocco began to feel compassion for Marina and was able to work at forgiving her. It took many months of hard work for him to experience a decrease in his social anxieties and resentment, but the personal commitment to the process produced concrete results. During that time, he was able to be honest with Marina about his social phobia, his resentment toward her, his desire to forgive, and his beliefs about the origin of her emotional pain.

OBSESSIVE–COMPULSIVE DISORDER

OCD encompasses a broad range of symptoms that represent multiple psychological domains, including perception, cognition, emotion, social relatedness, and diverse motor behaviors. This disorder is a multidimensional and etiologically heterogeneous condition (Leckman et al., 1997). The role of anger in OCD has not been extensively described. Snaith and Taylor (1985) reported irritability in the majority of patients with severe OCD symptoms. A subgroup of patients with OCD with impulsive features, including childhood conduct disorder symptoms and an increased rate of suicide attempts, has been reported (Hollander et al., 1996–1997).

Comorbidity with other psychiatric disorders is common. A lifetime history of major depression is present in two thirds of OCD clients. In one study of obsessions and compulsions associated with postpartum onset major depression, aggressive obsessional thoughts were the most frequently encountered (Wisner et al., 1999). This disorder coexists with a number of other Axis I disorders, including PD, social phobia, eating disorders, and Tourette's Syndrome (Rasmussen & Eisen, 1994). The majority of clients with OCD have at least one personality disorder, with most falling in Cluster C (Baer

& Jenike, 1992). In one study, participants with Cluster A personality disorder had significantly higher OCD severity scores at baseline, and this cluster was a strong predictor of poorer outcome (Baer et al., 1992).

Behavioral therapy is frequently helpful in the treatment of OCD (Greist & Jefferson, 1996) and, at present, selective serotonin reuptake inhibitors are the pharmacotherapy of choice for this disorder (Greist & Jefferson, 1998). However, these treatments sometimes result in only moderate patient response, and some clients with OCD do not respond at all (Rasmussen & Eisen, 1997). Rasmussen and Eisen have suggested that new procedures are needed for treatment-refractory clients.

In our clinical experience, a core feature that underlies obsessions and compulsions in some clients is the failure to recognize and deal adequately with anger. These individuals use powerful defense mechanisms to try to control their resentment and rage toward those who have hurt them. Perfectionistic tendencies as well as guilt and fear of the possible eruption of anger may interfere with their ability to deal honestly with their emotional pain. Subsequently, this anger leads to obsessions about aggressive fantasies or fears of becoming contaminated. In an attempt to reduce their anxiety or stress or to try to prevent some dreaded event from occurring, clients engage in compulsive behaviors.

Aggressive obsessions are often seen in OCD and are included as symptoms to be evaluated in the Yale Brown Obsessive Compulsive Checklist (Goodman et al., 1989). Also, Primeau and Fontaine (1987) reported that self-destructive behavior and OCD share some significant characteristics and that the driving force behind self-mutilation is relief from tension, which is similar to the performance of a compulsive ritual (Jenike, Baer, & Minichiello, 1990).

The clinical use of forgiveness can be helpful in both the identification and the resolution of the excessive anger in some clients with OCD. The majority of clients experience their resentment only after they have engaged in cognitive forgiveness toward those who have disappointed them at different life stages. However, clients with this disorder are so highly defensive that the work of forgiveness can be prolonged and difficult. These individuals often comment in the Work Phase that they found it easier to deal with their cleaning or washing compulsive behaviors than with their emerging anger, aggressive impulses, and desire for revenge.

Ashley, a 35-year-old married mother of two, sought treatment of her obsessive fears that her children might acquire terrible diseases from germs in the home. In an attempt to protect her children, she spent numerous hours cleaning the house each day. Early in treatment, she asked to be hospitalized after her fears of contamination became so extreme that she put her children's wool coats into the washing machine.

Initially, Ashley denied that anyone had hurt her. After explaining the value of forgiveness in the treatment of OCD, the therapist asked Ashley to think that she wanted to try to forgive anyone who had disappointed her or been insensitive to her in her childhood, adolescence, and adult life. It took months before Ashley could admit that she had been hurt by anyone. Finally, as she thought of forgiving anyone who had hurt her, her defenses diminished and her emotional pain emerged. She acknowledged that her husband Kurt had been extremely insensitive to her for years. In fact, he was extremely critical, and at times, he was verbally abusive. She recognized that she needed to deny her pain with him for many reasons, including fear of his anger, fear of divorce, and strong insecurities from the constant criticism that she had experienced during her youth.

Ashley also came to realize that she had been denying strong resentment from the time she was a child toward each of her parents. Her perception was that they had favored her other siblings and had treated her like a second-class citizen. She came to recognize that she had then married someone who was almost as critical as her parents had been. At this stage, she needed an antidepressant to deal with the sadness and strong rage associated with her betrayal experiences. At first, she felt so hurt that she was unable to think about forgiving anyone, but when she realized how essential it was for her to resolve her anger to overcome her germ phobia, she decided to make a decision to forgive even though she did not feel like doing so.

She realized that her true fears were not of her children being harmed by germs, but of her buried rage and the fact that she feared hurting her husband or someone else as a result of it. During the struggle with her powerfully angry impulses, in frustration Ashley responded, "I wish I was back dealing with my germ phobia—it was a lot easier than this." Ashley was able to continue to forgive Kurt because she was aware of his difficult life with an alcoholic father who continued to be a major source of stress even in their married life. She had always felt empathy for Kurt and, in the end, her compassion enabled her to decide to let go of her anger with him. Finally, her forgiveness was facilitated by his participation in therapy and acknowledgment of the mistakes he had made in their relationship.

The dynamics were explained to Kurt, and he was asked to consider that he might have been misdirecting anger at Ashley meant for his alcoholic father. He apologized to Ashley and committed himself to work at forgiving his father, which helped significantly in her recovery. However, Ashley continued to have difficulty in letting go of her anger with her parents. She came to believe that they never really wanted her and had always harbored a resentment against her. As she tried to tell herself that they were emotionally sick people who had no right to have a negative influence over her emotional life, she was able to make the cognitive decision to let go of her resentment toward them. She could not develop compassion for her parents, nor was she able to absorb the pain.

As Ashley's unconscious rage with her husband and parents decreased through the use of forgiveness, her obsessive fear concerning her children lessened also. Her husband felt guilty about his role in his wife's illness and made major changes in the way that he treated her; in addition, he decided to forgive his father and resolved not to act in a similar manner. After 2 years of treatment, Ashley's OCD symptoms were resolved.

POSTTRAUMATIC STRESS DISORDER

Some individuals with PTSD struggle with extreme anger and frequently have powerful impulses to seek revenge against those who traumatized them. The *DSM–IV* lists irritability and outbursts of anger as one of the persistent symptoms of increased arousal in PTSD (American Psychiatric Association, 1994). Chemtob, Novaco, Hamada, Gross, and Smith (1997) termed the anger type in some extremely hostile patients with PTSD as "ball of rage."

Excessive anger in PTSD is evident today among those who have lost their jobs through downsizing and are unable to locate comparable work or in people who were physically or sexually abused. Forgiveness can enable the victim to let go of rage and impulses for revenge while at the same time pursuing justice regarding the traumatic event. Forgiveness also can diminish the recurrent memories of the event, decrease fears, irritability, and obsessional thoughts of the offender. The failure to resolve the anger with the offender regularly places the perpetrator in a position of power over the victim.

Tiffany, age 28, was a victim of medical malpractice while giving birth. In a critical condition for a week, she almost died. As a result of her treatment and prolonged hospitalization, she developed a PTSD with recurrent nightmares and dreams of a near-death experience. In addition to extreme anxiety, she was left with a serious health problem as a result of careless treatment. The initiation of a lawsuit and the pursuit of justice did not provide relief from her symptoms and especially her rage against the doctors and hospital because they reported the loss of a critical biopsy report and medical records essential to her case.

Tiffany lived with the great fear that her doctors would never be held accountable for the malpractice, and she regularly thought about ways in which she could seek revenge. In the hope that forgiveness would help diminish her emotional pain, she tried to think about forgiving her offenders. Tiffany discovered that she was unable to use the word *forgive*: "I can't think of forgiving while I'm still in pain because of what they did and because of their arrogance and lying." Tiffany was a religious person and was helped by thinking that she was powerless over her rage and wanted to turn it over to God and that revenge belongs to God. Her ideas were not unlike those described in 12-step programs. Her PTSD symptoms diminished very slowly over a period of several years. After 5 years, her lawsuit against the doctors and hospital finally moved toward a trial date, and as the hope of justice increased, her powerful anger diminished significantly.

Earl, age 50, had a successful 28-year career with a large international corporation. He entered therapy after being told by his employer that he would no longer be a general manager but would have to return to sales. His corporation had a markedly small business in the limited territory that he was assigned. He realized that his new position would not be able to support his income, and it appeared that within less than a year he would be fired. As a result of the trauma associated with these events, Earl developed severe insomnia with recurrent dreams of the demotion. He constantly replayed the event and became depressed with markedly diminished interest in significant activities and extreme fears for the future.

In attempting to understand why his corporation took action against him, Earl became convinced that it was because he had blown the whistle when he spotted collusion between another highly successful salesman and someone from a different national corporation. An investigation revealed that his views were accurate, and the salesman lost his job and the regional general manager was demoted. He was convinced that their friends higher up on the corporate ladder were seeking revenge against him because of his honesty. His emotional and mental state were such that the therapist and he agreed to pursue disability rather than attempt to go into his new position with severe symptoms and face the loss of his career in a short period of time.

Earl made the decision to try to work at forgiving those who had betrayed him, not because he wanted to let go of his anger with them, but because he felt so guilty about regularly overreacting in anger against innocent people. He also came to understand the relationship that existed between his anger and the accompanying insomnia, depression, and mistrust. He tried to forgive to facilitate the recovery from his severe PTSD symptoms. Because he continued to view the actions of his employer as evil and motivated by revenge, Earl had great difficulty in forgiving his employer.

After a number of months in therapy and as a result of the diminishment of his anger, Earl decided to take legal action against the corporation for the manner in which it had treated him. He struggled with violent impulses against different members of the corporation and, at that time, he tried to think that he wanted to let go of these thoughts and not act on them. This was a difficult process for him. He realized that holding onto his strong anger would only harm him, but he was not able to use the word *forgive*.

Over the course of several months, he did find relief from thinking daily that he wanted to let go of his desires for revenge and not act on them.

The thought of obtaining justice through legal means was an additional encouragement to him. The trauma, however, was so severe that Earl remained in the process of forgiveness for several years, unable to absorb the pain or to find any meaning in his suffering. His major method for coping was regular reflection that he did not want his former employer to control him and that he had the desire to let go of his rage and impulses for revenge. These steps helped diminish his PTSD symptoms as he continued to pursue legal action against his employer.

TOWARD THE FUTURE

The case studies in this chapter suggest that forgiveness can be an effective psychotherapeutic technique that facilitates the healing of anxiety disorders by resolving the various degrees of anger associated with them. It is our hope that future research will empirically study the uses of forgiveness in the treatment of specific anxiety disorders. This research may clarify whether forgiveness is more helpful with certain anxiety disorders than others and if its use is more effective for certain age groups.

9

FORGIVENESS IN SUBSTANCE ABUSE DISORDERS

Henry, age 37, had a long history of alcoholism and cocaine abuse. He had been through several rehabilitation efforts and was aware that his anger and need to rebel played a major role in subsequent relapses. Even though Henry had known for years that forgiving his father for being controlling and punitive would help diminish his anger and benefit his recovery, he was unable to take that step. As long as he held onto his addiction and his anger with his father, he experienced a distorted sense of power. Henry's firm decision to work toward the understanding and resolution of anger and the subsequent benefits to his recovery is presented in this chapter. We also describe present methods for dealing with anger in addictive disorders; common origins of anger in substance abusers; the four phases of forgiveness; and the use of forgiveness in clinical cases in treating the anger in addictive disorders associated with depression, low self-esteem, anxiety, antisocial personality, rebelliousness and intense anger, and other personality disorders.

Substance abuse is a serious disorder, regularly associated with excessive anger. Annually, approximately 100,000 deaths in the United States are ascribed to alcohol abuse and alcoholism, making them the fourth leading cause of mortality after heart disease, cerebrovascular disease, and cancer (Stinson & DeBakey, 1992). Substance abuse disorder (SUD) is associated with social and psychological difficulties that give rise to anger in the user and others, including family conflicts, parental neglect, child abuse, social isolation, antisocial behavior, and unemployment (Kumpfer & Hopkins, 1993).

Studies support the clinical experience of many therapists that excessive anger is prevalent in those with SUD. Conduct disorders in adolescents, for example, have been shown to precede alcohol and drug abuse by several years (Huizinga, Loeber, & Thornberry, 1991). Substance abusers' levels of anger and violence are higher than levels found in the general population (Awalt, Reilly, & Shopshire, 1997), and substance abusers score far above national norms on the State–Trait Anger Expression Inventory (Potter-Efron, R. T. & Potter-Efron, 1991; Tivis, Parsons, & Nixon, 1998; Walfish, Messey, & Krone, 1990). Drug abusers have significantly higher scores on State and Trait Anger scales and are more likely to express anger toward other people or objects and have less control of their angry feelings than the general population (DeMoja & Spielberger, 1997). Also, subjective anger is an important correlate of alcoholism in men with depression and more closely related to alcoholism than antisocial personality (C. E. Lewis, Rice, Andreason, Endicot, & Hartman, 1986). Certain substances such as alcohol, PCP, amphetamines, and cocaine are associated with aggressive patterns of behavior (S. Cohen, 1985; Miller & Potter-Efron, 1989). Finally, adoption studies have identified a subtype of alcoholism characterized by high heritability and an aggressive and impulsive personality (Cloninger, Bohman, & Sigvardsson, 1981; von Knorring, von Knorring, Smigan, Lindberg, & Edholm, 1987).

Many therapists identify substance abusers as their angriest, most abusive, and most violent patients. Their resentment can interfere with both inpatient and outpatient recovery programs, playing a major role in relapse (Daley & Marlatt, 1992; Gorski, 1983; Potter-Efron, P. S. & Potter-Efron, 1991). Some in recovery relate that their sobriety is threatened because they lack an understanding of ways to cope effectively with their anger. Many substance abusers realize that they drink to control their anger or as a method to diminish their defenses so that they can more easily vent hostile feelings. According to Alcoholic Anonymous (AA, 1976),

> Resentment is the number one "offender." It destroys more alcoholics than anything else. . . . It is plain that a life that includes deep resentment leads only to futility and unhappiness. . . . [W]ith the alcoholic, this business of resentment is infinitely grave. We found that it is fatal. . . . If we were to live, we had to be free of anger.

METHODS OF DEALING WITH ANGER IN ADDICTIVE DISORDERS

A number of psychotherapeutic approaches have been recommended for the treatment of the anger in SUD (Awalt et al., 1997; Clancy, 1997; Daley & Marlatt, 1992; Lacks, 1988; Potter-Efron, P. S. & Potter-Efron,

1991; Reilly et al., 1994). However, a major difficulty at the present time is the failure of the majority of therapists to recommend to these patients a specific plan for coping with their resentment. Mental health professionals usually do not acknowledge or directly address the hostility in the substance abuser. Perhaps the therapists are hoping that the angry feelings, behaviors, and thinking will be addressed in the 12-step program. The 12 steps of AA for substance abuse disorders can be found in Exhibit 9.1.

The need for a specific plan to treat anger in the substance abuser is supported both by clinical experience and by research that reveals that feelings of anger have failed to subside after inpatient drug treatment (Powell & Taylor, 1992). Another difficulty in deciding which treatment plan to use is the lack of empirical research of the various treatment protocols for the excessive anger in substance abusers.

The expression of anger in patients continues to be the method most often recommended by therapists. Yet, the limitations and dangers of this approach have been described in the literature (Daley & Marlatt, 1992; Fitzgibbons, 1986; Potter-Efron, P. S. & Potter-Efron, 1991; Tavris, 1989). Unfortunately, many therapists are unaware of other anger management techniques available, and in particular, the use of forgiveness has received scant attention. Forgiveness, however, has been recommended as a way of

EXHIBIT 9.1
The 12 Steps of Alcoholics Anonymous

1. We admitted we were powerless over alcohol, that our lives had become unmanageable.
2. Came to believe that a Power greater than ourselves could restore us to sanity.
3. Made a decision to turn our will and our lives over to the care of God *as we understood Him.*
4. Made a searching and fearless moral inventory of ourselves.
5. Admitted to God, to ourselves, and to another human being the exact nature of our wrongs.
6. Were entirely ready to have God remove all these defects of character.
7. Humbly asked Him to remove our shortcomings.
8. Make a list of all persons we had harmed, and became willing to make amends to them all.
9. Made direct amends to such people wherever possible, except when to do so would injure them or others.
10. Continued to take personal inventory and when we were wrong promptly admitted it.
11. Sought through prayer and meditation to improve our conscious contact with God *as we understood Him,* praying only for knowledge of His will for us and the power to carry that out.
12. Having had a spiritual awakening as the result of these steps, we tried to carry this message to alcoholics, and to practice these principles in all our affairs.

working through past anger (Potter-Efron, P. S. & Potter-Efron, 1991). The model that the Potter-Efrons recommend is Smedes's (1984) approach, a pioneering first effort, but not a psychologically complete one, nor one that has been empirically validated.

BENEFITS OF FORGIVENESS

From our clinical experience, forgiveness can be highly effective in treating SUD because it may help diminish angry feelings, thoughts, and behaviors in the patient. The ability to understand the causes of anger and maintain control over it helps stabilize the mood of substance abusers and facilitates their recovery. Forgiveness also can diminish the anger in the comorbid disorders associated with SUD. The healing of this anger is important because it can inhibit the recovery process.

ORIGINS OF RESENTMENT IN ADDICTIVE DISORDERS

Numerous areas of conflict can give rise to strong anger in substance abusers. These include loneliness and depression, strong insecurities, anxiety and mistrust, work and career tensions and frustrations, rebelliousness, and bonding with hostile peers (Kumpfer & Turner, 1990–1991). Additional conflicts can be narcissism, posttraumatic stress disorder, antisocial and dependent personality disorders, unemployment, poverty, and self-hatred. Also a heritable biological factor may play a role in the resentment in some addicts (Cloninger et al., 1981; von Knorring et al., 1987).

AN OVERVIEW OF THE FORGIVENESS PHASES FOR SUBSTANCE ABUSERS

An examination of the typical problems and challenges faced within each of the four phases of forgiveness with case studies is presented as an aid to the therapist.

Uncovering Phase

In this phase of treatment, the challenge is not necessarily to identify anger because most substance abusers readily admit that they have problems with hostile feelings or impulses. Ascertaining with whom the addict is truly angry, however, can be a formidable task. Because passive–aggressive expression can be the major hidden method of venting resentment in some addicts, it is important to recognize both passive–aggressive and active anger.

The first step in identifying the true origin of the addicts' anger is to assist them in recognizing major disappointments in relationships throughout their lives. In our clinical work, the most significant anger arises from disappointments and hurts in the father relationship, but it can also develop from other relationships with mothers, spouses, sibling, peers, and employers. If the alcoholic is involved with AA, the Step 4 and 5 inventory can be invaluable in this phase when done with a sponsor or therapist.

The common complaints against fathers are that they themselves were alcoholic or that they were too distant, angry, controlling, narcissistic, or weak. Many addicts relate that they never expressed this anger directly to their fathers in childhood or adolescence, either because they feared him or because they worried about losing the relationship with him as a result of their honesty. Rebellious behavior in the home, school, or community was an easier path to choose.

Decision Phase

Addicted people in an inpatient treatment program often are unwilling to make the decision to forgive an offender because of ambivalence about their recovery or because of the benefits they derive from their resentment, including, in the case of men, the projection of a strong masculine image. One way to motivate such people to decide to work on forgiveness is to present the negative consequences of storing up their hostile feelings. As patients realize that harboring resentment gives the offender a controlling influence in their lives, those in recovery programs are more willing to consider forgiveness as an option. As a further complication, patients can feel guilty about ways in which their hostile behaviors have hurt other important people in their lives, including children, spouses, and friends. This, too, can serve as a motivation to forgive.

Work Phase

The fact that many addicts, whose parents had SUD, can quickly identify and empathize with their parents facilitates the work of forgiveness. The most challenging patients are those with physically and emotionally abusive parents because they often discover powerful impulses for revenge or violent thoughts and fantasies. When this type of strong anger emerges, many addicts feel powerless over their rage, but fortunately, their familiarity with 12-step programs can prove invaluable. In such circumstances they are asked to modify the first two steps and reflect that they are powerless over their rage and impulses for revenge and want to turn them over to God.

Those with strong repeated anger attacks benefit from treatment with a serotonin reuptake inhibitor.

The ability to resolve anger from the past and the present has numerous benefits for those in recovery and reinforces the decision to use forgiveness on a regular basis. Many substance abusers begin the work of forgiveness and relapse for a variety of reasons. Some of them need to hit rock bottom many times before they truly make a commitment to work on their recovery and on their resentment.

Anger management interventions for individuals struggling with substance abuse sometimes fail to address the significant early life conflicts that give rise to strong resentment. Therefore, the deep anger is never fully resolved and often emerges under the influence of the addictive substance.

Some of the common obstacles to the use of forgiveness in substance abusers include the following: the unwillingness to give up the addictive substance, the emotional high that comes from rebellious behavior, ambivalence about giving up the reliance on strong anger for a strong masculine identity, narcissism, lack of a desire to be healthy, the need for acceptance from peers who are addicted, difficulty in changing the habit of excessive use of anger when disappointed, and lack of a role model for forgiveness.

Deepening Phase

People who are addicted are often more motivated to make amends with those whom they have hurt and from whom they seek forgiveness as a result of their work on Step 5 of the 12 Steps of AA. Usually, these people find that in this phase their self-esteem begins to increase as a result of the resolution of anger from the past and their growing ability to deal with angry feelings in a healthy manner.

ANGER ASSOCIATED WITH DEPRESSION

Depression and loneliness are important clinical issues in those with addictive disorders. In a retrospective, blinded, case-controlled assessment of the drug and depressive history of depressed outpatients, alcohol dependence followed the onset of depression by 4.7 years, and among polydrug users, cocaine dependence occurred 6.8 years after the first major depressive episode (Abraham & Fava, 1999). Alcoholism, in particular, is strongly associated with depression and suicidality (Galanter & Castaneda, 1985; Schuckit, 1986). Major depression and dysthymia occur 1½–2 times more commonly in people with alcoholism than in the general population (Helzer & Pryzbeck, 1988). It also has been shown that opiate addicts have high rates of depression (Rounsaville, Weissman, Crits-Christoph, Wilber, & Kleber, 1982; Woody,

O'Brien, & Rickels, 1983). Because depressive illness is a major predictor of relapse (Pickens, Hatsukami, Spizer, & Suikis, 1985), the ability to resolve the anger associated with it can help substance abusers in their recovery and protect them from relapse. Clinical experience has shown that loneliness is one of the major factors influencing the development of depressive disorders in substance abusers.

Antone, age 39, had a 15-year history of alcoholism that included several inpatient treatment programs. After several sessions, he was able to acknowledge that he struggled with intense loneliness that had never been identified in his several rehabilitation experiences. Next, he was able to recognize very strong resentment toward former friends and family members as a result of his loneliness.

When asked if anyone in the past had hurt him, he recalled a painful relationship with a woman 6 years earlier. He believed that she had used him and then ended the relationship after having an abortion. His anger intensified when he began to recognize that he had become extremely fearful of vulnerability in a relationship as a result of her betrayal. At the same time, he uncovered anger with a narcissistic older brother who failed to support him emotionally.

Antone began to recognize a pattern of drinking as a way to escape from his severe loneliness and its associated anger. He decided to try forgiving those who had hurt him in the hope that it would help with his alcoholism, his recovery, and his loneliness. He was given past forgiveness exercises in which he tried to think of forgiving the woman who had betrayed him so profoundly. Initially, he found it difficult to forgive her. There were moments when he thought of getting revenge. His memories of her were so painful that he was reluctant to address them. After several months of struggling, he finally committed himself to forgive her because he realized that the pain was limiting his life. He realized how fortunate he was that she had left him, given her repeated pattern of selfishness. As his forgiveness deepened, he was surprised to feel compassion for her because he surmised that her extreme selfishness would probably limit her ability to ever enter into a healthy, loving relationship unless she changed.

In some ways he found it even more difficult to forgive his married older brother who was the father of several children whom Antone loved. He felt certain that his brother's extreme self-centeredness created the obstacle that prevented a relationship with the children. As he worked at forgiving his brother, he also came to feel some compassion for him.

Antone's increasing ability to control his anger through forgiveness helped him significantly in his recovery from alcoholism and loneliness. The most difficult aspect of the work of forgiveness was that of making the commitment to forgive. Also, he became more willing to trust a woman again as the influence of the past hurt diminished.

ANGER ASSOCIATED WITH LOW SELF-ESTEEM

Substance abusers have been noted to have low self-esteem (Washton, 1995). Many alcoholics relate using alcohol as a way to cope with their insecurities. Some go so far as to say that their confidence comes from the "bottle" and that they only feel good about themselves after drinking. Those with low self-esteem often have significant amounts of anger with parents, spouses, siblings, peers, employers, and significant others who failed to help them develop a positive identity or who damaged their self-respect.

Seth, a 20-year-old college student, entered a drug and alcohol inpatient treatment program for mixed addiction of alcohol and cocaine. Prior to his hospitalization, Seth was in treatment for his addictions and intense social anxiety. He felt that people were always looking critically at him and he dreaded any kind of embarrassment. His extreme social fear interfered significantly with his college life. Not only was he afraid of participating in class, but he also found himself needing to drink or use drugs before socializing with his peers. When he drank, he related that he felt very confident and did not fear being rejected.

Seth was the second child in his family and grew up in a home in which he felt comfortable. He had enjoyed a close relationship with his mother but did not feel particularly close to his father, although he liked him. In the first grade, Seth began experiencing strong rejection by his peers because of his inability to play sports. He was regularly the victim of intense criticism and at times ridicule by other children throughout his elementary and middle school years. Because of his extreme sensitivity and shame over this peer ridicule, he never informed his parents of the daily emotional trauma that he experienced at school.

The high school years were much better for Seth. He was not a scapegoat, but his anxieties were of such an extreme nature that he had great difficulty trusting in interpersonal relationships. Also, he began to drink excessively during these years.

Seth recognized that he was regularly misdirecting the anger meant for his peers at his family, particularly his mother. He also realized that the hurt he experienced from his peers as a child made him extremely fearful of being rejected as a young adult. His decision, after several months of therapy, to work at forgiving his peers from his childhood years was based on the hope that this would help with his recovery and diminish his excessive anxieties, which interfered with his college life.

In reframing and understanding, Seth tried to view his offenders as children and teenagers who were themselves troubled by excessive anger and possibly by a dislike for themselves, which they were misdirecting at him. His pain was so intense from his peer experiences that he was not able to experience any compassion or empathy toward those who hurt him. Also, he had great difficulty absorbing and accepting the pain because of its profound nature.

Seth was a strong young man who made the intellectual decision to let go of his anger to help his recovery even though he did not feel like it. Many days he felt that he really wanted to strike back, but he saw intellectually that revenge was ultimately useless and would only harm him. He felt benefit from reflecting on an old Chinese proverb that "He who seeks revenge builds two coffins."

As Seth continued the forgiveness process and felt stronger in dealing with his addiction, he experienced a diminishment of his insecurities, and over the course of several years he slowly felt more comfortable in peer relationships. As he grew in the ability to separate his childhood peers from his young adult peers, his trust increased and his compulsive need for alcohol or drugs to relax with his peers decreased. He also benefited from regular physical workouts during which time he would imagine expressing anger at those who had hurt him in the past. Developing a better body image was also beneficial to building his self-esteem.

ANGER ASSOCIATED WITH ANXIETY DISORDERS

Anxiety is very common in those with SUD (Bower, Cipywnyk, D'Arcy, & Keegan, 1984; Walfish et al., 1990). In one study, the lifetime prevalence rate of alcoholism in those with anxiety disorders was 13% (Regier, Boyd, & Burke, 1988). Alcohol use disorders and anxiety disorders demonstrate a reciprocal causal relationship over time, with anxiety disorders leading to alcohol dependence and vice versa (Kushner, Sher, & Erickson, 1999).

Some people who have been disappointed and hurt in important loving relationships resort to addictive substances to diminish their fears of being betrayed and their fears of commitment. This reaction is common when loving relationships end. The use of addictive substances as a means of coping with anxiety and work pressures is extremely common in US society.

Adolescents and young adults from divorced families can manifest trust difficulties, fears of betrayal, and hesitancy to commit in relationships (Wallerstein, 1991). They often resort to alcohol, marijuana, cocaine, or other substances to cope with these fears. In Wallerstein's 15-year follow-up of children of divorce, 20% of those in the study were drinking heavily (Wallerstein & Blakeslee, 1989).

Malcolm, age 25 and single, entered treatment for help with his cocaine addiction. He already had been to one inpatient treatment program, relapsing not long after his discharge. Malcolm was the third of four children, and he grew up in a home with a weak passive father and an unaffectionate mother who attempted to control him. Although he found himself attracted to women, in his therapy Malcolm came to understand that he found it safer and more pleasurable to do his lines of cocaine than to risk becoming vulnerable in a relationship of trust with a woman. After several failures in attempting to overcome his cocaine addiction, he had hit bottom and was now highly motivated to work on his recovery, and he subsequently was willing to examine all areas of emotional pain in his life.

In his therapy, a great deal of anger with his mother was uncovered, as well as, much to his surprise, a profound mistrust of women because of the way he had been treated by her. He related, "I hated the way in which she tried to dominate my life, my friendships, my future, even my breathing." This discovery initially intensified his anger with his mother. However, he came to understand that the resolution of this anger was essential to establishing healthy friendships with women and to his recovery. He decided to try forgiveness because neither denying nor overreacting in anger was beneficial to him. A major difficulty in applying forgiveness was that his mother had not changed her controlling ways, which reawakened his anger and mistrust.

He decided to use the forgiveness process to help him in his recovery and in his ability to establish healthy female friendships. Initially, in the Work Phase of forgiveness, Malcolm was unable to forgive his mother cognitively or emotionally. Instead he used a modification of the 12-Step program of AA and daily reflected that he was powerless over his cocaine addiction and intense anger with his mother and he wanted to turn them both over to God. He felt comfortable in this process because he had a strong spiritual life. His anger with his mother fluctuated significantly. There were times in the forgiveness process when he was unable to let go of his anger with her at all, especially when certain painful memories from the past emerged. However, he was determined not to be controlled by his past and, as he worked at giving up his resentment, he felt freer and less controlled.

His struggle with trusting female relationships was a lengthy one, but fortunately he was able to identify several trustworthy women in his life. The 2-year process of forgiveness proved beneficial in Malcolm's recovery from his cocaine addiction, and it opened him to healthier friendships.

REBELLIOUSNESS AND INTENSE ANGER

Substance abusers often identify their alcoholism and drug abuse as a type of rebelliousness against family members, employers, or society at large. Adolescents, in particular, discover that it gives them a sense of strength, freedom, and acceptance from other hostile, rebellious peers. Some, too, find that rebelliousness provides an excuse for avoiding responsibility or becoming dependent on others.

Henry, whom we introduced at the start of this chapter, had a 16-year history of alcohol and later cocaine substance abuse. He had several inpatient hospitalizations for alcoholism and spent weekend time in prison because of several arrests for driving under the influence of alcohol. After a period of 6 months of weekends in prison, he became truly motivated for the first time in recovery. The other incentive was that his wife had just given birth to their first child, a son.

Henry had significant psychological insights into the profound anger and rebelliousness that influenced his substance abuse. He was fully aware that he had grown up in a large family with a powerful, domineering father who had ruled his family with an iron fist. When Henry engaged in moderate rebellious behavior as a teenager, his father's response was swift and severe, grounding him for an extended period of time for even minor acts of rebellion. As an adolescent, Henry was fully aware that he derived great pleasure from drunkenness because, when he was intoxicated, his father had absolutely no ability to control him. Although he saw his present behavior as self-destructive, he had difficulty letting go of the deep resentment and bitterness he felt toward his father even though he realized that it played a major role in his struggle with alcoholism.

Henry had been in therapy a number of times during which the concept of forgiveness had been presented to him, but he admitted that in earlier phases of therapy he had only given lip service to the concept and had never truly made a decision to overcome his addictive disorder or to let go of his anger through forgiveness. He admitted that his reasons were that he enjoyed the sense of rebelling and that his anger helped him feel that he was stronger than his father.

The questions that the therapist repeatedly presented to Henry during his therapy were, "Why are you allowing your father to continue to control you? Why not let go of your anger with him and thereby break the control of the past?" Henry resolved to break the negative legacy passed on by the men in his family from one generation to the next, and for the first time he truly committed himself to try to understand and forgive his father. During the time when Henry worked at thinking of forgiving his father daily, his level of compassion toward his father increased and, in time, Henry really felt like forgiving him. He also slowly grew in his ability to accept the pain of the past and came to believe that his father had, in fact, attempted to love him as much as he was capable of loving him, given his own conflicts from his family of origin. Henry related, "My father had a difficult life with many heavy responsibilities, and he did the best he could given his family background."

As his anger slowly diminished, Henry grew in his ability to accept the pain of his past. As he continued forgiving his father, Henry's guilt from his rebellious anger diminished and his self-esteem improved. For the first time, he was able to relate to his father in a positive manner.

ANGER WITH ANTISOCIAL PERSONALITY

Studies reveal that 23–55% of children with conduct disorder develop antisocial personality disorder as adults (Robins, 1978; Robins & McEvoy, 1990), and more than 80% of those who go on to develop antisocial personality disorders have an associated SUD (Regier et al., 1990). Huizinga et al. (1991) recommended the simultaneous treatment of delinquency and substance abuse as more effective than a program focused only on one or the other. Forgiveness can be used with angry adolescent substance abusers to diminish their hostile feelings and impulses for revenge.

Those with antisocial personality disorders can have childhood and adolescent experiences of profound betrayal or abuse. The response to this betrayal pain is intense anger that can lead to violent fantasies and impulses and then destructive behaviors. In the treatment of anger stemming from antisocial personality, it is necessary first to uncover the intense rage from childhood and adolescence and to determine toward whom it is directed. Here the therapist will find value in exploring the depths of anger in all significant relationships by specifically asking if strong hatred, violent impulses, or a death wish has been entertained.

Throughout the process, strong hostile feelings emerge toward a parent, an abusive family member, or others with whom the patient had interacted. As a result of perceived benefits that these patients experience from their intense anger, there is often a major resistance to the resolution of the inner rage and tendency toward violent behavior. Factors that influence the decision to change the method that has previously been used to deal with inner fury and to consider the use of forgiveness include negative experiences with the law, a decision to stop acting like the offender, renewed commitment to family, or the emergence of guilt.

For individuals with violent fantasies, impulses, and behaviors, the release of rage can be facilitated by a process that begins with the physical expression of anger in a manner in which others will not be hurt; for example, the use of strenuous exercises, a punching bag, or breaking objects of little value. Men tend to be very comfortable with this approach to releasing their anger through their strength. Physical expression is followed immediately by making a decision to forgive offenders by cognitively relinquishing the desire for revenge. For some, the inner rage and impulse for revenge are so powerful that the word *forgiveness* cannot be used; this is particularly true in cases involving abusive fathers. As related earlier in this chapter in the Work Phase and in Malcolm's case of rage with his controlling mother, the therapist can suggest that when clients cannot use the word *forgiveness* that they modify Steps 1 and 2 of the 12 steps of AA. They can reflect that they are powerless over their rage and want to turn it over to God or think that they want to let go of their desire for revenge.

ANGER IN PERSONALITY DISORDERS

In one study, Rounsaville et al. (1998) found that the majority of substance abuse patients (57%) met the criteria for at least one comorbid personality disorder with Cluster B being particularly predominant, especially antisocial personality disorder and borderline personality disorder. Substance abusers who have narcissistic personality conflicts regularly manifest very strong anger and rage. These individuals are commonly encountered in drug and alcohol treatment programs and have been reported to respond poorly to individual psychotherapy (Washton, 1995). However, some of the patients do respond to a treatment protocol that challenges them to act more responsibly, to give themselves more fully to others, and to use forgiveness rather than ventilating their anger whenever they feel upset. This approach to treating the narcissistic personality is developed further in a case study in chapter 12.

The success rate is not particularly high in treating this subtype of addicts because their substance abuse is an important part of their compulsive, pleasure-seeking lifestyle. Some, however, do become motivated to change from their narcissism. The major factors that influence such a decision include an awareness of harm to the self, feelings of emptiness and depression, fear of losing a loved one or a job, or the emergence of guilt.

Narcissistic personality traits predispose these individuals to impulsive angry outbursts and violent behavior when their needs are not being met or when they are not the center of attention. Forgiveness is taught as an alternative method for coping with their anger and as a way to reach beyond themselves to other people. While supporting the appropriate expression of anger, we recommend forgiving and understanding when the patient feels upset with others as the first step in dealing with anger. The narcissistic person is asked to reflect on trying to be more patient and understanding with others and to act in a more mature and responsible manner. Also, past forgiveness exercises are used that concentrate on parents or other important people who facilitated the development of the patient's narcissism. Because forgiveness involves the giving of a moral gift to others, the narcissistic person learns to focus on care for others.

In one study (Valgum & Valgum, 1985), 30% of the female alcoholics met the criteria for borderline personality disorder. Forgiveness can be effective in diminishing the resentment and hostility in this personality disorder, which usually arises from early life betrayals. The ability of borderline patients to control their resentment is of great value in the treatment of SUD.

TOWARD THE FUTURE

Forgiveness has significant potential to help substance abusers not only with their recovery from alcohol and other drugs but also from associated comorbid disorders. Thus far, in the early stages of forgiveness studies, no research has been undertaken to demonstrate its effectiveness with substance abusers. However, a number of clinical case studies are forming the basis for that effectiveness. The ability of people who are addicted to learn how to resolve and control excessive anger and even violent impulses should facilitate their recovery and protect them from relapse.

Presently, in psychotherapy there is a need to address the serious and, at times, dangerous resentment in substance abusers. Unless this anger is faced and resolved, it may be directed toward others or even against the self, with the subsequent danger of serious disease or early death. The reliance on the expression of anger in treating SUD is inadequate because most people who are addicted have enormous amounts of buried resentment, and they regularly overreact when they express their anger.

No empirically supported protocols exist for the treatment of the excessive anger in people who are addicted, and important research needs to be done in that area. Psychotherapy research projects could compare the process of forgiveness in SUD with other treatment modalities of the anger in addictive disorders. After this research is completed, it would then be possible to develop empirically based programs for the treatment of this strong anger. The 12-step programs, particularly in working with a sponsor, do address some of the important issues on the journey toward forgiveness. Although not empirically supported, it is generally accepted that this program is effective for many, while other approaches have failed.

Fitzgibbons's clinical work leads to the opinion that by diminishing and even resolving hostile feelings, vengeful thinking, and angry behaviors, forgiveness will play an increasingly important role in the treatment of substance abuse disorders in the future.

10

FORGIVENESS IN CHILDREN AND ADOLESCENTS

Earl, age 7, was brought into therapy by his parents for the treatment of attention deficit hyperactivity disorder (ADHD). He was extremely impulsive, angry, and hyperactive, and his parents had great difficulty coping with his behavior. Major anger was uncovered with his parents because of their constant fighting and, in particular, with his mother for her physically abusive behavior toward his father. As a result of the intense anger within his home, the work of forgiveness was begun simultaneously with Earl and each of his parents. Although he was young, he understood what it meant to make a decision to forgive rather than to express his anger. His parents helped by starting to model slowly this change in dealing with their anger.

This chapter relates the treatment of Earl's anger and that of his parents with forgiveness therapy. We also discuss the three methods of dealing with anger, denial, expression, and forgiveness, that are important for children and adolescents to understand and to learn, as well as the common origins of anger in childhood. We also present the uses of the four phases of forgiveness therapy within the context of clinical cases of ADHD, conduct disorder (CD), oppositional defiant disorder (ODD), separation anxiety disorder, panic disorder (PD), obsessive–compulsive disorder (OCD), and adjustment disorder as a result of being bullied and in stepchildren and adopted children. Countertransference issues are also presented.

The excessive expression of anger in children and teenagers in US society seems to have increased since the 1980s. For example, a recent *Uniform Crime Reports* shows a greater number of arrests than 10 years ago in children and teens under age 18 in such areas as aggravated assault, murder, nonnegligent manslaughter, and burglary (Federal Bureau of Investigation, 1998). The number of juveniles arrested for violent crimes increased 64% between 1987 and 1994 (Snyder, 1994). Also, depression, suicide rates, CD, and substance abuse among adolescents have increased (Fombonne, 1998). The rates of suicidal behavior and substance abuse in adolescents almost doubled between 1979 and 1990 in Fombonne's study. Among psychiatrically referred children and adolescents, aggressive behavior patterns have shown a detectable increase over the past 2 decades (Achenbach & Howell, 1993) and are now the most common reason for referral regardless of ambulatory, or institutional setting (Carlson, 1995). We have witnessed the rapid escalation of news reports portraying youthful perpetrators of violence and murder in the home, the school, and the community at large. There is an urgent need to come to a deeper understanding of the nature of anger in youths and ways in which it can be resolved.

Unfortunately, clinical literature contains little on the use of forgiveness in children (Fitzgibbons, 1986, 1998; Hope, 1987). For the most part, children neither understand nor know how to deal with their angry feelings and impulses for revenge. They usually are aware of only two ways to handle their anger, either the denial or expression of it. Children as young as four are able to grasp the concept of forgiveness if the parents are cooperative and discuss and model forgiveness. Those who work with children should have special training in this area. Few understand that a third option is available to them—that of understanding and forgiving those who hurt them. When used appropriately, forgiveness can resolve the strong feelings of anger in children, including violent impulses, and assist in the treatment of numerous child and adolescent disorders. Therapists can provide valuable assistance to children by helping them develop an understanding of the three basic mechanisms used to cope with anger: denial, expression, and forgiveness.

DENIAL

During early childhood, the most common method for dealing with anger is denial. The dangers attached to denial include emotional harm to the child, increased feelings of sadness, guilt and shame, and the misdirection of the resentment toward others.

We find that the relationship in which a child has been most likely to deny anger was the one in which the young person was more fearful. This usually was the father relationship. However, in today's world, the father can sometimes be the nurturing parent and the mother the more distant. Unconsciously, children fear that the expression of anger toward the parent most removed will result in greater distancing in a relationship that may already appear somewhat tenuous. This is particularly true in single-parent homes in which the father does not live with the child.

EXPRESSION

The next method commonly used by children for dealing with anger is either to express it openly and honestly or to release it in a passive–aggressive manner. It is of benefit to review with children the numerous ways in which anger can be vented passively. The therapist might consider having the young patient complete an anger checklist to identify these behaviors. Many parents can also participate in the evaluation of their child's anger by completing an anger checklist in relation to their son or daughter and thus provide the therapist with additional information on the degree of the child's anger. Various checklists can be found in Appendixes 10A, 10B, 10C, and 10D.

It may be helpful to view actively expressed anger as encompassing three types: appropriate, excessive, and misdirected. Children benefit from learning the value of the healthy or appropriate expression of anger, such as healthy assertiveness, as well as the psychological harm from responding consistently to stress in an excessively angry manner such as through temper tantrums. It is important for them to realize that when they do not resolve anger from a particular hurt, they may later harm others without realizing it by misdirecting this resentment toward them. Such anger can damage friendships, interfere with learning, harm family relationships, and limit participation in team sports. In clinical practice, we find that the most common recipients of misdirected anger are younger siblings, peers, mothers, and teachers.

Concepts of displacement and the consequences of displacing anger can be difficult for children to understand and accept so concrete examples need to be used. At times, it can be helpful if parents or a therapist relate stories of misdirected anger from their own youthful experience.

Some therapists believe that they have been successful in treating anger in children and adolescents when their young patients express the anger they had previously denied. Actually, what has been accomplished is only one step toward resolution because, in itself, expression is incapable of freeing children from the burden of resentment that they carry. The experience of anger can lead to a desire for revenge, which does not diminish until the existence of the resentful feelings is uncovered and subsequently resolved. Without this uncovering and resolution, anger can be displaced for many years onto others and erupt decades later in loving relationships. Anger may not be fully resolved until a conscious decision is made to work on forgiving the offender.

FORGIVENESS

Not surprisingly, we need to clarify for children what forgiveness is not. We find that children need to learn the following issues. Specifically, forgiveness is not tolerating and enabling angry, abusive people to express their anger. In addition, children need to learn that forgiving does not mean being a doormat or acting in a weak manner. Forgiveness does not limit healthy assertiveness. It does not mean trusting or reconciling with those who are abusive, insensitive, or show no motivation to change their unacceptable behavior. Finally, forgiveness is not necessarily going to others and informing them that one is forgiving them.

ORIGINS OF ANGER

As already stated, clinicians often discover that the relationship in which children experience the greatest degree of disappointment, and subsequently the greatest degree of anger, is in the parental relationship, especially the one with the father. This is particularly true at the present time when almost 40% of children and teenagers do not have their biological fathers at home. Fortunately, the father involvement in the lives of children is moving in a more positive direction, at least in many middle-class families. Numerous studies have documented difficulties with resentment and aggressive behavior in the children of divorce (Block, Block, & Gjerde, 1988; Guidubaldi, 1988; Hetherington, 1989; Johnston et al., 1989; Wallerstein, 1983, 1985, 1991; Wallerstein & Blakeslee, 1989). Also, Clark et al.'s research (1997) has shown that boys whose fathers have SUD have increased rates of disruptive behavior disorders (CD, ODD, and ADHD) than boys without paternal SUD. One study of parental love deprivation and forgiveness revealed that most respondents implicated the father, not the mother, as being emotionally distant (Al-Mabuk, Enright, & Cardis, 1995).

In our clinical experience, the major cause of anger in the father relationship is the result of growing up with a father who had difficulty in communicating his love and in affirming his children. Misdirected father anger may be a contributing conflict in schools and homes today. Many children who have intense father anger present with CD, ODD, ADHD, and intermittent explosive disorders.

Difficulties in the mother relationship that lead to intense anger can be the result of children not experiencing enough love and praise, feeling controlled or criticized, or being made to feel that one does not measure up to some standard. At times, too, the child may have felt overly responsible for the mother, or may have come to the conclusion that she was overly critical of the father. Also, some children today have mothers who, due to the pressures of high-powered careers, are less available emotionally to them.

Other sources of anger sometimes result from hurts and disappointments from siblings or rejection by peers. Often an older child misdirects anger at a younger sibling that is really meant for a parent or peers. Many children and adolescents crave peer acceptance to develop a positive sense of self and to protect themselves from loneliness. Those children who are rejected regularly in school rarely tell their parents how they are being treated because they are so ashamed or because they believe that their parents cannot protect them. Therefore, parents need to be aware of the various ways in which this conflict can manifest itself. These include isolation, withdrawal, hostile treatment of others, social anxiety, or depression. When these symptoms are present, the parent should ask specifically if this child is being criticized, ridiculed, or bullied by others.

Some children have difficulties with their anger as a result of modeling after a parent who could not control anger. This excessive expression of anger is then passed from one generation to the next. In our experience, this modeling occurs most often with the father. Other practitioners have noted that mothers can tend to be as overly expressive of anger or that they express their anger passively or by being controlling. Parents typically do not know how to handle their anger in a psychologically healthy manner and, subsequently, unhealthy methods for dealing with this emotion, such as expressing anger excessively or misdirecting anger, are manifested by parents.

Many in the mental health field believe that the excessive anger seen in ADHD and other disorders in children is biologically determined (see, e.g., Hechtman, 1991). However, at this time, no specific neurotransmitters have been identified that cause excessive anger. Also, the use of addictive substances can trigger excessive anger as well as personality conflicts, especially narcissism.

We now examine some of the specific childhood and adolescent disorders with a focus on the treatment of the excessive anger in them that can be reduced or resolved through the use of forgiveness. The resolution of this resentment facilitates the healing of these disorders.

ATTENTION DEFICIT HYPERACTIVITY DISORDER

ADHD is the most prevalent psychiatric disorder of children presenting for treatment (Anderson, Williams, McGee, & Silva, 1987; Szatmari, Offord,

& Boyle, 1989). In Wolraich, Hannah, Pinnock, Baumgaertel, and Brown's (1996) study of 8,258 children, there was a predominance of boys ranging from about a ratio of 4:1 for ADHD–hyperactive/impulsive type to 2:1 for ADHD–inattentive types, predominantly inattentive types (Wolraich et al., 1996). The relatively high comorbidity (47–93%) of ADHD with CD and ODD (Biederman et al., 1996; Biederman, Newcorn, & Sprich, 1991; P. Cohen, Velez, Brook, & Smith, 1989; Fergusson, Hoorwood, & Lloyd, 1991; Jensen, Martin, & Cantwell, 1997; Offord, Boyle, & Racine, 1991; Velez, Johnson, & Cohen, 1989) implies the seriousness of anger in this disorder. Children with ADHD have also been shown to exhibit a high degree of comorbidity with depression and anxiety disorders (August, Realmuto, MacDonald, Nugent, & Crosby, 1996; Eiraldi, Power, & Nezu, 1997; Milberger, Biederman, Faraone, Murphy, & Tsuang, 1995).

Barkley (1990) stated that many, if not the majority of, children with ADHD have problems with aggression and emotional control. Also, the importance of identifying and treating the anger in this disorder is supported by studies that reveal that ADHD is associated with a 10-fold increased incidence of antisocial personality (Klein & Mannuzza, 1991; Weiss, Milroy, & Perlman, 1985), a 25-fold excess risk for institutionalization for delinquency (Satterfield, Hoppe, & Schhell, 1982), up to a 5-fold increased risk of drug abuse (Gittelman, Mannuzza, Shenker, & Bonagura, 1985; Klein & Mannuzza, 1991), and up to a 9-fold increased risk of incarceration (Mannuzza, Klein, Konig, & Giampino, 1989). Also, Scahill et al.'s (1999) research on the psychological and clinical correlates of ADHD demonstrated that children with ADHD were more likely to be male, to have mothers with a history of psychiatric treatment, to have fathers with a history of excessive alcohol use, and to live in families with higher levels of family dysfunction than non-ADHD children.

We have found that the therapeutic use of forgiveness is effective in diminishing the excessive anger in ADHD, particularly in the hyperactive and impulsive types. The expression of anger in ADHD children is not limited to the active release of this emotion. Some of the symptoms in the inattentive type of ADHD in some children may be the passive–aggressive expression of anger. These include not listening, failing to follow through with instructions, forgetfulness, or careless mistakes. Some youngsters engage in these behaviors deliberately by not cooperating with teachers or parents as a way to vent anger.

Many children and teenagers with ADHD are not aware of being overly angry or, if they are aware, they are unable to identify the origin of their anger. In the Uncovering Phase of treatment, they begin to identify major disappointments in their lives and the anger associated with the hurts that they experienced. Some decide to learn how to use forgiveness, although others discover benefits gained from holding onto their anger.

Old habits are hard to break, and the development of a new habit of using forgiveness to deal with anger is acquired slowly. Parents play a key role in the Work Phase by reminding their child to consider using forgiveness, as well as the appropriate expression of this emotion, when angry.

Earl, a 7-year-old who was finishing first grade, presented with symptoms of ADHD, hyperactive and impulsive types, and symptoms of ODD. He had almost no ability to control his angry behavior. Both of his parents were adult children of angry alcoholic fathers, and they had been in marital therapy for over a year working on controlling their tempers through the use of forgiveness. The level of excessive anger in the marital relationship had diminished significantly.

Earl was able to recognize that he had been very angry with his parents as a result of their fighting. His parents asked for his forgiveness and promised to try overcoming their bad tempers and curtailing their fighting. Earl nodded in agreement. The therapist responded, "Earl, I would like you to see whether you can tell your parents now that you want to try to forgive them." He proceeded to verbalize his desire to forgive them and then went over to them and gave each a hug.

The therapist next asked his parents to explain to him the causes of their fighting. They told Earl that each of them had brought a great deal of anger into their marriage from their family backgrounds from the paternal grandfather, the maternal grandfather, and the maternal grandmother. Without realizing what they were doing, they related that they had misdirected this anger toward each other. With an attempt at a smile, he said, "I'm glad you told me. At least I'm not the reason you're always mad." At the end of the session Earl was given a note from the therapist that suggested that daily he think "I want to forgive mommy and daddy for all their fights." At the succeeding sessions his ability to use forgiveness to control his anger was reviewed. Although he continued being angry, the episodes were somewhat less frequent and less intense.

Neither Earl, nor his parents were able to identify anyone else in the neighborhood or at school with whom he might be angry. After an initial diminishment in his anger, it erupted again, and he had great difficulty controlling his rageful feelings. Ritalin was then used. Shortly thereafter, another major source of previously denied anger was identified.

His mother visited the afterschool program he attended, and she was extremely upset by the way that the older boys taunted him. Earl was ashamed of this treatment and had never told his parents. After an attempt to remedy the situation failed because those in the afterschool program were unable to control the bullies, Earl's mother removed him from this program, and his explosive anger diminished greatly.

In the Deepening Phase, Earl was pleased that he had learned of a way to control his temper and that he was able to help his younger brother to work at controlling his anger by talking with him about forgiving others.

Nathan, a 13-year-old with a 7-year history of ADHD with inattention, hyperactivity, and impulsivity, had been treated with Ritalin but had a minimal response. In addition to his ADHD, Nathan also had an ODD and was depressed. In the Uncovering Phase of treatment, as his trust grew in the therapist, he admitted to feelings of intense anger for his father Carl because of his habitual absence from the family. His father worked 6 to 7 days a week and rarely came home before 9:00 p.m. Nathan insisted, "Dad doesn't care about us. The only thing he cares about is work." He stated that he felt cheated out of a father relationship and out of a normal family life. He complained to his father, "If the other men in the neighborhood can find time to play with their kids after supper and on weekends, why can't you?" His father had reacted in a defensive manner and attempted to rationalize his behaviors.

Nathan came to realize that he was misdirecting anger with his father at his mother and siblings, and he felt sincerely guilty about this. He hesitated telling his father how angry he was because he did not want to lose what little relationship he had with him. The major reason that Nathan began the Work Phase of forgiveness was guilt about his misdirected anger and about his deep resentment against his father, whom he loved in spite of his weaknesses and absence. Nathan also hoped that if his anger diminished, it might motivate his father to work at changing his behavior.

Nathan was receptive about making the attempt to use forgiveness to diminish his anger. He moved from cognitive forgiveness to truly feeling like forgiving his father when his mother explained to him in family sessions how painful his father's own family life had been. In addition, he realized that his dad had actually modeled after his own father (Nathan's grandfather), who was not an emotionally giving person.

When Nathan would feel unable to continue with the work of forgiveness because of his father's failure to change, he would try to picture a little boy or teenager inside his father who was never happy with family life and was driven to avoid the home. The pain in this wounded little boy motivated Nathan to continue. However, at times, he said, "That was a long time ago, why won't he give us a chance?" At such times he used spiritual forgiveness. His mother encouraged him to try to give his anger to God with his father. Whenever he felt that he could not control his anger, Nathan learned to turn in that direction.

Carl was highly defensive in sessions with Nathan and during individual therapy. He was encouraged to spend more time with Nathan, but an improvement in the father–son relationship occurred only after Carl lost his job and temporarily worked from the home. With the diminishment of his own anger, Nathan was able to use his excellent sense of humor with his dad to help him enjoy his place in the home, and Nathan began to see a slight change in his father.

Nathan's ADHD, ODD, and depressive symptoms diminished in part because of his use of forgiveness to control his angry feelings. He developed far more compassion for his father and overreacted less in the family and in the school.

CONDUCT DISORDER

Children with conduct disorders (CD) manifest the most extreme form of anger in childhood and adolescence. The anger intensifies as the child grows, and under stress it can lead to the development of fantasies and impulses of revenge and antisocial behavior. Two types of CD are distinguished by whether the first symptom appears before or after age 10. Childhood-onset CD is notoriously difficult to treat. The more severe childhood-onset CD is typically marked by more aggressiveness, more severely disturbed peer relations, and a lengthier course than seen with adolescent-onset CD (Lahey et al., 1995). Children who demonstrate this pattern often exhibit antisocial and criminal behaviors through adult life. In many cases adolescent-onset CD is confined to a stage of dalliance with delinquent behavior and remits with continued socialization and maturation (Moffitt, 1993).

Forgiveness can diminish the intense anger in these young people that often develops as a result of fatherlessness, poverty, abuse, association with delinquent peers, divorce (Amato & Keith, 1991; Wallerstein, 1991), and various types of family psychopathology (Frick, 1998; Kazdin, 1995). The parents of children with CD have high rates of psychopathology (Lahey et al., 1988), especially antisocial behavior (Faraone, Biederman, Keenan, & Tsuang, 1991; Frick et al., 1992) but also substance abuse and depression (Frick, 1993). Children with CD are at risk later in their adult lives for difficulties with substance abuse, anxiety, and mood disorders or the development of an antisocial personality.

Because many of these children and teenagers are unable to release their anger with those who have betrayed them, they regularly misdirect their rage and violent impulses against others through aggression, violation of rules, destruction of property, and theft.

The forgiveness process can be lengthy and difficult, and therapists encounter numerous resistances. These include expression of rage as a source of significant pleasure and, in the case of boys, as a sign of male strength. A misguided benefit these children discover in their fury is that rage bonds them to certain hostile peers who would reject them if they gave up their violent impulses.

Some of these children decide to use forgiveness only after they have developed serious problems in their schools or with the law. Others become motivated to change after recognizing that, if they fail to alter their behavior, they will be spending time in prison one day. Finally, some children and adolescents want to break the control of the past by working at forgiving their offenders.

Jorge, age 13, had angry behavior that was extremely disruptive at home and in the classroom. He remembered having a close relationship with his father until his dad abandoned his mother, Jorge, and a younger sibling. At the time, Jorge was 4 years of age, and since then he had no contact with his father. In addition, Jorge had a difficult relationship with his stepfather, who had entered his life when he was 7 years old.

After engaging in hostile behavior at home, in school, and in the community, Jorge was hospitalized after being unable to control his hostile behavior at home, in school, and in the community. In a session with his mother, he was asked to imagine what would happen if his father were present in the room and he expressed his anger with him. Jorge then sprang from his chair like a lion about to attack its victim; grabbed a chair; threw it against a wall while screaming "I hate you. I'd like to kill you"; and ran from the room.

After this session, Jorge admitted that he had harbored strong impulses of revenge against his father from a very young age because of all the hardships his family had endured and because he missed having a father. He viewed his father as a "spoiled brat" and "a creep." With the help of his mother in the sessions, Jorge came to understand that his father had grown up with a highly anxious and self-centered mother who neglected her children and that his father had repeated his mother's narcissistic behavior. Also, he learned from his paternal grandfather that his father had married several times more and was unable to maintain a commitment to anyone.

Jorge made a decision to let go of his impulses for revenge against his father to help himself and to break his father's influence over his emotional life. He knew that unless he could let go of his violent anger against his father, he would misdirect it at others or toward himself. However, in the Work Phase of forgiveness Jorge was not able to use the word *forgive* because he associated it with excusing his father's behaviors. The therapist then suggested that he try to think several times daily that he wanted to let go of his impulses for revenge against him.

After several months of working on his impulses for revenge, Jorge wanted to speak to his father. His paternal grandfather attended several sessions to attempt to help deepen his understanding of Jorge's father and asked his son to call in during a session to help Jorge. After his father agreed to call, the next several sessions focused on preparing Jorge for the possible responses of his father. During one session the therapist role played his father responding to him in a narcissistic manner. Jorge came to understand that his major motivation for speaking with his father was to tell him how much he had hurt him and the entire family. During the first telephone session with his father, Jorge acted like a nervous little boy who wanted to try to bond with his father again. His father seemed genuinely concerned about him and expressed a desire to help him in any way that he could.

In the next telephone session, Jorge's disappointments and anger emerged. He was assertive as he said, "Why did you leave us? It was really hard, and we hardly ever had money for anything, even at Christmas." Jorge surprised himself by his ability to be forceful with his father without losing control of his temper. His father did not apologize or try to explain his behavior. Instead, he acted in a narcissistic manner and related that he would not allow himself to be treated in such a way and that he was going to end the telephone call. Because he had worked to understand his father better, Jorge was not surprised by this reaction.

The exchange with his father was a further motivation for Jorge to let go of his violent impulses toward a man he now viewed as immature. Slowly, his rage diminished, but over the course of several years he had occasional relapses of excessive anger. By the time he finished high school, his violent anger had largely been resolved, and he had accepted the pain of the past. He moved on to military service and to a healthy relationship with a young woman. In the Deepening Phase, he found meaning in his suffering, in part, because he was able to help his girlfriend with her sadness and anger with her insensitive father.

The healing of the violent impulses in youngsters with CD is an arduous, lengthy, but rewarding process for those who are motivated and have at least one involved parent or parent-substitute to support them. It is far more difficult with children and adolescents without a healthy parent or grandparent.

OPPOSITIONAL DEFIANT DISORDER

According to the *DSM–IV*, ODD has been seen as a developmental precursor to CD and is more common in families in which there is serious marital discord (American Psychiatric Association, 1994). However, in one study of ODD associated with ADHD, two subtypes of ODD were identified: one that is prodromal to CD and another that is subsyndromal to CD but not likely to progress into CD in later years (Biederman et al., 1996). When ODD co-occurred with CD in this study, it preceded the onset of CD by several years. Also, higher rates of positive family histories for CD or antisocial personality were found among the children with CD compared with the children with ODD or ADHD.

The excessive anger seen in ODD children is not as severe as that in children with CD in that most of these youngsters with ODD do not yet struggle with violent impulses and fantasies. The psychotherapeutic use of forgiveness can play an important role in decreasing or resolving the hostile feelings, thoughts, and behaviors seen in children with ODD. If the strong anger in children with ODD is treated effectively, our experience indicates it may prevent the later development of CD.

Sean, age 7, became increasingly angry and rebellious with his mother after his father left the family. He regularly lost his temper, refused to listen to his mother, and provoked his sisters. He also became much more defiant and narcissistic and demanded that his mother buy him new toys several times weekly.

In the sessions with his mother and sisters, Sean admitted, "I'm really mad at dad. He doesn't care about us. All he ever did was watch TV anyway." Sean's mother told him that his anger was hurting her and his sisters and that it reminded her of his father's selfish temper tantrums. Sean became tearful and remorseful during the session and stated that he did not want to hurt anyone. He agreed to try to let go of his anger with his father on a daily basis and thus attempt to avoid repeating his dad's self-centered behaviors. This intervention seemed to motivate Sean, and when he slipped back into ODD, his mother would remind him to continue to forgive his father. Over the course of several months, the work of daily thinking that he wanted to understand and try to forgive his father helped Sean gain more control over his angry feelings and behaviors. However, there were times when, after spending a weekend with his selfish father, it would take several days to gain control over his sad and angry feelings.

While using forgiveness therapy in the treatment of the anger in ADHD, CD, and ODD, therapists encounter major obstacles, including the sense of control that their clients' anger gives them over others, modeling after their parents, and a sense of strength and self-esteem derived from the expression of anger. It is not uncommon, either, for the process of forgiveness to be blocked by parents who excuse all angry behaviors in their children with ADHD, claiming that their behavior is solely the result of biological factors over which their children have no control. Such parents may have serious problems with excessive resentment themselves, and therefore they attempt to undermine efforts made to teach their children to be responsible for their anger and to resolve their hostile feelings. Subsequently, therapy often focuses on encouraging parents to identify their own anger and to work on forgiving those who have hurt them. However, the fathers, in particular of those whose children have CD, are often highly resistant to participate in treatment and often have no desire to control their excessive anger. By modeling forgiveness, the majority of parents can bring about a marked improvement in the level of resentment and acting-out behaviors in their children with ADHD, CD, and ODD.

SEPARATION ANXIETY DISORDER

Separation anxiety disorder is common among children and teenagers, who experience excessive anxiety concerning separation from the home or from those to whom these youngsters are attached (DSM–IV, 1994). They often fear going to school and are fearful of being alone without a major attachment figure, particularly the mother. The DSM–IV indicates that these children may show anger or hit someone who is forcing separation. Also, the child's demands to be constantly close to the attached parent can lead to resentment and conflict within the family.

Studies of comorbidity in children with separation anxiety disorder reveal depression in one third and other anxiety disorders in one half of these children (Klein & Last, 1989; Last, Francis, Hersen, Kazdin, & Strauss, 1987). Studies of depressed prepubertal children and adolescents have found concurrent separation anxiety disorder in 30–60% of participants (Biederman et al., 1995; Kovacs, Gatsonis, Paulauskas, & Richards, 1989; Ryan et al., 1987).

Children, in our clinical experience, often develop separation anxiety disorder after some major life stress or traumatic experience, which can include a mother's serious illness, prolonged separation from the mother, excessive fighting between parents, marital separation or divorce, a serious illness in the child, change in school, move to a new neighborhood, or the death of a sibling. Children whose family histories are positive for depression, PD, and alcoholism appear to be at increased risk. Clinically, we find that ridicule and the experience of being a scapegoat by other children may lead to intense fears of betrayal outside the home and separation anxiety. Also, one study found that 83% of mothers of children with separation anxiety disorder had a lifetime diagnosis of anxiety disorder, 53% had a lifetime diagnosis of major depression, and 57% had a current anxiety disorder diagnosis (Last, Hersen, Kazdin, Francis, & Grubb, 1987).

Even though these youngsters are aware of their intense fears of separation from their mothers or fathers, most are unaware of the cause of their fears, and they are not conscious of the anger they have toward those who have hurt or disappointed them. The identification of the origin of their fears and the resolution of the anger associated with traumatic experiences through forgiveness therapy facilitate the treatment of these children's separation anxiety symptoms. Therapists can relate to these youngsters how their fears are tied into anger from various hurts and will diminish if they can learn to resolve their anger.

Marty, age 8, developed separation anxiety symptoms at the beginning of second grade. He had great difficulty leaving his mother and begged her to ride on the school bus with him. When she did not join him, he would fly into a rage and tell her that he would not talk to her when he returned from school. In the evenings, he became increasingly fearful and anxious. The history revealed that there had been no traumatic experiences with his peers that could produce such intense fears, but he had experienced chronic trauma in his home. His parents had been separated for a period of 6 months, and his father had only recently moved back home. For 2 years, Marty had witnessed such intense fighting between his parents that, at times, it subsided only with police intervention.

After several therapy sessions, Marty was able to identify that he was angry with his parents and that he had strong fear of another separation. He asked perceptively, "Don't you love each other anymore?" His parents were no longer fighting, but they had great difficulty trusting each other and, subsequently, they were not particularly affectionate.

In family sessions, Marty's parents apologized to him for their behavior and insisted that they were motivated to improve their marital relationship. They promised, "You don't have to be afraid. We're not going to separate again because we love each other, and we're going to work this out." Although these words comforted Marty, he realistically did not trust them fully.

When the therapist explained to Marty that the resolution of his own anger would help his fears diminish, he decided to work on thinking of forgiving his parents for the hurts of the past. His work on forgiving was aided by the fact that his parents regularly requested forgiveness from him for all of the stress they had caused him.

As Marty worked at forgiving his parents, he became aware that he had much more anger than he realized with each of them. The therapist made the recommendation that he should not feel guilty because the anger was justified, and if he worked regularly at forgiving, he would experience his anger diminishing in time. Over the course of several months, Marty experienced a much greater degree of comfort and sense of safety in going to school and found himself feeling much less angry with his parents.

At the same time, the therapist was seeing Marty's parents and attempting to strengthen the trust in their relationship and work on forgiveness between them. Consequently, the improvement in the marital relationship helped diminish Marty's separation anxiety disorder symptoms in a significant way.

PANIC DISORDER

A high incidence of depression has been reported among children and adolescents with PD (Alessi & Magen, 1988; Alessi, Robbins, & Dilsaver, 1987; Black & Robbins, 1990; Bradley & Hood, 1993). Adolescents with panic attacks have been found to be three times more likely to have expressed suicidal ideation and approximately two times more likely to have made suicide attempts than were adolescents without panic attacks (Pilowsky, Wu, & Anthony, 1999). Also, in a study of PD in children and adolescents, there was a high level of comorbidity with disruptive disorders (Biederman, Faraone, Marrs, & Moore, 1997). Specifically, 58% of the children and 71% of the adolescents met the criteria for ODD and 25% of the children and 29% of the adolescents met the criteria for CD. In our clinical work, children and adolescents with panic attacks have significant anger associated with various types of traumatic life experiences.

Alexis was 11 years old when she developed several severe panic attacks over a weekend. She awakened during the night with a rapid heart beat and feared that she might die. She was so agitated and frightened that her parents took her to an emergency room on two consecutive nights. Her medical evaluation indicated that there was no physical basis for her symptoms.

Alexis was the oldest of three children, her parents had a good relationship, and she enjoyed good friendships at school. Immediately after the panic attacks, however, she developed symptoms of separation anxiety disorder, and for the first time she began sleeping in her parents' bedroom. Also, during the day she clung to her mother and did not want her to leave her.

After several sessions, the major stress identified was the daily exposure in her school to an antagonistic teacher. Slowly she began to explain, "She's so mean. I don't want to go to school. She hasn't picked on me yet, but she probably will soon." After an explanation of the value of resolving her anger, she agreed to work on thinking that she wanted to forgive her teacher. Next, Alexis's mother helped her try to understand her teacher by telling Alexis that she knew that her teacher lived alone and her bad temper might be the result of loneliness. As a further step, her parents tried to protect her by going to the school and filing a complaint against the teacher. Although the school reassured the parents that they would monitor this teacher, Alexis's fears were so strong that she needed to remain at home for several months before she was able to return to school.

Alexis was given a written cognitive forgiveness exercise in which she was asked to try to understand her teacher and to make a decision to forgive her. Her mother worked with her regularly on these assignments. These exercises initially provided some relief, but later even stronger anger emerged with her teacher for the hurts of the past. For a period of time, it became difficult for Alexis to forgive the teacher at all. When Alexis learned that her teacher may have had a depressive illness, she was able to feel some compassion, and she returned to the work of forgiveness. Slowly, her panic symptoms decreased as well as the resentment she felt toward the teacher.

OBSESSIVE–COMPULSIVE DISORDERS

Symptoms of OCD in children and adolescents respond to both psychotherapy (American Academy of Child and Adolescent Psychiatry, 1998; March & Leonard, 1996; March & Mulle, 1998) and medication (March et al., 1998; March, Leonard, & Swedo, 1995). In a study of adolescents with OCD, there was a high comorbidity with disruptive disorders and tic, mood, and anxiety disorders (D. Geller, Biederman, Griffin, Jones, & Lefkowitz, 1996). The most frequently reported obsessions were those of violent or catastrophic events, often involving a loved one (60%). In this study, 53% of the participants had at least one disruptive disorder, 43% had ODD, 73% had major depression, and 33% had ADHD. Also, when present, the disruptive behavior disorders developed years before the onset of OCD. This study of excessive disruptive disorders in adolescents with OCD was consistent with another report of a 32% overlap between OCD and ADHD in a sample of juveniles (D. Geller, Biederman, Reed, Spencer, & Wilens, 1995). Geller et al. (1996) suggested that other studies of pediatric OCD comorbidity may not have reported higher comorbidity with disruptive behavior disorders and ADHD because of the use of numerous exclusionary criteria.

Most children and adolescents with OCD initially do not identify excessive anger as a serious difficulty in their lives. However, significant anger is regularly uncovered in them with parents, peers, or siblings. Obsessive–compulsive symptoms are often a defense against strong feelings of anger that the child is unable to face as a result of fear. Forgiveness helps resolve the anger and associated aggressive obsessions in these youngsters and thereby assists in their recovery from OCD.

Van, a 7-year-old first grader, developed a severe germ phobia and extremely compulsive behaviors. After going to the bathroom, he would regularly spend 20–30 minutes cleaning himself. At school he would not open or close any doors without first covering his hand with his sweater to protect himself from germs. He limited his play with his friends because of his fear of being contaminated by germs. His compulsive behaviors increased and required larger amounts of time. The only anger Van manifested was when his parents tried to shorten the time he spent in compulsive behaviors.

Initially, Van had no awareness of any difficulties that preceded the development of his symptoms. However, when his parents were seen alone, they related numerous stresses in their relationship. His mother had been sick over the previous year with severe chronic fatigue and numerous vague health problems that resulted in prolonged bed rest. She had had a stressful relationship with her own father as a child and had difficulty in trusting her husband. Also, even though Van's parents rarely quarreled, there was little affection in the marital relationship. Although each was dissatisfied with the marriage, they were not considering separation or divorce; neither were they working to improve their marital relationship.

Van denied having any fear that his parents might separate or divorce, although he had been informed by them that there was considerable stress in the marriage. He, in fact, called their relationship "good." When asked about his mother, who had been in bed for almost a year, he insisted, "I'm not worried about her. She'll be fine." His parents and the therapist suggested to Van that he might have developed a fear of something bad happening to him as a result of his mother's illness and of the stress in his parents' marriage. His parents told Van that he had the right to be angry and that they thought he did have some anger toward them. The therapist explained that his fears might have been too frightening to face, so instead of addressing them, Van acquired the fear that he might contract a serious illness from germs.

Van's parents made a commitment to work toward a resolution of their difficulties so that their relationship would improve. The therapist then told Van that he thought that he had also denied angry feelings toward his parents and validated those feelings as being normal. Then he was asked to think daily that he wanted to forgive his parents. Van reluctantly agreed to think of forgiving his parents for those times when they were not kind or loving to one another even though he was not consciously aware of being angry with them. After several months of therapy Van was able to admit having angry feelings toward his parents. Also, Van was encouraged to trust that his parents' marriage would become a happier one. Work on forgiveness and trust over a period of 6 months, in addition to participation in marital therapy by the parents, resulted in a significant improvement of Van's obsessive–compulsive symptoms.

ADJUSTMENT DISORDER WITH ANXIETY DUE TO BULLYING

Several studies cite that 21% of children in middle school (Boulton & Underwood, 1992) and 22% in elementary school (Austin & Joseph, 1996) report that they have been bullied. Children who are bullied by their peers often develop a number of psychological difficulties, including social isolation and loneliness (Boulton & Underwood, 1992), psychosomatic symptoms and hyperactivity (Kumpulainen et al., 1998), anxiety, social phobia (Gilmartin, 1987), depression and suicidal ideation (Rigby & Slee, 1999), fear of going to school, and low self-esteem. Also, their peers regularly side with the bullies against them, do not support them, and even develop strong anger toward them (Rigby & Slee, 1991). As a result of harsh treatment by their peers, these children and teenagers develop regularly intense anger and even violent impulses for revenge against their tormentors. These impulses can become obsessive even though usually they are not acted on. In some, this anger is misdirected into the home toward younger siblings or even parents. Embarrassment concerning the abusive treatment usually keeps the child from relating the feelings of anxiety to their parents, so there may be confusion on the part of the parents as to what is taking place.

Miguel, age 12, told his parents whenever other children made him a scapegoat at school or at sports. Although he was the smartest student in his class and a good athlete, he became increasingly anxious and angry as a result of the constant ridicule by peers. The apparent reason for the abuse was his protruding front teeth. They called him "Bucky the Beaver" at every opportunity. To his credit, even when he was outnumbered, Miguel was emotionally strong and had no difficulty responding in an assertive way to his tormentors. However, he developed symptoms of anxiety as a result of peer ridicule.

The anger with his peers regularly spilled over into his relationships with others in the family. Miguel knew that he was misdirecting anger and was motivated to try to resolve his resentment with his peers. He was asked daily to try to view his peers as being jealous of his intelligence and athletic abilities and then to think of forgiving them. He was helped in this process with his father's encouragement. Miguel's dad told his son that he had been subjected to similar treatment as a boy. Miguel actually came to feel compassion for his peers and viewed them as being weak boys who could not face him individually but needed to hide in a group.

Our clinical experience from treating bully victims for over two decades is that bullying has increased significantly in the schools and communities. Teachers, regardless of length of service, report not being confident in their ability to deal with bullying, and 87% want more training (Boulton, 1997). New programs need to be developed to protect children in schools, to help victims learn how to resolve their strong anger with impulses for revenge, to encourage peers to understand bullies and to support victims, and to provide treatment protocols for the hostility in bullies.

STEPCHILDREN

Conflicts with excessive anger in children from divorced families has been reported in many studies (Wallerstein, 1991). Some stepchildren harbor serious resentment toward their birth parents that is often hard to control. They may deny the anger, but it emerges in times of stress. Stepparents can also have difficulty with their anger as a result of a number of factors, including residual resentment from their previous marriage.

Rachel, age 35 and married, had, in addition to her own two children, two stepchildren in her home. The stepchildren had been deeply hurt by their alcoholic mother and her abusive boyfriend before they had come to live with their father. The children's anger that was meant for the adults with whom they had formerly lived was frequently misdirected toward Rachel and the other children. Their angry behaviors created enormous tension in the home. Rachel became so exhausted and overwhelmed that she even considered separating from her husband Aaron. She began therapy and, after the first session, took steps to become assertive with her stepchildren. She identified the origin of their anger and encouraged them to try to let go of their resentment by forgiving their mother and her boyfriend rather than by misdirecting their feelings.

It was particularly difficult for Rachel's stepson Brad to let go of his anger with his mother's physically abusive boyfriend. Brad viewed this man as being emotionally sick, and his opinion was validated by the therapist. The treatment of his anger was facilitated by punching a pillow and then by thinking that he wanted to let go of his impulses to strike back.

This work of forgiveness was a lengthy and difficult process for the children and, at times, they continued to overreact in anger toward Rachel. When that would happen, Rachel would remind them that she did not deserve their anger and would encourage them to try to let go of their resentment with their mother by forgiving her. They were helped in the process by trying to recall that much of their mother's behavior was the result of her illness of alcoholism. Finally, Rachel modeled forgiveness in the home by asking for forgiveness for any ways in which she may have disappointed the children and by granting it to others who hurt her, including their father.

Some children from divorced families harbor rage and some have violent impulses against a parent. Often these young people are unable to use the word *forgiveness* because they sincerely believe that the parent, stepparent, or parents' partner should not be forgiven. In lieu of using the word *forgiveness*, when these children choose the spiritual form of forgiveness, they are asked to think that they are powerless over their anger and want to turn it over to God. It is important for such strong anger to be addressed, because the failure to do so can result in hostile impulses becoming misdirected internally or outwardly toward the family, school, or community. Also, the failure to face and resolve the anger predisposes these children to depressive episodes and difficulties in trusting.

ADOPTED CHILDREN

Adopted children and adolescents can have difficulty with excessive anger. In our experience, this anger originates from a number of sources, including traumatic memories with their birth parents or other caregivers, shame, a profound difficulty in trusting, or other experiences of rejection.

These youngsters can exhibit angry behavior and usually lack an understanding of the origin of their resentment. Their anger can diminish by discussing the early-life, unconscious betrayal anger that may have developed after separation from a birth parent. The youngster should be encouraged to consider making a decision to work at forgiveness rather than venting anger in an excessive manner. In some cases, forgiveness exercises are given to them in which the young people are asked to think of forgiving one or both birth parents for abandoning them.

The hostile feelings in such children are often a defense against their feelings of vulnerability and fear of further betrayal. These youngsters often will only work at changing hostile behavior after their trust in the adopted parents has grown significantly.

Amber, an intelligent 9 year old, was adopted from Russia at the age of 5 with her 2-year-old brother. After being taken away from her drug-addicted mother who was a prostitute, Amber was placed in a strict Russian orphanage and later related being treated in a harsh manner there. Her adjustment to her adoptive family and community in the United States was difficult. She distanced her adoptive parents, children in the neighborhood, and anyone who tried to befriend her. She became increasingly angry and later engaged in violent behavior toward her adoptive mother.

The therapist told Amber, "You have every reason to feel very angry about what happened to you in Russia with your mother and in the orphanage. However, that anger has never left you and now you are misdirecting it at your mother and others. Why not try to think that you want to forgive your birth mother rather than take that resentment out on your mother? I have seen forgiveness diminish the anger in other adopted children." Amber denied this anger for months. At home her mother was told to tell her that she did not deserve her hostile aggressive treatment and that if she could forgive her birth mother her anger would diminish and they might have a good relationship.

Amber slowly acknowledged that she had felt a great deal of resentment toward her birth mother for her addictive behavior and for failing to protect both her and her brother. She also expressed anger toward the caretakers of the orphanage in Russia. Painful memories emerged in which she recalled hitting her birth mother in Russia when her mother was drunk. It was suggested to Amber that at the present time she was misdirecting intense hostile feelings that she had for her birth mother toward her adoptive mother and was using her anger as a defense to keep everyone at a distance.

Amber was given handwritten forgiveness notes to take home and work on between sessions which her mother reviewed with her. These notes stated (a) "I want to stop misdirecting my anger at those who don't deserve it," (b) "I want to try to understand that my birth mother was sick with a drug addiction, and I want to try to forgive her," (c) "I want to let go of the anger from Russia so that I can be free and not controlled by the past." She was challenged to trust people more than her mother had ever been able to trust. It was stated that unless Amber took these steps, she might be as lonely, unhappy, and fearful as her birth mother.

As she worked on trust and forgiveness of past hurts, Amber became aware that some good could come from her pain. She expressed the desire to become a health professional and someday go back to Russia to help children who had suffered in the same manner as she. As her resentment diminished and her trust grew, she became much less defensive and hostile toward her adoptive mother and toward her peers.

TOWARD THE FUTURE

The study of anger and forgiveness in children is in its infancy, and there is a clinical indication to proceed with it given the amount of excessive anger seen in child and adolescent disorders and in youngsters in society today. Because the great majority of mental health professionals have not received specialized training in the nature and treatment of excessive anger in children (Fitzgibbons, 1998), there is a compelling need for training. This requires the development of clinically applicable subjective and objective measures of active and passive–aggressive anger in children.

Future research should attempt to measure the degree of anger in children with each disorder and in their parents. Different psychotherapeutic and pharmacological approaches used in the treatment of this anger could be evaluated. Then, empirically based treatment protocols could be developed and assessed both for the child and for the parent, when indicated. Finally, a major challenge in the years ahead will be the development of evaluation and treatment protocols for dealing with bullies in schools and their victims, which will include the involvement of parents, teachers, and school administrators.

Thus far, there have been no scientific studies of forgiveness in the treatment of childhood and adolescent disorders. However, based on the clinical evidence of the ability of forgiveness to decrease excessive anger in extensive clinical cases, there is reason to believe that its effectiveness with children and adolescents will be shown as clearly and convincingly as it has with adults. Its regular use in the treatment of excessive anger in childhood and adolescent disorders perhaps may help prevent the later development of mood and anxiety disorders, personality disorders, and substance abuse disorders in adult life.

APPENDIX 10A
Active Anger in Children Checklist

Mild

☐ Is irritable
☐ Often loses temper
☐ Is impatient
☐ Is regularly annoyed
☐ Blurts out answers before questions have been asked
☐ Is impertinent; talks back
☐ Is verbally aggressive
☐ Pouts and sulks
☐ Is uncooperative with teacher

☐ Constantly teases
☐ Has difficulty waiting one's turn
☐ Is frequently frustrated
☐ Intrudes on others
☐ Is defiant
☐ Argues, quarrels
☐ Acts "smart"
☐ Is negative
☐ Is disobedient

Moderate

☐ Lies
☐ Is a chronic violator of rules at home or school
☐ Is overly aggressive
☐ Initiates fights
☐ Cheats
☐ Stays out at night
☐ Shows excessive recklessness
☐ Tries to dominate others

☐ Is hostile
☐ Excessively swears
☐ Hits others
☐ Is rude
☐ Is the class clown, disruptive at school
☐ Makes violent threats
☐ Is spiteful, vindictive
☐ Has "bad" companions

Severe

☐ Was suspended from school
☐ Steals
☐ Perpetrates violent acts against people, animals, or property
☐ Runs away from home
☐ Perpetrates violent acts against oneself

☐ Is constantly truant
☐ Was expelled from school
☐ Abuses substances
☐ Sets fires
☐ Forces sexual activity
☐ Carries a weapon

Appendix 10B
Oppositional Defiant Disorder Checklist

☐ (1) Often loses temper
☐ (2) Often argues with adults
☐ (3) Often actively defies or refuses to comply with adults' requests or rules
☐ (4) Often deliberately annoys people
☐ (5) Often blames others for his or her mistakes or behavior
☐ (6) Is often touchy or easily annoyed by others
☐ (7) Is often angry and resentful
☐ (8) Is often spiteful or vindictive

Appendix 10C
Conduct Disorder Checklist

Aggression to people and animals

- ☐ (1) Often bullies, threatens, or intimidates others
- ☐ (2) Often initiates physical fights
- ☐ (3) Has used a weapon that can cause serious physical harm to others (e.g., a bat, brick, broken bottle, knife, gun)
- ☐ (4) Has been physically cruel to people
- ☐ (5) Has been physically cruel to animals
- ☐ (6) Has stolen while confronting a victim (e.g., mugging, purse snatching, extortion, armed robbery)
- ☐ (7) Has forced someone into sexual activity

Destruction of property

- ☐ (8) Has deliberately engaged in fire setting with the intention of causing serious damage
- ☐ (9) Has deliberately destroyed others' property (other than by fire setting)

Deceitfulness or theft

- ☐ (10) Has broken into someone else's house, building or car
- ☐ (11) Often lies to obtain goods or favors or to avoid obligations (i.e., "cons" others)
- ☐ (12) Has stolen items of nontrivial value without confronting a victim (e.g., shoplifting but without breaking and entering; forgery)

Serious violations of rules

- ☐ (13) Often stays out at night despite parental prohibitions, beginning before age 13 years
- ☐ (14) Has run away from home overnight at least twice while living in parental or parental surrogate home (or once without returning for a lengthy period)
- ☐ (15) Is often truant from school, beginning before age 13 years

Appendix 10D
Attention Deficit Disorder/Attention Deficit Hyperactivity Disorder Checklist

1. Inattention

- ☐ Often fails to give close attention to details or makes careless mistakes in school work, work, or other activities
- ☐ Often has difficulties sustaining attention in tasks or play activities
- ☐ Often does not seem to listen when spoken to directly
- ☐ Often does not follow through on instructions and fails to finish school work, chores, or duties in the workplace
- ☐ Often has difficulty organizing tasks and activities
- ☐ Often avoids dislikes or is reluctant to engage in tasks that require sustained mental effort
- ☐ Often loses things necessary for tasks or activities
- ☐ Is often easily distracted by extraneous stimuli
- ☐ Is often forgetful of daily activities

Continued

2. Hyperactivity

☐ Often fidgets with hands or feet or squirms in seat
☐ Often leaves in classroom or in other situations at which remaining seated is expected
☐ Often runs about or climbs excessively in situations in which is inappropriate
☐ Often has difficulty playing or engaging in leisure activities quietly
☐ Is often "on the go" or often acts as if "driven by a motor"
☐ Often talks excessively

3. Impulsivity

☐ Often blurts out answers before questions have been completed
☐ Often has difficulty waiting turn
☐ Often interrupts or intrudes on others

11

FORGIVENESS IN MARITAL AND FAMILY RELATIONSHIPS

Helen, age 36, and Mike, age 38, sought counseling for assistance in dealing with their marital conflicts. Helen complained that Mike was emotionally distant and that he had difficulty showing affection and offering praise. He, in turn, criticized Helen's lack of care for their children and their home. In the uncovering phase of treatment, Helen identified anger not only toward Mike, but also toward her father, who had always been emotionally distant, and she wanted to begin the process of forgiveness. Mike, on the other hand, was slower coming to an awareness of the depth of his anger. As with many husbands, his denial of modeling after a distant father and of being angry with him was intense.

As Helen and Mike worked at trying to understand their parents and each other, their substantial marital anger began to diminish through using forgiveness daily for the anger from family of origin and from marital hurts. Their marital healing is discussed later in this chapter.

We also discuss major sources of marital anger, the danger of the excessive expression of anger, and the uses of the four phases of forgiveness, within the context of clinical cases with spouses who are emotionally distant, controlling, angry, passive–aggressive, physically abusive, narcissistic, and unfaithful, as well as in separation and divorce and in other family relationships.

The psychotherapeutic use of forgiveness can play an effective role in marital and family therapy. In our clinical work, forgiveness is recommended throughout the course of marital therapy to assist in the resolution of anger from past and present hurts that divide couples. When forgiveness is used, it diminishes the excessive anger that regularly creates serious difficulties between spouses. Only in recent years has the process been described in marital and family therapy (Ashleman, 1996; Coleman, 1989, 1998; DiBlasio, 1998; Fitzgibbons, 1986; Hargrave, 1994; Reed, 1998; Walrond-Skinner, 1998; Worthington, 1998; Worthington & DiBlasio, 1990). Other methods of treating marital anger have been advocated (Christensen & Jacobson, 1999; Ellis, 1976; Mace, 1976; Margolin, 1979). In this chapter, we discuss the role of forgiveness in assisting in the resolution of marital anger and conflicts.

UNDERSTANDING ANGER IN MARRIAGES

The complex and powerful emotion of anger is one of the major reasons why couples seek counseling. Because spouses are often unable to understand and resolve their excessive anger, love and trust begin to deteriorate in the relationship, and varying degrees of sadness, anxiety, and insecurity develop.

Nature of Anger

To prevent serious conflicts in marital relationships, the therapist and couple must determine whether existing anger is appropriate, excessive, or misdirected. To make this distinction, the partners must understand the nature of anger and develop the ability to express anger toward a spouse in a healthy manner. Assertiveness protects one from being treated in an insensitive way and in addition helps the other person face his or her own conflicts and become motivated to change. Healthy feelings of anger can energize couples to work harder to correct difficulties in a marital and family relationship. People who are appropriately assertive actually lead healthier lives than those who are unable to express their anger. Self-help books on assertiveness that clients might read are Lloyd (1995) and McFarland (1992).

Unfortunately, some spouses have the mistaken idea that expressions of anger are always healthy for the relationship. They must be cautioned that this powerful emotion can quickly get out of control. Actually, many spouses overreact in anger because of the failure to resolve resentment from past hurts with the partner, from their family of origin, or from other relationships. Such resentment is regularly released under certain types of stress and pressures.

Common origins of this unconscious anger are from hurts with parents, significant others from the past, or difficulties with peers in the workplace. Clinical experience indicates that in a marriage each partner has some degree of buried anger that they bring to the relationship and there is more resistance in the Uncovering Phase of the treatment of marital conflicts than in the treatment of any individual disorder. The resolution of anger from different stages of life is essential and can be accomplished through the use of forgiveness. Often, it is helpful to ask each partner to resolve anger with a parent who had disappointed or hurt them.

Just as there are two types of lipoproteins in the body, one of which is healthy (high density) and one which is damaging (low density), so there are two basic types of anger in marital relationships, one healthy (appropriate anger) and one damaging (excessive or misdirected anger). For the health of the marriage, it is essential that the destructive anger be eliminated.

Certain instructions within therapy can assist the spouses when conflicts arise. After experiencing anger, the spouse who expressed anger or the recipient of the anger is asked to think about whether the emotion is deserved and appropriate or whether it might be excessive and misdirected. Distinguishing between these two different and yet similar types of anger is crucial because each calls for an entirely different response. The response to appropriate anger may be an apology or the effort to be more sensitive to the partner in the future.

The process of distinguishing appropriate and misdirected anger takes a deep understanding of one's spouse as well as patience and wisdom and may entail help from close friends. It is important to look for the truth in what a partner is saying. Spouses, who regularly overreact or misdirect their anger, tend to blame their partner for the painful feelings that they experience. Overreacting spouses usually are unwilling to examine how they themselves contribute to the relational difficulties. Some seem to take a certain pleasure in criticizing their spouses and have difficulty making an apology. They do not admit that they overreact, and there can be a stubborn refusal to consider that they, too, may have unresolved family-of-origin or other conflicts.

Major Sources of Marital Conflict

In attempting to determine whether one is dealing with appropriate or excessive anger, one must understand the principle sources of marital anger. Gottman and Levenson's (1992) research with couples has identified a number of sources of marital conflict including lack of satisfaction, stubbornness and withdrawal from interaction, defensiveness, and negative emotional expression. Many factors to be considered are disappointments in the marital relationship, hurts from the family of origin or conflicts regarding trust, and the lack of communication of love and praise. Feelings of inadequacy and narcissism can also play a role in such displays of anger. Depression can also contribute to marital anger. A study by Pan, Neidig, and O'Leary (1994) showed that, for every 20% increase in depressive symptoms, the odds of being severely aggressive toward the spouse increased by 74%.

Other common sources of anger are the inability to cope with difficult children or in-laws, work stress, or an excessive sense of responsibility. Frequently, it can be determined that anger originates from unreasonable expectations placed on one's spouse, a lack of emotional support, or a lack of balance in one's life. As shown in chapter 8, a frequent manifestation of the imbalance in one's life is the result of excessive time spent by some spouses on children's sporting activities to the neglect of the other spouse.

Finally, in trying to understand marital anger, the therapist can review the defensive functions of anger as a shield against profound mistrust in relationships, feelings of insecurity, feelings of sadness and loneliness, chronic disappointment, and feelings of hopelessness.

The Danger of Excessive Expression of Anger

The excessive expression of anger can separate spouses by making them even more angry and aggressive toward one another (Straus, 1974). It can adversely affect children (Gardner, 1971), reinforce inappropriate ways of relating (Tavris, 1984), aggravate psychosomatic illness, and increase guilt and shame (Horowitz, 1981). When attempting to reconcile a marital relationship, if the other spouse has difficulty in trusting, the partner has to be cautious about the expression of anger because it can interfere with the partner's willingness to be vulnerable and seek reconciliation. In such situations, it can be in one's best interest to process the anger inwardly, through understanding and forgiveness, rather than by expressing it. Coping with anger in this manner does not result in any damage to the individual, contrary to the popular belief that the failure to express anger causes harm.

The four phases of forgiveness therapy are presented next within the context of the following clinical cases of spouses who are emotionally distant, controlling, angry, passive–aggressive, abusive, unfaithful, and narcissistic, as well as in cases of separation and divorce and other family conflicts.

THE EMOTIONALLY DISTANT SPOUSE

Numerous life difficulties can limit the ability of some spouses to become emotionally close, self-giving, and supportive. When one has unknowingly modeled after a parent who has the same conflict, the spouse can benefit from working at forgiving that parent. This is particularly the case with men who model distant fathers and, subsequently, have difficulty with self-giving.

After overcoming significant resistance to uncovering the anger present in themselves, these individuals eventually use forgiveness daily to resolve the betrayal anger from the life stage or stages at which the hurts occurred. Thus, they may spend time each day using both understanding and forgiving for the healing of the marriage. The resolution of anger combined with cognitive–behavioral therapy usually results in an improved ability to be emotionally giving and loving.

The Distant Husband

Helen came into treatment for depression which she believed was the result of severe marital loneliness. Her husband Mike loved her but was not physically affectionate and rarely told her that he cared for her. Also, she grew up in a home in which she felt little affection from either parent. Her depression resulted in chronic fatigue, and she began to neglect her children and home. To escape from her loneliness, she met a man and had an affair with him. As a result, Helen felt guilty and became even more motivated in her attempts to improve her marriage.

In the marital sessions, Mike stated that he had justifiable anger with his wife for acting in an irresponsible manner regarding the care of the home and children. Her behavior was interpreted by the therapist, in part, as a manifestation of depression and of passive–aggressive anger toward him.

Initially Mike was resistant in examining his own weaknesses from his family of origin. He was loyal to his father, whom he viewed as an excellent role model in most ways. It took several months before he could admit that when he was young, he wished often that his father had been more affectionate and affirming. Slowly, Mike came to understand Helen's needs and the fact that he had difficulty in being sensitive to her as a result of modeling after a father who was markedly limited in his ability to communicate love and praise. The uncovering of Mike's childhood and adolescent anger with his father was a lengthy process.

When he understood that his unconscious anger with his father was an important factor that interfered with his ability to love his wife, Mike tried to understand and forgive his father to improve their marriage. He was given a written cognitive forgiveness exercise in which he was asked to picture himself as a child and as a teenager and think, "Dad, I want to try to understand you and to forgive you for not giving more affection, praise, and warmth to mom and me." Then he was asked to imagine communicating to his father, "I want to model after your good qualities, but not your weaknesses. I don't want to be emotionally distant like you." Mike came to realize that his father's style of relating was the result of modeling after Mike's grandfather and that he had not meant to hurt his family.

As Mike worked at forgiving his father and committing himself to act differently, he began to feel freer from the weakness that he had acquired from his father. Slowly, he grew in his ability to communicate more with Helen and, during this process, he was able to apologize to her and express remorse for the ways in which he had hurt her by his aloofness.

At the same time, Helen was struggling with her anger and tried daily to understand and to forgive Mike for being distant. She did not want to continue to vent anger at him in passive–aggressive ways. After forgiveness was explained as a method for letting go of her anger, which would help in the healing of her marriage, she agreed to try it. Initially, she did not truly feel like forgiving Mike because she was so angry, but she made the cognitive decision to do so after the benefits of forgiving were repeatedly conveyed. As her understanding of Mike's family conflicts grew and as she saw him work to change his behavior, she felt much more compassion and was able to genuinely want to forgive.

Helen also came to recognize that she had been overreacting in anger at Mike as a result of her failure to resolve her childhood and adolescent anger with her emotionally distant father. Helen's father had lost his own father (Helen's grandfather) when she was young and had grown up with unaffectionate relatives. Helen was asked to try to understand and to forgive her father. In the process of using past forgiveness exercises, Helen imagined herself as a child and teenager thinking, "Dad, I want to try to understand and to forgive you for being so emotionally distant." The resolution of Helen's anger with her father and with Mike for past hurts diminished her resentment, and as her anger decreased, her husband then felt emotionally safer with her.

The resolution of the anger associated with the conflicts in Mike and Helen's relationship took several years of treatment. The psychotherapeutic use of forgiveness was used successfully with each partner and led to a marked improvement in their marital relationship.

In the Deepening Phase, each came to a greater understanding of the partner, and their trust in each other grew. Each realized that the spouse did not deliberately want to inflict hurt but had acted out of unresolved emotional conflicts from the family of origin. They also grew in a greater sensitivity to their own weaknesses that had created tensions earlier in their married life. They were more hopeful as a result of a greater confidence in their ability to resolve marital conflicts in a more peaceful and positive manner. Finally, forgiveness became an important tool in protecting their communication and their marital love.

In our clinical experience, the resistance in many married men in facing their issues with their fathers can be formidable. Unlike Mike, a number of men steadfastly refuse to examine the influence of their own father's relationship on them and their marriages. Uncovering father anger in these men can be facilitated if the therapist shares how he or she worked to break through denial to understand and forgive a parent or significant other. For example, the therapist may relate briefly the process of uncovering and deciding to forgive a parent who had difficulty in communicating love or praise.

The Distant Wife

Walter, age 35, entered therapy for the treatment of severe depression, and it required the use of several antidepressants to restore his sleep and cognitive abilities. The history disclosed that he had been extremely lonely in his marriage. Walter complained that his wife Susan was acting more and more like her unaffectionate mother. He was conflicted because he still loved his wife and feared that a divorce would severely harm their two young children.

Susan, age 35, thought the marriage had deteriorated after the birth of their oldest child 9 years earlier. She believed that she had developed a postpartum depression at that time, but it had gone untreated. Susan, too, was upset about the emotional distance in their marriage. She admitted that she had great difficulty in feeling good about herself and in offering emotional support to Walter. However, she also believed that his anger kept her at a distance.

Susan had a good deal of insight and was aware that she had unresolved conflicts with her critical and cold mother and was highly motivated to resolve them. She believed that her mother had never been emotionally supportive of her and never would be. When asked what she had done with her anger with her mother, she related, "I tried to bury it as deeply as possible within." However, she intuitively knew that this denial did not free her from the anger or the sadness associated with it.

Each spouse recognized inner excessive anger and was motivated to overcome it. After forgiveness was explained to them, they demonstrated no resistance in making a decision to use it in their marriage. Then a forgiveness assignment was given to each of them. Walter was asked to try to think of being patient with his wife and of forgiving her for the weaknesses that she had acquired from her mother. Susan was requested to use past forgiveness exercises for her anger with her mother in which she would reflect daily that she wanted to both understand and forgive her mother for childhood, adolescent, and adult disappointments.

Because her mother was such a controlling and difficult woman, Susan did not want to involve her in the Work Phase of the forgiveness process. Instead, psychodrama techniques were used in which Susan would visualize her mother seated in a chair and relate to her, "Mom, I've hated your insensitive and controlling manner of treating me from the time I was a little girl. I can't express fully how much you have disappointed me as a mother. I don't want to act like you. I want to let go of my anger with you." Then, even though she did not feel like doing so, she would try to think that she wanted to forgive her. This phase of forgiveness was difficult for Susan: "This is the most difficult thing I've had to do in my life, but I know I have to let go of my anger with her if I want a good marriage." She was able to move ahead in the work of forgiveness, in part, because she came to view her mother as an emotionally sick woman.

In Walter's Work Phase of the forgiveness process, anger emerged with his father who kept everyone at arm's length. Walter came to realize that at times he may have overreacted to his wife's distancing because of similar pain he had felt as a boy and as a teenager with his own father. Then, Walter asked, "Please forgive me for being short tempered and for misdirecting anger at you that was meant for my father." After granting forgiveness, Susan responded, "Walt, please forgive me for acting like my mother and for overreacting in anger also."

Slowly the anger diminished in this marriage. However, Walter told Susan, "I'm afraid of trusting again because I'm afraid you're going to pull away again and put up walls." It took many months before he felt comfortable being vulnerable to her. However, as he saw her becoming warmer and more giving, Walter felt more comfortable in being vulnerable. Susan grew in her ability to communicate love and affection as she resolved her anger with her mother and as she committed herself to act in a different manner than had her mother. Fortunately, she was able to identify a loving aunt as a healthy role model for emotional giving and tried each day to model after her. Susan had great difficulty in absorbing the years of pain with her mother, but the rediscovered relationship with her aunt was very comforting.

THE CONTROLLING SPOUSE

In our clinical experience, forgiving the distant or unaffectionate spouse is an easier task than forgiving the controlling spouse because the latter one is usually more rigid and arrogant. The domineering spouse is much more resistant to therapy because often he or she is defending the self against serious unconscious emotional conflicts. Also, when this person enters therapy, initially there is an attempt to control the therapist. It is not unusual during treatment of such cases that therapists experience anger toward a controlling client. The therapist may benefit by forgiving such clients during or after the sessions and by being direct and clear with them.

The most common causes of controlling behavior in a spouse are the result of modeling after a controlling parent or a narcissistic personality. Another reason is a stressful and traumatic childhood and adolescence as a result of having a distant, addicted, neglectful, extremely angry, or narcissistic parent. Also, many of those abandoned in childhood will be highly controlling in their adult lives as a compensation for the lack of security that they experienced. Finally, some spouses are extremely controlling because of their narcissistic personalities, which result in their insistence on always having their own way.

It is challenging and difficult to resolve the emotional conflicts of controlling spouses and help those individuals let go of their excessive anger. One reason for this is that most of these individuals have a weak foundation in trusting others as a result of their childhood and adolescent traumas with neglectful or hostile parents.

Once the client is aware of the origin of the spouse's need to control, it is possible to become more confident and assertive and point out the weakness of the controlling partner. In the Work Phase, the offended partner needs a great deal of patience because a significant change in this type of behavior can take a considerable amount of time. Also, it is usually difficult to continue forgiving the controller because domineering behavior is repeated on a regular basis.

When one forgives a controlling spouse, it does not mean that the individual decides to tolerate insensitive treatment (see chapter 3). Instead, forgiveness can remove the stress of anger, strengthen the spouse to be assertive and to make the necessary decisions that need to be made to protect oneself and one's children, and improve the marital relationship. Finally, if the spouse is unwilling to give up the controlling behavior, marital separation might be indicated. Such a step may be the only thing that will motivate some spouses to work on their compulsive need to control.

The Controlling Husband

Jed, age 28, was controlling, overly critical of his wife, and irresponsible in the home. His wife Violet, age 26, entered therapy because she could no longer tolerate his behavior. For a long time he refused to participate in marital counseling and only agreed after Violet threatened separation and divorce.

Initially, Jed blamed Violet for his anger. He was highly resistant to examine any conflicts from his family of origin and accused Violet and her family background for causing the stresses in their marriage. For months, Jed reluctantly came to therapy and did little work because he wanted to maintain control over his wife and the therapist. His attempt to control the sessions was interpreted by the therapist as a defense against the fears of uncovering conflicts from his family of origin.

Violet accused him of not working in therapy and again threatened marital separation unless he worked on his own conflicts. It took many months for Jed to accept that his difficulties with trusting and anger were a major source of the marital conflicts. Until that time he tried to pressure Violet to end therapy and, when that failed, he attempted to control most of the sessions by blaming her for the stress in the marriage, by using humor to defend against his own weaknesses, and by not following the advice of the therapist to face honestly his emotional pain from his childhood and adolescence.

Violet had great difficulty coping with her anger with Jed because, for months, he did not appear truly motivated to change. She was asked to try to resolve her anger for the good of the marriage by forgiving him each day. She would reflect daily that Jed was not strong enough to face his childhood and adolescent hurts. Then, she thought she wanted to try to forgive him for this weakness and for how he was misdirecting family-of-origin mistrust and anger at her. This forgiveness did not limit her ability to be assertive with him. She was able to express her anger in an appropriate way when he was being controlling.

Under the threat of separation, Jed finally admitted that he had grown up in a family with a very controlling mother and with several older sisters who treated him in the same manner as his mother had. He reluctantly accepted that he might have an unconscious fear of being controlled by his strong wife, as he had been by his mother and older sisters. Even though he would not admit the presence of anger with these women, he was given a cognitive forgiveness exercise in which he was asked to reflect that he hated being controlled when young and that he wanted to try to think of forgiving the controllers in his world.

Again Jed manifested a great deal of resistance, not truly entering into the work of forgiveness. He continued to try to control numerous aspects of his and Violet's life together, including the care of their home, their time together, and their leisure activities, and he regularly overreacted in anger when he was unsuccessful. His ability to trust was so limited that he did not begin the hard work of forgiveness until he felt considerably safer with the therapist. To build that trust, the therapist would regularly reiterate that he did not want to control Jed and was not an agent of his wife. Also, the therapist expressed the view based on many years of clinical work that unless Jed resolved his anger with the offenders of his childhood and adolescence, they might control him for the rest of his life. Specifically, they would limit his ability to enjoy a trusting, relaxed relationship with Violet. The fear of being controlled by others motivated Jed to finally work on letting go of his deep resentment and to try trusting his wife.

Jed grew in trust as he reminded himself daily that his wife was a trustworthy woman who did not desire to control him. The growth in trust facilitated his ability to let go of the resentment toward his mother and sisters, which he had been misdirecting for years toward Violet. The recovery process was stormy, with intense quarreling and threats of separation necessitating several years of therapy because Jed, like many controllers, was ambivalent about giving up the control.

Violet, during this period, worked daily at trying to forgive Jed so that she would not overreact each time she saw his controlling behavior manifest itself. Jed, in the Deepening Phase, grew to become more trusting of Violet and felt greater love for her. Furthermore, he regularly expressed remorse to his wife for all the ways in which he had hurt her.

The Controlling Wife

Several months into their marriage, Dave, 53 years old, and Marsha, 50 years old, came into therapy because of their marital fighting. Dave complained that Marsha was driving him crazy because of her constant criticism and because of what he viewed as her compulsive need to control every part of his life. Dave was profoundly discouraged and talked about giving up on their new marriage. Marsha disagreed with him and claimed that her criticisms were fully justified. However, Marsha grew slowly to understand that she had difficulty trusting Dave because of all the ways she had been betrayed by her first husband, who had left her for another woman, as well as by her own mother, who had been an extremely controlling and critical person.

Because Dave was more receptive to understanding the concept and benefits of using forgiveness, he was asked to use it first to resolve his strong anger with his wife. Marsha was resistant to uncovering her anger, but she eventually agreed to use past forgiveness exercises, which were written down by the therapist, for hurts from her mother, and her former husband. After a number of sessions, she became motivated to resolve her anger toward her mother. She knew that this process was essential to reestablishing a healthy, loving relationship with Dave.

Marsha had far more difficulty in forgiving her former spouse, whom she was trying to forgive at the same time she was forgiving her mother, because she had never fully recovered from the pain of betrayal that he had caused. She related, "I gave myself totally to him, and he used me and left me for a former friend. Thinking of forgiving him is so hard. He should be punished and suffer for what he did to me." However, Marsha committed herself to the very hard work of forgiveness because, as she stated, "I don't want him to control me, and I want to be freed from that part of my life." As her anger with her former spouse diminished, she was able to admit that she feared that Dave would betray her as severely as her ex-husband had and that this fear gave rise to a need to control.

Other therapeutic interventions that helped improve this marital relationship were for Marsha to reflect daily that she wanted to avoid being as controlling and critical as her mother, to trust Dave and not control him and to ask Dave for forgiveness for her compulsive need to control. Their love became stronger as anger lessened and trust grew.

THE ANGRY HUSBAND

Carmen, age 40, and Javier, age 43, had a stormy 13-year marital relationship during which they had several separations. In spite of their intense emotional battles, they had a deep love for one another and for their four children. Javier had an explosive temper, and in times of stress would be exceptionally critical of his wife. He had been verbally abusive for years and recently had been physically abusive. Carmen responded by obtaining a protection-from-abuse order from the courts that prohibited Javier from coming into the house for 1 year. This order motivated Javier to honestly face his excessive anger.

The family histories revealed that each spouse had had extremely difficult experiences with the parent of the same sex. Javier's father and Carmen's mother were both angry and domineering toward their spouses and children. Javier's father was much more demeaning toward his wife than Carmen's mother had been toward her father. However, as a teenager, Carmen would regularly ask her father why he tolerated such abusive treatment from her mother and would suggest that he leave her.

Javier was highly resistant about examining ways in which he was acting like his hostile father, instead wanting to blame Carmen for all of the marital stress. Also, as a result of his experiences with his father, he was insecure and used his rage to boost a weak masculine identity. In view of these conflicts, the approach taken was to suggest that each of them had failed to resolve their childhood and adolescent anger with the parent of the same sex. Each was asked to think about modeling after the parent of the opposite sex, both of whom were kind and sensitive people.

The course of treatment was difficult, and Javier periodically had great difficulty controlling his anger in the sessions. At that point he was advised by the therapist to stop acting like his father and cautioned that unless he could get his temper under control, he might not be allowed to move back into the family. Carmen's major motivation for reconciliation, besides her love for Javier, was that her 16-year-old son treated her as Javier did. This was painful for her because, in view of the terrible relationship she had with her mother, she had always wanted to have a close relationship with her children. Carmen hoped that if Javier could learn to overcome his bad temper and treat her in a more loving manner, her son might model such behavior.

Javier began the work of forgiveness because he wanted his marriage to work and he wanted to move back with his family. The pressure of painful loneliness resulted in a lessening of his defenses. He hit bottom living by himself in an apartment, as he began to face how badly his father had treated his mother. He realized he was unconsciously repeating that behavior toward his wife. Then he began to follow written forgiveness instructions given by the therapist, which stated that he should imagine himself as a boy and teenager telling his father that he wanted to be loyal to his good qualities but not his anger and that he wanted to forgive his father for ways in which he had hurt him and his mother with his hostility. His work of forgiveness proceeded slowly, and on some days he slipped back into acting like his angry, critical father. It took approximately 6 months of hard work before Javier could deal with his anger in an appropriate manner. When he felt angry, Javier was encouraged to try to ask himself if his anger was appropriate or excessive. Then, he was asked to discipline himself to be understanding and forgiving toward Carmen before expressing what was upsetting him. Because Javier had relied on anger as a defense against his feelings of insecurity, cognitive–behavioral therapy also was used to build his self-esteem. As his confidence improved, he had less need of anger to bolster his masculine identity.

Finally, Carmen and Javier were asked to forgive the offending in-laws because both harbored powerful anger and resentment against them for what they viewed as intrusive and critical behaviors. The resolution of their excessive anger through the use of forgiveness over an 18-month course of therapy strengthened their marital love and trust. There were fewer episodes of excessive anger; when they erupted, they were resolved in a swift and effective manner.

THE ANGRY WIFE

Kareena, a 35-year-old mother of three, came into therapy because of her periodic episodes of explosive rage. She related a long history of marital conflict. During the arguments, which Kareena often initiated, she would verbally and, at times, physically abuse her husband Dennis. Kareena's motivation for entering therapy was that her oldest child, 10-year-old Brian, was manifesting uncontrollable anger episodes toward his siblings, parents, and peers. She felt guilty about his behavior, believing that she was responsible for it.

Kareena was the oldest of four children and had been in the parental role for her siblings from an early age. She had little emotional support from her mother and was subjected to abusive behavior from her alcoholic father. She thought that the awareness of her anger with an alcoholic father was sufficient to control this emotion in her own life. She came to recognize, however, that she had buried a great deal of anger with each parent and that in times of stress, in particular, she was repeating her father's worst behaviors. Also, she came to understand that, at times, her anger was used as a defense to keep her husband at a distance because she feared that he would betray her emotionally as her father had.

Kareena had no knowledge of how to deal with her anger other than through expression. In the first several sessions, she was asked to think about the possibility of understanding and forgiving before she expressed her anger. Then she was asked to think daily about forgiving each parent for how they had hurt her. In the evening after the first session, Kareena called her therapist and was upset and guilty because she had just verbally and physically abused her husband. She related remorsefully that she had just learned in therapy about using forgiveness for her rage but had not been able to apply it.

Once she understood the process of forgiveness, she decided to begin immediately by working to break the negative influence that the anger with her father had over her marriage and family life. Kareena tried daily to understand her father's behavior as the result of his own childhood experiences with an alcoholic father and came to appreciate more the emotionally wounded and probably abused little boy within her father. As this reframing and understanding increased, she grew in her ability to forgive him for all the hurts of childhood and adolescence. However, in this process she discovered that she had buried violent impulses toward him. In the early phases of therapy, she had no desire to forgive him and was quite angry, even though intellectually she was making a decision to forgive him. Kareena was also given a serotonin reuptake inhibitor to help diminish her anger attacks.

Over a period of several months, there was a significant decrease in Kareena's angry behavior. Also, she grew to accept the pain of her family background and to appreciate that in spite of that suffering she was fortunate to be in a good marriage and to feel basically positive about her life. At the same time, her son was participating in therapy in the same practice and experienced a diminishment in his anger. In the Deepening Phase, the quality of the marital and family life increased significantly. The children were no longer exposed to damaging behavior from their mother. Kareena was pleased that she had learned of a way to resolve her anger from the past and to control her excessive anger in daily life.

PASSIVE–AGGRESSIVE ANGER IN MARRIAGES

In many marriages the major method through which anger is expressed is in the passive–aggressive manner. In these cases the spouse pretends that he or she is not angry while at the same time acts passively to vent anger in a covert way toward the partner. Many individuals of this type try to portray themselves as understanding and loving while at the same time expressing their anger in a veiled manner. The most painful way in which passive–aggressive anger is expressed in the marriage is by withholding love.

Frequently, the victim of passive–aggressive anger is unaware that he or she is on the receiving end of clandestine resentment. The victim of this resentment often reports feelings of anxiety, sadness, exhaustion, anger, and various psychosomatic symptoms. Because the victim is seen as frustrated and irritable, that person may be wrongly identified by others as the angrier partner. Meanwhile, the passive–aggressive spouse tries to paint a self-portrait of a calm and relaxed person.

Passive–aggressive anger can be difficult to identify, and there may be major resistance on the part of the offender in admitting the release of resentment in this manner. One way in which this type of passive resentment can be recognized is through reviewing with spouses the common ways in which passive–aggressive anger is expressed in marriages. We regularly ask spouses to rate their partners' passive–aggressive anger by completing an anger checklist on them. (See Exhibit 11.1.)

The Uncovering Phase can be extremely difficult because the passive–aggressive individuals can be manipulative and highly defensive. They are often reluctant to admit that they are expressing resentment through passive behaviors. Despite this resistance, such clients are asked to engage in forgiveness therapy based on the history. For example, the individual may be asked to forgive a controlling or insensitive parent if that person is identified as a possible origin for such anger. Many spouses have never resolved anger with a neglectful or controlling parent and misdirect it into the marriage by acting in an irresponsible and insensitive manner. Cognitive forgiveness with these parents can result in the diminishment of the anger, especially when the passive–aggressive behavior is noted regularly and clearly identified as such.

There are some spouses who will not forgive because they fear becoming vulnerable again, because they enjoy using their passive–aggressive anger to cling to the victim role to both control and distance their partner, or because they find pleasure in rebelling in a passive manner. Some of these marital cases have resulted in separation and divorce because of the refusal to part with this veiled anger.

LIMITATIONS OF FORGIVENESS WITH ABUSIVE SPOUSES

Unfortunately, there are many individuals who are unwilling to work on the basic conflicts that give rise to their abusive anger. They often will

EXHIBIT 11.1
Passive–Aggressive Anger Checklist

MILD

- ☐ Is always late/leaves early
- ☐ Is deliberately sloppy
- ☐ Has an uncooperative attitude
- ☐ Is forgetful
- ☐ Procrastinates, deliberately puts things off
- ☐ Twists the truth
- ☐ Refuses to do what is reasonably expected

- ☐ Rehashes the past
- ☐ Bangs doors
- ☐ Is withdrawn
- ☐ Is deliberately slow
- ☐ Pretends not to hear or see
- ☐ Walks out on people
- ☐ Refuses to listen
- ☐ Always controls the television
- ☐ Is manipulative

MODERATE

- ☐ Refuses to clean the home or oneself
- ☐ Acts sick or helpless
- ☐ Is overly stubborn
- ☐ Withholds love or support
- ☐ Earns work or school grades markedly below one's ability
- ☐ Is impulsive, fails to plan ahead
- ☐ Avoids or ignores someone deliberately
- ☐ Refuses to function as a responsible parent or person
- ☐ Dates someone for the sole purpose of upsetting others

- ☐ Is always negative
- ☐ Refuses to praise or compliment
- ☐ Makes mistakes deliberately
- ☐ Gives the silent treatment or refuses to speak
- ☐ Is absent from work or school frequently
- ☐ Refuses to be responsible
- ☐ Refuses to work regularly
- ☐ Enjoys seeing people become upset
- ☐ Is divisive

SEVERE

- ☐ Refuses to eat
- ☐ Fails in school or work deliberately
- ☐ Refuses to take care of a serious health problem
- ☐ Attracts someone and then drops him or her as a way to punish emotionally

- ☐ Fails to care about anything
- ☐ Tries to be sick deliberately
- ☐ Fails to pay bills
- ☐ Is a con artist
- ☐ Makes false accusations

not give up anger because it makes them feel strong and in control of the spouse. They experience pleasure in punishing someone, and at some level they recognize the benefits that they experience from the use of abusive anger. Their partners need to make a decision as to the most effective way to protect themselves from this abusive anger. Frequently used responses are demands for therapy, protection-from-abuse orders, marital separations, and divorce. Sometimes, interventions of this nature result in a commitment on the part of the abuser to work toward the resolution of the anger. If the angry spouse has demonstrated extremely impulsive and violent behavior, interventions must be planned carefully in regard to choice and timing to protect the abused spouse and any children in the family.

Yvette, age 45, was victimized for many years by her husband Morgan, age 49, who exhibited excessive anger. He was not only verbally abusive, but also at night, while feigning that he was dreaming, became physically abusive. He had often pushed her out of bed and struck her during his "dreams." After many months of therapy, Morgan was finally able to admit that his father had always been overly demanding, highly manipulative, and physically abusive in his youth. Although he admitted these difficulties with his father, he refused to acknowledge that he had unresolved anger with him that he had been misdirecting at Yvette. The therapist told Morgan that his behaviors indicated that he had powerful rage within himself, which he was misdirecting at Yvette. If he failed to commit himself to resolve this anger, he was told that it would be in his wife's best interest to separate and to end their marriage.

Despite his resistance, Morgan was asked to think of forgiving his father for the good of the marriage. When it became apparent that he was not working to forgive his father, the therapist suggested that the reason he was unable to take such a course was because he was relying on his anger to control his wife. Then he was asked to try to view Yvette as a woman who did not want to control him as his father had and as a woman who was trustworthy. These attempts to build up his trust in Yvette did not lead to any change in his behavior. Morgan simply refused to trust her or to resolve his anger with his father, continuing in his verbal and covert physical abuse.

His abusive behavior began to take a greater toll on Yvette, and she developed symptoms of depression. At that time the therapist recommended that she consider separating from him because of his refusal to work on his rage and because of his clever and cunning expression of physical abuse while pretending to be asleep. This covert abuse made it impossible for Yvette to pursue a protection from abuse order. The therapist warned her that her depressive illness could become more severe unless she took strong steps to protect herself. She refused to follow this advice and ended therapy. It can only be hoped that at some later point in time Yvette can become more assertive and that Morgan will work on the techniques recommended to him to let go of his rage and violent impulses and to build his trust.

THE NARCISSISTIC SPOUSE

One of the major causes of excessive anger in marriages is the result of narcissistic conflicts in a spouse. These individuals regularly overreact in anger when they cannot have their way or when their partner does not give in to their extreme selfish demands.

Charles, a 32-year-old father of three and a successful professional, manifested periodic explosive anger in his marital relationship, particularly when his needs were not met immediately. Charles was overly demanding, insensitive, and self-preoccupied, and he had difficulty in giving himself to his wife Kimberly, age 28. As the oldest of two children, he was always his mother's favorite and, according to his wife, he had always been spoiled. In addition, Kimberly believed that her mother-in-law had never accepted her, and Kimberly found her to be intrusive in their marriage.

In marital therapy, it was pointed out to Charles that he manifested a number of narcissistic personality traits of lacking empathy, being selfish, setting unreasonable expectations of favorable treatment, and taking advantage of others that predisposed him to excessive anger. He was highly resistant to therapy and attempted to blame all of the marital problems on his wife. It was suggested to him that when he felt extremely angry, he should try to act in a more mature and giving manner and to think about forgiving his wife rather than expressing his anger.

Kimberly was an intelligent, giving wife and mother. She was highly committed to making her marriage work. She came to realize that her major emotional conflict was that of being an enabler to her husband's narcissistic behavior and, by doing that, she was damaging their marriage. She embarked on a course of healthy assertiveness with her husband. For a number of months, the tensions intensified in their relationship to the point that Charles threatened to divorce her. She viewed this threat as highly manipulative and challenged him to proceed. At the same time, Kimberly tried to forgive Charles regularly for all of the hurts of the past caused by his narcissistic behavior even before he made a commitment to try to change. She also tried to work at being more assertive with her mother-in-law and at forgiving her to protect herself from the damaging effects of her own resentment toward her.

The possibility of divorce created enormous stress and anxiety for Charles and motivated him to work on his narcissistic anger. When angry, he began to forgive and think of being less selfish. He came to understand that he had developed strong narcissistic tendencies because of his childhood and adolescent relationship with his mother. Then he was asked to work at trying to forgive his mother for spoiling him and for depending too much on him as a source of happiness in her life. He also apologized to Kimberly and asked for her forgiveness and trust. Charles's impulsive and explosive behavior diminished.

Unfortunately, many narcissistic spouses are reluctant to change, and their marriages end. Some individuals would rather give up their spouse and children than give up their self-centered behaviors. They believe that they can be happy only with individuals who support their narcissistic lifestyle and who do not expect them to give themselves too much in a relationship with a significant other or with children.

INFIDELITY

Episodes of infidelity often emerge during the course of marital therapy owing to significant guilt on the part of the spouse who has been unfaithful and because of the desire to be honest in an attempt to strengthen the marriage. The first step in resolving the anger related to infidelity is to uncover the fundamental conflict that led the partner to seek out another person to express or fulfill unmet needs. If the offended spouse is able to realize the emotional pain in his or her partner, such as loneliness or feelings of insecurity or stress, it becomes much easier to move toward the decision to attempt to forgive the other. Usually the offended person is able to consider forgiveness only if his or her spouse shows significant remorse and understanding of the conflicts that caused the infidelity and is motivated to work on resolving them.

Marital infidelity results in some of the most powerful anger that one can encounter. The betrayal pain is so strong for some that the response is one of enormous rage coupled at times with violent impulses toward the offending partner and the other person. As a result of the intensity of emotion, this type of anger diminishes slowly and requires a prolonged use of forgiveness.

Many individuals feel so betrayed that they cannot think about forgiving their spouse. When this happens, sometimes spiritual forgiveness can be initiated, when appropriate, by one or both partners. One partner, for example, may begin to ask God's help. Sometimes one partner will ask God to forgive the other. Also, the work of forgiveness is facilitated by seeing the offending partner work to make changes. During the Work Phase, intense anger is often expressed in and out of therapy sessions. At the same time, it is important that the offender express remorse regularly, ask for forgiveness, and express confidence that he or she is going to be able to resolve the conflicts that led to infidelity.

In cases in which the infidelity is the result of extreme loneliness in the marriage, the person involved in the affair can have more anger than his or her partner. This is because individuals who are intensely lonely can have considerable rage with their partner for failing to communicate more affection, love, and praise. In those cases, it is the person who has had the affair who has the greater difficulty in forgiving, and it is the offended partner who needs to do the hard work in therapy of growing in the ability to be more emotionally giving.

A research study by Reed (1998) has shown that those who forgive the unfaithful spouse have greater psychological well-being than those who do not forgive. Clinical experiences also indicate that forgiveness has significant value in diminishing the betrayal pain and enabling couples to work at resolving emotional conflicts that predispose their marriage to infidelity.

SEPARATION AND DIVORCE ANGER

The anger associated with separation and divorce can be intense and damaging to both spouses and children (Buchanan, Maccoby, & Dornbusch, 1991; Johnston et al., 1989; Kalter, 1987). Children can show psychomotor agitation when parents are in conflict and usually feel deeply hurt when they hear one of their parents criticizing the other. Protecting children from this harmful anger is a major reason that parents consider the use of forgiveness during the separation and divorce process. Another incentive to resolve anger is to protect a future relationship from being harmed by resentment from the past. Research has shown benefits to the children and the forgiver. Forgiveness of a former spouse is linked to better mental health for single mothers, less punitive parenting behaviors, and more positive family relationships (Reed et al., 1999).

The divorce process is often associated with powerful feelings of sadness, anger, and mistrust. Although some feel relieved to be apart from an offending spouse, they frequently go through a mourning process that may be associated with strong feelings of betrayal rage. Others struggle with hatred and impulses to get revenge. Resolving such violent impulses is important for all people involved and for society as a whole. The ability to deal with anger during the divorce process is extremely helpful to the maintenance of emotional health. Self-help books relating to forgiveness and divorce are Hootman and Perkins (1982), and Enright (in press).

With especially difficult divorces, few people in the short run have the ability to forgive an offending spouse either cognitively or emotionally because it is too hard to let go of the anger. Many are bitter and resentful because they believe that their spouses did not try to put forth sufficient effort to make the marriage work. The use of spiritual forgiveness exercises in which the person reflects that he or she is powerless over the bitterness and hatred and wants to turn it over to God can be beneficial. These exercises may be coupled with regular expressions of anger, supported by the therapist, at an offending spouse. Finally, antidepressant medications can be of value in diminishing the sadness and rage in some clients.

Unfortunately, many individuals experience the periodic emergence of extremely strong anger and rage meant for their ex-spouses years or even decades after the relationship has ended. Those same individuals may feel guilty when they realize that their anger often is displaced toward a significant other who does not deserve it, such as a spouse, a child who reminds them of the ex-spouse, or coworkers. The resolution of such resentment is essential to their personal health and to the maintenance of healthy, loving relationships.

Rosanna, age 34, had an exceptionally controlling ex-husband Nick, whom she divorced after 6 years of marriage because he was far more loyal to his domineering mother than he was to her. She thought that she was no longer resentful of him. However, Rosanna discovered that she would overreact with strong anger toward anyone who was insensitive to her. These experiences demonstrated to her that she had been denying a great deal of anger toward Nick. She realized that she had not fully overcome her resentment toward him. After forgiveness was explained to her, she recognized that her coping strategies were not working and clearly saw the benefits to be derived from forgiving him. As she continued the forgiveness process, she found herself feeling more compassion for Nick and related, "He'll never be freed from the control of his mother and will probably act like her for the rest of his life."

Rosanna had been sufficiently hurt by Nick during their 6 years together that she did not want him to continue having a negative influence on her emotional life. As she committed herself to forgive her ex-spouse, her mood became much more stable, and she overreacted less often in anger. The reward for her hard work was that of being able to move on to a new, more mutually rewarding relationship. This is a common experience for many who work to break the control that their former spouse has in their emotional lives.

FORGIVENESS IN OTHER FAMILY RELATIONSHIPS

In addition to its therapeutic role in marital therapy, forgiveness can also be useful in diminishing and resolving the excessive anger that creates conflicts and divisions in many other family relationships. Specifically, it can help in the healing of strained and damaged parental, sibling, and in-law relationships (DiBlasio, 1998).

The conflicts in many parent–child relationships are the result of unresolved anger in a parent in their family of origin, most often with the father but at times with the mother, which is then misdirected at a child. The uncovering of this resentment is challenging because of the significant resistance in most people to admitting anger with their parents for failing to meet their needs for affection, praise, or support. Many parents eventually begin the work of forgiveness after the therapist explains that their failure to admit and to resolve their parental resentment leads them to overreact under stress and interferes with their ability to be loving and positive with their children.

The conflicts in many sibling relationships are also the result of misdirected anger that is meant for a parent, most often the father. This unconscious, inappropriate expression of hostile feelings in sibling relationships often begins in childhood and continues into adult life. Also, those who were rejected or ridiculed by their peers as children and teenagers regularly misdirect their peer anger into the home at a sibling. Recognizing the denial and the inappropriate expression of this resentment at a sibling, coupled with working at forgiving the offending parent or peer and asking for forgiveness of the sibling, can result in the strengthening of sibling relationships. Unfortunately, the important issue of sibling anger and abuse has received very little attention in the literature.

A major source of conflict in relationships with in-laws is the result of their attempt to control their adult offspring, spouse, and even grandchildren, and it can result in significant marital stress and increased family conflict. Couples benefit from being both assertive and forgiving toward the controller. However, forgiving these individuals does not mean that one should trust them. In fact, because the motivation for controlling individuals to change their behaviors is minimal, those offended regularly need to distance themselves from the offender. This stance may have to be taken for years, with the clear explanation that the offenders will not be trusted and welcomed until they change. In other words, forgiving and reconciling are not the same thing. Forgiving such offenders helps break their emotional influence and strengthens one in dealing with them.

Marriages and families are under significant stress as a result of resentment and hostile feelings. Excessive anger is one of the major reasons for marital conflict, marital separations, and divorce and for conflicts in parent–child, sibling, and in-law relationships. In this chapter, we demonstrate forgiveness as an effective psychotherapeutic approach that can help individuals to both understand and resolve their resentment, thereby protecting and strengthening marital and family relationships.

12

FORGIVENESS IN EATING DISORDERS

Millie, a 35-year-old divorced mother of two children, sought treatment for anorexia and depression. Millie had experienced a series of betrayals in her family (sexual abuse) and in her marriage (physical abuse) that severely damaged her ability to trust. She denied her powerful angry impulses against those who had hurt her and misdirected this anger at herself. Uncovering and validating her anger were major challenges in her treatment and took many months of therapy. Later, she feared making a decision to forgive and to begin the work of forgiveness because she thought this process might result in her becoming vulnerable to being hurt again. In this chapter, we discuss working on the phases of forgiveness with Millie and the many resistances encountered in her lengthy therapy. We also relate the role of active and passive–aggressive anger in eating disorders and the uses of the four phases of forgiveness therapy primarily in the context of clinical cases with patients with anorexia and those with bulimia.

EATING DISORDERS AND ANGER

Anorexia nervosa and bulimia nervosa are serious disorders with an outcome that is often severe. The anger in patients with eating disorders often originates from negative life events with parents (Horesh et al., 1995) and peers and is influenced by their comorbid conditions. Horesh et al. (1995) found that patients with anorexia showed significantly more negative life events concerning parents compared with patients in other psychiatric diagnostic categories. In Herzog, Keller, Sacks, Yeh, and Lavori's (1992) study of comorbidity, 73% of participants with anorexia nervosa, 60% of those with bulimia nervosa, and 82% of those with mixed anorexia nervosa/ bulimia nervosa had a current comorbid Axis I diagnosis. These comorbid disorders include major depression (Casper, Hedeker, & McClough, 1992; Herzog, 1984; Herzog et al., 1992), obsessive–compulsive disorder (OCD; Hecht, Fichter, & Postpischil, 1990; Jenike et al., 1990), anxiety disorders (Herzog et al., 1992), and personality disorders (Gartner, Marcus, Halmi, & Loranger, 1989; Herzog et al., 1992; Levin & Hyler, 1986; Mitchell, Hatsukami, Eckert, & Pyle, 1985; Wonderlich, Swift, Slotnick, & Goodman, 1990; Zanarini et al., 1998). Herzog et al. (1992) reported a prevalence of 63% for lifetime major depression in patients with anorexia nervosa and those with bulimia nervosa.

As is the case with most psychiatric disorders, little is known about the relationship between anger and eating disorders. However, in Fava, Rappe, West, and Herzog's (1995) study of 132 women with eating disorders, 31% of the patients reported an average of 4.8 anger attacks per month. The patients with anger attacks had significantly more depressive symptoms than patients without these attacks. Among patients with bulimia, there was a trend for anger attacks to be associated with greater severity of illness. In a study of adolescent girls, eating disturbances were significantly associated with aggressive behaviors (Thompson, Wonderlich, Crosby, & Mitchell, 1999). Girls who endorsed binge eating and purging or dietary restrictions had aggressive behavior two to four times higher than those who did not endorse these behaviors. Also, the constellation of eating disturbances and aggressive behavior was associated with a greater risk of drug use and attempted suicide.

Patients with bulimia and anorexia have been shown to be more depressed, anxious, and angry than participants without eating disorders (Breaux & Morino, 1994). However, patients with bulimia and those with anorexia did not differ significantly from each other in depression, anxiety, and anger. Brunner, Maloney, Daniels, Mays, and Farrell (1989) found that hostility was significantly greater in patients with anorexia than in control patients. Rebert, Stanton, and Schwarz (1991) observed that a greater state of depression and hostility were significantly associated with daily binge eating and purging. Also, bulimia nervosa is associated with behaviors involving poor impulse control, such as kleptomania and substance abuse (Beary, Lacey, & Merry, 1986; Bulik, 1987; Mitchell et al., 1985). Mitchell et al. (1985) found that 23% of women with bulimia reported a history of substance abuse. Hudson, Pope, Jonas, and Yurgelun-Todd (1983) found that 24% of patients with bulimia met the diagnostic criteria for kleptomania.

Lacey and Evans (1986) observed in their review of the literature that there is much evidence suggesting that impulsivity is common in eating disorders. Finally, the Minnesota Multiphasic Personality Inventory profile of patients with bulimia showed elevated scores on impulsivity and anger (Hatsukami, Owen, Pyle, & Mitchell, 1982).

In clinical experience, it has been noted that patients with bulimia and patients with anorexia express their anger in markedly different ways. Patients with bulimia are more likely to be honest about their anger and release it in an active manner, whereas patients with anorexia tend to mask their resentment and release it in a passive–aggressive manner. This clinical view is supported by the study of Fava et al. (1995) that patients with severe bulimia may be prone to develop irritability and anger attacks. However, that research did not measure the passive–aggressive expression of anger in the patients with anorexia. In a therapeutic setting, we have noted that many patients with anorexia are angrier and harbor stronger impulses for revenge than those with bulimia; however, their resentment is more controlled and released in covert ways not easily identified. Also, we have found that patients with eating disorders often use anger as a defense mechanism against their fears of being hurt by others.

PASSIVE–AGGRESSIVE ANGER IN PEOPLE WITH ANOREXIA

At the present time, passive–aggressive anger has yet to be measured empirically in eating disorders. When that happens, we anticipate that the prevalence of this type of anger will be more clearly recognized as a major clinical issue, especially for patients with anorexia. Clinical experience indicates that the passive–aggressive expression of anger is manifested more strongly in patients with anorexia than those with any other mental disorder, with the possible exception of certain personality disorders, such as the borderline, antisocial, and hysterical.

Passive–aggressive anger is a method of expression by which one attempts to hurt or provoke others and to obtain revenge while acting as though one is not angry. This expression of resentment in patients with eating disorder can be evaluated regularly by having patients and family members complete an anger checklist. Common manifestations of this type of anger include refusing to be responsible, acting helpless or sick, deliberate forgetfulness, tardiness, refusing to do what is reasonably expected, withholding love, deliberately failing and refusing to care for serious health problems, and refusing to eat.

The identification of passive–aggressive anger is difficult with patients with anorexia. They display denial and great restraint in emotional expression (Casper, 1990), and they manifest strong behavioral and emotional control (Casper et al., 1992; Garner, Garfinkel, & O'Shaughnessy, 1985; Haimes & Katz, 1988). In our clinical experience, patients with bulimia and patients with mixed anorexia nervosa/bulimia nervosa are much less defensive and more readily admit and express their anger, although at times such expression is excessive and inappropriate. This clinical experience is consistent with Herzog et al.'s (1992) research findings, which show a relationship between impulse-related behaviors and bulimic symptomatology.

PHASES OF FORGIVENESS IN PEOPLE WITH ANOREXIA

We observe that patients with anorexia use strong denial or obsessive–compulsive defenses to cope with intense anger from negative life experiences. Their strong need for emotional control offers a major challenge to the uncovering of the anger associated with the emotional trauma in their lives. In addition, they use their passive–aggressive anger as a tool to distance others because of fear of betrayal and an unwillingness to become vulnerable. Even though they can often identify their important life hurts and disappointments, most are reluctant to admit feeling angry as a result of these conflicts.

Hecht et al. (1990) and Jenike et al. (1990) described a strong relationship between anorexia and OCD with the combination of marked obsessive–compulsive and anorexia behaviors coinciding with more severe disturbances and chronicity. Casper et al. (1992) suggested that treatment efforts focus on addressing the patient's shyness and fear of relationships and on offering the hope that self-actualization can take place through expression of feelings and thoughts and not exclusively through self-control. This approach has value. However, some patients with anorexia are reluctant to admit the depth of their anger and are unwilling to work toward change because of secondary gains obtained from passive–aggressive anger. These include a sense of pleasure in seeing others agonize over their weight loss, their ability to distance others and to limit vulnerability to others, or a lack of desire to be in good health. Other patients have been hurt so deeply that they refuse to give up their compulsive behaviors because, in themselves, they provide a sense of safety and control.

In the Uncovering Phase of treatment, one approach to these resistances is to challenge the clients' compulsive need for control by suggesting that if they do not resolve their anger with those who hurt them that these individuals may control them for the rest of their lives. Family therapy sessions can be beneficial when family members ask the patient with anorexia for forgiveness for negative and painful emotional experiences such as neglect and promise to work toward making changes in their relationship. Also, psychodrama techniques are helpful in the Uncovering Phase when denial is very strong and when anger is vented primarily in a passive–aggressive manner. In attempting to break through this denial, the therapist has the option of role playing as the patient and verbalizing the emotional pain that the patient cannot or will not express, including the desire to see others suffer because of the patient's illness. The therapist can also role play as the person who has hurt the client, express sorrow, and ask for forgiveness for hurts that were inflicted.

Chad, a withdrawn 13-year-old with anorexia, who had been the victim of intense peer ridicule and physical abuse for years. Therefore, in this case, the therapist role played as his peers. In doing so the therapist stated, "You were the smartest boy in class, and I was jealous because you made me feel dumb." The patient responded by crying quietly. The therapist continued, "Chad, you must want to get even with me because I was rotten to you. I don't have any excuse; I used you to make me feel big with the rest of the gang. If it does any good, I'm sorry." As a result of much hard work in therapy, the power of this role-play exercise allowed Chad to become emotionally expressive in therapy for the first time.

Powerful angry feelings and the impulse for revenge can actually overwhelm the individual at such times, and he or she may even get out of control. In some instances, patients can become so obsessed with bitterness that they turn it on themselves. They need, therefore, to be warned regularly that unless they work on letting go of their anger and impulses for revenge, they may destroy themselves and thus allow those who have hurt them continued control over them.

The goal in the Uncovering Phase is to help people identify family, peers, or others who have hurt them in the past. Meetings with some of those mentioned may be necessary to obtain needed information, particularly with controlling patients with anorexia. Also, people in therapy need to understand that the use of forgiveness will be a gift not only to those who hurt them but also to themselves because it will enable them to express anger in a healthier, more assertive manner through the resolution of past resentment. Without forgiveness, the buried anger can result in either the overreaction or the misdirection of anger, which are both regular occurrences in bulimia nervosa and mixed anorexia nervosa/bulimia nervosa.

In addition to the factors already mentioned, some patients with anorexia nervosa decide to begin the forgiveness process because of a sense of shame that can appear when their passive–aggressive and controlling behaviors are identified or because they may have the desire to work on comorbid conditions such as depression. In some instances, there may be a recognition of the fact that controlling behaviors are not really helpful.

The major difficulty in the Work Phase of forgiveness is the emergence of intense fear at the beginning of the process. First, patients worry that if they forgive they might have to become vulnerable to someone who has hurt them deeply. The therapist can alleviate this anxiety by explaining that forgiveness and trusting are two different processes and that one can forgive to help oneself and not necessarily trust an offender who has not changed. The therapist should at this point distinguish forgiveness and reconciliation.

The next obstacle encountered is the strong fear of life betrayal. This fear is much more difficult to treat, but through the work of forgiveness, these patients begin to feel less depressed and more healthy. Because many have felt somewhat safe from betrayal in relationships as people having anorexia, they need to make a decision to return to the mainstream of life and abandon the sick role. In the midst of this conflict, even though they have begun to experience some benefit from forgiveness, many patients with anorexia need growth in their ability to trust so that they can maintain healthy relationships with others before they can commit themselves fully to the process. This growth in trust can begin to occur in the relationship with the therapist and with loved ones in family therapy sessions.

Several young women developed anorexia nervosa after a series of painful betrayals by their peers during high school, such as severe peer ridicule or rejections. These adolescents initially became depressed because of their loneliness and fear of betrayal in relationships, but their symptoms progressed into loss of appetite, social isolation, and anorexia. Initially these patients are often so completely obsessed with their weight and food intake that they have no conscious awareness of how much they had been hurt by their peers. In the course of their therapy, most are surprised at the depth of their rage and their desire to strike back.

The cycle continues, however, because after deciding to forgive their offenders to overcome the hurts of the past and to deal with their anorexia, they often become fearful of being hurt again if they become healthy and return to ordinary socialization. Growth in trust is facilitated by the support of loving parents and slow development of friendships with sensitive and trustworthy peers. Actually, the growth in trust with one's peers can become a more serious and difficult clinical issue than other issues already encountered. However, as these young people work to forgive the peers who hurt them, they usually grow in their ability to feel free and begin to recall other relationships with trustworthy peers from the past. The therapist needs to challenge such patients to stop avoiding personal relationships and to carefully select friendships in which they can develop trust.

Psychodrama techniques are effective with these adolescents who have been badly ridiculed by peers or terribly hurt by a parent or sibling through neglect or abuse because through them the patient has the opportunity to verbally express anger and rage with a peer, sibling, or parent. The exercises are followed immediately by an attempt to help patients understand how to cognitively forgive those who have hurt them. As a result of forgiveness therapy, the young people often grow in their ability to be assertive, but it is not unusual for them to spend 18–24 months or longer in intensive therapy.

When powerful inner rage in patients with anorexia is a result of severe betrayal experiences, such as sexual or physical abuse, the therapist can discuss the possibility of spiritual forgiveness exercises. We find that encouragement from loved ones and a past history with spiritual/religious education are helpful to the person who wishes to explore spiritual forgiveness. In this process, the person tries to turn the anger over to God.

Unfortunately, some patients with anorexia are unwilling to make a decision to give up their passive–aggressive resentment, their compulsive need for control, their mistrust of others, or their chosen isolation from the world in the sick role. These patients often have a burning, sick desire for revenge within themselves. Some fantasize attendance at their own funerals and enjoy imagining the suffering of those who have hurt them. We have seen some patients take quiet inner delight in seeing the shocked faces of those who look at their emaciated frames. Might it be the case that some people with anorexia who actually die, are in the end destroyed by their own passive–aggressive hatred and their decision never to trust anyone?

Millie, introduced in the beginning of the chapter, had been the victim of sexual abuse by her father and later physical abuse by her ex-husband. As a result of these traumatic experiences, she developed major depression, profound mistrust, and a severe fear of betrayal. Initially, she was treated with an antidepressant. She denied feeling overly angry; however, under stress she began to cut herself. An attempt was made to identify her anger with those who had betrayed her and to stop misdirecting it at herself.

Millie's self-cutting was interpreted, in part, as misdirected, violent rage, perhaps even murderous, which was meant for her father and her ex-husband. Additional reasons that many people give for self-cutting include (a) to break through a deadening feeling of numbness and (b) to transfer the pain on the inside that they feel powerless to express to a pain on the outside that they can articulate and others can see. For Millie, the most difficult aspect of dealing with her anger was confronting her buried rage. She was initially unable to accept that she might be harboring violent impulses against these two important people in her life. However, as she came to examine more clearly her childhood experiences with her father and her marital memories with her ex-husband, she slowly came to acknowledge that the development of violent impulses and the desire for revenge would be a natural response to such trauma. This understanding diminished her guilt, shame, and self-hatred.

Because of the severity of her rage, Millie was not asked to try to forgive either cognitively or emotionally. Instead, she was asked to think that she was powerless over her rage and impulses for revenge and that she wanted to turn them over to God. She first practiced this spiritual forgiveness exercise, which was a modification of the first two steps of Alcoholics Anonymous, in therapy, before it was assigned as to be used between sessions. These exercises brought her great relief because they provided a method through which she could admit the depth of her rage and at the same time release it without harming herself or others. This process continued for many months before she experienced symptomatic relief. The slow resolution of her hatred decreased her self-mutilation impulses and helped with the treatment of her anorexia. As her resentment diminished, she was able to use cognitive forgiveness in which she daily made a decision to forgive those who had hurt her.

FORGIVENESS IN PATIENTS WITH BULIMIA

In patients with bulimia, who are often very emotionally expressive, the challenge as Casper et al. (1992) suggested is to learn to establish control over the emotions. This can involve exploring the limitations of expressing anger as the sole method for handling resentment (Fitzgibbons, 1986; Tavris, 1984) and examining the benefits of forgiveness as a way to both control and resolve their anger.

Difficulties with impulse control are indicators that patients with bulimia struggle with strong anger. Although they often have difficulty trusting in relationships, they tend to be much more open, vulnerable, and less controlling than patients with anorexia. Because patients with bulimia are able to be more trusting of the therapist and identify the major disappointments and traumatic events of their lives, therapists do not need to rely as much on the family members for an accurate history.

After disappointments and betrayal experiences are identified, forgiveness is recommended as a method to help them in the treatment of their eating disorder and their comorbid condition. Most patients are willing to try using forgiveness, in part, because they want to overcome the hurts of the past and also because they have come to understand the limitations of reliance on expression for dealing with their angry feelings. Cognitive forgiveness exercises can be assigned in which the therapist gives written instructions for the patient to think of understanding and forgiving offenders for both recent and past disappointments and hurts in relationships. In working on forgiving others, many patients with bulimia nervosa and mixed anorexia nervosa/bulimia nervosa also become anxious about giving up the use of their anger as a defense mechanism to distance others. In this phase they struggle, too, with the fear that by resolving their anger they will risk becoming vulnerable. This process of forgiving and struggling to grow in trust can take years of work in therapy.

Abbie, age 35, developed bulimia as a college student after the death of her mother and resultant feelings of intense isolation and fear. She had never felt close to her father and described him by saying, "He thinks he's the center of the world. He really doesn't care about anyone except himself." No one in the family provided support or helped her cope with the loss of her mother. As college life continued, Abbie began to feel increasingly isolated, frightened, mistrustful, lonely, and depressed. After several disappointing dating relationships, her bulimia intensified and resulted in several hospitalizations while in her 20s. She responded fairly well to cognitive–behavioral interventions during the hospitalizations but relapsed quickly. During her hospitalizations, she was encouraged to express anger at her father, but she feared doing so because of the fragility of their relationship. She was treated with antidepressants and later developed poor impulse control and almost lost her job as a result of stealing.

Initially, Abbie had little conscious awareness of the depth of her anger with those whom she felt had betrayed her. However, she slowly came to view her bulimic symptoms as her way of isolating herself from others, especially men. As long as she was binging and vomiting several times weekly, she could not possibly consider involvement in a relationship. Attempts at family therapy were fruitless because of her father's narcissistic conflicts and his inability to be sensitive to her. Despite his behavior, she committed herself to forgive him because she did not want him to control her any longer. The most difficult aspect of the forgiveness process was that of accepting and absorbing the pain of betrayals with her father and a former boyfriend. There were times when she committed herself intellectually to forgiving these men, but shortly afterward she would feel strong anger that prevented her from continuing the process. At those moments she would tell herself that she had to give up her resentment if she wanted to be healthy. This cognitive step provided symptomatic relief over time.

After several years of therapy, the slow resolution of Abbie's anger and intense fear of betrayal enabled her to risk becoming more vulnerable in relationships. She no longer felt as strong a pull to hide from the world in her bulimic illness. Abbie came to realize that the resolution of her bitter feelings toward her father and her former boyfriend gave her a new lease on life and protected her from the toxic effects of resentment and mistrust.

Excessive anger is a serious problem in patients with eating disorders and can interfere with their treatment and recovery. The psychotherapeutic use of forgiveness has value in diminishing what appears to be severe passive–aggressive anger in those with anorexia nervosa and the active anger in those with bulimia nervosa and mixed anorexia nervosa/bulimia nervosa and in the treatment of the comorbid disorders associated with eating disorders. It is our hope that future research will measure the degree of active and passive–aggressive anger in these patients.

13

FORGIVENESS IN BIPOLAR AND OTHER MENTAL DISORDERS

Demi, age 26 and single, had a 4-year history of Bipolar Disorder I with only manic episodes. During her manic episodes, she was extremely angry. She identified the source of her anger and began the work of forgiveness with those who had hurt her in the past because she quickly realized its benefits. The regular use of forgiveness helped both control her anger and stabilize her mood. Her treatment is discussed in greater detail in this chapter.

We present the role and prevalence of anger in bipolar disorders, impulse control disorders, and Tourette's syndrome. In each disorder difficulties with excessive anger have been well documented both in research studies and in clinical experience. The uses of the four phases of forgiveness therapy in the treatment of patients with these disorders are described.

ANGER IN BIPOLAR DISORDERS

Irritability, a manifestation of anger, is one of the more common mood symptoms seen during manic episodes, and it is often the predominant mood. As reported in the *DSM–IV*, the lability of the mood between euphoria and irritability is frequently seen in mania (American Psychiatric Association, 1994). In Goodwin and Jamison's (1990) summary of numerous studies, 80% of adult clients manifested irritability during mania (see Table 13.1).

225

TABLE 13.1
Mood Symptoms During Mania: Frequency of Symptoms per Episode

Study	Clients N	Irritability %	Euphoria %	Depression %	Lability %	Expansiveness %
Clayton et al., 1965	31		97			
Winokur et al., 1969	100[a]	85	98		95	
Beigel & Murphy, 1971a	12		67	68[b]		
Kotin & Goodwin, 1972	20			92		
Carlson & Goodwin, 1973	20	100	90	100	90	
Taylor & Abrams, 1973	52	81	31	55		
Murphy & Beigel, 1974	30					66
Winokur & Tsuang, 1975	94	70	92[c]	90		
Abrams & Taylor, 1976	78	76	44			
Leff et al., 1976	63		97		59	
Loudon et al., 1977	16	75	81[d]	63[e]	56	
Taylor & Abrams, 1977	123[f]	81	39		52	44
Carlson & Strober, 1979	9[g]	100	89			60
Prien et al., 1988	103			67[h]		
Weighted M		80	71	72	69	60

Note. From *Manic-Depressive Illness*, by F. K. Goodwin and K. R. Jamison, 1990, pp. 30–31. Copyright 1990 by Oxford University Press. Reprinted with permission.
[a]100 episodes, 61 clients. [b]Depressive delusions in 24%, suicidal ideation in 7%. [c]Irritable only (8%), euphoric only (30%), irritable and euphoric (62%). [d]"Hypomanic affect." [e]Suicidal ideation in 25%. [f]Calculations based on N = 119. [g]Adolescents. [h]Mild depression (45%) moderate to severe depression (22%).

Excessive anger and irritability also are present in child and adolescent bipolar disorder. Davis (1979) observed that children with bipolar disorder were highly irritable and had prolonged and aggressive temper outbursts. In Carlson's (1995) study, children with bipolar disorder were severely irritable, dysphoric, and agitated. Biederman (1998) stated that children with bipolar disorder may not present with the classic adult manic picture, but instead, as several studies have shown, they present with a more chronic, irritable, and dysphoric course (McElroy, Strakowski, West, Keck, & McConville, 1997; Weinberg & Brumback, 1976). In a study (Wozniak et al., 1995) of preadolescent children who met the diagnostic criteria for mania, the clinical picture was characterized by severe irritability, and their presentation was predominantly mixed with symptoms of major depression and mania co-occurring.

In the review of 10 years of research into child and adolescent bipolar disorder, B. Geller and Luby (1997) suggested that prepubertal-onset bipolar disorder may be comorbid with attention deficit hyperactivity disorder (ADHD) and conduct disorder (CD) or have features of ADHD or CD, or both, as initial manifestations. Wicki and Angst (1991) reported in their longitudinal community cohort study that hypomanic cases presented more disciplinary difficulties at school when they were young and had reported more frequent thefts during their adolescent years than the rest of the cohort. In Kutcher et al.'s (1989) study of the comorbidity of CD with other Axis I conditions, they found that 42% of the bipolar clients had secondary CD. Also, comorbid CD in bipolar youths appears to be associated with a worse clinical course (Kovacs & Pollock, 1995). In another study of mania in children, 91% had lifetime comorbid oppositional defiant disorder and 86% lifetime comorbid ADHD (Biederman et al., 1998). Manic episodes in adolescents may be associated with excessive anger as manifested in school truancy, antisocial behavior, school failure, or substance use.

Our clinical experience indicates that the majority of clients with Bipolar II disorder, in which one or more major depressive episodes are accompanied by at least one hypomanic episode, periodically struggle with strong anger. This anger is associated with their depressive disorder and may or may not manifest itself in a more extreme manner as an anger attack (Fava, 1998). However, there is no empirical research yet to support this clinical view. Research has shown that depressed bipolar clients are less angry than unipolar clients (Beigel & Murphy, 1971b). Also, Jain, Leslie, Keefe, Sachs, and Fava (1997) found that clients with unipolar major depressive disorder were significantly more likely to report anger attacks than bipolar clients during a depressive episode.

Goodwin and Jamison (1990) identified a number of organic causes of manic and hypomanic symptoms (see Exhibit 13.1). Neuroendocrine studies may later identify a neurotransmitter abnormality that influences the excessive irritability and, at times, rage seen in clients with bipolar disorders.

The psychological origins of the anger in these clients is similar to those in other disorders presented in earlier chapters. However, in grandiose male clients we find that the most often identified source of anger is from conflicts and hurts in the father relationship. Numerous manic young men in their late teens and early 20s have reported very painful father relationships in which they were never affirmed in their masculinity or in which they were subjected to excessive unwarranted criticism. The resultant anger

EXHIBIT 13.1
Organic Causes of Manic and Hypomanic Symptoms

Drug related
Isoniazid[a]
Procarbazine[a]
Levodopa[a]
Bromide[a]
Decongestants
Bronchodilators
Procyclidine
Calcium replacement
Phencyclidine
Metoclopramide
Corticosteroids and ACTH[a]
Hallucinogens
Sympathomimetic amines
Disulfiram (Antabuse)
Alcohol
Barbiturates
Anticholinergics
Anticonvulsants
Benzodiazepines

Metabolic disturbance
Postoperative states[a]
Hemodialysis[a]
Vitamin B_{12} deficiency
Addison's disease
Cushing's disease
Postinfection states
Dialysis
Hyperthyroidism

Neurological conditions
Right-temporal seizure focus[a]
Multiple sclerosis
Right-hemisphere damage
Epilepsy
Huntington's disease
Postcerebrovascular accident

Infection
Influenza[a]
Q fever[a]
Neurosyphillis
Post-St. Louis Type A encephalitis[a]
"Benign" herpes simplex encephalitis
HIV/AIDS

Neoplasm
Parasagittal meningioma[a]
Diencephalic glioma[a]
Suprasellar craniopharyngioma[a]
Suprasellar diencephalic tumor[a]
Benign spheno-occipital tumor[a]
Right-intraventricular meningioma
Right-temporoparietal occipital metastases
Tumor of floor of fourth ventricle

Other conditions
Postisolation syndrome
Right-temporal lobectomy
Posttraumatic confusion
Postelectroconvulsive therapy
Deliriform organic brain disease

[a]Meets criteria of Krauthammer and Klerman (1978) for secondary mania.
Note. From Lazare (1979) and Stasiek and Zetin (1985).

from such disappointments in the father relationship is associated with a profound sense of male inadequacy. The resentment is rarely directed at the father for numerous reasons; instead, these young men overreact in anger at others who are undeserving. Both grandiose thinking and hyperactivity in these men seem to be an unconscious attempt to compensate for their profound sense of male inadequacy.

In many young women with bipolar disorder, a frequently encountered source of irritability and rage is strong, disabling loneliness. This loneliness is associated with strong feelings of sadness that have been denied regularly. These young women present a labile mood alternating between great irritability and euphoria, which is a reaction formation to their underlying loneliness and sadness. They may be angry with men who have hurt them or even at God. Also, it is not unusual to uncover anger arising from childhood and adolescent experiences of loneliness in a parental relationship.

FORGIVENESS IN BIPOLAR CLIENTS

Forgiveness can provide a new method for dealing with angry feelings and can play an important role in helping stabilize the mood of bipolar clients by diminishing their intense irritability or rage. Therapists usually encounter little resistance in these clients regarding the uncovering of their resentment. After their mood has been stabilized, when asked to describe who has disappointed them most in childhood, adolescence, and adulthood, bipolar clients usually are open and cooperative. However, until they have begun to work at forgiving on a regular basis, their anger can sometimes be misdirected at the therapist.

Ben, age 19, had a manic episode during the summer after his second year of college. He was the oldest of 3 children, had been a straight-A high school student, and had enjoyed his first 2 years of college. He was seen in consultation on an inpatient unit during the third week of his psychiatric hospitalization. His mood continued to be labile, alternating between euphoria and depression, and he had not responded well to medications. In addition, he had developed a number of troubling side effects from the antipsychotic drugs.

During the first session, Ben was asked if he could identify anyone who had hurt him over the course of the summer. He responded by crying uncontrollably for a prolonged period of time. He then began cursing his father for the constant ridicule to which he had subjected him during the summer: "My father was always calling me a dumb shit, just because I couldn't do the kind of things he can do with his hands." He added, "I have more brains than he'll ever have." The history revealed that Ben had never felt close to his father but, in time, he came to recognize that his dad was an unhappy and depressed individual, and he came to better understand him.

After forgiveness was explained as a method that could provide freedom from his anger toward his father, Ben quickly committed himself to working at forgiving him. At times, he felt so angry with his father that he had to live with his anger and discuss it at length before continuing the work of forgiveness. After his anger diminished, sessions were held with his father during which Ben was able to express how hurt he had felt in their relationship. Later, he expressed his desire to let go of his resentment toward his father in the hope that their relationship might improve. His moods during these sessions alternated between intense sadness with prolonged periods of crying and strong irritability toward his father. This catharsis with his father helped Ben greatly. Initially defensive, his father was able to apologize, in time, and commit himself to the process of recognizing his son's abilities and learning to encourage rather than belittle him.

The slow resolution of Ben's strong anger with his father over several months resulted in emotional stabilization. This young man spent several years working to understand how hurt his father had been as a boy, trying to resolve his anger toward a sad, overly critical parent. The most difficult aspect of the forgiveness process was to accept the pain of never having the type of father relationship he had hoped for when he was a boy and adolescent. He did, however, feel hopeful that the relationship with his father would improve if they both focused on the opportunities ahead rather than the failure behind.

Demi, introduced at the beginning of the chapter, was an extroverted and warm 26-year-old professional who had had two previous manic episodes that required brief hospitalizations. She recovered quickly and returned to her work after her medication was increased. When her mood was stable, she related that she was rarely angry. During her manic episodes, however, she manifested uncharacteristic hostility and explosive rage. When she was asked at her first session what she thought was the cause of her anger when she was manic, she responded angrily, "I want to get married and have a family, but there doesn't seem to be a decent man out there. In the end everyone I go out with winds up hurting me."

Demi came to recognize that in the past she had been spending a great deal of energy in the attempt to deny her anger. She liked the idea of honestly facing this emotion and trying to resolve it in a manner in which neither she nor others would be harmed. Enthusiastically, she began the work of forgiving the men who had hurt her because, intuitively, she sensed that it would help heal the pain of the past and free her from unnecessary baggage. However, she was not able to accept the loneliness associated with being single. Even though she worked at forgiving, she still periodically hated the pain of loneliness in her life.

Her mood was stable for many months until the approach of mid-November of that year. Then she began to obsess about spending Thanksgiving, Christmas, and New Year's without a special boyfriend whom she could really trust. After Thanksgiving, she suddenly became manic and was hospitalized again. During that time she was surprised to discover within herself a strong anger against God: "Why hasn't God brought the right man into my life? He's done this for many of my friends. What does He have against me? What have I done wrong?"

The expression of this anger was very helpful for her, although at first she was uncomfortable with the notion of thinking of forgiving God. However, Demi had come to realize that this was the most effective method of resolving her anger, and she committed herself to this unusual type of forgiveness, especially when she felt lonely or cheated.

After her hospitalization, Demi returned to work and continued to use forgiveness to help control anger and stabilize her mood. Although she continued to struggle with loneliness for years, she had no depressive episodes. She eventually married, and there have been no further manic episodes for the 5 years of her marriage.

Irritability and excessive anger are major mood disruptions that are common in clients with bipolar disorder. The failure to resolve and control this anger results in marked mood instability and in significant morbidity. Forgiveness is an effective psychotherapeutic practice that therapists can use to assist clients of all ages with bipolar disorder to overcome and to control their strong anger.

IMPULSE CONTROL DISORDERS

According to the *DSM–IV*, the essential feature of impulse control disorders (ICDs) is described as the failure to resist an impulse, drive, or temptation to perform an act that is harmful to the person or to others (American Psychiatric Association, 1994). The individual feels an increasing sense of tension or arousal before committing the act, and then he or she experiences pleasure, gratification, or relief at the time of committing the act. Following the act there may or may not be regret, self-reproach, or guilt. These disorders include intermittent explosive disorder (IED), kleptomania, pyromania, pathological gambling, and trichotillomania (hair pulling). Most of these disorders begin in adolescence or early adult life, except for trichotillomania, which often begins in childhood. All have an episodic or chronic course (American Psychiatric Association, 1994).

McElroy, Hudson, Pope, Keck, and Aizley's (1992) review of ICDs suggests that the phenomenology, family history, and response to treatment indicate that these disorders may be related to mood disorders, substance abuse disorders, and anxiety disorders, especially obsessive–compulsive disorder (OCD). Also, the biological studies indicate that IED and pyromania may share serotonergic abnormalities similar to those reported in mood disorders.

The impulsive behavior is seen by some as a failure of self-soothing mechanisms or as an attempt to relieve a variety of uncomfortable symptoms (Favazza & Rosenthal, 1990; Lacey & Evans, 1986). Lacey and Evans observed that multiple impulsive behaviors are seen in a number of disorders, including substance abuse disorders, eating disorders, self-harm, and personality disorders. They termed these individuals *impulsivists* and suggested that they had multi-impulsive personality disorder.

In our clinical experience, the strongest anger and aggressive impulses in ICDs are seen in IED, kleptomania, and pyromania. Those with these disorders, from early adolescence, tend to harbor aggressive impulses and vengeful thoughts against others. Their hostility is often the result of childhood and adolescent emotional trauma, especially neglect and abuse. Also, many model after a parent or family member with aggressive behaviors. Biological factors, too, may be important in the client's aggressiveness.

Although they may describe the aggressive impulses as irresistible when they emerge, in fact, in our clinical experience, these individuals often look forward to the release of their aggressive impulses. For example, a number of young men anticipate going out and engaging in violent behavior apart from the use of alcohol or drugs. Also, individuals with kleptomania and pyromania often enjoy fantasizing about stealing and setting fires before they actually release their hostile impulses. Many report feeling an emotional high after they perform aggressive and destructive acts. Some, after having been in therapy, become honest and even describe themselves as "anger addicts" because of the repeated pleasure and emotional high they experience from their aggressive deeds.

The degree of anger observed in the majority of clients with trichotillomania and pathological gambling is significant, but usually less than that seen in IED, pyromania, and kleptomania. The majority of clients who pull their hair met the criteria for other mental disorders, particularly anxiety and mood disorders (Schlosser, Black, Blum, & Goldstein, 1994). In one study, 35% of clients with pathological gambling also had another ICD (Specker, Carlson, Christenson, & Marcotte, 1995), and gambling is often comorbid with substance abuse disorder, depression, and sometimes with antisocial personality disorder (Bland, Newman, Orn, & Stebelsky, 1993; Crockford & el-Guebaly, 1998). Most do not have a strong inner desire to hurt others or to rebel against societal norms. However, some clients with trichotillomania have significant unconscious anger against offenders who have hurt them, which they misdirect at themselves. Their actions provide some relief from the tension that arises as a result of harboring strong resentment.

Therapy with clients with IED, kleptomania, or pyromania is challenging but also rewarding. In our clinical experience, there are secondary gains in these individuals that make them highly resistant to changing their impulsive behavior. Some of these gains include false feelings of strength and superiority, enjoyment from getting revenge against individuals and society, greater acceptance by hostile peers, and a distorted sense of loyalty to aggressive and violent family members. Clients with trichotillomania and pathological gambling are much less resistant and more open to admit their anger and begin the work of forgiveness.

Forgiveness can help these clients control their aggressive impulses and vengeful thoughts and resolve the anger with others who betrayed them, especially in childhood and adolescence. Forgiveness also can be a method for dealing with aggressive impulses that has more to offer them than the methods they acquired when young, which have caused serious difficulty and pain in their own lives and in the lives of others.

INTERMITTENT EXPLOSIVE DISORDER

The *DSM–IV* describes IED as discrete episodes of failure to resist aggressive impulses that result in serious assaultive acts or destruction of property (American Psychiatric Association, 1994). The degree of aggressiveness expressed during an episode is grossly out of proportion to any precipitating psychosocial stressor. In one study of IED clients, the childhood histories revealed high frequencies of problematic temper tantrums, impaired attention, hyperactivity, and other behavioral difficulties, such as stealing and fire setting (McElroy, Soutullo, Beckman, Taylor, & Keck, 1998). Also, 56% of the participants in this study had first-degree relatives with an ICD and 32% had a first-degree relative with probable IED.

In McElroy et al.'s (1998) study of IED in 27 participants, 88% experienced tension with their impulses, 75% felt relief from their aggressive acts, and 48% experienced pleasure with these acts. Ninety-three percent had a lifetime *DSM–IV* diagnosis of mood disorders, 48% substance abuse disorders, 48% anxiety disorders, 22% eating disorders, and 44% other ICDs other than IED. Finally, 60% receiving therapy with an antidepressant or mood stabilizer reported a moderate or marked reduction of their aggressive impulses, episodes, or both.

A major focus of therapy is to motivate the person to want to learn to control their aggressive impulses and to change behavioral patterns that harm others and the self. In our clinical experience, many have no interest in changing because of the secondary gain from the release of anger. For those willing to try controlling their aggression, the release of inner rage begins by incorporating some physical activity, such as hitting a punching bag. While hitting the bag, the person is encouraged to reflect, "I want to let go of my inner aggression and rage without harming others," "I want to let go of my rage and not seek revenge against others," "I don't want to hurt others as I was hurt when I was young," "I want to stop relying on my hatred as a source of strength," or "I don't want to continue to be as aggressive as my father was or peers are."

This exercise is followed by a cognitive decision to try letting go of impulses for revenge. As understanding the offenders deepens, they are encouraged to consider forgiveness. This step can be difficult if they were neglected or abused as children. However, if they persevere, even though they may not feel like forgiving, relief from aggressive and vengeful impulses slowly begins to occur. The ability to control their aggressive symptoms usually requires many years of therapy and is marked by periodic relapses into aggression. The most difficult aspect of the treatment of men with IED is that of strengthening their self-esteem so that they do not need to rely on anger and aggression as a source of strength.

Those with trichotillomania and pathological gambling usually are receptive to learning how to forgive. They report that diminishing anger does help with their impulse control and with comorbid mood disorders.

TOURETTE'S SYNDROME

In Tourette's syndrome, both multiple motor and one or more vocal tics are present at some time during the illness. The tics occur many times a day nearly every day or intermittently throughout a period of more than 1 year and during which time there was never a tic-free period of more than 3 consecutive months. The disturbance causes marked distress or significant impairment in social, occupational, or other important areas of functioning, and the onset is before age 18. The tics typically involve the head and other parts of the torso and upper and lower limbs. The disorder is 1.5 to 3 times more common in male clients, and the duration is usually lifelong, although long periods of remission may occur.

Episodic rage attacks with symptoms of sudden, uncontrollable, and explosive anger, irritability, temper tantrums, and aggression have been estimated to occur in 30% of clients with Tourette's syndrome (Comings & Comings, 1988; Wand, Matazow, & Shady, 1993). These rage symptoms are atypical of baseline character and have been reported to resemble what has been described in the adult neurologic literature as "episodic dyscontrol" (Elliot, 1984). They also resemble IED. The symptoms may occur spontaneously but more often appear as a response to seemingly trivial frustration or intrusion. The victim of the rage attack is often the child's mother, although the person can be someone outside the home. These episodic rages are a leading cause for psychiatric consultation for clients with Tourette's syndrome at one center (Bruun & Budman, 1998). The episodes present major problems in the patients' lives and are significantly diminished by the use of the SSRI Paroxetine (Bruun, Budman, Olson, & Park, 1998).

It has been estimated that OCD occurs in approximately 50% of clients with Tourette's syndrome (Singer & Walkup, 1991), and ADHD occurs in approximately 40–60% of those with Tourette's syndrome (Comings & Comings, 1988; Peterson, 1996; Singer & Walkup, 1991). In Budman, Bruun, Park, and Olson's (1998) study, all of the children with Tourette's syndrome and rage met the diagnostic criteria for both ADHD and OCD, and one third were diagnosed with a comorbid conduct disorder.

The cause of the rage in Tourette's syndrome is not clear and may be related to both psychological and biological factors. Budman et al. (1998) showed that the presence of comorbid disorders are correlated with increased incidence of rage attacks. In the chapter on child and adolescent disorders, difficulties with excessive anger in the comorbid disorders of ADHD, OCD, and other anxiety disorders are presented.

In our clinical work with clients with Tourette's syndrome, we have found that the tics in some young children relate to the presence of signifi-cance anxieties and fears, often as a result of conflict in the parental relation-ship, neglect by a parent, or fear of separation from a parent, particularly the father. As in the treatment of children with ADHD, these children, too, initially are reluctant to admit anger with a parent. After anger has been explained as a natural response to hurt and disappointment, their sense of shame and guilt decreases, and they become more comfortable accepting their anger. Inquiring about the fantasy lives of these children is important because it often reveals aggressive fantasies that can be interpreted.

In addition to anger with parents, some children with noticeable motor tics discover strong feelings of resentment with peers who have rejected them or even ridiculed them because of their motor or vocal tics. Painful isolation experienced by these children can give rise to aggressive fantasies and impulses against peers that can then be misdirected into the home, especially toward the mother or siblings. Children who are scapegoats of their peers rarely inform their parents of these painful experiences, therefore, it is important for parents to consider this, especially if the child is manifest-ing intense anger and rage for which there is no apparent cause.

In the treatment of the intense anger and explosive rage in some of these children, the approach we take is similar to that used in the treatment of anger in other childhood disorders. After the anger has been uncovered, often with the assistance of the parents, both child and parents are informed about the nature of anger and the three basic mechanisms for coping with this powerful emotion: denial, expression, and forgiveness. Then the benefits of using forgiveness are conveyed, and the client is encouraged to consider using it for the resentment associated with hurts from a parent, peer, or sibling. Parents are asked to monitor the child's anger and to encourage the use of this method for coping with excessive anger on a regular basis.

Specifically, when the parent sees the child as filled with strong anger, he or she might suggest, "Let's try to understand why you are angry and who you are angry with so that you don't misdirect the anger into the home when we don't deserve it," and "Now let's try to understand the person you're upset with and, hopefully, try to let go of the anger by forgiving him or her." If a parent learns that the child is angry as a result of rejection by peers at school or because of an absent or neglectful parent, it is important for a parent to tell the child, "We don't deserve your anger and hostility. You are angry with X or Y and need to work at understanding and forgiving him/her."

In conjunction with medication when working at regularly forgiving an identified offender, a diminishment in the degree of aggressive anger usually occurs after several months of treatment. However, if the child is subjected to ongoing peer rejection or ridicule as a result of motor or vocal tics, the resolution of the aggressive impulses is much more challenging and can require years of therapy. A child who experiences constant peer rejection or ridicule may have aggressive and violent fantasies against the offender on a regular basis. These young people can spend long periods of time engaged in such fantasies, watching violent movies or listening to music that extols violence and vengeful actions.

The diminishment of aggressive fantasies and impulses occurs in some children who have spirituality in their family background through reflecting on the fact that revenge belongs to God and that God can aid in the forgiving. A major obstacle to resolving the aggression in these clients (which is similar to that of children with conduct disorder and oppositional defiant disorder and adults with borderline personality disorder, antisocial personality disorder, and IED) is that they derive pleasure from their episodes of rage. Although medication can diminish the episodes of rage and is invaluable in the treatment of clients with Tourette's syndrome it does not resolve the significant impulses for revenge.

TOWARD THE FUTURE

McElroy et al. (1998) recommended further research to clarify the relationships among IED, rage outbursts in general, mood disorders, other Axis I and various Axis II disorders. The rage episodes in Tourette's syndrome are similar to those seen in IED. The management of the excessive anger in these disorders is essential for both the emotional well-being of the individual and for the good of society. Forgiveness studies have not yet been empirically evaluated in treatment of these disorders. However, on the basis of successful clinical experiences, there is a strong possibility that forgiveness will be demonstrated as an effective method for dealing with the aggressive feelings and behaviors in ICDs and in Tourette's syndrome.

14

FORGIVENESS IN PERSONALITY DISORDERS

Louise, a married 40-year-old mother of one child, has been in therapy for 15 years for the treatment of anxiety, depression, unstable interpersonal relationships, intense fears and mistrust of others, poor sense of self, and frequent anger attacks. She had been sexually abused repeatedly in her latency years by an uncle and also had been physically and emotionally abused by an older brother. She had never felt the emotional support of either of her parents, who divorced during her adolescence. Her difficult and demanding therapy is related in this chapter.

We also present the role and prevalence of anger in Cluster A, B, and C personality disorders (PDs). In these disorders, difficulties with excessive anger have been well documented both in research studies and in clinical experience. The lengthy and challenging process of helping clients with PDs to resolve and control their angry feelings, impulses, and ideation, which lead to significant stress and impairment, is developed in this chapter. The effectiveness of psychotherapy for PDs has been demonstrated (Perry, Banon, & Ianni, 1999), and the use of forgiveness can enhance the treatment of these clients. The use of the four phases of forgiveness therapy in the treatment of patients with these disorders are described.

Many clients with PD have conflicts with poor impulse control, episodes of aggressive behavior, and anger attacks (Fava, Rosenbaum, et al., 1993; Gould et al., 1996; Kernberg, 1992; Millon, 1996), especially those within cluster B (borderline, histrionic, antisocial, and narcissistic) and Cluster C (avoidant, dependent, and obsessive–compulsive). See Exhibit 14.1. However, Cluster A personality disorders are also, at times, associated with acts of strong resentment and violent impulses and behaviors. The difficulty with self- and other-directed impulsive aggression in clients with schizotypal and paranoid PD, borderline and histrionic PD, obsessive–compulsive PD, avoidant PD, and antisocial PD has been attributed to reduced central serotonergic function (Coccaro et al., 1989). Selective serotonin reuptake inhibitors (SSRIs) and other medications have been shown to reduce the impulsive aggressive behaviors seen in clients in all three personality disorder clusters (Coccaro, Astill, Herbert, & Schut, 1990; Coccaro & Kavoussi, 1997); Kavoussi & Coccaro, 1998; Kavoussi, Liu, & Coccaro, 1994; Markovitz, Calabrese, Schulz, & Meltzer, 1991).

Several studies have examined comorbidity between PDs and Axis I disorders. Oldham et al. (1995) reported that mood disorders co-occurred

EXHIBIT 14.1
Personality Disorder Definitions

Cluster A

Paranoid personality disorder is a pattern of distrust and suspiciousness such that others' motives are interpreted as malevolent.

Schizoid personality disorder is a pattern of detachment from social relationships and a restricted range of emotional expression.

Schizotypal personality disorder is a pattern of acute discomfort in close relationships, cognitive or perceptual distortions, and eccentricities of behavior.

Cluster B

Antisocial personality disorder is a pattern of disregard for, and violation of, the rights of others.

Borderline personality disorder is a pattern of instability in interpersonal relationships, self-image, and affects and of marked impulsivity.

Histrionic personality disorder is a pattern of excessive emotionality and attention seeking.

Narcissistic personality disorder is a pattern of grandiosity, need for admiration, and lack of empathy.

Cluster C

Avoidant personality disorder is a pattern of social inhibition, feelings of inadequacy, and hypersensitivity to negative evaluation.

Dependent personality disorder is a pattern of submissive and clinging behavior related to an excessive need to be taken care of.

Obsessive–compulsive disorder is a pattern of preoccupation with orderliness, perfectionism, and control.

---

significantly with avoidant PD and anxiety disorders co-occur with border-line PD and dependent PD. Substance abuse disorders co-occur with border-line and histrionic PDs. Eating disorders co-occur significantly with PDs in all three clusters (schizotypal, borderline, and avoidant). Unipolar affective disorder has been reported to co-occur with borderline, dependent, and avoidant PDs (Jackson et al., 1991). Other research has shown a strong connection between substance abuse and antisocial PD (Koenigsberg, Kaplan, Gilmore, & Cooper, 1985), between restricting anorexia and obses-sive–compulsive PD, and between normal-weight bulimia and histrionic PD (Wonderlich et al., 1990.)

Many PD patients report histories of childhood neglect or abuse. In one study, people with documented childhood abuse or neglect were shown to be more than four times as likely as those who were not abused or neglected to be diagnosed with PD in all clusters during early adulthood (Johnson, Cohen, Brown, Smailes, & Bernstein, 1999). Childhood disrup-tive disorders, anxiety disorders, and major depression increase significantly the odds for the development of a young adult PD (Kasen, Cohen, Skodol, Johnson, & Brook, 1999). Childhood conduct problems are an independent predictor of adolescent PDs in all three clusters (Bernstein, Cohen, Skodal, Bezirganian, & Brook, 1996). Adolescents with PDs have been shown to be more than twice as likely as those without PDs to have disruptive and substance abuse disorders during early adulthood (Johnson, Cohen, Skodol, et al., 1999).

The excessive anger in PD clients manifests itself early in life as conflicts in interpersonal relationships, extreme and inappropriate affecti-vity, impaired cognition with thoughts of revenge, and poor impulse control. In most PD clients, there is significant unresolved anger from childhood and adolescent experiences of parental neglect and abuse, especially in the borderline PD (Zanarini et al., 1997).

In our clinical experience, clients with narcissistic PD and dependent PD regularly overreact in anger and aggressive behaviors when their needs are not met immediately or when they face frustrations and stresses in their lives. In marked contrast to other clients with PD, individuals with these two PDs do not have significant residual resentment from childhood and adolescence that is misdirected later. They manifest little empathy or under-standing for others, resent giving themselves emotionally, and are obsessed with controlling the important people in their lives. The dependent PD individual often seeks to control their loved ones or important others by acting helpless or sick.

In our clinical experience, passive–aggressive anger is frequently seen in histrionic, dependent, narcissistic, and borderline PD clients. This type of anger tends to be difficult to treat in these PD clients for many reasons, some of which were described in the passive–aggressive section in Chapter

11. Passive–aggressive resentment is so prevalent that we believe consideration should be given to reestablishing it as a PD.

The resolution of the anger from past disappointments and hurts resulting from neglect and abuse through the use of forgiveness can be beneficial in stabilizing the impulse control, interpersonal functioning, affectivity, and cognition in these individuals. Because the treatment of Axis I conditions is often complicated by Axis II pathology (Reich & Green, 1990; Reich & Vasile, 1993), the management of the excessive anger in PD clients can assist in the healing of their Axis I disorders.

CLUSTER A PERSONALITY DISORDERS: PARANOID, SCHIZOID, AND SCHIZOTYPAL

The people with Cluster A PDs demonstrate mistrust, detachment, and acute discomfort in close relationships often as a result of betrayal experiences in childhood, adolescence, and adulthood. In our clinical experiences, these clients with paranoid, schizoid, or schizotypal PD can be so mistrustful and defensive that they have great difficulty in admitting their anger, with the exception of the client with paranoid PD. The *DSM–IV* classification describes the client with paranoid PD as someone who bears grudges, that is, is unforgiving of insults, injuries, or slights (American Psychiatric Association, 1994). Millon (1996) described the resentment and hostility in the clients with paranoid PD. Initially clients with schizoid and schizotypal PD do not appear to be angry. However, these individuals often harbor violent impulses for revenge against those who victimized and offended them. Under certain types of stress, these isolated and withdrawn individuals can erupt in intense anger and can commit violent acts of revenge against their tormentors in schools, families, and communities.

Clients with PD have not been noted to demonstrate significant rates of anger attacks; however, their mistrust and shame about their repressed resentment and impulses for revenge may lead these clients to make dishonest responses to subjective evaluative measures. Other methods of evaluating anger are necessary with these clients, including those done by family members and significant others.

Therapists often do not identify anger in the client with schizoid or schizotypal PD as an important clinical issue. However, in our clinical experience it definitely is. Children and adolescents with these personality traits and adults with paranoid PD sometimes harbor aggressive impulses for revenge that can be misdirected with tragic consequences at innocent people. The uncovering of anger in Cluster A clients is challenging because they are so mistrustful and defensive. Role playing as an offender can facilitate this process, as can asking the client to begin forgiving individuals in the past identified by the therapist who neglected or hurt the client.

The use of forgiveness with these clients can assist in the diminishment of their angry or violent impulses against those who have hurt them. The Work Phase, however, is arduous and lengthy. A major obstacle is that their anger is used to distance others. The development of trust first in the therapist and then in others is essential to help these clients learn to control their resentful feelings and angry impulses. Most individuals simply will not work at forgiveness until they feel safer in relationships, which may take a number of years in therapy. However, once trust is established, the majority of Cluster A individuals are willing to use forgiveness and derive benefit from it.

At this stage in the study of anger and forgiveness, a reasonable hypothesis can be made that, in the future, significant degrees of anger will be identified in the clients with schizoid or schizotypal PD.

CLUSTER B PERSONALITY DISORDERS: ANTISOCIAL, BORDERLINE, HISTRIONIC, AND NARCISSISTIC

In our clinical experience, clients with antisocial PD and borderline PD are among the angriest, regularly manifesting great difficulty in the control of their hostile feelings and impulses. Many enjoy striking out in anger at innocent people, including therapists. Initially, individuals with histrionic PD and narcissistic PD may not be viewed as having problems with excessive anger; however, most do. Fava, Rosenbaum, et al. (1993) found that the presence of anger attacks in clients with unipolar depression was associated with higher rates of comorbid Cluster B PDs, in particular borderline PD. Also, borderline PD clients have been shown to manifest more severe anger compared with dysthymic control clients (Snyder & Pitt, 1985), and male clients high in narcissism are likely to express anger physically (McCann & Biaggio, 1989). Clients with histrionic PD often can manifest their anger in a passive–aggressive manner, at times, through eating disorder symptomatology.

Many individuals in Cluster B enjoy their ability to influence and control others with their anger and therefore are often reluctant to deal with this emotion in a healthier manner. Subsequently, there is great resistance in these clients to the use of forgiveness. In our clinical experience, less than 50% in this cluster will even consider the concept of forgiveness. Those who do decide to use forgiveness usually only do so after a major difficulty occurs in their lives, such as the loss of a loved one, serious conflicts in interpersonal relationships, refractory depressive or anxiety disorders, career failures, arrest, imprisonment, or financial problems.

The treatment of the hostile feelings, vengeful thoughts, and aggressive impulses in a person with antisocial PD has been described earlier. In our clinical experience, antisocial PD clients often harbor violent impulses against a parent, most often their father, and others who have hurt them. Unfortunately, they regularly misdirect these impulses. With those who attempt to try forgiveness in therapy, the major factors are the desire to break the emotional control of those who have hurt them and the wish to be freed from the guilt arising from their hostile actions. To date, no double-blind psychotherapy studies have been done on the treatment of anger in antisocial PD.

Individuals with histrionic PD have family backgrounds similar to those with antisocial PD (Spalt, 1980). They lack the ability to handle their anger effectively and are reluctant to admit their hostile feelings. Instead of honestly discussing their hurts and subsequent resentment, they often somatize their difficulties and present themselves as victims. Although they periodically erupt in anger attacks, this usually is not the preferred way for handling their angry feelings.

Once the anger in people with histrionic PD is uncovered, they, more than the clients with antisocial PD, become more willing to attempt the use of forgiveness. In part, this is because they do not depend on their anger to project a strong image or identity as do those with antisocial PD.

The treatment of a client with narcissistic PD is described in chapter 11. Children and adolescents with strong narcissistic PD traits can be extremely disruptive to family and marital life. People with these symptoms at every life stage are reluctant to change and are insensitive, self-centered, and manipulative. When the opportunity presents itself, these clients are encouraged to use forgiveness to control their impulsive angry outbursts.

CLUSTER C PERSONALITY DISORDERS: AVOIDANT, DEPENDENT, AND OBSESSIVE–COMPULSIVE

The anxious and fearful individuals of Cluster C often experience anger attacks. Gould et al. (1996) found that Cluster B, Cluster C, and self-defeating personality traits significantly predicted the presence of anger attacks. In another study, depressed clients with anger attacks had significantly higher rates of dependent, avoidant, narcissistic, borderline, and antisocial PDs compared with depressed clients without anger attacks (Tedlow et al., 1997).

In this cluster, the individual with avoidant PD is most aware of being angry and most honest about admitting struggles with hostile feelings. In our clinical work, we have found that the dependent client with PD often expresses anger in a passive–aggressive manner by avoiding responsibility, by acting helpless, or by embracing the sick role. The perfectionistic thinking, rigidity, and need for control in clients with obsessive–compulsive PD result in strong resistances against anger. These individuals have great difficulty admitting their resentment, and the uncovering process can be lengthy and challenging.

After the anger has been uncovered, most clients with avoidant PD and obsessive–compulsive PD are willing to work at forgiving those who hurt them. However, dependent PD individuals are highly resistant to forgiving because of their belief that if they let go of their resentful feelings, they may have to change, become healthier, and act in a more responsible manner.

FORGIVENESS THERAPY IN BORDERLINE PERSONALITY DISORDER

Clients with borderline personality disorder (BPD) are among the angriest, most unstable, and difficult individuals whom mental health professionals treat. The importance of anger as a central affective feature of BPD has been emphasized in the literature (Gunderson & Singer, 1975; Snyder & Pitt, 1985). Many BPD clients who work in therapy come to attribute their strong resentment and aggressive impulses to childhood and adolescent experiences of neglect and abuse by parents and other caretakers (Zanarini, Gunderson, Marino, Schwartz, & Frankenburg, 1989; Zanarini et al., 1997). Thus far, Wolberg (1973) is the only mental health professional to recommend forgiveness for the anger in clients with BPD.

These individuals who experience an ongoing sense of abandonment, unstable relationships, a weak sense of self, chronic feelings of emptiness and loneliness, and stress-related paranoid ideation are easily angered by stresses that might not provoke others. Then, they often have great difficulty in controlling their hostile feelings, but their anger and aggressive behavior do respond to treatment with antidepressants and other medications (Fava, 1997; Salzman et al., 1995).

BPD is diagnosed predominantly in female clients (about 75%), co-occurs with other PDs, and ranges in prevalence from 30% to 60% among PD clinical populations as reported in DSM–IV. Also, there is an increased familial risk of antisocial PD and substance abuse disorders in these clients.

BPD clients often meet the DSM–IV criteria for a number of common Axis I disorders, particularly major depression and substance abuse. In a study of Axis I comorbidity of BPD (Zanarini et al., 1998), anxiety disorders were almost as common as mood disorders. Also, posttraumatic stress disorder was found to be common but not universal, and men and women were found to differ in that substance abuse disorders were significantly more common among male clients with BPD, whereas eating disorders were significantly more common among female clients. Fifty-three percent of the male clients and 62% of the female clients with BPD had eating disorders. Also, the pattern of complex lifetime Axis I comorbidity evidenced by clients with BPD is a useful marker for the borderline diagnosis. Seventy-five percent of clients with BPD exhibited the pattern for both a disorder of affect and a disorder of impulse. This has a strong sensitivity and specificity for the borderline diagnosis. Zanarini et al. (1998) concluded that a history of several Axis I disorders, particularly if they had an early onset, may have a role in the development of what is commonly seen as borderline psychopathology.

Clients with BPD regularly misdirect anger at their therapists, more so than in any other Axis I or Axis II disorder, especially when they have recently felt hurt again in a relationship, when painful material emerges during therapy, when they want to hurt others as they have been hurt, and when they perceive the therapist does not care or give enough. Not uncommonly, these clients relate to the therapist, "I'm furious with you. Why do you talk to me that way (implying a devaluation of them)? I'd really like to hit you or throw something at you."

In such cases, it is essential for the therapist to label this anger as misdirected, attempt to uncover the true offender, and suggest who actually deserves the anger. Then the client is encouraged to consider the limitations of relying solely on the expression of anger as the major way for dealing with this emotion and to consider to begin the Work Phase of forgiveness. In addition, many clients are encouraged at this stage in therapy to take an SSRI for their strong resentment.

Many clients with BPD who work at forgiveness discover enormous rage with and violent impulses toward parents and significant others as a result of feelings of neglect, abuse, or betrayal from childhood, adolescence, and adulthood. They are often motivated to begin letting go of their deep resentment to extricate themselves from the pain of the past and to help in the treatment of their Axis I disorder or disorders. Diminishing their resentment from childhood and adolescence can assist in stabilizing their mood and can give them a way to control their anger. However, these clients are very fragile and have great difficulty in trusting and, under stress, can quickly relapse, misdirecting strong resentment at therapists and others.

These clients with BPD then are encouraged to continue the work of forgiveness with new offenders. However, some refuse to take the next step, and for a period of time they may blame what they perceive as insensitivity from the therapist for their hostile feelings. In such cases, when anger is misdirected regularly at the therapist, it may be necessary to develop a therapeutic contract in which the client agrees to work on forgiveness daily in relationships indicated by the therapist, if therapy is to continue. At times it is in the client's best interest to be referred to another mental health professional if the client refuses to stop misdirecting anger at the therapist.

The treatment of the anger in the BPD client is one of the most challenging tasks in psychotherapy. The process of assisting these clients in letting go of their violent and vengeful impulses from childhood, adolescence, and adulthood can take many years of treatment. The course of treatment can be stormy. The therapist often needs to be assertive and to set clear limits. The therapist can tell clients with BPD, "I am not your neglectful, insensitive, or abusive parent. I do not deserve your hostility." The response might be, "Yes, you do. You don't really care about me." With such resistance, the therapist might reply, "I cannot allow you to treat me as you were treated by an offender."

Fortunately, the majority of clients with BPD are able to recognize that they are misdirecting their anger and then recommit themselves to the work of forgiveness with those who have hurt them. The most difficult aspects of the work of forgiveness for BPD clients are reframing (e.g., understanding why their parents were neglectful or abusive) and giving up the desire for revenge and associated aggressive impulses. The latter is also a major challenge in the treatment of a number of clients with PD, particularly those with antisocial, schizotypal, or paranoid PD. Initially, clients with BPD are encouraged to make a cognitive decision to abandon the desire for revenge, which will break the emotional control of offenders from the past. As they grow in understanding their offenders, these clients usually experience relief from buried aggressive fantasies and thoughts. However, the diminishment of the powerful anger in these clients can take many years.

Clients with BPD are so fragile that they can misperceive rejection at every turn. At times it can be helpful for the therapist to apologize or ask forgiveness for disappointments, such as not returning a call for several hours or running late in the office. Also, countertransference anger is important to address with BPD clients. Therapists can regularly experience justifiable anger toward clients who misdirect anger at them or who violate boundaries by intruding into the personal life of the therapist in numerous ways, including coming to their homes or communities and contacting the family members. Other common countertransferrance reactions to BPD clients are anxiety, acting out through being late, lack of empathy, or feeling victimized.

Louise, whom we described at the beginning of the chapter, entered therapy at age 25 for treatment of depression, intense fears, and excessive anger outbursts after ending a one-year relationship with her boyfriend Mike. She had been in therapy intermittently since her adolescence for depression and anxiety. Her history revealed repeated experiences of emotional neglect and sexual and physical abuse from her childhood. She had struggled with profound feelings of worthlessness, emptiness, sadness, suspiciousness, mistrust, and intense anger.

Louise initially was angry with Mike and with her uncle, who had sexually abused her. Later in her therapy deep resentment emerged toward her older brother and her parents. Louise was troubled by her anger, yet believed that it was fully justified. She was interested in exploring forgiveness as a new method for dealing with her anger because she was not comfortable with the approach recommended by her previous therapists of releasing anger primarily through expression. This method of handling her anger had resulted in her feeling frustrated, guilty, and somewhat frightened of the depth and power of her inner rage.

Louise was asked initially to try to think of understanding and of forgiving Mike. She was aware of his weaknesses, which helped her begin this work of forgiveness and experience some initial relief from the pain in that relationship. She then began to think of other men who had hurt her in her life, including her uncle, brother, and father, and as a result began to feel more depressed and angry.

After she complained of feeling completely empty and mistrustful of others, she began to direct anger toward the therapist. At the end of sessions she complained of not being helped enough and was reluctant to leave the office. Louise was asked to consider that she might be misdirecting anger at the therapist meant specifically for Mike, her brother, her uncle, and her father. At times she could consider this, but not always. She would then be asked to consider thinking of wanting to let go of her justified resentment.

Louise often responded, "I have been hurt so deeply I really can't forgive them even though I know it might help me." Because she recently had developed religious beliefs, she was comfortable thinking that she was powerless over her justifiable resentment and wanted to turn that feeling over to God. This method of handling the rage arising from her repeated experiences of neglect and abuse proved to be invaluable in her treatment.

The work of forgiveness with her brother, uncle, and father went on for years. She felt emotional relief from the slow resolution of this justifiable resentment. However, anger attacks were not uncommon both in her personal relationships and in her therapy sessions. In an attempt to deal with her pain with her brother she was assertive with him. Unfortunately, he would not admit his past emotional abuse. However, at this time she met Kent, the man she would marry, and the comfort in that relationship helped her cope with the sadness and anger toward her brother.

Her deep resentment toward her mother for not protecting her from the sexual abuse of her uncle and the emotional abuse and neglect of her brother and father emerged regularly over the course of many years of treatment. Her mother was able to apologize to Louise. She related that she had been very depressed in her marriage and had difficulty in giving to others.

Louise had difficulty in trusting Kent. As she attempted to grow in her trust in him, periodically painful memories of hurts from her childhood and adolescence would emerge, which would make her fearful of being hurt further. She would attempt to forgive those who had hurt her as a way of diminishing the influence of the emotional pain from the past.

The development of trust in Kent occurred slowly. Under stress in their relationship she would become very suspicious and fearful. Louise would overreact in anger, but as her trust improved, her irritability lessened. In therapy she would often relate, "I've never been able to trust anyone in my family. They all betrayed me. Won't Kent let me down also?"

The use of forgiveness in her therapy helped Louise resolve the intense anger from her past, facilitated her growth in trust, enhanced her self-esteem, helped her control her anger, and improved her ability to hope.

TOWARD THE FUTURE

Research is needed to clarify the origins of excessive anger in clients with PD associated with Axis I disorders. Fava and Rosenbaum (1997) observed that increased rates of comorbid PD diagnoses in depressed clients with anger attacks suggest that these clients' behavior and attitudes may bias the clinician to view the attacks as secondary to PD, as opposed to a unipolar depressive disorder. However, Gould et al.'s (1996) findings support the hypothesis that anger attacks are associated PD traits. In their study, they found that self-defeating traits were the best predictors of anger attacks.

There has been little research into the treatment of antisocial PD and almost no funding for such work (Black & Larson, 1999). This oversight should be corrected and future research should be directed at those with antisocial PD, given the serious problems of crime and of a high prison population in the United States. Also, Black and Larson (1999) recommended that prevention efforts should target those at greatest risk for antisocial PD, namely, children with conduct disorders. Forgiveness research in clients with antisocial PD in the criminal justice system has begun recently (Chapman & Maier, 2000).

Forgiveness holds many benefits for clients with personality disorders. The resolution of their strong anger from different life stages and their impulses for revenge against offenders can stabilize their mood, improve interpersonal relationships, enable them to gain control over their angry feelings and impulses, diminish their impulsive and self-destructive behaviors, and assist in the healing of their Axis I disorders.

III

PHILOSOPHICAL FOUNDATIONS AND EMPIRICAL INVESTIGATIONS

15

MORAL, PHILOSOPHICAL, AND RELIGIOUS ROOTS OF FORGIVENESS

The academics in particular reading this book will need to delve more deeply into the meaning of forgiveness because the concept is richer and deeper than we have portrayed to this point. If you research the topic, you owe it to yourself to avoid superficial operationalizations of the construct. Deeper understanding will translate into sounder and more meaningful research. Clinicians, too, owe it to their clients to know the many facets of forgiveness so that, as a client or patient becomes more reflective on the topic, the therapist will be a few steps ahead, aiding the client's learning.

We begin with some refinements from our definition, presented in chapters 1 and 2, focusing primarily on forgiveness as a moral virtue. We then present ancient views and modern philosophical ideas that bolster our definition of forgiveness.

REFINEMENTS IN OUR DEFINITION FROM PHILOSOPHY: IS FORGIVENESS A MORAL VIRTUE?

The study of moral virtue has had a robust discussion since the publication of Alister MacIntyre's (1984) and Yves Simon's (1986) work. Both draw on Aristotle's analysis of what constitutes a virtue. We present Simon's interpretation of Aristotle's definition to ascertain whether forgiveness qualifies as a virtue. We address eight points on the matter.

1. *Virtue as goodness.* Because moral virtues are centered on character, they are concerned with goodness. As we have seen, the focus of forgiveness is on the overarching principle of beneficence with corollary principles of unconditional worth and moral love. Also included in the definition of forgiveness are the moral emotions of compassion and the expression of generosity. All of these qualities, properly understood and practiced, are concerned with human welfare and, therefore, qualify as good.

2. *Virtue as inclination.* In possessing character or in practicing a virtue, the person wants to do good; there is an inclination to be forgiving. The person must want to and be motivated to forgive. In other words, one does not forgive just because his or her parents (or therapist) advocate it.

3. *A virtuous person understands what he or she is doing.* One who forgives from a moral position understands forgiveness as moral or good. The person must have some sense of what he or she wants. This should be determined by a "rational principle": Why do I think it is good to forgive?[1] This does not necessarily mean that the forgiver holds to a conscious statement about such principles, as a moral philosopher might, but there is some sense of awareness of the moral goodness involved in forgiveness.

4. *A virtuous person practices the virtue.* One is said to possess character or to be demonstrating a virtue when he or she is practicing this quality. A forgiver forgives. Yet, it is not so simple that a forgiver always forgives in the same way, with the same effort, and with the same swiftness. The situation and person one faces determine the quality of the forgiving at any given time.

5. *A virtuous person need not be perfect in the expression of the virtue.* One who practices a virtue rarely does so with perfection. It takes time to be transformed, to perfect the quality of the virtue. One may be a better forgiver at age 60 than at age 40 if the virtue is embraced and practiced regularly.

6. *Different people demonstrate different degrees of the virtue.* There are varying degrees of any virtue that different people possess. We know that forgiveness is not an all-or-none phenomenon based on our studies with the Enright Forgiveness Inventory

---

[1] See Simon (1986, p. 105).

(see chapter 19). In other words, expect individual differences in forgiveness.

7. *A genuine expression of a virtue avoids extremes.* The genuine practice of virtues is expressed within what Aristotle calls a mean, not underrepresented or overrepresented to the point of distortion. For example, a forgiver does not just wave passively at the idea of giving up resentment (a negative extreme) or embrace the notion of living with a physically abusing person at all costs in the name of forgiveness (an extreme that may go beyond the positive pole of forgiveness).

8. *A virtuous person tries to be consistent.* A person who genuinely practices the virtue strives for consistency within similar situations. If one forgives a brother for being an hour late to the scheduled meeting, then one strives to forgive the stranger who was similarly late. Of course, even though one tries to forgive people in a similar way in very different situations, one may not be successful. For example, forgiving a tardy brother may be quite different from forgiving a parent who was continually abusive for many years.

Summary and Problems Created

It appears that forgiveness fits within the criteria of a moral virtue. Forgiveness can be unambiguously placed within each of the above eight criteria without contradiction. Nevertheless, we now have two problems. If forgiveness is a virtue and if virtues are good to be expressed, is it not the case that we have now created the idea that forgiveness is a duty? If so, then all who are unfairly treated must forgive if they are to maintain their status as moral people. The notion that forgiveness is the choice of the forgiver has vanished.

We have two responses to this problem. First, it is possible to place certain virtues under the status of supererogatory. By this we mean that they are good, but at the same time go beyond duty or obligation. Charity to the poor might be an example here. If one must decide whether to give $5 to the poor or to use that money to feed his or her family, it cannot be said that the lack of charity is immoral. The particular expression of charity is supererogatory. Forgiveness has this same quality. Although it is a moral good when someone properly expresses forgiveness, it is not immoral to withhold it in many cases. The would-be-forgiver may be too angry or fearful at present to entertain the thought of forgiveness. In other words, it is possible to retain the idea of choice and the idea of morality together for certain virtues. Of course, some people who see forgiveness as a morally principled decision will hold themselves to forgiveness-as-obligation, without necessarily insisting that all must forgive.

Our second problem is in making aretaic judgments (see Lapsley, 1996, p. 46). An *aretaic judgment* is a way of forming opinions about people on the basis of their character. If we as therapists are not careful, we may become judgmental of people as we give them forgiveness scales or watch them as they refuse to forgive. All psychological applications of the moral virtues are vulnerable to such judgments, which, of course, contradict one of the major tenets of psychotherapy—do not judge the client. Although such judgments are always lurking in the background, we believe that they are avoided and rationally eliminated when we have recourse to the vitally important idea that forgiveness is supererogatory and always the choice of the one offended.

New Concept Created

If forgiveness is the expression of a moral virtue and if that expression is good, then the psychological view of forgiveness changes. We mentioned earlier that forgiveness has the combined attributes of a skill, coping strategy, and commitment, but now we must deepen our understanding. If the practice of a moral virtue says something about one's character, then forgiveness, at least in part, is a quality somehow connected to oneself. In psychological terms, the act of forgiving eventually may form a part of the person's identity as he or she practices forgiveness, knows it is good, and realizes that forgiveness is not some quality that exists independently of the self or even outside the self but is part of who one is. At this point, forgiveness ceases to be only an act that one performs and becomes part of the moral self (see Lapsley, 1996, on the psychology of the moral self). If this is true, then forgiveness therapy, at least in part, is the deliberate attempt to transform character and identity in the client by expressing goodness toward an offending person (or people).

FURTHER REFINEMENTS IN OUR DEFINITION BASED ON PHILOSOPHY

We add four other ideas about forgiveness as derived from philosophy.

1. *Secondary forgiveness is possible.* Marietta Jaeger forgave the murderer of her daughter (Jaeger, 1998). Because Jaeger was not the one physically injured, does she have the right to forgive? Brakenhielm (1993) made the distinction between anonymous and personal forgiveness within the context of

forgiving someone who did not directly hurt you. In *anonymous forgiveness*, the person forgives someone who did not hurt the one forgiving or a loved one. For example, a person in Wyoming hears on television of a murder in Florida and forgives the murderer. In *personal forgiveness*, the person forgives someone who hurt a loved one, as in Jaeger's case. Although she cannot forgive on behalf of her daughter because, after all, this is her daughter's business, Jaeger can forgive because of the direct pain that the killer caused her as the mother of the victim. To Brakenhielm, there is a certain intimate quality to forgiveness that makes room for a loved one's secondary experience and subsequent pain.[2]

2. *Exceptions to supererogation.* There are two exceptions to the idea that forgiveness is supererogatory. First, some religions see forgiveness of other people as a duty. For example, Landman (1941) and Shapiro (1978) claimed that forgiveness is mandatory for Jewish believers under certain circumstances, especially when a fellow believer repents and asks for forgiveness. Some Christian denominations see forgiveness as a moral duty once a more complete understanding of the interplay between divine and human forgiveness is understood (see the gospel of Matthew 18:21–22; Vine, 1985, p. 251). Even here, the idea of free will plays a part, as the person chooses to obey or not.

Second, there is something churlish about Shakespeare's Shylock as he continually seeks his pound of flesh, especially if he never extends mercy. In a modern-day example, suppose Agnes is sorrowful for stealing $5 from Ray. She replaces the funds, with interest, and quietly awaits his forgiveness. She has asked, almost begged, for forgiveness on at least 10 occasions. After 3 years, he is unresponsive and cold toward her. There may be a sense of Ray operating outside the Aristotelian doctrine of the mean here, showing an extreme form of resentment without a balance of understanding and compassion.

We must further remember that a person who will not forgive may decide later that forgiveness now is appropriate. According to Simon (1986), people are usually influenced by "practical wisdom," a quality that helps them know when to

---

[2] For further discussion on Brakenhielm's ideas, see Enright (1997). In some cases, we can see where anonymous forgiveness is appropriate. For example, if a dictator in a distant land withholds food from a starving community, a person reading about this may become resentful and forgive.

go ahead with the practice of forgiveness. The more practice, the more practical wisdom is developed.[3]

3. *The offender need not apologize.* Although some disagree with this, such as Adams (1989), we claim that forgiveness can be unconditional primarily because it is one person's individual choice to be moral to another. There is nothing in any environment that can prevent one from giving a gift to another if one so desires. Also, holding to the view that forgiveness is conditional on another's apology (or related response) might make some clients suffer twice: once from the offending act and again because he or she is not free to begin forgiveness therapy, or perhaps to continue it, until an interloper apologizes. For a discussion of the unconditionality of forgiveness, see Holmgren (1993).

4. *The offender need not have intended the wrong.* We base this concept on Downie (1965), and we say this because, in our experience, many people did not intend to hurt someone else by their actions.[4] In our clinical experience, this is the case especially within marriages and families. If Fred, who is not paying attention while driving, slams into Frieda's car and this accident results in her breaking her leg, it seems unfair to now say that she cannot forgive him. Given our definition that a forgiver rationally determines wrongdoing, if Frieda decides that Fred should have been paying more attention, despite his plea that he "just made a mistake," it is Frieda's call about whether to forgive him.

IN DEFENSE OF OUR DEFINITION: ANCIENT VIEWS

Literature from the ancient world, especially from Hebrew, Christian, Islamic, Hindu, and Buddhist viewpoints, illustrates that forgiveness occurs within the context of moral right and wrong, involving reduced resentment and increased compassion and moral love, culminating in transformation.

Moral Right and Wrong

The monotheistic traditions of Hebrew/Jewish, Christian, and Islamic faiths unambiguously connect forgiveness from God with human wrong or

---

[3]See Simon (1986, p. 106).
[4]O'Shaughnessy (1967) and Murphy (1982) disagree with us on this point.

sin. In fact, forgiveness is one specific response by a holy God to reestablish harmonious relations with the people who have done wrong. In the Hebrew Bible, the word *salah* (appearing 46 times) refers to God removing sin from the people (Vine, 1985). In ancient Hebrew culture, a complex system of animal sacrifice accompanied people's repentance as atonements for sin (see the book of Leviticus in the Hebrew Bible). As people experienced mercy from God, they, too, were to show mercy (Newman, 1987; Shapiro, 1978).

The primary ancient Greek word for forgiveness in the Christian Bible is *aphiemi* (appearing 22 times), meaning that God removes sin and reestablishes unity with the people following their repentance and acceptance of Christ's saving act of redemption. As in the Hebrew writings, a forgiven Christian was expected to forgive others (see Matthew 18:21–22).

In the Koran, Islam's primary book of instruction, Allah is seen as "all-pardoning, all-forgiving" (from Williams's 1961, p. 50, translation of the Koran). This beneficent state occurs if the believer has faith, repents, and then does good works. In contrast to the Hebrew and Christian systems, no blood sacrifice is necessary to show the abomination of sin in Islam. As in the other two traditions, a Muslim believer is to follow Allah's expression of morality (see Williams, 1961).

The Bhagavad Gita, an instructional book for Hindus, discusses the importance of forgiving within the context of right and wrong. For example, when counseling people following war—a clear example of fighting against wrong—the Bhagavad Gita suggests that it is good to forgive under certain (unspecified) circumstances (Prabhup-āda, 1984, p. 528).

Buddhism, a philosophical system that does not have a word specifically translated as "to forgive," illustrates the virtue of compassion within stories. For example, in one such story, a Buddhist is caught instructing the king's harem on the fine points of philosophy. The enraged king binds and whips the ascetic, who, even near death, displays no anger but instead wishes the king well (Tachibana, 1926, p. 136). Although Buddhists would not ascribe wrong, but rather ignorance, to the king, it is important to note that the kinds of stories appearing in Buddhism are not dissimilar to those in other traditions in which cruelty precedes forgiving and compassion. We should also note that forgiveness is not a word foreign to Buddhists. Loving-kindness is a Buddhist term that often encompasses forgiveness. While in the United States giving a series of lectures following his receipt of the Nobel Peace Prize in 1989, the Dalai Lama referred consistently to the importance of forgiveness. See, as one example, *The Chicago Tribune*, October 13, 1989, section C, p. 10, in which he called for conferences of "educators and other concerned people to come together to discuss peace, love, and forgiveness."

Reduced Resentment and Increased Beneficence

When the ancient traditions illustrated forgiveness in stories, they invariably included examples of the forgiver abandoning resentment and offering beneficence in its place. Consider the classic story from the Hebrew Bible in which Joseph forgave his brothers (Genesis 37–45). Jealous of his favored status in the family, his brothers sold Joseph into Egyptian slavery. When they all met years later, the brothers did not recognize Joseph, who certainly recognized them. Joseph at first struggled with his anger, holding some of his brothers captive when they visited Egypt in the hope of finding relief from famine. Eventually, he broke down in tears of compassion, hugging his brothers and helping them obtain food. Abandoning resentment was only half of the result.[5]

The story of the Prodigal Son in the Christian Bible is similar. A father, abandoned by his younger son, expresses unconditional love for him on seeing him from a distance returning home. Love and kindness accompanied forgiveness. In the Buddhist story of the ascetic above, the ascetic showed loving-kindness for the king even as he lay dying from the king's torture.

The Interconnectedness of Thoughts, Feelings, and Behaviors

The Hebrew and Christian Bibles show the interplay among the various human responses that constitute forgiveness. Consider a passage from Deuteronomy 6:5. There the Hebrew nation is counseled to love God "with all your heart, and with all your soul, and with all your might." The heart was the seat of emotions, the soul of wisdom, and the might of one's behaviors. Also consider a parallel passage in Mark 12:30, in which the Christian is counseled to love God "with all your heart, and with all your soul, and with all your mind, and with all your strength." The ancient writers were not as quick to carve up the person into psychologically distinct parts as we are today. In both traditions, the love expressed to God extended to people as well (Leviticus 19:18; Mark 12:31).

Transformation

Joseph experienced the transformation of anger with his brothers into love for them and estrangement in relationships to renewed affection. The father of the Prodigal Son experienced a similarly renewed relationship

---

[5] It is interesting to note that Joseph forgave unconditionally, without repentance or apology from his brothers. In the story, the brothers' one expression of remorse came because they got caught, not because they so wronged their brother years before.

260   *HELPING CLIENTS FORGIVE*

with his son. The Buddhist ascetic, while not encountering a transformed relationship with the king, did experience transcendence of anger in which he had no bitter feelings.

IN DEFENSE OF OUR DEFINITION: MODERN PHILOSOPHICAL VIEWS

Modern philosophy rarely has consensus about moral issues. Nonetheless, there is considerable agreement by a number of modern philosophers regarding the nature of forgiveness. Consider a number of philosophers' statements in Exhibit 15.1. As we have seen in our own definition and in North's (1987), forgiveness includes the abandonment of resentment and the application of beneficence. Downie (1965), too, equated forgiving with the principle of beneficence, especially as it is expressed in moral love. The relational quality of forgiving is seen in both North's and Downie's views.

Twambley (1976), Hughes (1975), and M. Lewis (1980) emphasized the dual qualities of abandoned "hostility" and resentment while adopting "equality," "friendlier attitudes," and moral love toward a wrongdoer. The principle of beneficence, again expressed in moral love, appears in the philosophy of Kolnai (1973–1974). Richards's (1988) main point is that one cannot restrict the negative emotions only to resentment; there are many other ways of expressing displeasure toward an offender. Holmgren (1993), while agreeing that forgiveness involves the beneficent emotion of compassion, introduced the important idea of unconditional respect for a wrongdoer, not because of the hurtful act, but because he or she is a person and all people are capable of, or have the potential for, goodwill. Thus, forgivers can unconditionally respect offenders. Note further Holmgren's emphasis on "intrinsic value," which is the same idea that we label as "intrinsic worth" in our definition.[6]

Finally, Yandell (1998), as all the others do in Exhibit 15.1, places forgiveness within a moral context. He took the additional and unique position that the process of forgiveness can, at times, occur spontaneously. There is a reported case that supports this idea (Ten Boom, Sherrill, & Sherrill, 1971).

Clinicians may be wondering at this point about the relevance of the depth to which we have gone in explaining the moral dimension of forgiveness and also whether their client needs to forge his or her understanding

---

[6] Holmgren's (1993) idea of "intrinsic value" was derived from a Kantian analysis of forgiveness and persons. Ours was derived from a Piagetian cognitive analysis of forgiveness and persons (Enright & the Human Development Study Group, 1994). Our analyses were performed independently with the same conclusion.

EXHIBIT 15.1
Philosophers' Statements About Interpersonal Forgiveness

North (1987)

If we are to forgive, our resentment is to be overcome not by denying ourselves the right to that resentment, but by endeavouring to view the wrongdoer with compassion, benevolence and love while recognizing that he has willfully abandoned his right to them. (p. 502)

Downie (1965)

An injury involves the severing of the relationship of *agape*, and forgiveness its restoration. . . . *Agape* involves the treatment of other people not just as sentient beings but as beings who are rational and able to obey moral rules and pursue moral values just as the forgiver himself can. The forgiver is required to prevent any barrier remaining permanently between him and the forgivee (at least on his side . . .) and to renew trust in him. (p. 133)

Hughes (1975)

Forgiveness is the cancellation of deserved hostility and the substitution of friendlier attitudes. It has important consequences for which it is highly valued—socially, in that the offender can hold up his head again, and inwardly, in the quietening of remorse (p. 113)

Twambley (1976)

You are within your rights to resent his action. In forgiving him, you relinquish that right, you adjust your relationship to one of equality. [Forgiveness has a gift-like quality]. (p. 9)

Lewis (1980)

[Drawing on Kierkegaard's ideas, Lewis stated that] forgiveness cannot be understood without explicit reference to the commandment "you shall love. . . ." It means a consent to renounce one's own attitudes, one's own desires for revenge and retaliation, the pain of indignity and feelings of resentment. (pp. 242–243)

Kolnai (1973–1974)

[T]he more virtuous I am the more *disposed* I am to forgive. This is so simply because forgiving is an exquisite act of charity or benevolence in a meaningful context. . . . (p. 104)

Richards (1988)

To forgive someone for having wronged one is to abandon all negative feelings toward this person, of whatever kind, insofar as such feelings are based on the episode in question. (p. 79)

Holmgren (1993)

[T]he victim's forgiveness brings valuable understanding, acceptance and compassion to the offender. (p. 345)

The person who reaches a state of genuine forgiveness determines that regardless of whether she repents, the wrongdoer is a valuable human being who has made a mistake and done wrong. (p. 348)

Further, the appropriate attitude to adopt towards persons in light of their intrinsic value is respect. (p. 349)

Yandell (1998)

Forgiveness is a morally significant process that occurs between persons. This is not to deny that forgiveness can be spontaneous. Theoretically, a spontaneous act of forgiveness can be understood as the minimal limit on a process. (p. 35)

Note. Some of the material in this table was taken from Enright, Eastin, Golden, Sarinopoulos, & Freedman (1992). Adapted with permission.

of forgiveness in such depth. The definition of forgiveness expresses the ideal; people are imperfect, rarely reaching the ideal. Yet, the definition of genuine forgiveness presents a goal for everyone. Surely it is a goal many will not reach, but without that goal, forgiveness is likely to degenerate into meaning whatever any given client (or clinician) wishes it to mean. Such relativism must be resisted, otherwise where reason may have prevailed, there is chaos.

THE QUESTION OF THE MORAL EMOTIONS

We already have seen that ancient Hebrew and Christian conceptions of forgiveness easily accommodated the interplay of emotions, thoughts, behaviors, and one's spiritual attributes into a whole response toward another who has offended. Modern philosophy is less clear on such interplay. Consider four of Emmanuel Kant's ideas. First, moral principles are primary in determining moral character. Because principles are derived from rational thought, people's cognitions are primary. Second, Kant considered the emotional aspects of moral responses to be a kind of window dressing (Sherman, 1990). As someone smiles in bringing kindness, it is the will to be kind, not the smile, that determines the moral quality of the response. Third, emotions can be inconsistent and, in some cases, can obstruct a moral response, as in the event of someone who is compelled by duty to save a drowning child but fears loss of one's own life. Fourth, emotions are passive. People do not will to be angry or afraid. These are passive to the extent that they are reactive (Sabini & Silver, 1987). Morality is willed and active, not passive.

Our acceptance or rejection of the Kantian position is of great importance and cannot be underestimated. If we conclude that Kant is correct, then we engage in cognitive therapy only. Our assessment devices will ask questions about thoughts or even behaviors but will be devoid of questions about affect.

We have four responses against the Kantian position. First, Kant has an excellent point that rationally determined principles are at the core of morality. Much of the moral development research of the 20th century centered on the importance of rationality (Kohlberg, 1969; Piaget, 1932). Yet, can rationality alone lead to a complete morality, especially in the appropriation and expression of beneficence? Consider an example. Clarence is hurt by Martha's insensitive remark. He says to her, "You should not have done that." Martha, if she is aware of her own insensitivity, would agree, but she would feel no sense of support or affirmation from Clarence. His words do not convey affect or, if they do, it is a stern, perhaps cold expression. Nothing in Clarence's sentence suggests beneficence. On the other hand, suppose Clarence said, "You should not have done that, but I dearly love you anyway." The second clause, focused on emotion, conveys an entirely different attitude toward Martha. The second sentence may repair a relationship, whereas the first may drive them further apart. It seems odd to say that the expression of a principle (you should not be insensitive) apart from emotion is complete. It seems odd to say that the expression of emotion is not required in the sentence (on the use of language to convey moral emotions, see B. Williams, 1973).[7]

Second, to claim that emotions are only window dressing is to miss the point that morality, especially beneficence, conveys not only fairness but also support. Again, consider an example. Corey, Clarence's 2-year-old son, erroneously slams the car door on his own thumb. In one scenario, Clarence, as a morally principled, rational parent, walks over to the boy and, out of a sense of duty, offers with his left hand a handkerchief to temporarily stop the bleeding while with the right hand calls his broker on the cellular phone. In another scenario, Clarence rushes to the boy and cradles him, communicating a sense of heartfelt concern, not only out of duty but also out of love. Duty is not the only moral response, and in some cases when it is devoid of appropriate affect, it may not suffice as moral.[8] Our point is this: Just because one can imagine a thousand instances in which action born out of duty is honorable does not mean that there are no exceptions. Examples of beneficence, as in the car door incident, constitute the bulk of the exceptions (on the interplay of emotions and principles within the context of beneficence, see Sherman, 1990).

Third, Kant makes an important statement when he demonstrates how emotions at times can obstruct justice (as in the case of a fearful rescue worker who refuses to save a child). Such examples, although well taken, do not adequately address the specific instance of beneficence. We must remember that Kant's primary mission was to validate duty. Beneficence, as a moral expression that goes beyond duty, does not fit so neatly into his examples. It seems hard to imagine people persevering year after year in working at a soup kitchen, giving lavishly to charity, or setting up hospice care for the destitute in India devoid of the motivating elements of love and caring. Can duty alone make people persist in such activities, especially for many years? Even if some might, will most continue without yoking emotions to the principles?

---

[7] We are not claiming that language centered on emotions is required in all sentences that communicate morality. Yet, if the goal is the accurate communication of beneficence, mercy, or love, then including such language is more often than not better than its absence.

[8] Perhaps this distinction between rationality and sincere, expressive concern is at the heart of the justice and caring debate between Kohlberg (1969) and Gilligan (1993) regarding the scientific study of moral reasoning.

Fourth, not all philosophers reject the importance of affect. Aristotle, whose basic definition formed the foundation for Simon's (1986) and our analysis of moral virtue, made an explicit place for the passions. We can control the expression of anger or resentment. Do many therapies not emphasize the learning of appropriate expressions of sadness, anger, resentment, and related emotions? Can there not be considerable relief realized in people who begin to learn more appropriate expressions of these? It is clear that the emotions are not as passive as Kant believed. We have a certain degree of willed control over them. Philosophers, even those sympathetic to the Kantian position (such as Sherman, 1990), are moving away from the strained orthogonality of emotions, cognition, and behavior within the sphere of morality (see also Sabini & Silver, 1987).

ON THE DECONSTRUCTION OF OUR DEFINITION

A variant on our definition has been in the published literature since 1991 (Enright & the Human Development Study Group, 1991). We question how long it or even a better one, if it surfaces, will last. Enright, Freedman, and Rique (1998) predicted that forgiveness would fall victim to "definitional drift." In other words, across the generations of scholars, the construct of forgiveness will become distorted beyond recognition. As Erik Erikson (1968) noted for his own involved, subtle construct of ego identity, scientists do not always preserve original meanings when they operationalize a construct, especially one that is difficult to understand in the first place. His statement about ego identity became prophetic as he watched the scientific community operationalize his construct to the point at which it no longer resembled the ideas expressed in his 1968 classic.

If these observations are correct, then we predict that, across the decades, our definition and its defense from ancient and modern philosophical writings will be almost unrecognizable within the published literature, especially if writers do not scrutinize previous work. We say this because the recent self-help and social scientific writings on forgiveness indicate that some writers are not studying other authors' work to any great extent. At the very least, people are not incorporating existing ideas into their work but instead are each "reinventing" a definition of forgiveness as they proceed.

We would not at all mind if the shifts in definition followed the rational scheme outlined by the philosopher of science, Lakatos (1978). When disagreements arise about meaning within a scientific context, Lakatos recommended that answers to the following questions be considered: (a) Is there an apparent contradiction or problem within an existing definition? (b) Is there a new definition that corrects the old, flawed definition? (c) What new information is added with the incorporation of the new view?

and (d) Are there any new contradictions or problems created as we accept the new view? If we proceeded to change definitions in this way, chaos is avoided.

However, if the field advances the way Hannah Arendt (1969) saw some academic fields "progressing" decades ago, then chaos is inevitable. She lamented the almost obsessive push for "original scholarship" (p. 30) to such an extent that in some fields people destroy existing knowledge to make room for the new. Therapists who do this in the area of forgiveness do so at the expense of clients' health.

As we will see in the next chapter, definitional drift already is beginning to happen within the study of forgiveness. To avoid further deterioration in the meaning of this rich and subtle construct, it is imperative that we examine those published works that may be contributing even now to a drift in meaning.

16

SKEPTICAL VIEWS OF FORGIVENESS

Therapists may be surprised at how well-read some clients will be as they come into forgiveness therapy. Forgiveness both as a topic in philosophy and self-help became popular in the 1990s. As a result, numerous articles and books, some for the general public, are available. Unfortunately, not all publications are accurate or deep in their treatment of the subject. Some clients, therefore, will come to therapy with misinformation that they have read, heard about, or even learned at a workshop or seminar. Part of the therapist's job, then, will be some reeducation to challenge client or patient to rethink prior ideas about forgiveness.

There are a number of current skeptical views about forgiveness. Although some skepticism is healthy and aids in the learning of a difficult concept, much of the skepticism about forgiveness that we see is based on misunderstandings of just what forgiveness is. These misunderstandings do not aid understanding but cloud it. This chapter looks at some of these skeptical views for two reasons: (a) so that a therapist might anticipate a client's skepticism and (b) so that the therapist might take some time to examine any personal doubts about the topic. Such examination should deepen the understanding of just what forgiving entails and help the therapist better decide whether forgiveness is appropriate for clients or patients.

FORGIVENESS AS A WEAK AND INFERIOR RESPONSE TO INJUSTICE

The basic thrust of these arguments is that either the forgiver or the forgiven loses something important and so it is best not to enter into forgiveness in the first place.

The Forgiver as Weak

In the late 19th century, Friedrich Nietzsche (1887) made the intriguing claim that those who forgive are weaklings with no other recourse than forgiveness. For example, Alice may continually "forgive" her husband Derek, who is emotionally distant and verbally abusive, not out of moral principle, but out of the family's need to cash his paycheck every week.

For Nietzsche (1887), most forgiveness examples are like the above. Timid people, who have nowhere to turn, forgive. If Alice were morally strong, she would assert her right to a just solution with Derek. This is a serious challenge to forgiving because it calls into question the moral character of the forgiver and thus questions the entire enterprise of forgiveness itself. We would like to challenge Nietzsche's assertion with two main points.

First, consider the Hebrew story of Joseph forgiving his brothers for selling him into slavery, discussed in chapter 15. Was Joseph being timid and feeble when he forgave his brothers? It seems that he was in the position of power, not submission, when he forgave. In fact, not only did he have the power to punish them but also he did so more than once. If anything, Joseph was demonstrating courage, not moral timidity, when he finally revealed himself to the brothers and initiated reconciliation without a guarantee on the brothers' part that their tricks would cease. Alice's forgiveness need not be timid but can flow from the same kind of courage that Joseph demonstrated.

The second rebuttal to Nietzsche (1887) involves a modern psychological finding rather than a philosophical argument. Trainer (1981/1984) did one of the first scientific studies of forgiving. Her adult participants were interviewed about their motives for forgiving an offender. She found that some people actually misunderstood the quality of forgiving and distorted its meaning.

For example, Trainer (1981/1984) labeled one group as *expedient forgivers*, who forgave only as a means to an end. They retained a certain condescension and hostility toward the offender, not unlike Hunter's (1978) description of the *pseudoforgiver*. In other words, the "forgiving" was not a freeing act at all but one that bound the person further in chronic anger. Perhaps this is the pattern that Nietzsche described in the 19th century.

Trainer, in her scientific study, found a different group, which she labeled *intrinsic forgivers*, who forgave out of moral principle. Trainer found less anger in the intrinsic forgiver group compared with other groups. Alice's exasperation at Derek may lessen if she forgives in this way.

In sum, those who expediently forgive may be on a path that looks suspiciously like the real thing. The major difference is that an expedient forgiver is doing so for extrinsic reasons, for reasons of keeping a job or protecting oneself only. The genuine forgiver does so for morally principled reasons, regardless of the external consequences. Such forgiveness for its own sake suggests genuine courage and strength, not retreat and weakness.

The Forgiven as Weakened

In contrast to the Nietzschian position, some warn that receiving forgiveness can leave the forgiven weakened, in a one-down, "I owe you one" position (see Augsburger, 1981; Cunningham, 1985). A forgiver who so manipulates the one who did wrong actually is not forgiving at all. Where is the generosity or moral love in continually requiring recompense? Moral restraint not only is absent, but also a sinister form of punishment reigns in the relationship as the forgiver reminds the forgiven of the "gift."

The Forgiver as Inferior

When someone forgives so rapidly that he or she glosses over a legitimate period of anger, that person is not showing self-respect, as Murphy (1982) reminded us. Murphy's concern, however, is not with forgiving per se but instead with the short-circuiting of the process. As long as the process of forgiving makes room for this legitimate period of anger, Murphy and those who agree with him should not be troubled by forgiveness.

The Forgiven as Inferior

Even if a forgiver does not try to dominate the offender, the latter may nonetheless feel very badly about having to be forgiven (see Droll, 1984/1985; O'Shaughnessy, 1967). Derek may feel that Alice, by her forgiving, is morally superior to him. Yet, Alice need not tell Derek of her gift, as we discussed in chapter 1. Even if he should suspect forgiveness on her part and then pine over this, Alice has done nothing wrong. Her gift remains a gift regardless of Derek's response. If a child wails in protest over the gift of socks on Christmas morning, does this present then not count as a gift given just because the child wanted a popular CD-ROM game and did not receive it?

Forgiving as Alienating to Self

Droll (1984/1985), who did one of the early doctoral dissertations on the psychology of forgiveness, made the intriguing claim that humans' essential nature is more aggressive than forgiving allows. Those who forgive are thwarting their basic nature, much to their detriment. We wonder, however, whether the hostility that blows apart already established families also is against that which is fundamentally good for the human condition. Because forgiving may restore important relationships, it is actually the antithesis of alienation (Enright & the Human Development Study Group, 1991).

Forgiving as Disrespectful to the Offender

One argument states that when someone is hurt by another, it is best to show some resentment because it lets the other know that he or she is being taken seriously. If forgiveness cuts short the resentment process, the forgiver is not taking the other seriously and, therefore, is not respecting the other. Nietzsche (1887) also devised this argument. We disagree with the basic premise here that forgiveness does not involve resentment. As a person forgives, he or she starts with resentment.

We also disagree that resentment is the exclusive path to respecting. Does a person show little respect if he or she quells the resentment in a day compared with 2 days? Is a week of resentment better than the 2 days? When is it sufficient to stop resenting so that the other feels respected? Nietzsche (1887) offered no answer. If a person perpetuates the resentment, certainly he or she is not respecting the other.

Forgiving as Producing Hypersensitivity to Hurt

Both Downie (1965), a philosopher, and Droll (1984/1985), a psychologist, raised the challenging possibility that someone who practices forgiveness may become overly sensitive to slights and minor hurts. As a forgiver begins to scrutinize injustices, he or she may begin to falsely see these at every turn. Yet, those who genuinely forgive try to see exactly what happened in the original offense. If anything, true forgiving would seem to correct hypersensitivity as the forgiver strives for an accurate understanding of offender and offense.

FORGIVENESS AS A FORM OF INJUSTICE

Four arguments, discussed below, attack forgiveness as thwarting justice. Such accusations, of course, may be serious if true, because they imply an incompatibility between justice and forgiveness; an individual may have to choose one or the other.

Forgiving Perpetuates Injustice

Suppose Nietzsche overstated his case by describing what Trainer (1981/1984) would call expedient forgiving rather than intrinsic forgiving. This does not invalidate Nietzsche's point about moral weakness, because even an intrinsic forgiver, in Alice's example above, does not necessarily exert her right to a fair solution. Alice may intrinsically forgive and then face business as usual with Derek. Forgiveness may quell anger, but it is a sorry truce indeed, because Derek wins. In fact, if business as usual continues, Alice will be contributing to the reprehensible family condition.[1]

A key rebuttal to the above argument is that, as we saw in chapter 3, genuine forgiveness and reconciliation are not synonymous. Joseph forgave first, then reconciled with his brothers as we saw in chapter 15. When someone forgives, he or she may or may not reconcile with the offender. In this example, the offenders, Joseph's brothers, were more than willing to accept the peace offering.

If Alice in our modern example truly forgives, there is nothing in the forgiveness rule book that says that she cannot now seek fair treatment from Derek. In fact, were she to first forgive and then attempt a fair solution, her quest may prove to be more compassionate; the outcome may be more favorable than if she charged ahead, seeking justice while fuming.

One of the loudest assertions against forgiving as morally sound concerns the situation involving Alice and Derek. Suppose Alice forgives a husband who continues his pattern of abuse. Is she not now open to even deeper abuse? If she misunderstands forgiveness and confuses it with reconciliation, then, yes, she is open to further and dangerous abuse. Yet, if she is first clear that forgiving is an internal, moral response to unfairness and that reconciliation involves both parties in mutual agreement, then she need not blindly reconcile.

If Derek insists on reconciliation without any sense of repentance and a willingness to seek help, one can hardly call this reconciliation. If Alice forgives in her heart and then decides not to reconcile, she may be taking an important step toward personal health. If she does not forgive, she may be trapped with an inner hatred that could affect both her and the children.

Does forgiveness, then, perpetuate injustice? We can now see that blind reconciliation (or should we say pseudoreconciliation) is the culprit making all of this philosophical trouble for forgiveness. It is not forgiving per se that is immoral, but hastily reentering an abusive situation before

---

[1]Lauritzen (1987) argued that forgiving is inappropriate under such circumstances.

the offender understands the offense, is genuinely willing to change, and shows some evidence of that change.

Forgiving Reverses Social Justice

Perhaps an excessive focus on forgiveness will lead to opening the jail cell doors, paroling all criminals, and imposing a new form of societal injustice as society refuses to take a stand against wrongdoing. Philosophers such as M. Lewis (1980) and Roberts (1971) raised these issues. The major problem with such arguments is their confusing forgiveness with legal mercy or pardon. A juror is never the one wronged. Legal pardon takes place, in theory, apart from personal offense for the one pardoning. Forgiveness always takes place within a context of personal hurt for the one forgiving. Therefore, even if one forgives regularly, this should have no bearing on one's competence as a juror or judge in which other parties are the ones injured.

Forgiving Blocks Personal Justice

Even if societal justice can exist alongside forgiveness—one can seek fairness while on a jury, for example—is it not true that a forgiver relinquishes certain rights? After all, a forgiver no longer has a claim on that pound of flesh. If Alice forgives, even though she may have a right to treat Derek in a way that is less than generous, she will refrain.

We must distinguish a *personal right* from a *community right* or even a *family right* (see Yandell, 1998, p. 9, on this point). Alice does not give up her right to a fair alimony settlement when she forgives. What she may give up is the personal right for compensation for all of the pain caused by Derek's insensitivity. Otherwise, she may try both to forgive and to punish for her own sake, a contradictory situation (Yandell, 1998). Does the abandonment of this personal right, then, make forgiving immoral? We think not, because as one deliberately gives up an entitlement—in this case, some compensation for emotional damage—this is done as a gift to Derek and perhaps to others upset by Alice's plight. A gift given, even under this circumstance, is hardly immoral because genuine gift giving is not immoral. As Alice forgives, presuming that she chooses to do this, she does so with a full awareness that Derek was unfair, thus operating within the moral realm. Furthermore, if the intent of the forgiveness is to help the children and herself move on as a family, this, too, is hardly immoral.

Forgiveness Blinds the Forgiver to What Is Just or Unjust

Safer (1999) presented a case of family dysfunction in which "forgiveness" plays a major role in perpetuating deep injustice. Two middle-aged parents ask their adult daughter to "forgive and forget" her brother's sexual abuse toward her. The daughter, of course, is aghast at the parents' apparent attempts to downplay and deny the offense. The parents in this case study do not seem aware of the enormity of the offense. Their quest for forgiveness is an attempt at distortion of reality, a cover-up for their son, and oppression of their daughter.

If Safer (1999) had shown this as a case of pseudoforgiveness in which people are deliberately distorting the meaning of forgiveness for some unspecified gain, we would have no problem with the case or the analysis. Safer, however, used the case as an illustration of the dangers of actual forgiveness.

In our experience, true forgiveness helps people see the injustice more clearly, not more opaquely. As a person breaks denial, examines what happened, and allows for a period of anger, he or she begins to label the other's behavior as "wrong" or "unfair." The parents in the above case, however, have minimized what is wrong with their son's behavior. They are using pseudoforgiveness as a weapon. Certainly, therapists should be aware of such distorted thinking in a client or patient. The therapist, however, need not condemn genuine forgiveness because a client twists its meaning.

In sum, forgiveness is no obstacle to justice. Forgiving acts do not perpetuate injustice or prevent social justice from occurring. Forgiveness may thwart attempts at extracting punishment for emotional pain, but this usually turns into a gift for the offender and a release of potentially hurtful anger for the forgiver. There are at least four other basic challenges to forgiving within our modern era, which we discuss in the following sections.

FORGIVING AS LOGICALLY IMPOSSIBLE

Immanuel Kant raised the possibility that forgiving was not possible because the wronged party cannot erase the injustice: The wrong happened, there is nothing that a forgiver can literally do to rid oneself of the wrong, and because forgiving tries in vain to so rid the wrong, forgiving is therefore futile. Yet, as North (1987) instructed, forgiving does not try to literally obliterate the wrong but instead to alter the effects of that wrong. Properly understood, forgiving is a reaction to a wrong, not some magical formula that tries to pretend that the wrong never occurred in the first place. A forgiver tries to change the distorting effects on the relationship in forgiving.

WOMEN ARE CONTROLLED BY MEN IN FORGIVING

Women are asked to forgive far more often than men. Even in our case study in this chapter, Alice does the forgiving. The self-help books target women; research sometimes targets women. Forgiveness is asking women to tolerate men's injustice; men would not be asked to do this toward women. Therefore, forgiving is playing out the power differential in the new societal struggle (which, to Marx, belonged once to ownership and labor in industry), which is the battle of the sexes.

The argument is helpful if clinicians and researchers ever focus attention on only one gender. In actuality, however, the pioneering research and interventions have been concerned about both genders. For example, Al-Mabuk et al. (1995) educated both college men and women in forgiving deep hurts. The first empirical study on forgiveness published in psychology included both men and women (Enright, Santos, & Al-Mabuk, 1989). Although it is true that some self-help books are geared toward women only, most talk to both genders (see Smedes's 1984, 1996, books as examples).

One cannot help but see a particular assumption in the argument that targeting women for forgiveness is a gender bias. The argument seems to imply that forgiving is a way for the offender to keep a sinister control over the forgiver. If forgiving led automatically to reconciliation, then the argument would have weight. We already saw, however, that forgiving an offense and reconciling with an offender are two separate issues. The argument has a false first premise, that forgiveness and reconciliation are synonymous.

If, on the other hand, forgiving is a choice freely made and, once made, releases one from a host of psychological problems, then a predominant focus on women would actually be a bias against men. In actuality, however, forgiveness therapy and research target both genders.

ONE MUST NOT FORGIVE CERTAIN OFFENSES

This idea against forgiving is centered on controlling just what a forgiver can and cannot forgive. For example, one of us was giving a workshop when a patron stopped the proceedings to ask an intriguing—and loaded—question. A father is estranged from his 16-year-old daughter because she is heterosexually active, the argument began. We all know that sexual activity outside marriage is no offense to many in contemporary society. If the father forgives his daughter, the father is perpetuating a myth about the offending nature of that which should not offend, the questioner clarified. Would you, Mr. Speaker, encourage the father to continue in his forgiveness effort?

This is a great question for the following reason: No matter how one answers the yes–no question, someone will be offended. There are at least three responses that can offend those hearing the answer. First, if one says yes, the father, who is deeply hurt by his daughter's actions, should forgive, then one is closed-minded in the eyes of those siding with the daughter.

One would be considered closed-minded because one sees an offense, whereas they see no offense. Second, if one says no, the father should be discouraged from forgiving because the daughter did nothing wrong, then one encourages wrongdoing in the eyes of those siding with the father. Third, if one says no, the father should be discouraged from forgiving if the daughter intends to maintain her present objectional behavior, one is, again, closed-minded from the viewpoint of the daughter's advocates. How would anyone answer?

Our response went something like this. Suppose, instead of engaging in sexual behavior, the daughter were robbing banks. Could the father forgive his daughter the pain caused him? All agreed that forgiving was appropriate there. Without debating whether sexual behavior outside of marriage is right or wrong, it was obvious that the audience members were more than willing to let the father forgive as long as his views were consistent with that audience's views. In other words, there was an implicit sense of the audience's controlling the father's own forgiving.

We then asked, "Will you only allow people to forgive, without condemning them, if their values are in agreement with your own?" Because few people wish to appear controlling, the answer was a clear no. Then, if the father is rational, operating from a particular worldview that sees mid-adolescent sexual activity as wrong, and if the daughter's behavior frightens the father who worries about pregnancy or even AIDS, then is it not reasonable to let him forgive? Perhaps the father must take time to determine exactly what he is forgiving. Perhaps he would forgive her lack of communication with him or her disobeying rules of the household. If the daughter continues the behavior, does the father start by forgiving a particular incident in the past that he finds most troubling?

The consensus was to let the father forgive, although not all in the audience would themselves forgive. Some, if they were the father, would not forgive because they see the daughter's behavior as no offense. Others would not forgive because the daughter's behavior was ongoing and, therefore, continued to be an offense to them.

The lesson of this argument is that there are many shades of gray in today's society regarding what is and is not offensive. People, without realizing it, seem to balk at others forgiving what they themselves would not. Is this not one more subtle twist on the theme of control? Perhaps each forgiver must decide what is in his or her best interest to forgive, presuming that the person is rational and not engaging in a form of pseudoforgiveness.

FORGIVING AS PASSIVE

The final argument, more from psychology than philosophy, does not present a moral attack but does portray forgiving as negative. The gist of the argument is that forgiving always commences after injustice. It does not prevent injustice from happening in the first place, and so it is a passive form of communication and action. Our response is a question: What is effective in stemming injustice in this imperfect world? No form of communication, no problem-solving strategy to date, can prevent all injustice. Is it not reassuring to know that there is a potentially helpful response to injustice?

Furthermore, we must ask why forgiveness is considered passive just because it comes after an injustice. When one examines the struggle to overcome anger, the struggle to offer undeserved compassion to an injurer, one can hardly label forgiving as passive. Finally, as one forgives, is it not possible that the offender may be transformed through the forgiving, thus making that form of injustice less likely in the future? In such cases, forgiveness precedes issues of justice and injustice and acts as a preventive of further abuse.

17

EMPIRICAL SUPPORT FOR THE SOCIAL–COGNITIVE MODEL OF FORGIVENESS

As we saw in the previous chapter, not all who think about the topic of forgiveness envision it in the same way. As we saw in chapter 4, there appears to be a developmental progression of how people come to understand certain features of forgiveness, such as the conditions under which one is most likely to forgive. Therapy may progress more slowly or more smoothly depending on how a person thinks about forgiveness. Someone who has a lower level understanding of forgiveness, for example, may insist on embracing resentment until he or she can get even in some way. In other words, a client's basic understanding of forgiveness is important to the therapy itself. We, therefore, believe that it is vital not only to describe a social–cognitive developmental sequence of forgiveness (which we did in chapter 4), but also to provide scientific validation for the model.

To test whether our model of styles of forgiveness was developmentally sound and cross-culturally relevant, we and others carried out five studies, which we describe in this chapter. In general form, they give the practitioner a good basis for assessing the validity of our developmental model of forgiveness.

As we did in chapter 6, we provide here considerable detail of the scientific method and results of the studies done with our social–cognitive developmental model of how people develop in their thinking about forgiveness. The detail is provided so that academics may not only understand but also critique or even replicate the research efforts. The practitioner should have a good basis for assessing the usefulness of our developmental model by reviewing those studies.

THE INITIAL STUDIES

Enright, Santos, and Al-Mabuk (1989) assessed people's thinking about forgiveness by presenting two hypothetical dilemmas, in the tradition of Piaget and Kohlberg. We were attempting to validate the developmental sequence described in Exhibit 4.1 in chapter 4. The participants were 4th, 7th, and 10th graders; college students; and adults, with a total sample size of 59 in Study 1 and 60 in Study 2, which was an exact replication of the first study. The groups were equally divided by gender, except in the case of the college student group in Study 1, which had one fewer male participant.

In one of Kohlberg's famous dilemmas, Heinz must decide whether to steal a drug to save his dying wife. We altered the script so that the greedy druggist hid the drug, making it impossible for Heinz to steal it. His wife then died. Heinz now must decide about forgiving the druggist. We asked questions such as these:

- *Style 1*. If Heinz got even with the druggist by causing him to lose his business, would that make Heinz less sad than he is now? Would it help Heinz forgive the druggist? Why or why not? What does it mean to forgive?
- *Style 2*. Suppose that the druggist gave Heinz lots of money. Will this make Heinz feel better? Will it help him forgive? Is this the best way for Heinz to forgive the druggist?
- *Style 3*. Suppose all of Heinz's friends come to him and say, "Please be more mature about this. We want you to be friends with the druggist." Would this stop his sadness and anger and make him like the druggist? Would it help him forgive the druggist? Why or why not?
- *Style 4*. Suppose Heinz is a very religious man. His religious leader points out to him that he should not stay so angry with the druggist. Would this help Heinz forgive the druggist? Why or why not?
- *Style 5*. Are there benefits (good things) that happen when an angry or sad person like Heinz forgives the druggist? If yes, what are the benefits?
- *Style 6*. Suppose Heinz starts feeling friendly toward the druggist, and Heinz even feels love. Now the druggist hides another drug

when Heinz is sick. Could Heinz forgive the druggist now? Why or why not?

The second dilemma, adapted from Rest's (1986) Defining Issues Test, has Thompson, an escaped prisoner, living a law-abiding life in a quiet town. In our version, he never committed the crime for which he was accused, judged guilty, and imprisoned. Jones, a neighbor, recognizes him as the one who escaped years ago. She reports him to authorities, and Thompson is rearrested.

Each person's interview was presented in written form to two judges, who independently assigned a style to each scorable response. For each dilemma, all scorable responses were averaged into a dilemma score. The two dilemma scores were then averaged for the overall style score. All protocols were scored without awareness of the person's age, gender, and score on the other dilemma.

Besides the forgiveness measure, Rest's (1986) Defining Issues Test of Kohlbergian justice reason was given, along with a modified religiosity scale, based on Allport, Gillespie, and Young (1953). The 10-point, Likert-type scale asked questions about attendance at religious services, reading scriptures, and having religious discussions with peers.

The findings for Study 1 are as follows. The correlations between the two forgiveness dilemmas was .83. The age group differences were assessed in a 5 (age group) $\times$ 2 (gender) analysis of variance (ANOVA) in which there were strong differences among the age groups, $F(4, 49) = 21.32$, $p < .0001$. The 4th-grade cohort was significantly different from the college students and adults. Seventh graders were significantly lower than the college and adult cohorts. Finally, 10th graders were significantly lower than the adults. The means and standard deviations are in Table 17.1, first column. As is evident, the 4th- and 7th-grade students tended to think of forgiveness in terms of restitution or compensation. Apologies were not only important, but also seen as necessary to forgiveness. By 10th grade, the participants were more influenced by peer pressure to forgive. The college students and adults focused more on the obligations inherent within belief systems and the impact that forgiveness may have on social harmony. Only in adulthood did we see instances of Style 6 reasoning in which forgiveness was filtered through the moral principle of love. No gender differences were observed. The forgiveness reasoning scale was significantly correlated with justice reasoning ($r = .54$) and in a modest way with religiosity ($r = .33$).

Study 2 replicated the first study. The correlation between the two forgiveness dilemmas was .71. Age groups again were different from one another, $F(4, 50) = 9.45$, $p < .0001$. The exact pattern of cohort differences as in Study 1 were observed here (see Table 17.1, right half, for means

TABLE 17.1
Means and Standard Deviations for the Forgiveness Styles by Age in Enright, Santos, and Al-Mabuk (1989)

Grade or age group	Study 1 forgiveness style			Study 2 forgiveness style		
	M	SD	n	M	SD	n
Grade 4						
Male	2.29	0.21	6	2.08	0.13	6
Female	2.19	0.29	6	2.04	0.64	6
Total	2.24			2.06		
Grade 7						
Male	2.05	0.37	6	2.36	1.49	6
Female	2.75	0.23	6	2.83	0.58	6
Total	2.40			2.59		
Grade 10						
Male	3.24	0.53	6	2.96	1.31	6
Female	2.91	0.52	6	2.82	0.63	6
Total	3.08			2.89		
College						
Male	3.93	0.38	5	3.75	0.85	6
Female	4.01	0.86	6	3.81	0.83	6
Total	3.96			3.78		
Adult						
Male	4.37	1.38	6	4.07	0.55	6
Female	3.94	0.73	6	3.95	1.29	6
Total	4.16			4.01		

and standard deviations). Again, no gender differences were found. The forgiveness scale correlated with justice reasoning ($r = .40$) and again with religiosity ($r = .54$).

Because these findings were observed in the midwestern United States, we did not yet know the extent to which we may observe similar patterns across cultures. Also, we must keep in mind that the stimulus materials were all hypothetical. People may appear to be more forgiving or need fewer conditions to forgive on hypothetical problems than on actual injustices perpetrated against them. The next three studies reported below examined the findings cross-culturally. The study in Korea was intended to examine the extent to which answers on hypothetical situations relate to actual forgiveness of real injustices.

THE TAIWANESE STUDY

In 1990, Huang did a doctoral dissertation on the theory of forgiveness in Taiwan, Republic of China, to examine the extent of similarity between

TABLE 17.2
Comparison of Means From Taiwan and the United States on Forgiveness Styles

Grade or age group	U.S. sample	Taiwan sample
Grade 4	2.24	2.66
Grade 7	2.40	2.43
Grade 10	3.08	3.18
College	3.96	3.60
Adult	4.16	4.47

the U.S. findings and those in Asia. Although this was a convenience sample of sorts (Huang is from Taiwan), it was thought to be an interesting comparison because of the differences between the two cultures. The Confucian idea of community harmony and tolerance may produce different responses than in the United States, where issues of justice and righting individual wrongs may be stronger. Of course, these are cultural stereotypes, but observers of Asian and Western cultures have written about the differences in these broad ways (see, e.g., Dien, 1982; Duck, 1983).

Huang's (1990) replication of Enright et al. (1989) is in Table 17.2. For purposes of comparison, the Study 1 findings from Enright et al. (1989) are included (see "U.S. sample" in table). In all cases except for the college sample in the United States ($N = 11$), the sample size was 12 per age group, with equal numbers of male and female participants in each group. Note that the age group means are similar between the cultures. The correlation of the five means in the United States with the five in Taiwan was .94, showing strong statistical correspondence among the scores of the two cultures.

THE KOREAN STUDY

In a study on forgiveness in Korea, Park and Enright (1997) reported on a different reasoning sequence than that in Exhibit 4.1. Their intent was to examine not only people's understanding of the conditions under which they may forgive but also their understanding of the basic meaning of forgiveness and the strategies they may use in actually forgiving. These three reasoning categories would have resulted in an inordinately lengthy interview for the participants, who were 30 junior high school and 30 college students in Korea equally divided by gender, if the six-style sequence were the unit of analysis. We would have had to probe for the existence of six styles across three domains for a total of at least 18 reasoning patterns. To simplify the procedure, Park and Enright collapsed Styles 1 and 2, Styles 3

EXHIBIT 17.1
Development of Forgiveness as Discussed in Park and Enright (1997)

Pattern 1: Revengeful forgiveness	Physical or psychological revenge or compensation must occur before forgiveness is possible.
Pattern 2: External forgiveness	Pressures from social groups to forgive are sufficient to elicit forgiveness.
Pattern 3: Internal forgiveness	Forgiveness occurs unconditionally when incorporating moral principles of beneficence, particularly the principle of love.

Note. Pattern 1 is equivalent to Styles 1 and 2, Pattern 2 is equivalent to Styles 3 and 4, and Pattern 3 is equivalent to Styles 5 and 6 in Enright, Santos, and Al-Mabuk (1989).

and 4, and Styles 5 and 6 from Exhibit 4.1 into only three patterns, as seen in Exhibit 17.1. For the sake of simplicity, we present only the sequence for the conditions under which people may forgive (and not the sequences for the meaning of forgiveness or strategies used when forgiving).

The study was intended to address three questions:

1. Were there cohort differences as were found in Taiwan and the United States?
2. Does an adolescent's style (or what the researchers called a pattern) relate to the ecological validation issue of how he or she actually resolves interpersonal conflicts with friends?
3. Does one's developmental understanding of forgiveness relate to the actual degree of forgiveness experienced in a friendship in need of repair?

The measure paralleled that in Enright et al. (1989). Following a screening questionnaire in which all of the participants had to have experienced a significant hurt from a same-sex friend within the past 6 months, the respondents were given the other scales. The Understanding Forgiveness Interview presented two hypothetical dilemmas, as in Enright et al. (1989). The students' scorable responses were collapsed across the categories of conditions under which one would forgive, the meaning of forgiveness, and the strategies one would use in forgiving to create one composite developmental pattern score.

The Restoring Friendship Strategy Scale was a 10-item Likert-format questionnaire intended to assess the degree to which the participant tried to reconcile with the friend who was unfair ("I tried to see the good qualities in my friend"). The Degree of Forgiveness Scale, again in a 10-item Likert format, was intended to assess how much he or she forgave the friend ("To what extent will you help if your friend is in need?").

Regarding Question 1, the Pearson correlation between age group and developmental pattern was moderately strong ($r = .51$, $p < .001$). A 2 (age group) $\times$ 2 (gender) ANOVA revealed age group differences ($M = 2.01$, $SD = 0.36$ for the college students and $M = 1.65$, $SD = 0.28$ for the junior high school students), $F(1, 56) = 18.47$, $p < .05$. The range of scores showed variability across the sample. For example, 10 participants were averaging in the 1.00–1.50 range, 39 participants in the 1.51–2.16 range, and 11 participants at 2.17 and above (showing at least one Style 3 response). There were no gender differences.

Regarding Question 2, a Pearson correlation between the Understanding Forgiveness Interview and the Restoring Friendship Strategy Scale was statistically significant ($r = .55$, $p < .001$). The more advanced the participant's understanding of forgiveness on the hypothetical dilemmas, the more he or she actually tried to forgive the friend who was unjust. This is an interesting finding, especially as an answer to people who may think that the hypothetical dilemmas lack ecological validity. This finding suggests that there is a link between hypothetical reasoning and how one actually forgives.

For Question 3 (developmental pattern compared with the degree of forgiving a friend), the researchers found one statistically significant correlation ($r = .34$) using the mode as the scaling metric on the Understanding Forgiveness Interview and one nonsignificant finding ($r = .23$) using the mean. This result is not as strong for the ecological validity issue as is Question 2.

In general, the results from this study are similar to those in Taiwan and the United States. People seem to develop in their understanding of forgiveness. The pattern is from the simple to the more complex and from more distorted to more accurate views of forgiveness.

THE FRENCH STUDY

In a study on forgiveness with a French sample, Girard and Mullet (1997) extended our work by providing a more complex analysis of people's responses than we have done to this point. Applying a variation of Norman Anderson's (1976) functional theory of cognition, they were able to ascertain the interplay of the various conditions under which a person might forgive. Our approach was to describe the best condition the participant thought necessary to forgive. With Anderson's model, Girard and Mullet were able to assess the relative influence of all conditions of interest at the same time. Seven conditions were simultaneously assessed: intent of harm, severity of the consequences, cancellation of consequences, social proximity to the offender, apologies from the offender, attitude toward the offender, and the unconditional situation. Adolescents and young (25–39), middle (40–55), and older adults (60–96) primarily from Orleans, France, were the participants ($N = 236$).

To create situations in which the various conditions were present, Girard and Mullet (1997) created complex hypothetical dilemmas. Consider one example:

> Marie-Noelle and Josiane are sisters (proximity). They both worked in the same firm. Josiane, who had been working in the firm for several years, asked for a promotion. Marie-Noelle, who was very talkative but not mean (intent to harm), disclosed some information about Josiane's professional life. Josiane's section head heard about this information and began to doubt the working qualities of Josiane, so he refused her promotion (severity of consequences). Marie-Noelle was truly remorseful about what happened and asked Josiane to forgive her (apologies). Josiane's best friend, who knows Marie-Noelle well, also asked her to forgive her sister (attitudes of others). Josiane asked another section head for a promotion, again, which she has gotten at the present time (cancellation of consequences). Right now, do you think that you would forgive Marie-Noelle, if you were Josiane?

The following are some of the basic findings. First, there was a developmental trend in the unconditional forgiveness situation. The elderly participants were the most unconditional forgivers (58% of the sample). Second, the peer-pressure condition (what Girard and Mullet, 1997, called the "attitude of others") was important only for the adolescent group. Third, participants, regardless of age, did not focus only on one factor but balanced several factors in their decision to forgive. The majority of participants were likely to forgive when the negative consequences were canceled, the intent to harm was absent, social harmony was restored, and an apology ensued. We wonder, however, about the extent to which people were actually willing to forgive or simply to condone. After all, if no harm was intended and no genuine injustice occurred (because negative consequences were canceled), what was left to forgive? Fourth, apologies were weighted as important in the forgiveness process. Whether such apologies were seen as an absolutely necessary or simply as a sufficient condition is unclear from the research. Finally, as in the previous studies, no gender differences were observed.

An important aspect of this study is the finding that people do not focus only on one condition when they forgive. In our previous research, we, too, found that people attend to more than one condition. This was evident as we took mean scores, which imply an average around different levels. Yet, this French research by Girard and Mullet (1997) is the first to make this point more formally. It is an important finding, suggesting that stages or styles that supposedly are developmental are not occurring in isolation from other thought forms. A client who seems to require an apology from an injurer still may be capable of understanding the issues on the higher levels. In other words, one cannot assume that the concept of unconditional forgiveness is lost on someone who is seeking revenge or who demands an apology as a necessary condition of forgiveness. These issues have direct bearing for the cognitive theory of unconditional forgiveness that we presented at the end of chapter 4.

18

OTHER FORGIVENESS
INTERVENTIONS

Other research groups have developed and tested clinical interventions involving forgiveness. In this chapter, we review those that have been scientifically tested. There are other interventions, not subjected to any empirical tests, that are more difficult to evaluate because they have not been tested.

As with our own interventions, we provide in this chapter a significant amount of detail about other interventions on forgiveness so that the researcher may have a sufficient amount of information to evaluate the studies. Note that we provide additional information on some of the measures that we and others use in research in the following chapter.

We also believe that the details of the therapeutic aspects of the programs may be of considerable interest to clinicians, who may come away with some strategies to either incorporate or avoid in their work. Following the description of each program, we attempt to draw some preliminary conclusions about what seems to work and what does not. We begin with two studies that fall under the heading of "Brief Therapy." We think that it is vital that clinicians be able to judge, from a scientific standpoint, the effectiveness of brief therapy. We say this because of the trend in managed health care for shorter interventions. As readers will see, shorter is not usually better where forgiveness therapy is involved. Following our examination of brief therapy, we then turn to four other studies: two with college students, one with high school participants, and one with children. As readers will see, some programs are effective, whereas others are not.

BRIEF THERAPY

Two studies have been done with a brief format. The first one published (McCullough & Worthington, 1995) concerned 86 college students (76% female, 24% male) who were nonrandomly assigned to one of three 1-hour interventions. Two of the experimental conditions were explicitly focused on forgiveness. The third was a waitlist control group. All of the participants reported that they have wanted to but have been unable to forgive a particular person. The depth of the unforgiveness or the nature of the interpersonal hurt was not discussed in the article.

The two forgiveness interventions differed in the following way: Participants in Group 1 (called interpersonal intervention) were told that forgiveness may improve relationships with the offender and others. Group 2 participants were told that forgiveness may improve one's own emotional state. Both forgiveness treatments were designed to foster empathy toward an offender. Within the 1-hour period, participants in the forgiveness group formed into therapy groups of about 7–14 people in each; each experimental condition, then, had an unspecified number of such groups. People in the two experimental conditions considered the "frailties and weaknesses of the offender" (McCullough & Worthington, 1995, p. 57) as a means of promoting empathy. The exercise is reminiscent of our reframing unit as described in the previous two chapters, 5 and 6. The difference, of course, between ours and the current procedure is the time element. Our reframing exercises, in some cases, unfolded over weeks or even months, whereas here the exercise was part of a multifaceted 1-hour exercise.

The participants in the forgiveness conditions also wrote letters (which were not sent) to the offender describing their feelings and intent to forgive. Within the hour, participants further reflected on their own need to be forgiven and the difference between forgiveness and reconciliation. Two male doctoral students in counseling psychology were the leaders of the groups.

The Wade Forgiveness Scale (see chapter 19 for a detailed description) served as the dependent measure. There are nine subscales assessing the degree to which the participant has forgiven an offender. Items are on a 5-point Likert scale, assessing the participants' thoughts, feelings, and behaviors toward the person.

Statistical analyses involved an analysis of covariance, using pretest scores as the covariate for the posttest and 6-week follow-up scores on the Wade scale. It was expected that the two forgiveness interventions would show statistically significantly higher means at the combined posttest and follow-up than the waitlist control group. A Time × Condition effect could indicate one of two possibilities: Either the forgiveness groups had a washout effect at follow-up or they continued to improve significantly in forgiveness. Another area of interest was whether either of the two forgiveness conditions outperformed the other in the combined posttest and follow-up analysis or even in the posttest to follow-up comparison.

The results are summarized in Table 18.1. This table is an analysis only of the collapsed data from the posttest and the follow-up, which generated the most statistically significant results. Basically, there are 27 statistical tests performed to examine the pairwise group differences. Their reason for so many statistical tests is that the authors chose to examine the Wade Forgiveness Scale on the subscale level rather than on the total score level. In only 33% of the tests did the interpersonal and self-enhancement conditions show statistically significant differences from one another as seen in the second column of the table. In other words, the two forgiveness manipulations do not show major differences in people's ability to forgive.

Columns 2 and 3 in Table 18.1 explicate the differences between the two forgiveness conditions and the waitlist control group. In column 2, when self-enhancement forgiveness was compared with the control condition, the forgiveness condition led to higher forgiveness scores less than half the time: Four of nine tests (a 44% success rate) statistically differentiated the conditions. In column 3, when interpersonal forgiveness was compared with the control condition, the forgiveness intervention produced higher forgiveness scores in only three of nine comparisons. When all 18 tests of forgiveness condition are compared with the control group, we see that the hypothesis was statistically supported only 7 of 18 times (39% success rate).

TABLE 18.1

Areas of Statistical Significance on the Nine Forgiveness Subscales in McCullough and Worthington (1995)

Subscale of Wade's Forgiveness Scale	1 Self-enhancement forgiving condition compared with interpersonal forgiving condition	2 Self-enhancement forgiving condition compared with control group	3 Interpersonal forgiving condition compared with control group
Revenge	Yes	Yes	Yes
Freedom from obsession	No	No	No
Affirmation	Yes	Yes	No
Victimization	No	No	No
Feelings	No	Yes	Yes
Avoidance	No	No	No
Toward God	No	No	No
Concilation	Yes	Yes	Yes
Holding a grudge	No	No	No

Note. A "yes" response signifies statistical significance between two groups, whereas a "no" signifies no difference between the groups. Of the 9 statistictical tests in Column 1, 3 (or 33%) of the comparisons were statistically significant. Of the 18 statistical tests in columns 2 and 3, 7 (or 39%) of the comparisons were statistically significant.

The effects themselves, when statistical significance was observed, were small. For example, consider the means for only one subscale, Revenge, which did show differences across all three pairwise statistical comparisons. Keep in mind that the subscale has a range of possible scores from 10 to 50, a 40-point range. Yet, the self-enhancement condition realized a gain on this subscale of only about 3 points from pretest to posttest and of less than 5 points from pretest to follow-up. Similarly, the interpersonal forgiveness condition realized a gain in forgiveness on this scale of only about 1 point from pretest to posttest and about 3 points from pretest to follow-up.

The results were modest. Perhaps the results are encouraging because McCullough and Worthington (1995) found anything at all that was statistically significant after only 1 hour of intervention. Keep in mind, however, that the researchers eliminated from participation anyone with a substantial hurt (such as incest) because of the short nature of this program. In all likelihood, the interveners worked with participants who were not exhibiting clinical symptoms because of a lack of forgiveness (although we do not know this with any certainty because it was not assessed). If a person has deep hurt and is showing psychological compromise, then the reasonable conclusion is that a 1-hour intervention probably is not sufficient for that person's needs. Even considering the participants in this study, one cannot conclude that they forgave deeply, given the pattern and strength of results.

The second of the three brief interventions is reported in both McCullough (1995) and McCullough et al. (1997). Over 100 college students (80% female, 20% male) were randomly assigned to one of three conditions: (a) an empathy-based forgiveness program, (b) an advocacy-based approach in which the relational and personal benefits of forgiveness were emphasized, and (c) a waitlist control group. Presenting problems worthy of forgiveness included boyfriend or girlfriend issues (34%), problems with a close friend (21%) or parents (17%), and others (28%). Each intervention occurred over one weekend with a total of eight 1-hour sessions. A 6-week follow-up assessed possible gain, maintenance, or washout of the results.

The first three sessions of the empathy seminar were spent establishing rapport and examining each person's targeted issue for forgiveness. Sessions 4–8 centered on empathy toward the one who was unjust. Empathy was taught as a promoter of forgiveness and as a prosocial, relationship-enhancing activity. Each participant wrote about the offending person's psychological state prior to and after the incident. Near the end of the weekend, the participants were encouraged to see the offender as a needy person who may benefit from being forgiven. The final session distinguished forgiveness from repentance and reconciliation.

The 60-item Enright Forgiveness Inventory (EFI) served as the dependent measure of forgiveness. As in the previous study, the statistical procedure examined the posttest differences among the experimental conditions and simultaneously assessed for gain or loss from posttest to follow-up, with the pretest scores serving as a covariate. The researchers assessed the empathy condition against the forgiveness advocacy and control conditions. At posttest, the empathy-based program was statistically superior to the other two groups.

This result is surprising, because the empathy-based program showed a gain of only 12 points on the EFI, whereas the advocacy-based approach showed more than twice that gain, about 28 points. The fact that the empathy-based group started 47 points higher than the advocacy-based group on the EFI at pretest may be partially responsible for these seemingly anomalous statistically significant findings. It seems as though there was an unfortunate randomization with wide differences between the forgiveness conditions on the EFI means at pretest. In examining the posttest EFI means themselves (not the gain scores), we see that the forgiveness advocacy group remained almost 25 points behind the empathy group, despite the greater gain by the advocacy group from pretest to posttest. In any event, at follow-up the two forgiveness seminars were statistically equivalent but still statistically higher than the control condition.

Although the central condition was an empathy condition, the short-run results are not indicative that empathy alone is responsible for the encouraging results, given the emphasis on both reframing and empathy during the weekend's activities. Perhaps the combination of cognitive reframing and affective empathy exercises can be beneficial to participants in the short term. The long-run results, however, present a different picture of equivalence between the two forgiveness conditions.

On the dependent variable of mental health, as measured by a brief symptom checklist (Derogatis & Spencer, 1982), the advocacy-based forgiveness group was statistically superior to the waitlist control group, but the empathy-based forgiveness program was not.

When presented in published form, McCullough's (1995) study analyzed only 5 of the items from the EFI despite the fact that the participants were given all 60 items (see Enright, 1999, for an explanation of this dependent measure and its use in McCullough et al., 1997). Results generally were similar to those reported in the dissertation with the 60-item scale.

When researchers of Kohlbergian justice education programs were experimenting with the variable of time, one clear finding began to emerge: The shorter the program, the greater the likelihood of smaller effects or even a washout effect at follow-up (see Enright, Lapsley, & Levy, 1983). It appears that the same kind of problem is befalling forgiveness programs. For example, Coyle and Enright (1997) in their 10-week program recorded gains of about 55 and 85 points on the EFI for the experimental groups exposed to forgiveness, whereas McCullough's (1995) weekend seminar reported gains of about 12 and 28 points. The relationship to psychological health did not exist at all for the empathy-based forgiveness group in McCullough's weekend seminar, whereas others with longer forgiveness programs reported positive results with psychological health (see Al-Mabuk et al., 1995; Coyle & Enright, 1997; Freedman & Enright, 1996; Hebl & Enright, 1993). Finally, the hypothesized superiority of the empathy-based group as a way of fostering forgiveness was not realized in McCullough (1995) because of the washout of the posttest findings at follow-up when the two forgiveness programs were analyzed on the dependent variable of forgiveness.

Interventions of short duration on moral issues do not seem to be the answer. After all, changing either one's views of justice or one's level of forgiveness is not a psychological response that can be altered quickly. Both take time. Blasi and Milton (1991) wrote of the moral self as a sense of identity that needs time if adjustments are to be made in how one views the self as moral (or more deeply moral than before). A 1-hour intervention or even a quick series of lessons over one weekend may not be enough time to alter the moral self as a forgiving person.

AN INTERVENTION WITH COLLEGE STUDENTS

Luskin (1998) reported a study with 55 university students (10 men, 45 women). All passed initial screening criteria, indicating that they have been unjustly treated by another person. The age range was between 18 and 30 years. Anyone who experienced the deep trauma of physical, sexual, or violent abuse was excluded from the study. The participants were randomly assigned to one of two identical forgiveness interventions or to a waitlist control group.

Following the pretest, the forgiveness participants received six 1-hour training sessions (once per week). This was followed by the posttest and 10 weeks later by a follow-up test. The contents of the six sessions are as follows:

- *Session 1*. The participants were first introduced to the author's definition of forgiveness, which is described below.

  Forgiveness is the moment to moment experience of peace and understanding that occurs when an injured party's suffering is reduced as they transform their grievance against an offending party. This transformation takes place through learning to take less personal offense, attribute less blame to the offender and, by greater understanding, see the personal and interpersonal harm that occurs as the natural consequence of unresolved anger and hurt. Through the practice of open heartedness and clear thinking the injured party becomes capable of determining how long and often they will experience this moment to moment peace and understanding (pp. 29–30, italics added).

Luskin (1998) relied principally on the work of Ellis (1994) for his exposition on what is meant by "clear thinking" and "greater understanding." He relied on Childre's (1998) HeartMath techniques for his exposition of "peace" and "open heartedness." Forgiveness, in his view, is a learned response, including reduced resentment and the offering of beneficence to the offending party.

Following this introduction, the participants were instructed in "Freeze Frame" and "heart lock-in" approaches to forgiveness. HeartMath's Freeze Frame technique involves the following five steps: First, recognize a stressful experience and take time out from it; second, make an effort to switch focus from one's racing emotions and mind to one's heart, and bring attention to the area around the heart; third, reflect on a loving feeling that may have occurred in the past, and try to reexperience that feeling; fourth, once centered in this way, ask your heart what would be a better response to the stressful situation; and fifth, take seriously the response generated from the heart.

Heart lock-in uses the lessons from the Freeze Frame exercise in a 15–20 minute meditation exercise. The person first relaxes; shifts focus from thoughts to heart; recalls the loving feeling; sends that feeling of love or appreciation to self or another person; and if thoughts intrude, the person continues focusing on the heart exercise. The participants were asked to practice these techniques regularly.

- *Session 2.* The techniques above were placed directly within the forgiveness context and the participants were encouraged to apply them to their own forgiveness situation.
- *Session 3.* The principles of rational emotive therapy (RET) were introduced. The basic point of RET is to challenge irrational thoughts. The participants were asked to examine what happened in light of RET's challenges not to stereotype the offending person or the self. In addition, two other HeartMath issues were taught: appreciation and what is called "neutral." The former asks participants to see the good in the situation, even if the good consists of the fact that the offense could have been even worse than it was. Neutral is a technique that asks the person, not necessarily to maximize positive effect, but to minimize negative effect of an experience by focusing on the area around the heart.
- *Session 4.* There was continued practice in RET and Freeze Frame, focused on the offending person.

- *Session 5.* Empathic listening was introduced. In conversation with others (including the one who hurt the participant), the participants were encouraged to shift to the area of the heart as a way of neutralizing negative effect and increasing beneficence.
- *Session 6.* All of the techniques were reviewed and applied to the participants' forgiveness situation.

The direct measure of forgiveness was the Interpersonal Distance Scale (McCullough, Rachal, & Sandage, 1997, as cited in Luskin, 1998), which assesses one's conciliatory behaviors toward an offender as well as one's desire to end estrangement and harm toward him or her. Other measures given at all three testing periods were the Willingness to Forgive Scale and the Hope Scale (see Al-Mabuk, 1990/1991; Al-Mabuk et al., 1995), state and trait anger and a self-efficacy measure designed to assess the participants' confidence on managing negative feelings toward the offending person and others in the future. Other scales given at only one or two of the testing times are not discussed here.

Analyses used change scores from pretest to posttest and then from pretest to follow-up. For the Interpersonal Distance Scale, no differences were found between treatment and control conditions for either the pretest to posttest or the pretest to follow-up test comparisons. In other words, the forgiveness treatment did not lead to greater forgiveness than the waitlist control condition. The Willingness to Forgive Scale, which assesses one's desire to forgive in hypothetical situations (not directly related to the offender and offense of the participant) showed no difference between groups from pretest to posttest, but there was a difference favoring the experimental group in the pretest to follow-up comparison. In contrast, there were significant differences favoring the experimental group in trait (but not state) anger, hope, and self-efficacy in both comparisons from pretest to posttest and from pretest to follow-up testing.

The pattern of results is not straightforward for concluding that the forgiveness program was effective. The fact that forgiveness, as a central dependent variable, was not statistically significant calls into question whether the intervention actually was about forgiveness or whether it was about anger reduction or some other issue. Even the Willingness to Forgive Scale, although not directly related to one's offender, showed mixed results. On the other hand, trait anger, self-efficacy, and hope all were statistically significant, suggesting that the program was beneficial to the participants. Effect sizes, in most cases, were adequate to strong. Whether the benefit was caused by forgiveness itself or some other psychological variable is ambiguous. Yet, the results are encouraging and potentially important. Further research with HeartMath and RET in the context of forgiveness is indicated.

COLLEGE WOMEN HURT IN ROMANTIC RELATIONSHIPS

Rye (1997) reported on a study of 58 college women from a medium-size midwestern public university. All were hurt by a romantic partner and were between 18 and 23 years old. Approximately 70% were in their freshman year. The most frequently reported hurt was infidelity (69%), followed by verbal abuse, physical abuse, or threats and other offenses.

All of the participants were randomly assigned to one of three conditions: (a) a "secular" forgiveness condition, (b) a religiously based program in which Christian principles were integrated into the secular forgiveness program, and (c) a no-contact comparison group. The forgiveness groups met once per week for six 90-minute sessions. Three female graduate students, trained in the forgiveness principles, led the groups and were supervised by a licensed, PhD clinical psychologist and an advanced clinical psychology doctoral student.

A brief description of each session is as follows:

- *Session 1*. Following introductions and group guidelines, the group leaders led participants in a "guided meditation" (p. 45) of the wrong done and the wrongdoer. The point was to examine one's feelings, thoughts, and behaviors toward the offender. Homework consisted of a letter written, but not sent, to the offender. The religiously based program followed the same guidelines with the addition of the request for the participants to examine how their religious and spiritual lives had been affected by the injustice.
- *Session 2*. Homework assignments were first reviewed, and then the participants explored their angry feelings. For homework, they made an inventory of the grudges that they still maintained. The religiously based program also focused on how anger is portrayed in the New Testament.
- *Session 3*. Following an examination of the participants' grudge list, dyads were formed for the purpose of role playing issues of "negative self-statements" (p. 46). The purpose was to analyze how self-statements can facilitate anger control. They were then introduced to the author's definition of forgiveness, which is "the overcoming of negative thoughts, feelings, and behaviors in response to an offender's considerable injustice" (p. 114). Forgiveness was contrasted with forgetting, condoning, legal pardon, and reconciling. The homework consisted of reflecting on the lessons one can learn from emotional pain.
- *Session 4*. The participants once again reflected on the author's definition of forgiveness and then discussed the potential bene-

fits and drawbacks to forgiving someone. A reflection on the offender's positive qualities then ensued.

- *Session 5.* The session focused first on how the group members may have hurt other people. A challenge to begin forgiving the offender was then made.
- *Session 6.* The group discussed the issue of reconciliation and reflected on how far along the forgiveness process they were as individuals. A final opportunity to forgive during the intervention itself was presented.

Fourteen measures were given at pretest, posttest (1 week after intervention), and follow-up (approximately 6 weeks later). Measures included anger, anxiety, depression, hope, anticipation of the future, hostility, fear of intimacy, loneliness, religious well-being, existential well-being, the likelihood that one would forgive, feelings of forgiveness (focused on the offender in particular), forgiveness cognition (focused on the offender), and concepts of forgiveness learned in the sessions.

The results were analyzed in four ways. First, all groups were collapsed to examine the change across pretest, posttest, and follow-up. Second, the groups were separated and a Time (pre-, post-, and follow-up tests) × Condition analysis of variance was run. Unfortunately, the statistical tests that were significant were not followed with a test of the interactions but instead with within-condition examinations across the time periods. Thus, one cannot assess which conditions differed from which other conditions across time. Third, the groups were separated, and a Time × Condition test was done from pretest to posttest only. Finally, the same statistical design was run for the pretest to follow-up comparison.

Consider the results in each of the four statistical designs. For the first comparison (collapsing across conditions to examine change from pretest to posttest to follow-up), all 14 variables showed statistically significant gains. Of course, this could be caused not by the effectiveness of the forgiveness interventions but by time itself.

In the second comparison (separating condition across pretest, posttest, and follow-up), 9 of the 14 variables were statistically significant at the $p < .05$ level. When the more conservative approach is taken ($p < .01$), four of the variables show statistical significance (existential well-being, feelings of forgiveness, forgiveness cognition, and the forgiveness test regarding intervention content).[1] Again, because the interactions were not tested, it is unclear exactly which conditions are different from which other conditions; an examination of means suggests that the forgiveness interventions (secular and religious) outperformed the comparison group, but the two

---

[1] Because there were four groupings of 14 analyses each, $p < .01$ seems appropriate.

forgiveness groups do not appear to differ from one another. In essence, the forgiveness interventions led to an increase in forgiveness variables but not to a change in clinically relevant variables such as anxiety or depression.

For the third comparison (separating condition and comparing pretest to posttest), 4 of the 14 variables showed that the forgiveness interventions outperformed the comparison group in anger and the three forgiveness variables. Here anger, as a clinically relevant variable, does differentiate the groups. Finally, the fourth comparison (pretest to follow-up) showed a more favorable pattern, with 6 of the 14 variables showing statistical significance favoring the forgiveness interventions over the comparison group. Those variables included avoidance of hope (changing toward a more hopeful stance), anticipation of the future, religious well-being, existential well-being, cognitive forgiveness, and the forgiveness test from the intervention. Apparently it took some time following intervention for the students to assimilate the information and to apply it to their own romantic relationship. Once this occurred, however, those in the forgiveness groups seemed to benefit in a number of positive ways.

We find it interesting that positive results were obtained when the definition of forgiveness included only the absence of negative responses toward an offender rather than what (to us) is a more complete definition including the presence of positive responses toward that offender. It is still unclear whether the definition used here, when applied within a clinical context, can effect change in such variables as anxiety, depression, and hostility. We know that when a more complete definition is presented to people (see chapter 6), such results can be observed. More research is needed here.

HIGH SCHOOL STUDENTS HURT IN ROMANTIC RELATIONSHIPS

Gassin's (1995) research with high school students is unique in that no other researcher has assessed such a young population to date. Her 19 participants (15 young women and 4 young men) were all hurt by a romantic partner. A randomized experimental and no-contact control group format was used. There was a pretest, followed by an 8-week intervention in which the participants met once per week. The experimental group engaged in a strictly cognitive approach to forgiveness. The instruction was based on a psychological education curriculum in which the participants learned principles of psychology and then were encouraged to apply the knowledge to their particular situation.

Unique to this study is the fact that the instructor deliberately avoided using the word *forgiveness*. The point was to ascertain whether the psychological principles that, in theory, underlie forgiveness, could, by themselves, induce a forgiveness response. The no-contact control group received no instruction. A posttest and an 8-week follow-up were included. Dependent measures included forgiveness, state anger, psychological depression, hope, and social cognitive complexity.[2]

The eight experimental sessions are described below.

- *Session 1*. Exploration of the hurtful situation and its personal consequences.
- *Session 2*. The nature and impact of psychological defense mechanisms were discussed.
- *Session 3*. Ecological and systems models of psychology were presented, showing the interconnectedness among, for example, conflict among spouses, displaced parental anger onto a child, and that child's anger. The point was to examine the many factors that may influence someone's behavior and thoughts.
- *Session 4*. Introduction to social perspective taking and empathy. Because a number of previous interventions have linked forgiveness with these variables, Gassin (1995) believed that the students' introduction to these variables may promote forgiveness of the romantic partner.
- *Session 5*. Discussion of attribution theory. The goal was to aid the students in identifying the various types of psychological variables that may explain another's unfairness. Attribution errors were examined so that the students could examine whether their current perceptions of the former partner are accurate.
- *Session 6*. Discussion of the core worth of people regardless of their behavior.
- *Session 7*. Finding a sense of meaning in the unfairness and subsequent hurt.
- *Session 8*. Review and summary of the psychological principles covered in the course.

The results were analyzed with change scores from pretest to posttest and then from posttest to follow-up. Only the social–cognitive complexity scale showed any differences between the experimental and control groups. The experimental participants developed more sophisticated conceptions

---

[2]The social–cognitive complexity scale, created by Gassin (1995), was an open-ended essay, asking the participants to describe themselves and the romantic partner who allegedly was unfair to them. The degree of psychological differentiation of one's own and the other's personality comprised the gist of the complexity measure.

of self and other as a result of the course, and this was statistically significant on the pretest to posttest group comparison.

It is unclear why the intervention did not improve forgiveness or lead to a change on the assessments of psychological health. We have several speculations. First, it may be the case that younger participants require more time in a forgiveness intervention. Younger participants may need the time to learn and reflect on the psychological concepts more than adults do. Second, the fact that the word *forgiveness* was not used at all in the intervention may be a reason for the lack of differences between the groups. *Forgiveness* is a powerful word with deep meaning for some people. That word may need to be used by interveners if psychological progress is to be made. Third, adolescent pride may result in a need to minimize the effect of rejection. If denial is strong, resentment will not be uncovered. Fourth, it may be that romantic injustice is not as compelling an issue for high school students as it might be for adults. Once the person who was treated unfairly finds another partner, it may be the case that psychological injury fades quickly. The pretest means suggest this. The experimental group's pretest mean on the EFI was 238.85. This is over 40 points higher than the EFI mean in Coyle and Enright (1997), for example. Finally, the small sample size may have obscured statistical significance on forgiveness. For example, the experimental group showed a gain on the EFI of about 46 points from pretest to follow-up, whereas the control group gained only 15 points, yet no significance was observed. Statistical power may be playing a part here.

INNER-CITY 5TH GRADERS AND FORGIVENESS

Hepp-Dax (1996) conducted the first empirical study of forgiveness with children. Twenty-three 5th graders, 11 boys and 12 girls, served as participants. Nine boys were Hispanic, and 2 were African American; 11 girls were Hispanic, and 1 was African American. The majority of participants cited peers (61%) as the offender. The offenses included such injustices as verbal (52%) and physical (17%) attacks. The children were randomly assigned to a forgiveness group or a control group assigned to an ecology curriculum. The boys and girls met separately in different groups. Each group met for eight 45-minute sessions within a 4-week period.

The forgiveness intervention was based on the process model (discussed in chapter 5). A manual describing the processes was prepared for the intervener, a female school psychologist with 17 years of experience. The forgiveness curriculum is as follows: .

- *Session 1*. Participants were introduced to issues of fairness and unfairness along with the right to feel and be safe.

- *Session 2*. Emotional pain as a result of unfairness was discussed. The children learned, in a rudimentary way, about psychological defenses and coping strategies. For example, the instructor read a story of a child who was bullied by another. The one who was attacked responded by denying what happened (a psychological defense). Eventually, the child got angry. Different kinds of anger were discussed: temporary annoyance, deeper anger that can affect a person's mood, and even deeper anger that seems to last and can turn to hatred. The children then learned about their choices when angry. They can choose to try to let the anger go, or they can hold onto it.
- *Session 3*. The children were introduced to the idea of what forgiveness is and is not. Forgiveness was introduced as a positive, compassionate gift that can be given to those who are unfair. Forgiveness was distinguished from reconciliation so that the children would continue to feel and be safe, depending on their particular circumstance. To concretely illustrate the power of forgiveness, the instructor filled a bowl with water and had the children empty small bottles of food coloring into the bowl. The food coloring represented the anger and resentment of unforgiveness. The instructor then poured a small bottle of bleach into the water darkened by the food coloring, and the substance turned clear again. She pointed out how forgiveness can act on the darkened emotions in one's heart and clear them.
- *Session 4*. The commitment to forgive was discussed. The children generated two lists: one stating why they might want to forgive and another stating why they might not want to forgive. Discussion followed.
- *Session 5*. The children engaged in discussions intended to reframe who the unfair person is. The mind was compared to a television set: Some stations show violence, whereas other stations show supportive people helping each other. The children were told, "When you are seeing the one who hurt you as an entirely bad person, it is like you are on the TV channel with violence. Try turning the channel in your mind regarding the person. Turn to a channel that shows some of his or her good points." The instructor challenged the students to think of the injuring person in broader contexts than just the injury.
- *Session 6*. One's own emotional pain, empathy, and compassion as feelings were introduced. Empathy was discussed as trying to feel what the other person feels. Questions such as the following were asked: What do you think it would be like to be in (the offending person's) skin? The point was to have the

children see someone who may be confused, or unhappy, or afraid. Compassion was introduced first by having the children focus on people they know who are poor. They then thought about someone who was physically ill. Finally, they considered these feelings of love toward the offending person. The instructor stated that as the child begins to feel even a little compassion toward him or her, then the change of heart that is forgiveness is emerging.

- *Session 7.* The children's need to be forgiven by others was discussed. This was done to show them that they, too, have needed and in the future may need others' understanding and forgiveness. If this is so, then it may serve as a motivator to forgive.

- *Session 8.* The ideas of letting go of the grudges and angers were discussed. Forgiveness can reach beyond the fights and bitterness with one person to affect the whole world. The idea of teamwork in forgiving and the spreading of love and compassion were introduced and discussed.

The ecology program focused on living systems, solar energy, plant growth, and one's place in preserving a good world. The program included a combination of lectures, discussion, and group activities.

As in other programs, once the experimental group finished the forgiveness education, the ecology control group began the forgiveness work. A 7-month follow-up was also administered. Dependent measures included the EFI for Children, self-esteem, anxiety, and a teacher behavior-rating scale.

Following the first 4 weeks, the forgiveness experimental group was statistically significantly higher than the ecology control group in forgiveness. This was the first demonstration that children as young as age 10 can be taught to forgive. There were, however, no demonstrable improvements in the psychological variables. Once the ecology group began the forgiveness intervention over the next 4 weeks, their improvements on the dependent measures were compared from the first 4 weeks (when they served as the control group) to the second 4 weeks (when they were the experimental group). No statistically significant differences were evident for any measure, including forgiveness. In other words, this second experimental group did not replicate the gains in forgiveness observed with the first experimental group.

At follow-up, all children who were still attending the school ($N = 23$) were reassessed. The statistical test combined all participants after the second posttest (at 8 weeks) and compared this with the scores at the 7-month follow-up. There were statistically significant gains on the Negative Cognition subscale in forgiveness, but not on the total scale or any of the other subscales. In other words, the children thought less negatively about their offender at follow-up than they did at the 8-week posttest. Self-esteem also increased significantly. One cannot claim that the forgiveness intervention alone is responsible for these positive results. It may be that the combined forgiveness and ecology curriculum, which half of the students experienced, played a part. It also is possible that time alone aided the children's improvements in forgiveness and self-esteem.

HYPOTHESIS-FORMING CONCLUSIONS

Because forgiveness research is yet in its infancy, different researchers are experimenting with approaches to intervention that are different from one another. Because most empirical attempts are assessed once only, it becomes impossible to draw definitive or even reasonably confident conclusions, especially when the null hypothesis is not rejected. For example, why did Luskin (1998) fail to induce forgiveness in his participants? Factors of time, the nature of the offenses being considered, the nature of the curriculum, and the particular makeup of the participants all could have played a part and interacted with one another. Similarly, why did Gassin (1995) not find positive results with the high school students hurt in romantic relationships? All of the variables possibly affecting Luskin's study could be present here, as well as the fact that the intervention was exclusively cognitive and the instructor deliberately avoided using the word *forgiveness*. Conclusions become difficult.

Nevertheless, let us in a spirit of hypothesis-forming musings (not in a spirit of drawing conclusions) speculate about the qualities within the various interventions that may prove important in the future. Consider six issues.

First, we are of the opinion that longer term approaches will prove to be more effective than short-term efforts. As we have seen, brief forgiveness therapy has not shown itself to be powerful in two studies to date. Of course, depending on the nature of the problem, brief forgiveness therapy may be successful. We predict that participants who are highly motivated to forgive, who have problems that are not deeply and seriously unjust, who have a history of understanding and even practicing forgiveness, and who are not experiencing clinical levels of anxiety or depression may benefit more from brief therapy than those who do not show this pattern. In other words, brief therapy may be for only certain kinds of clients or patients.

Second, the younger the person, the longer the intervention may have to be, as when dealing with children and college-age adults. Fifth graders may need more time to understand the subtleties of forgiveness than college students. Nevertheless, age alone should not be the determining factor. College students, who are used to learning and applying that learning, may require less time than middle-aged adults, who have been absent from the classroom for many years. Certainly, forgiveness therapy is not only about learning, but that learning component may add time to the process for some people.

Third, it may be best, as is the case with the vast majority of interventions, to explicitly let the client know that this, in fact, is a program about forgiveness. *Forgiveness* is such a meaningful word for many people that the introduction of the word itself may prove to have some therapeutic benefit.

Fourth, we are unconvinced that forgiveness can be defined by the absence of resentment without the presence of beneficence. The ancient literature and modern philosophical discourse on forgiveness are more in agreement than disagreement with us on this point. The arguments that forgiveness is only the abandonment of resentment (see McGary, 1989) seem less convincing as arguments than those, say, of North (1987) or Holmgren (1993) that make room for unconditional love or respect of the offender. We challenge each future researcher to defend his or her position regarding the definition being used as the basis for the intervention.

Fifth, programs that address the patient's cognitive, affective, and even behavioral approach to the offending person may prove more effective than programs that reduce forgiveness only to the cognitive, or affective, or behavioral. Reframing seems essential to us, as does the cultivation of compassion and empathy. Learning how to set behavioral boundaries and establish trust are important when the offender's behavior that led to the unfairness is deemed unacceptable to the person.

Sixth, there seems to be a wide variety of approaches for introducing reframing, empathy, and compassion to clients. Hepp-Dax's (1996) exercise with the bowls, bottles, and bleach with children to show how forgiveness works on anger is wonderfully creative. Luskin's (1998) use of HeartMath strikes us as important and worthy of further study. McCullough et al.'s (1997) use of empathy training should be pursued. In other words, even though there may be important essentials underlying forgiveness, there is no one external expression of each essential. Researchers and clinicians should be encouraged to experiment with creative manifestations of the forgiveness essentials and to share these with the scientific and therapeutic communities.

FUTURE RESEARCH

As some final thoughts on interventions, we would like to speculate on new directions that dissertators and other researchers might take. An ideal study may be the following. First, select a sample that has clinical symptoms (such as high anxiety and low self-esteem). In the ideal, it is best to select a group that has suffered unambiguous hurts, such as those who have been hurt in a traffic accident and now have spinal cord injuries and in which the other driver has been found guilty of causing the accident. Participants in clusters of three should be yoked on age, gender, social class, type of injury, severity of injury, and time since the injury. The three are then randomized to one of three groups: (a) a forgiveness program, (b) a support program, and (c) a no-contact control group. Our field, although young, is ready for this three-group investigation.

The interventions should be one-to-one for at least 12 weeks; we say this because of the strong results in Freedman and Enright (1996) and Coyle and Enright (1997), which were individualized and long term. Even better, the ending point should be geared to each individual's response in the forgiveness group that he or she has forgiven. With the yoking procedure, then the posttest can commence for the three yoked participants once the experimental participant, by self-report, forgives. The forgiveness and support conditions should each have written manuals for the intervener and, ideally, for the participants as well. In our view, control groups after posttesting should be exposed to forgiveness for ethical reasons.

The forgiveness manual should include information on what forgiveness is and is not; the importance of a decision to forgive; and training in reframing, empathy, compassion, bearing pain, and finding meaning in suffering, at the very least. Other components could be added as described in chapter 5. If sufficient numbers of participants are located, then assessing different forgiveness interventions with different facilitators, randomly assigned, would be important to detect experimenter effects.

A generation of research beyond this might include discerning which aspects of forgiveness intervention (reframing, empathy, and so forth) are vital to statistically significant outcomes and which are not. Are reframing and empathy both necessary for improved psychological health in participants? Only carefully constructed experiments that vary one or two themes at a time will be able to answer such a question. Do certain kinds of problems (incest, sibling rivalry, spinal cord injury) require longer interventions? Does length of intervention vary with time since the injury? Perhaps those with more recent injustices are the most angry, requiring the most time in treatment. The next generation of researchers should begin refining the work done to date so that clients and patients can expect the most efficient treatment possible. Research can increase such treatment efficiency.

19

MEASURES OF INTERPERSONAL FORGIVENESS

As we have seen throughout this book, definition matters. If therapists are to help a patient forgive, they must have an adequate understanding of what forgiveness is and how people go about forgiving (Enright & North, 1998). If therapists are interested in getting an initial assessment of the degree to which a person has forgiven someone, then they need to have a good scale that accurately reflects the definition of forgiveness. After all, if a patient shows, through a screening assessment, that he or she is deeply unforgiving toward, for example, a parent, then therapy will start at a different point than if the patient shows some degree of forgiveness toward the parent.

Important considerations for any busy helping professional are whether the assessment device reflects the construct well; is easy to administer and score; and has excellent psychometric properties, showing strong reliability and validity. These same considerations hold both for researchers, whose statistically significant data depend in part on the reliability and validity of the scales, and for test constructors, whose goal ought to be the creation of a better measure. To assist therapist, researcher, and test constructor, we provide considerable detail on a variety of existing measures of forgiveness. The information should aid the clinician who is seeking a good screening or even a post-therapy assessment. The information should aid the researcher in determining whether to incorporate a scale into a scientific investigation and the test constructor who may wish to build a measure of forgiveness.

Our purpose here is to review the existing measures of forgiveness that have been used in published research. After describing each, we offer our recommendation for the use of the instrument.

ENRIGHT FORGIVENESS INVENTORY

The Enright Forgiveness Inventory (EFI) is based on the construct of forgiveness discussed in chapter 2. In devising the scale at the University of Wisconsin–Madison, we presumed that forgiveness is in the context of a personal injustice that the respondent has experienced (see Subkoviak et al., 1992, 1995). When forgiving, the participant offers a degree of positive affect, cognition, and behavior toward the offending person. Also, when forgiving, the person should demonstrate, at least to a degree, the absence of negative affect, cognition, and behavior toward the offending one. When assessing for forgiveness, researchers must distinguish between the respondent's genuine overtures of forgiveness and false responses or pseudoforgiveness. Thus, any good measure of forgiveness, in our opinion, must rule out that the person is not condoning, excusing, or denying what happened. Otherwise, the respondent may assent to such statements as "I am no longer angry" or "I like the person," not because forgiveness is taking place but because he or she sees no problem at all.

We began our work by convening a seminar with eight graduate students and two professors, one of whom is a specialist in measurement, who met for over a 2-year period to study and understand the construct of forgiveness. Following this period of study, we generated a pool of potential items that reflected the six subscales described above (absence of negative affect, cognition, and behavior, and the presence of positive responses in these same three areas).

The panel then decided on 25 items in each of the six subscales that best seemed to represent forgiveness. For example, "I think of ways to get even" assessed the presence of negative cognition toward the offender. The 150 items were then placed into a 6-point Likert format from *strongly disagree* (1) to *strongly agree* (6). The higher the score, the more forgiveness is being offered to the one who acted unfairly. The goal, through item analysis, was to reduce the number of items to 60, 10 within each subscale, with a range of scores from 60 to 360.

Prior to considering the forgiveness items, the participants completed a cover sheet asking them to consider the most recent hurt in which a person was unfair to them. Note that we labeled the EFI as the "Attitude Scale" for participants so that the exact nature of the assessment would not be so obvious. A series of questions about the person and the event follows on this sheet. See Exhibit 19.1 for an example of this cover sheet and

EXHIBIT 19.1

Description of the Enright Forgiveness Inventory (60-item version)

ATTITUDE SCALE

We are sometimes unfairly hurt by people, whether in family, friendship, school, work, or other situations. We ask you now to think of the *most recent* experience of someone hurting you *unfairly* and *deeply*. For a few moments, visualize in your mind the events of that interaction. Try to see the person and try to experience what happened.

How deeply were you hurt
when the incident occurred?
(Circle one)

| Not hurt | A little hurt | Some hurt | Much hurt | A great deal of hurt |

Who hurt you? (Circle one)

Child   Spouse   Relative   Friend of same gender

Friend of opposite gender   Employer   Other (specify) _____

Is the person living?   Yes   No

How long ago did this hurtful event happen? (Please write in the number of days or weeks, etc.)

_____ days ago   _____ months ago

_____ weeks ago   _____ years ago

Please briefly describe what happened when this person hurt you:

_____

_____

_____

_____

Now, please answer a series of questions about your current attitude toward the person. We do *not* want your rating of past attitudes, but your ratings of attitudes *right now*. All responses are confidential so please answer honestly. Thank you.

EXAMPLES OF AFFECT ITEMS

This set of items deals with your current *feelings* or *emotions* right now toward the person. Try to assess your actual *feeling* for the person on each item. For each item please check the appropriate line that *best* describes your current feeling. Please do not skip any item. Thanks.

I feel _____ toward him/her.
(Place each word in the blank when answering each item.)

	Strongly disagree	Disagree	Slightly disagree	Slightly agree	Agree	Strongly agree
1. Warm	1	2	3	4	5	6
2. Negative	1	2	3	4	5	6
3. Kindness	1	2	3	4	5	6
4. Happy	1	2	3	4	5	6
5. Hostile	1	2	3	4	5	6

20 items total on Affect subscale (10 positive and 10 negative affect items).

Continued

EXHIBIT 19.1
Continued

EXAMPLES OF BEHAVIOR ITEMS

This set of items deals with your current *behavior* toward the person. Consider how you *do act* or *would act* toward the person in answering the questions. For each item please check the appropriate line that *best* describes your current behavior or probable behavior. Please do not skip any items. Thanks.

Regarding the person, I do or would _____. (Place each word or phrase in the blank when answering each item.)

	Strongly disagree	Disagree	Slightly disagree	Slightly agree	Agree	Strongly agree
21. Show friendship	1	2	3	4	5	6
22. Avoid	1	2	3	4	5	6
23. Ignore	1	2	3	4	5	6
24. Neglect	1	2	3	4	5	6
25. Help	1	2	3	4	5	6

20 items total on Behavior subscale (10 positive and 10 negative items).

EXAMPLES OF COGNITIVE ITEMS

This set of items deals with how you currently *think* about the person. Think about the kinds of thoughts that occupy your *mind* right *now* regarding this particular person. For each item please check the appropriate line that *best* describes your current thinking. Please do not skip any item. Thanks.

I think he or she is _____. (Place each word or phrase in the blank when answering each item.)

	Strongly disagree	Disagree	Slightly disagree	Slightly agree	Agree	Strongly agree
41. Wretched	1	2	3	4	5	6
42. Evil	1	2	3	4	5	6
43. Horrible	1	2	3	4	5	6
44. Of good quality	1	2	3	4	5	6
45. Worthy of respect	1	2	3	4	5	6

20 items total on Cognition subscale (10 positive and 10 negative items).

THE PSEUDOFORGIVENESS SCALE
Items Are Listed Below

In thinking through the person and event you just rated, please consider the following final questions:

	Strongly disagree	Disagree	Slightly disagree	Slightly agree	Agree	Strongly agree
61. There really was no problem now that I think about it.	1	2	3	4	5	6
63. The person was not wrong in what he or she did to me.	1	2	3	4	5	6
65. What the person did was fair.	1	2	3	4	5	6

Continued

EXHIBIT 19.1
Continued

CONSTRUCT VALIDATION QUESTION

We have one final question. To what extent have you forgiven the person you rated on the *Attitude Scale*?

Not at all		In progress		Complete forgiveness
_____	_____	_____	_____	_____

examples of items in the Affect, Behavior, and Cognition domains of forgiveness from the final 60-item version of the scale. All items with negative material ("I resent the person") are reversed scored. Note also that the word *forgiveness* appears nowhere on the scale so that the participants cannot easily ascertain the exact nature of the questionnaire.

A 5-item pseudoforgiveness scale is included at the end of the questionnaire and is scored separately from the first 60 items. This scale is intended to assess for instances of condoning, excusing, and denying on the part of the respondent. As a general rule, anyone scoring 20 or higher on this scale should have his or her data removed from further analysis because, in all likelihood, he or she is not demonstrating genuine forgiveness. We arrived at the cutoff of 20 because this value suggests that the participant is checking the "agree" side of the scale, on the average, for each of the five responses. Examples of the pseudoforgiveness scale are also in Exhibit 19.1.

In the initial study (Subkoviak et al., 1992, 1995), we selected items for the final 60-item version of the EFI as follows. First we examined an item's correlation with its corresponding domain score (of Affect, Behavior, or Cognition). In other words, we summed the 50 items within the Affect domain, subtracted that item from the domain, then correlated the item of interest with the remaining 49 items within the domain. Each selected item correlated above .65 with its respective domain score. Then we examined the correlation of each item with the total score from the Crowne–Marlowe (1960) Social Desirability Scale. Each selected item correlated below .17 with social desirability. An added constraint was to select the 10 best items within the six subscales (negative affect, positive affect, negative cognition, and so forth) that fit our correlational criteria with the domain and social desirability. The resulting scale, in theory, should be internally homogeneous and be free of social desirability response bias.

This initial study assessed 394 participants, 204 women and 190 men, half of whom were college students (mean age = 22.1 years) and the other half the same-sex parent of the student (mean age = 49.6 years). Besides the EFI and social desirability, the participants were given the Spielberger State–Trait Anxiety Scale (Spielberger et al., 1983), the Beck Depression Inventory (Beck & Steer, 1987), and a religiosity scale assessing behavioral practice of one's religion (Subkoviak et al., 1995). A final question—always given last—"To what degree have you forgiven the person whom you identified on the Attitude Scale?," examined the construct validity of the EFI.

Table 19.1 gives the values for the Cronbach's alpha of internal consistency and the correlation between the EFI and the one-item question about forgiving the offender, not only for this initial validation study but also for other studies using the EFI within the United States. The EFI is highly internally consistent across diverse studies. There also is strong construct validity. Keep in mind that the one-item test about forgiveness, as any one-item scale does, restricts the value of the correlation to a maximum of about .70. The correlations across the studies suggest that the EFI unambiguously measures forgiveness and not some other construct.

Table 19.2 gives the internal consistency estimates and the construct validity correlations for samples across other cultures. Again, we see strong internal consistency reliability and construct validity for the EFI. It seems that this scale can be used as a measure of the degree to which a person forgives another in a wide variety of cultural settings.

TABLE 19.1
Reliability and Validity of the Enright Forgiveness Inventory, U.S. Samples

Study	Sample size	Cronbach's α	Correlation of EFI and 1-item forgiveness question
Subkoviak et al. (1995)	394[a]	.98	.68
Gassin (1995)	19[b]	.99	.74
Wilson (1994)	118[c]	.97	.64
Holeman (1995)	63[d]	.98	.59
Sarinopoulos (1996)	219[e]	.99	.60
Ashleman (1996)	30[f]	.98	.69
Coyle & Enright (1997)	10[g]	.95	1-item question not given
Nousse (1998)	32[h]	.98	.63

Note. EFI = Enright Forgiveness Inventory.
[a]204 female and 190 male participants; half of the sample was college students (mean age = 22 years), the other half was their same-sex parent (mean age = 50 years). [b]15 females and 4 male high school students (estimated mean age = 16.5 years). [c]Women who survived sexual abuse (mean age = 40 years). [d]63 women who survived sexual abuse (mean age = 38 years). [e]157 female and 62 male participants; half of the sample were college students (mean age = 21 years), the other half were their same-sex parent (mean age = 49 years). [f]30 divorced mothers (mean age = 40 years). [g]Men hurt by partner's abortion decision (mean age = 22 years); alpha was based on the average of three pretests. [h]Women with an injustice regarding an abortion decision or procedure (mean age = 35 years).

TABLE 19.2
Reliability and Validity of the Enright Forgiveness Inventory in Five Cultures

Culture	Sample size	Cronbach's α	Correlation of EFI and 1-item forgiveness question
Austria	376[a]	.98	.78
Brazil			
Sample 1	200[b]	.98	.74
Sample 2	399[c]	.98	.70
Israel	164[d]	.98	.71
Korea	326[e]	.97	.68
Taiwan	321[f]	.97	.68

Note. EFI = Enright Forgiveness Inventory.
[a]190 male and 186 female participants; half of the sample was college students (mean age = 23 years), the other half was their same-sex parent (mean age = 52 years). [b]100 male and 100 female participants; half of the sample was college students (mean age = 22 years), the other half was their same-sex parent (mean age = 49 years). [c]200 male and 179 female high school students (mean age = 15 years). [d]100 male and 54 female participants; half of the sample was college students (mean age = 23 years), the other half was their same-sex parent (mean age = 52 years). [e]161 male and 165 female participants; half of the sample was college students (mean age = 21 years), the other half was their same-sex parent (mean age = 51 years). [f]151 male and 170 female participants; half of the sample was college students (mean age = 21 years), the other half was their same-sex parent (mean age = 49 years).

Other findings of note from the initial study are as follows. The EFI did not generally correlate with anxiety. In other words, when a participant is hurt by a person who is not particularly important to the participant, he or she does not experience emotional distress. On the other hand, when parents are hurt by close family members and when college students are hurt in partner relationships, there is a significant and moderate (−.30 to −.48) negative relationship between the EFI and state anxiety. It seems that forgiveness matters for emotional health when one experiences hurt in what we called *developmentally appropriate* relationships, those relationships that many people in a given age group identify as important. Depression and the EFI were not related in general, and one possible explanation is that we had a restriction-of-range problem with the depression variable. Few in the sample were in the clinical range of depression. Nonetheless, parents who were deeply hurt by a family member showed a correlation of −.43 between the negative affect subscale of the EFI and depression.

A 2-week examination of the EFI's test–retest reliability with 36 college participants was reported in this initial study. The correlation from Time 1 to Time 2 for the entire 60-item scale was .86. It was expected that this value would be lower than the internal consistency value, because the latter was an observation at one point in time, which diminished measurement error.

Given the strong internal consistency reliability and construct validity across cultures for this scale, we recommend its use when the researcher or clinician wants an index of the degree to which a respondent has forgiven someone. The directions on the cover sheet can be altered to fit the intended purpose. For example, the user may not be interested in knowing about the most recent hurt experienced by the respondent but instead desire information on a spouse or parent. The directions can be altered accordingly. Our research group has done so, and the psychometric properties have remained strong (see Coyle & Enright, 1997, as one example).

Let us end this section with an idea raised in chapter 15 about the nature of forgiveness as a virtue. The cross-cultural evidence in Table 19.2 suggests that forgiveness possesses certain features common to a wide variety of cultures. Certainly each culture may express forgiveness differently and to varying degrees. Yet, when we asked participants to rate the degree to which they forgave the person targeted on the Attitude Scale, all cultures showed strong correlations between the forgiveness question and the EFI total score. Apparently, the words used in the EFI convey the concept of forgiveness to people in Eastern and Western cultures, in the Northern and Southern hemispheres and across diverse religions, at least in the cultures chosen. We doubt that forgiveness is a convention, subject to such deep and divergent cultural interpretations, as to render the concept unrecognizable when taken out of one cultural context and placed in another.

WADE FORGIVENESS SCALE

When we were developing the EFI, we were unaware of Wade's (1989/1990) efforts to devise a scale that assesses the degree of forgiveness toward an offending other.[1] Likewise, Wade was unaware of our efforts. It is, therefore, intriguing that the two scales have certain important features in common: (a) Both assess the degree of forgiveness in the areas of affect, behavior, and cognition; (b) both are on Likert scales for each item (ours on a 1–6 scale and Wade's on a 1–5 scale per item); and (c) both ask the respondent to focus on one person only. In contrast, the two scales differ in the following: (a) The Wade scale asked 150 respondents to think about a person they already have forgiven, and another 150 respondents were asked to consider a person they had not forgiven, which makes the responses retrospective; (b) Wade includes items focusing on the respondent's relationship with the divine ("I prayed for them, asking God to bless them"), whereas the EFI focuses only on the offending person; and (c) within the scales of Affect, Behavior, and Cognition, we devised six subscales for the EFI (positive affect,

---

[1] Although our goal in this chapter is to review only those scales that have been used in published research, we make an exception with the Wade Forgiveness Scale. The dissertation project in which the scale was developed is unique at this point, focused on the construction of a forgiveness scale.

negative affect, positive behavior, negative behavior, positive cognition, and negative cognition); Wade, in comparison, created only one Affect subscale (positive and negative items), four Behavior subscales (8 items assessing avoidance, 5 assessing issues with God, 12 conciliation items, and 4 items concerning grudge-holding), and four Cognition subscales (10 items assessing revenge, 4 assessing freedom from obsession, 9 affirmation items, and 5 victimization items).

As we did in the development of the EFI, Wade (1989/1990) went through a laborious test construction process. First, she interviewed 20 professionals, including professors, psychologists, and pastors to understand their views of what forgiveness and unforgiveness are. On the basis of these interviews, Wade generated 451 items that seemed to reflect the constructs of forgiveness as brought out in the interviews. Ten nursing students then rated each of the 451 items to judge whether they reflected forgiveness or not. Eight of 10 raters had to agree on any given item for it to be retained, which reduced the pool of items to 242.

Next, Wade (1989/1990) asked 10 adult students from Sunday school classes to further rate the items regarding their appropriateness for a scale of forgiveness, which resulted in a total of 118 items being retained. Because the subscale categories of Affect, Behavior, and Cognition were based on Wade's and the original interviewees' basic understanding of what constitutes forgiveness, these subscales were retained throughout this item reduction process.

Finally, 150 college students were asked to consider someone whom they had forgiven and another 150 were asked to specifically consider someone whom they had not forgiven in rating the 118 items. Wade then analyzed (two-tailed analysis of variance) each item by comparing the variances from the group that had forgiven with the group that had not forgiven, eliminating 18 items. The remaining items were then subjected to a factor analysis, out of which emerged the subscales within each of the larger subscales of Affect, Behavior, and Cognition. If an item did not correlate at least .50 with the factor's total score, that item was eliminated from the scale. Through this process, the final, 83-item Wade Forgiveness Scale (WFS) was developed.

In this original development, the WFS was not correlated with other scales to establish construct validity. However, Sarinopoulos (1996) did correlate the 83-item scale with the 60-item EFI in a sample of 111 college students and 108 of their same-sex parents, similar to the Subkoviak et al. (1995) design. The two forgiveness scales correlated .87, suggesting considerable convergence of constructs between the two scales. The Affect, Behavior, and Cognition subscales between the two measures correlated between .71 and .84. Both scales showed high internal consistency reliability (EFI = .99, WFS = .97) and no relation to social desirability. Sarinopoulos, in contrast to Wade, asked each participant to think about a person who has recently hurt the participant deeply and unfairly, following the EFI directions. No mention of forgiveness or unforgiveness was made. This change in directions for the Wade scale may have led to a stronger relationship between the two scales than may have been the case if her original wording was retained.

It appears that the EFI and the WFS tap similar constructs. This was somewhat surprising to us because we see important theoretical differences between the EFI and WFS. Consider five differences between the two scales. First, the WFS does not have a pseudoforgiveness scale. Thus, a person may be condoning or excusing the offender, a situation the scale will not detect. Second, there is no distinction made between forgiveness and reconciliation. The Behavior subscale of conciliation has at least 5 of 12 items focused on reconciliation (Item 8: "I took steps toward reconciliation: wrote them, called them, expressed love, showed concern, etc."; Item 24: "I did my best to put aside the mistrust"). From a philosophical perspective, one can forgive and not trust, as when a friend forgives a compulsive gambler but then will not make loans to him or her anymore.

Third, a person's motive in offering conciliation is important to discern, yet such motives are not assessed in this measure. For example, suppose a person strongly agrees with Item 25 in the Behavior subscale: "I was willing to forget the past and concentrate on the present." Is it not possible for a person to show such conciliation to gain an advantage of some kind, not because of beneficence directed at the offender? Trainer (1981/1984) discussed the issue of expedient forgiveness, a form based on improving one's own situation ("forgiving" a supervisor to retain the job) and not on moral goodness.

Fourth, some items in the WFS are asking for the respondent's past judgment, not his or her present judgment ("I was victimized"). Many people may say that they were victimized without feeling victimized now. Fifth, in our view, some of the items in the Behavior subscale seem to belong more appropriately in the Cognition subscale ("I wished them well").

What do we make of the apparent differences on a theoretical level and the strong correlation between the scales? What seems to be happening is this: When completing a scale, respondents do not make the fine-grained theoretical distinctions that researchers and scholars do when constructing the scale. It matters not to a respondent if an item is misplaced into one subscale rather than another. It apparently is rare, at least in the United States, for respondents to condone when the directions ask about a person who has hurt them deeply and unfairly. In many cases, people try to reconcile when they forgive. Thus, retaining such items in the WFS does not have an appreciable effect on a total score. In our opinion, however, researchers must strive to be as faithful to a construct as possible, despite the more global, less-refined judgments of participants. Our task as researchers is to be as accurate as possible. We never know what sources of error, no matter how subtle, we are introducing into a scale when we allow items to be retained that have obvious flaws on the level of theory.

Do we recommend the use of Wade's scale? This is not an easy call, because the psychometric properties are strong while the conceptual flaws remain. We suggest that the WFS be reworked in light of the above criticisms so that the psychometrics and underlying theory are both strong. The reworking, we suspect, could be accomplished rather easily.

INTERPERSONAL RELATIONSHIP RESOLUTION SCALE

Hargrave and Sells (1997) described the Interpersonal Relationship Resolution Scale (IRRS) as a self-report instrument designed to assess a person's pain caused by both an interpersonal injustice and the subsequent work of forgiving and reconciling. Hargrave's (1994) views of "relational pain" are based on the family systems model of Boszormenyi-Nagy (1987), which is not centered on forgiveness. Instead, it emphasizes the theme of relational ethics, focused on the balance of justice, loyalty, merit, trustworthiness, and related values. Relational ethics are based on the belief that people have an intuitive sense of the balance between rights and obligations. When the rights and obligations within a relationship are balanced, that is, both parties are aware of their entitlements and their obligations toward others, then trustworthiness and a strong relationship are more likely to exist.

When an imbalance occurs within the relationship, trust breaks down and must be reestablished. *Forgiveness*, defined as "the release of blame and reconciliation" (Hargrave & Sells, 1997, p. 43), restores the balance. Further in the article, forgiveness is described as an "effort in restoring love and trustworthiness to relationships so that victims and victimizers can put an end to destructive entitlements" (p. 43). This definition places the work in a fairly specific context, that of ongoing relationships, primarily within the family, in which reconciliation is desired. The definition would not include, for example, a person forgiving a thief, who disappears into the night never to be seen again. It also would not include a person forgiving a physically abusive spouse, who refuses to change and reconcile. The definition, in fact, excludes all of those special cases in which trust is unlikely to occur. As we have stated, it is possible to forgive someone and then not trust in certain areas, as when a friend who is a compulsive gambler asks for your credit card.

The framework places the work of forgiveness into two broad categories, that of exoneration and forgiving itself. *Exoneration* is defined as lifting the load of culpability from the offending person through insight and understanding. *Insight* helps the victim realize (a) that he or she has been hurt by another, (b) how this injury occurred in the first place, and (c) that he or she might become a victimizer unless there is a deliberate attempt to reduce anger and bitterness. *Understanding* is similar to our concept of reframing in that the forgiver scrutinizes both the offender's actions and the offender as a person. Understanding can reduce condemnation and blame once the reframing takes place.

Forgiving is defined similarly to what we and many of the philosophers (and writers of the ancient texts) called *reconciliation*. The act of forgiveness, in this view, requires that the offender and offended interact in such a way to reestablish love and trust in the relationship. Hargrave and Sells (1997) were clear on their point that a forgiver demands specific actions on the victimizer's part to reestablish trust. The offender, in the victim's process of forgiving, is given the opportunity for compensation. Here, the victim allows the victimizer to work off the debt in slow increments. Also in forgiving, the victim offers an overt act of forgiveness. This often is ritualized so that the offender acknowledges the offense and apologizes and the victim accepts the apology.

In summary, Hargrave (1994) encompassed both exoneration and forgiving into his model. Exoneration is broken down into the subcomponents of insight and understanding. Forgiving is broken down into the subcomponents of the opportunity for compensation and the overt act of forgiveness. The IRRS has four subscales reflecting these four subcomponents of forgiveness.

In addition, Hargrave and Sells (1997) intended to assess, separate from the forgiveness scale, the way that pain was manifested as a result of the original offense. Hargrave (1994) distinguished four areas for assessment: shame, rage, control, and chaos. Each is on a continuum from high to low. For example, low rage would suggest that a person does not overtly manifest anger, whereas high rage suggests the externalization of inner pain. These four dimensions, representing the manifestation of inner pain, constitute four other subscales on the IRRS.

In the initial development of the scale, Hargrave and Sells (1997) generated 162 items reflecting the eight constructs. The items are in the form of statements, to which a person responds "yes" or "no." Examples of items across the eight subscales are in Exhibit 19.2. For the preliminary validation study, 164 participants from psychology classes and occupational sites completed the scale. A factor analysis with varimax rotation revealed eight factors, corresponding to the eight constructs described above. Those items with the highest loading on their own factor were included in the final version of the IRRS. In the Forgiveness scale, the Insight, Understanding, and Overt Act of Forgiving subscales each has 5 items, whereas the Opportunity for Compensation subscale has 7. In the Pain scale, the Shame, Rage, and Chaos subscale each has 6 items, whereas the Control subscale has 4. The Cronbach's alpha of internal consistency for the 22 items of the

EXHIBIT 19.2
Examples of Items From the Hargrave and Sells (1997) Interpersonal Relationship Resolution Scale

FORGIVENESS SCALE

Insight

Item 16. I know how to effectively stop this person from causing me pain.

_____ Yes, most of the time   _____ No, almost never

Understanding

Item 20. If I had come from this person's background, I might do some harmful things to people.

_____ Yes, I might have made the   _____ No, I think I would have done
           same mistakes.   better.

Opportunity for Compensation

Item 19. Our relationship is improving a little each time we are together.

_____ Yes, I find this mostly true.   _____ No, this is mostly false.

Overt Act of Forgiving

Item 4. I believe this person would not intentionally hurt me again because he or she is now trustworthy in our relationship.

_____ Yes, this is true much of the   _____ No, this is hardly ever true.
           time.

PAIN SCALE

Shame

Item 26. I am ashamed of what has happened to me.

_____ Yes, I feel this way much of the   _____ No, I seldom feel this way.
           time.

Rage

Item 31. I feel like smashing things.

_____ Yes, I feel this way often.   _____ No, I hardly ever feel this way.

Control

Item 36. It is often better to cover up your feelings.

_____ Yes, I believe this is mostly   _____ No, I hardly ever feel this way.
           true.

Chaos

Item 25. I easily misplace things.

_____ Yes, I do this much of the time.   _____ No, this is hardly ever the case.

Note. From "The Development of a Forgiveness Scale," by T. D. Hargrave and J. N. Sells, 1997, *Journal of Marital and Family Therapy, 23,* pp. 41–63. Copyright 1997 by the American Association for Marriage & Family Therapy. Adapted with permission.

Forgiveness scale is .92 and for the Pain scale is .95. Subscale alphas ranged from .63 to .87. The correlation between the Forgiveness and Pain scales was −.15, strongly suggesting that the two are unrelated constructs.

Four scales were used as correlates in establishing what the authors called concurrent validity for the IRRS: the Personal Authority in the Family System Questionnaire (assessing spousal intimacy and related issues), the Relational Ethics Scale (assessing trust, loyalty, and entitlements) (Hargrave & Bomba, 1993), the Fundamental Interpersonal Relations Orientation–Behavior Scale (assessing expressed and wanted inclusion and related constructs) (Schutz, 1958), and the Burns (1994) Depression Checklist. Each scale other than the depression inventory has 6 to 8 subscales, all of which were correlated with the IRRS and its 10 subscales (a total Forgiveness scale and its 4 subscales and a total Pain scale and its 4 subscales), for a total of 230 Pearson product–moment correlations.

Only 33 of the 230 statistical tests reached significance at the $p < .01$ level. When we examine only the correlations between the various measures and the Forgiveness scale and its four subscales within the IRRS, we see that of the 150 tests, only 9 reached statistical significance at the $p < .01$ level. The strongest and most frequently significant relationships were between subscales of the Forgiveness scale and subscales of the Personal Authority in the Family System Questionnaire. Those who show understanding to a victimizer (which is one of the subscales of forgiveness) are more likely to have spousal intimacy. Those who give the opportunity for compensation and show an overt act of forgiveness (both of which are forgiveness subscales) are more likely to have intergenerational intimacy. The 22-item Forgiveness scale itself was given 23 tests with the other measures and showed statistical significance only once. These results are not strong and, therefore, do not scientifically establish the validity of the IRRS.

Next, Hargrave and Sells (1997) gave the IRRS to 35 participants constituting a clinical sample (acknowledging family conflicts) and 63 representing a nonclinical sample. Of the 10 tests between the two groups (the Forgiveness scale and its four subscales and the Pain scale with its four subscales), all differentiated the clinical and nonclinical samples at $p < .05$. The clinical sample was less forgiving, as defined by the IRRS, and reported more emotional pain than the nonclinical group.

Hargrave and Sells (1997) claimed that, on the basis of the factor-analytic pattern, the IRRS possesses significant construct validity. We disagree with this interpretation. Yes, when subjected to the factor analysis, the scale divides into the eight subscales that have been established a priori, but this tells nothing of whether the scale assesses forgiveness in particular. What is needed is evidence that the scale relates to other, psychometrically established scales of forgiveness. We suspect that the IRRS indeed would be statistically significantly related to the EFI and the WFS, but the conclusion must await the evidence. We also suspect that there would be convergence because, in a random sample, most would be struggling with family issues. If, on the other hand, the IRRS were examined with the EFI and WFS under the specific constraint that the offender was a stranger or someone who was not interpersonally close to the participant, we suspect that the scales would not correlate highly because of the reconciliation themes embedded into the IRRS.

Would we recommend use of this instrument? Yes, under limited circumstances. If the researcher or clinician were interested in family themes in particular and reconciliation issues that go beyond forgiveness, then the scale appears to be useful. We would not recommend that the user see the IRRS as one scale but instead as two, assessing the independent constructs of forgiveness/reconciliation and emotional pain. Our recommendation for use is centered only on the forgiveness/reconciliation subscale because the emotional pain scale, as is evident in Exhibit 19.2, asks, at least in some of the items, about one's general affective state, not about a specific offense from a particular offender. Of course, more validation work must be done before we are more confident that the scale actually assesses its intended purpose.

FORGIVENESS OF OTHERS SCALE

A research group from Georgia State University developed the Forgiveness of Others Scale (FOS) as part of a larger inventory to assess personality disordered behaviors (Mauger et al., 1992). It is unclear from the article why the researchers embedded forgiveness within a personality disorder framework. Perhaps the extreme lack of forgiveness suggests personality deficits. In any case, we get a glimpse of the authors' definition of forgiveness by an examination of their items because, in their view, the "items for each scale [forgiveness of other and forgiveness of self, the latter of which is not discussed here] can be taken as empirically operational definitions of forgiveness" (Maugher et al., 1992, pp. 172, 174). Fifteen true–false items constitute the FOS. We will not describe the empirical efforts undertaken to arrive at the 15 but instead refer the reader to the original article. Examples of the items are as follows: "If another person hurts you first, it is all right to get back at him or her," "When other people insult me, I tell them off," and "I often use sarcasm when people deserve it."

In our view, the FOS is a measure of revenge or perhaps of incivility or even narcissism rather than forgiveness. The participant does not center on a particular offender or offense. Instead, the person answers rather general questions about typical tendencies when annoyed or hurt by others. We should realize that even if a person responds "false" to the 11 items written in the above fashion, he or she is not necessarily showing a forgiveness response. For example, one may not wish to "get back" or "tell them off" because the offender is seen as not worth the effort. One can reject the idea of revenge but still dismiss that person without forgiving him or her.

There are four questions written from a positive stance, in contrast to the negative images of the first 11 items. Even the positively stated items, however, do not necessarily assess the respondent's forgiving attitude or behavior. Consider two examples. The first example says, "I feel that other people have done more good than bad for me." This could be true, yet a respondent nonetheless might refuse to forgive those who "have done more . . . bad for me." The scale does not assess this possibility. The second example says, "I believe that when people say they forgive me for something I did they really mean it." Here the assessment focuses on the respondent as receiving forgiveness, not doing the forgiving.

In our view, the FOS does not assess a respondent's forgiving feelings, thoughts, or behaviors and thus should not be used for that purpose. Even so, we find this scale to be intriguing because it was the first one ever published that attempted to measure forgiveness. Pioneers do not always come to the most accurate conclusions because there are no models that can form the basis of reflection or reaction. This is truly a pioneering effort for which the authors deserve much credit.

CONCLUDING REMARKS ABOUT MEASUREMENT

The issue of *definitional drift*, about which we mused in chapter 15, is alive and well within the measurement area. We have four different measures and at least three different constructs represented. Although the EFI and the WFS look reasonably similar, they differ substantially from the other two scales reviewed here. Hargrave and Sells (1997) seemed to emphasize reconciliation more than forgiveness in their scale, whereas Mauger et al. (1992) emphasized the diminution of revenge as the gist of forgiveness.

We predict that this trend of drift in the meaning of forgiveness will grow greater rather than smaller in the future. There are at least two reasons for this prediction. The first concerns the nature of academic inquiry itself. As far as we can discern, academic rewards go to those who produce unique products, not to those who borrow from others, at least in the scholar's own generation. If this is true, then the pressure on scholars new to the field of forgiveness studies will be to create their own scales. The more researchers who enter the field, the more scales we are likely to see in the future.

We recommend that anyone who is considering the development of a new forgiveness scale first ask these questions:

1. Why is there a need for a new scale?
2. Does the new scale correct some fault in the older scale or scales?
3. Is the flaw in the older scale (a) embedded in the definition and operationalization, (b) contained in the structure of the scale itself, or (c) observed within the psychometric properties of the scale?
4. How will the new scale correct the flaw or flaws?
5. Beyond correcting existing flaws, does the new scale add something to definition, scale structure, or psychometric properties that the older scales did not possess?

The incessant striving for uniqueness within academia may create more rather than less problems for this new field unless researchers take the time to answer the above questions before proceeding.

A second reason why we are likely to see definitional drift is seen in the construct itself. The meaning of forgiveness is to be found in a variety of disciplines that do not at present have scholars who talk regularly across the disciplines. Forgiveness belongs to theology, philosophy, psychology, sociology, and the varied applied professions such as social work, medicine, psychiatry, and clinical psychology. A researcher must know something of the meaning of forgiveness from each of these perspectives. The failure to be an interdisciplinary scholar within forgiveness holds a vital consequence: The scholar will not understand the multifaceted nature and deeper meaning of forgiveness if he or she stays locked within his or her own discipline. Surely distortions in the areas of measurement are likely to follow.

In the future, we recommend that different types of scales begin to be developed. At present the only type of scale is that which assesses the degree to which one person forgives another. We now need assessments of where a person is, for example, within the process model of forgiveness (chapter 5). If a person, say, is currently in the Work Phase of forgiveness and is struggling with the issue of reframing, a researcher or clinician should be able to measure this. One person may be in two different units simultaneously of the process model, whereas another person may be currently working on only one unit. One person, who is in two different units, may not be struggling much at all with these units but is moving slowly and smoothly through them; another person, who is working within only one unit, may be struggling mightily. Thus, it may be important to discern (a) which unit or units a person is currently working on and (b) the ease or difficulty he or she is having in dealing with the unit or units. Work of this nature has commenced at the University of Wisconsin–Madison.

EPILOGUE: THE FUTURE OF FORGIVENESS

It is worth repeating from our Preface that the scientific study of forgiveness began in the mid 1980s. In our view, the studies should have commenced in the 1890s when scholars began scouring both ancient texts and contemporary philosophical writings on moral issues (see Hall, 1891, as one example). How the topic of forgiveness was overlooked by social scientists far into the next century still is a mystery to us. The consequence, of course, is that we should have had a head start of about 100 years on our knowledge about this vital topic. Instead, recent explorers are the pioneers.

FORGIVENESS AS INTERDISCIPLINARY STUDY

Science, of course, is not the only basis for knowledge about forgiveness. Philosophy and theology have had considerably longer histories inquiring into forgiveness than has psychological science. We find it significant that the ancient wisdom literature from Judaism, Christianity, Islam, and other systems considerably overlaps in the meaning ascribed to person-to-person forgiveness. This is so despite the use of different languages to communicate its meaning and different cultures in which the meaning emerged. Although the ancient literature showed considerable variation in the manifestation of forgiveness across different religions, there still existed substantial convergence on underlying concepts. In other words, forgiveness does seem to possess the features of a virtue with very specific meanings.

Modern philosophy, using appreciably different language in another historical era under dissimilar cultural conditions, shows meaningful convergence with the ancient underlying ideas. Our contemporary scientific analysis of meaning through the cross-cultural data collections of the Enright Forgiveness Inventory (EFI) in Austria, Brazil, Israel, Korea, Taiwan, and the United States reveals more similarities than differences among the various cultural groups. This occurs despite the EFI being administered in German, Portuguese, Hebrew, Korean, Chinese, and English. Taken together, the ancient literature, modern philosophical inquiry, and psychological science all suggest that forgiveness has a certain meaning to it that we should preserve. It remains to be seen whether the concept can withstand the modern skepticism found in historical relativism (all knowledge is bounded by time), cultural relativism (all meaning is embedded in culture; there are no universals), and scientific absolutism (facts alone matter, metaphysical notions are false or irrelevant).

We are especially concerned about pragmatism and forgiveness. If we incorrectly (in our view) equate forgiveness only with its usefulness in therapy, then the moral principles underlying the concept may be slowly lost. Forgiveness is not a technique, but a process developing out of a moral sense of the other person's goodness. The meaning of that process is to be found in the philosophical study of ethics. If we lose sight of the interdisciplinary nature of forgiveness and focus only on its pragmatic outcomes, we may conclude that forgiveness is what therapists and clients or patients do, not a moral principle founded on beneficence. Ironically, our own work may accelerate the equating of the *meaning* of forgiveness with its *consequences* of reduced anger, anxiety, and related emotions. We do not intend to leave such an impression. We must continue to differentiate what forgiveness is from what happens once a person does forgive. The issues, although related, are distinctly different.

If we are to move forward well, we should consider opening up dialogue among scholars who represent disciplines that too rarely exchange information. Philosophers, theologians, social scientists, and practitioners must begin to give the best of their disciplines to others who are willing to listen. We will know more deeply as we learn the assumptions, techniques, and scholarship of other fields of study.

There is much to learn from a scientific examination of forgiveness, and our learning time probably will accelerate as more join this field. There are seven major questions, among others, awaiting answers:

1. What place does anger have in clinical disorders, and are there specific disorders for which forgiveness is more important than others?

2. How do clients and patients forgive, as they reflect and report on their own forgiveness process?
3. Which units of the process model are the most important for clients to use in effecting forgiveness?
4. Which of the units are the most difficult to confront and master or overcome in the forgiveness process?
5. Are there certain kinds of anger that need prerequisite therapies before forgiveness therapy commences?
6. On which disorders should we begin to accumulate scientific knowledge about forgiveness?
7. How can we proactively prevent excessive anger from developing so that clinical symptoms do not emerge?

Let us briefly address each in turn.

THE PLACE OF ANGER IN CLINICAL DISORDERS

Anger is associated with all the clinical disorders presented in this book. We are not claiming that anger alone or even predominantly is the cause of each disorder discussed in chapter 7–14, but it is comorbid with them. At this point, we are only making the modest claim that, on the basis of observation in clinical settings, there is more anger present in clinical disorders than the field is currently acknowledging. There is much we need to know.

For example, suppose Enrique and Warren both had verbally abusive, alcoholic fathers and both now are unemployed for similar reasons, say company downsizing. But only Warren is depressed. In fact, Enrique seems to be thriving psychologically while Warren is seething with anger. Why does one person become enraged over genuine injustices, whereas another avoids the deep, pervasive anger associated with psychopathology? Both may get angry, but only one manifests anger so intensely as to compromise his emotional well-being. We need to know what accounts for a person staying healthy in the face of considerable unfairness. Family background, ways of coping, one's philosophy of life and religious experiences, and support from others all must be examined. We suspect that one's nervous system and the production of certain brain chemicals (such as serotonin, for example) also play a part.

Might it be the case that those with fewer community, family, and friendship supports need more than others to learn about and practice forgiveness? Might it be the case that those whose physiological constitutions place them more at risk for anger attacks and profound resentment need, more than most, to learn about and frequently practice forgiveness? We are not claiming that those without environmental support or those with vulnerable physiology should be more virtuous. We are taking the clinical perspective here, not the philosophical or theological, in speculating that the more vulnerable person particularly needs forgiveness for emotional or mood stability. Such practice, as we argued in chapters 2 and 15, actually may play a part in transforming personality and character because forgiveness seems to play a part in one's identity.

Another area of research on anger is this: If anger pervades all disorders discussed here, then why do the symptoms vary widely across the disorders? Why does David, who is deeply resentful about being teased by peers, exhibit conduct disorder, whereas Jennifer, also deeply resentful about being teased, exhibit anorexia nervosa? We certainly are aware of the issue of comorbidity (both David and Jennifer may share symptoms of a secondary disorder), but why does one show aggression predominantly, whereas the other strives for rigid control of self and perhaps others? It might be the case that Jennifer's anger is more of a passive–aggressive anger, whereas David's is more overt, but why does one respond to injustice with passivity and another with demonstrable aggression? We do not yet know the answer.

Why do some get depressed and others anxious when treated unfairly? Why do some drink, whereas others displace their anger onto loved ones? If anger is a common theme, then anger alone cannot explain the emergence of specific symptoms. Surely there are explanations outside of anger to answer these questions, but a focus on anger in addition to other factors may lead to a deeper, more satisfying answer.

CLIENTS' AND PATIENTS' REFLECTIONS ON THE FORGIVENESS PROCESS

To date, the forgiveness models developed have been generated by theorists and clinicians, not by patients themselves. New methodologies such as grounded theory, cooperative inquiry, participatory inquiry, and similar approaches have involved the participant in the construction of knowledge (see, e.g., Reason, 1988; C. Smith & Nylund, 1997). Rather than an imposed structure from outside, the researcher and participant both strive to understand the nature of the issue. In our case, that issue is how one goes about forgiving. In the development of our process model of forgiveness, we used feedback from people who have forgiven and material from case studies, as well as philosophical and psychological analyses of forgiveness. In other words, our explicit model was formed, to a large degree, from an examination of people's implicit understandings of forgiveness. Yet, we can do more as the numbers of patients going through forgiveness therapy increases.

We should realize that certain ideologies have become attached to these emerging methods. Although any social scientific method can be ideologically neutral, such neutrality has not been part of the new participant interview strategies. Many using the new methodologies adhere to the belief that morals are conventions, culturally and historically bound. The focus often is on the outward expressions of behavior and language, not on the underlying similarities across cultures and history. We urge philosophical and ideological neutrality in the use of the in-depth interview strategy. Valid data will help form our understanding of those aspects of forgiveness that, on the one hand, are shaped by history, culture, religion, and similar variables, and those, on the other, that are constant across these conditions.

IMPORTANT UNITS OF FORGIVENESS

It is possible that certain units of the process model of forgiveness are considered by clients and patients to be more vital to emotional healing than other units. If we ask people who have gone through the process to reflect on that process, perhaps certain units will emerge as more central, more important for them. It may be the case that people from different cultures or religions will target different units as important. Male and female participants may differ under certain circumstances; children and adults may differ. Our point is that all people probably do not experience forgiveness therapy in the same way. A focus on what is important to people may be a first step in documenting what is therapeutically effective and what is not.

DIFFICULT UNITS OF FORGIVENESS

That which is important to a client or patient is not necessarily a unit through which he or she easily passes. For example, in therapy, George realized that if he were to overcome his anger at his insensitive supervisors, then he had to bear the pain of the unfairness. George inquired into the various meanings of "bearing" or "absorbing" the pain and spent months in therapy trying to apply the ideas in his own circumstance. This unit was important, but certainly not easy for him. We must begin to understand people's views on difficult processes, including a sense, if this is even possible, of the average time lengths needed to work through these processes. Again, historical, cultural, religious, age, and gender variables may contribute to our knowledge in this area.

PREREQUISITE THERAPIES

Although anger is associated with all clinical diagnoses as described here, we wonder whether the causes of this anger differ in important ways. For example, people with certain personality disorders, such as the narcissistic personality, may be angry not only because of injustice but also because of perceived injustice. Even as an adult, Sally would explode in anger when people did not say "yes" to her wants and needs. Unable to secure a raise from her employer, she fantasized revenge on a daily basis. One problem is that virtually all employees at her particular company were underpaid compared with employees in other similar companies. Although she was treated unfairly, her reaction was extreme. Sally, in therapy, finally realized how she insisted on her own way starting as a young child. Her single-parent mother, exhausted from holding two jobs, tried for but did not demand a change in Sally's acting-out behavior. Rather than first forgiving her mother, Sally worked on her own feelings of guilt. She realized in therapy that she created an intolerable family environment for her mother, siblings, and even for herself. As she became aware of her guilt and of her past pattern of temper tantrums, she approached the problem with her supervisor in a new way. She saw him not as an ogre but as a person doing the best he could at the time. She, nonetheless, made the decision to forgive him, but she did so with far less anger than previously.

Sally's anger was not the result solely of another's unfairness. She had to confront her own narcissism first. In the future, those clinicians engaging in forgiveness therapy may begin to amass knowledge on other prerequisites needed for patients prior to suggesting forgiveness.

ON WHICH DISORDERS SHOULD WE BEGIN TO FOCUS?

Throughout the clinical section of this book, we have been outlining a research agenda that will take many years to achieve. In our view, fruitful areas in which to start are the substance abuse disorders and the childhood disorder, attention deficit hyperactivity disorder (ADHD). Those with substance abuse are among the angriest of patients whom we have seen in our practice, yet there are few, if any, formal, professional protocols developed for dealing with substance abuse in general or such abuse and anger. The use of forgiveness, as we have suggested, may prove to be effective here. Because we already have valid tests of the process model of forgiveness in other areas, it is time to scientifically test the hypothesis that a forgiveness protocol will help substance abusers. Such a protocol could be helpful to thousands of people.

ADHD is an area of interest for us because the underlying anger of these children is being ignored for the most part. Certainly medication is called for in many cases, but we are concerned that the exclusive focus on the biological may obscure the underlying anger in need of treatment and resolution. If we do not look for this anger, we will not be motivated to develop alternative or conjoint therapies that directly address the anger in children suffering from ADHD. Perhaps it is time to contrast the psychopharmacological approach with forgiveness in a randomized experimental and control group study.

PREVENTION

Science and clinical observation both suggest that forgiveness may be helpful in ameliorating anger, related emotions, and their effects when people have suffered injustices. Yet, most work to date has centered on helping people after they have developed clinical symptoms. How can forgiveness be introduced in a systematic fashion to those who are emotionally healthy? Perhaps one place to start is with children in classrooms and families. Helping children learn about forgiveness (what it is and is not and how one goes about forgiving) is important. Such learning may aid children in coping with injustices and angers now and may carry forgiveness into adult areas of career, spousal relationships, and instruction of their own children. The cases we presented in this book show how emotional pain can pass through the generations. It is our hope that forgiveness, soundly applied, in therapy and as a form of psychoeducation may be one very potent way of transmitting emotional health through many generations. In this way, not only the individual but also the family and the larger culture should benefit.

REFERENCES

Abraham, H. D., & Fava, M. (1999). Order of onset of substance abuse and depression in a sample of depressed outpatients. *Comprehensive Psychiatry, 40*(1), 44–50.

Abrams, R., & Taylor, M. A. (1976). Mania and schizoaffective disorder, mania type: A comparison. *American Journal of Psychiatry, 133,* 1445–1447.

Achenbach, T. M., & Howell, C. T. (1993). Are American children's problems getting worse? A 13-year comparison. *Journal of the American Academy of Child and Adolescent Psychiatry, 32,* 1145–1154.

Adams, J. E. (1989). *From forgiven to forgiving.* Wheaton, IL: Victor Books.

Alcoholics Anonymous. (1976). *The big book.* New York: Alcoholics Anonymous World Services.

Alessi, N. E., & Magen, J. (1988). Panic disorder in psychiatrically hospitalized children. *American Journal of Psychiatry, 145,* 1450–1452.

Alessi, N. E., Robbins, D. R., & Dilsaver, S. C. (1987). Panic and depressive disorders among psychiatrically hospitalized adolescents. *Psychiatry Research, 20,* 275–283.

Allport, G. W., Gillespie, J. M., & Young, J. (1953). The religion of the postwar college student. In J. M. Seidman (Ed.), *The adolescent* (pp. 266–285). New York: Dryden.

Al-Mabuk, R. H. (1991). The commitment to forgive in parentally love-deprived college students (Doctoral dissertation, University of Wisconsin–Madison, 1990). *Dissertation Abstracts International A, 51*(10), 3361.

Al-Mabuk, R., Enright, R. D., & Cardis, P. (1995). Forgiveness education with parentally love-deprived college students. *Journal of Moral Education, 24,* 427–444.

Amato, P. R., & Keith, B. (1991). Parental divorce and the well-being of children: A meta analysis. *Psychological Bulletin, 110,* 26–46.

American Academy of Child and Adolescent Psychiatry. (1998). Summary of practice parameters for the assessment and treatment of children and adolescents with obsessive–compulsive disorder. *Journal of the American Academy of Child and Adolescent Psychiatry, 37,* 1110–1116.

American Psychiatric Association. (1994). *Diagnostic and statistical manual of mental disorders* (4th ed.). Washington, DC: Author.

Anderson, J. C., Williams, S., McGee, R., & Silva, P. A. (1987). *DSM–III* disorders in preadolescent children: Prevalence in a large sample from the general population. *Archives of General Psychiatry, 44,* 69–76.

Anderson, N. H. (1976). Equity judgements as information integration. *Journal of Personality & Social Psychology, 33,* 291–299.

Angold, A., & Costello, E. J. (1993). Depressive comorbidity in children and adolescents: Empirical, theoretical, and methodological issues. *American Journal of Psychiatry, 150,* 1779–1791.

Apter, A., Bleich, A., Plutchik, R., Mendelsohn, S., & Tyano, S. (1988). Suicidal behavior, depression and conduct disorder in hospitalized adolescents. *Journal of the American Academy of Child and Adolescent Psychiatry, 27,* 696–699.

Apter, A., Gothelf, D., Orbach, I., Weizman, R., Ratzoni, G., Har-Even, D., & Tyano, S. (1995). Correlation of suicidal and violent behavior in different diagnostic categories in hospitalized adolescent patients. *Journal of the American Academy of Child and Adolescent Psychiatry, 34,* 912–918.

Arendt, H. (1969). *On violence.* New York: Harcourt, Brace & World.

Ashleman, K. A. (1996). *Forgiveness as a resiliency factor in divorced or permanently separated families.* Unpublished master's thesis, University of Wisconsin, Madison.

Augsburger, D. (1970). *The freedom to forgive.* Chicago: Moody Press.

Augsburger, D. (1981). *Caring enough to forgive: True forgiveness.* Chicago: Moody Press.

Augsburger, D. (1988). *The freedom of forgiveness* (2nd ed.). Chicago: Moody Press.

August, G. J., Realmuto, G. M., MacDonald, A. W., Nugent, S. M., & Crosby, R. (1996). Prevalence of ADHD and comorbid disorders among elementary school children screened for disruptive behaviors. *Journal of Abnormal Child Psychology, 24,* 571–595.

Austin, S., & Joseph S. (1996). Assessment of bully/victim problems in 8 to 11 year-olds. *British Journal of Education and Psychology, 66,* 447–456.

Awalt, R. M., Reilly, P. M., & Shopshire, M. S. (1997). The angry patient: An intervention for managing anger in substance abuse treatment. *Journal of Psychoactive Drugs, 29,* 353–358.

Baer, L., & Jenike, M. A. (1992). Personality disorders in obsessive compulsive disorder. *Psychiatric Clinics of North America, 15,* 803–812.

Baer, L., Jenike, M. A., Black, D. W., Treece, C., Rosenfeld, R., & Greist, J. (1992). Effects of Axis II diagnoses on treatment outcome with clomipramine in 55 patients with obsessive–compulsive disorder. *Archives of General Psychiatry, 49,* 862–866.

Baker, M., Dorzab, J., Winokur, G., & Cadoret, R. J. (1971). Depressive disease: Classification and clinical characteristics. *Comprehensive Psychiatry, 12,* 354–365.

Barkley, R. A. (1990). *Attention deficit hyperactivity disorder: A handbook for diagnosis and treatment.* New York: Guilford Press.

Beary, M. D., Lacey, J. H., & Merry, J. (1986). Alcoholism and eating disorders in women of fertile age. *British Journal of Addiction, 81,* 685–689.

Beck, A. T. (1976). *Cognitive therapy and emotional disorders.* New York: International Universities Press.

Beck, A. T., & Steer, R. A. (1987). *Beck depression inventory.* San Antonio, TX: Psychological Corporation.

Beck, A. T., Ward, C. H., Mendelson, M., Mock, J., & Erbaugh, J. (1961). An inventory for measuring depression. *Archives of General Psychiatry, 4,* 561–571.

Beigel, A., & Murphy, D. L. (1971a). Assessing clinical characteristics of the manic state. *American Journal of Psychiatry, 128,* 688–694.

Beigel, A., & Murphy, D. L. (1971b). Unipolar and bipolar affective illness: Differences in clinical characteristics accompanying depression. *Archives of General Psychiatry, 24,* 215–220.

Bergin, A. E. (1988). Three contributions of a spiritual perspective to counseling, psychotherapy, and behavior change. *Counseling and Values, 33,* 21–31.

Bernstein, D. P., Cohen, P., Skodal, A., Bezirganian, S., & Brook, J. S. (1996). Childhood antecedents of adolescent personality disorders. *American Journal of Psychiatry, 153,* 907–913.

Biederman, J. (1998). Debate: Mania is mistaken for ADHD in prepubertal children. *Journal of the American Academy of Child and Adolescent Psychiatry, 37,* 1091–1093.

Biederman, J., Faraone, S. V., Marrs, A., & Moore, P. (1997). Panic disorder and agoraphobia in consecutively referred children and adolescents. *Journal of the American Academy of Child and Adolescent Psychiatry, 36,* 214–223.

Biederman, J., Faraone, S. V., Mick, E., & Lelon, E. (1995). Psychiatric comorbidity among referred juveniles with major depression: Fact or artifact? *Journal of the American Academy of Child and Adolescent Psychiatry, 34,* 579–589.

Biederman, J., Faraone, S. V., Milberger, S., Jetton, J. G., Chen, L., Mick, E., Greene, R. W., & Russell, R. L. (1996). Is childhood oppositional defiant disorder a precursor to adolescent conduct? Findings from a four year follow-up study of children with ADHD. *Journal of American Academy of Child and Adolescent Psychiatry, 35,* 1193–1204.

Biederman, J., Mick, E., Bostic, J. Q., Prince, J., Daly, J., Wilens, T. E., Spencer, T., Garcia-Jetton, J., Russell, R., Wozniak, J., & Faraone, S. V. (1998). The naturalistic course of pharmacologic treatment of children with maniclike symptoms: A systematic chart review. *Journal of Clinical Psychiatry, 59,* 628–637.

Biederman, J., Newcorn, J., & Sprich, S. (1991). Comorbidity of attention deficit hyperactivity disorder with conduct, depressive, anxiety, and other disorders. *American Journal of Psychiatry, 148,* 564–577.

Black, A. E., & Pedro-Carroll, J. (1993). Role of parent–child relationships in mediating the effects of marital disruption. *Journal of the American Academy of Child and Adolescent Psychiatry, 32,* 1019–1027.

Black, B., & Robbins, D. R. (1990). Panic disorder in children and adolescents. *Journal of the American Academy of Child and Adolescent Psychiatry, 29,* 36–44.

Black, D. W., & Larson, C. L. (1999). *Bad boys, bad men: Confronting antisocial personality disorder.* New York: Oxford University Press.

Bland, R. C., Newman, S. C., Orn, H., & Stebelsky, G. (1993). Epidemiology of pathological gambling in Edmonton. *Canadian Journal of Psychiatry, 38,* 108–112.

Blasi, A., & Milton, K. (1991). The development of the sense of self in adolescence. *Journal of Personality, 59,* 217–242.

Block, J., Block, J. H., & Gjerde, P. F. (1988). Parental functioning and the home environment in families of divorce. *Journal of the American Academy of Child and Adolescent Psychiatry, 27,* 207–213.

Boszormenyi-Nagy, I. (1987). *Foundations of contextual therapy: Collected papers.* New York: Brunner/Mazel.

Boulton, M. J. (1997). Teachers' views on bulllying: Definitions, attitudes and ability to cope. *British Journal of Education and Psychology, 67,* 223–233.

Boulton, M. J., & Underwood, K. (1992). Bully/victim problems among middle school children. *British Journal of Education and Psychology, 62,* 73–87.

Bower, R. C., Cipywnyk, D., D'Arcy, C., & Keegan, D. (1984). Alcoholism, anxiety disorders and agoraphobia. *Alcoholism: Clinical and Experimental Research, 8,* 48–50.

Bradley, S. J., & Hood, J. (1993). Psychiatrically referred adolescents with panic attacks: Presenting symptoms, stressors, and comorbidity. *Journal of the American Academy of Child and Adolescent Psychiatry, 32,* 826–829.

Brakenhielm, C. R. (1993). *Forgiveness* (T. Hall, Trans.). Minneapolis, MN: Augsburg Fortress.

Bray, J. H., Williamson, D. S., & Malone, P. E. (1984). *Manual for the personal authority in the family system questionnaire.* Houston, TX: Houston Family Institute.

Breaux, C. A., & Morino, J. K. (1994). Comparing anorectics and bulimics on measures of depression, anxiety and anger. *Eating Disorders: The Journal of Treatment and Prevention, 2,* 158–167.

Bristol, G., & McGinnis, C. (1982). *When it's hard to forgive.* Wheaton, IL: Victor Books.

Browne, A., & Finkelhor, D. (1986). Impact of child sexual abuse: A review of the research. *Psychological Bulletin, 99*, 66–77.

Brunner, R. L., Maloney, M. J., Daniels, S., Mays, W., & Farrell, M. (1989). A controlled study of Type A behavior and psychophysiologic response to stress in anorexia nervosa. *Psychiatry Research, 30*, 223–230.

Bruun, R. D., & Budman, C. L. (1998). Paroxetine treatment of episodic rages associated with Tourette's disorder. *Journal of Clinical Psychiatry, 59*, 581–584.

Bruun, R. D., Budman, C. L., Olson, M. E., & Park, K. S. (1998). Rage attacks in children and adolescents with Tourette's disorder: A pilot study. *Journal of Clinical Psychiatry, 59*, 576–580.

Buchanan, C. M., Maccoby, E. E., & Dornbusch, S. M. (1991). Caught between parents: Adolescents' experience in divorced homes. *Child Development, 62*, 1008–1029.

Budman, C. L., Bruun, R. D., Park, K. S., & Olson, M. E. (1998). Rage attacks in children and adolescents with Tourette's disorder: A pilot study. *Journal of Clinical Psychiatry, 59*, 576–580.

Bulik, C. M. (1987). Drug and alcohol abuse by bulimic women and their families. *American Journal of Psychiatry, 144*, 564–577.

Burns, D. (1994). *The therapist's toolkit: Comprehensive treatment and assessment tools for mental health professionals.* (Available from David Burns, 11987 Morietta Lane, Los Altos, CA 94022).

Busch, F. N., Shear, M. K., Cooper, A. M., Shapiro, T., & Leon, S. (1995). An empirical study of defense mechanisms in panic disorder. *Journal of Nervous and Mental Disorders, 183*, 299–303.

Calian, C. S. (1981). Christian faith as forgiveness. *Theology Today, 37*, 439–443.

Carlson, G. A. (1995). Commentary: National plan for research on child and adolescent mental health disorders. *Archives of General Psychiatry, 52*, 724–726.

Carlson, G. A. (1995). Identifying prepubertal mania. *Journal of the American Academy of Child and Adolescent Psychiatry, 34*, 750–753.

Carlson, G. A., & Goodwin, F. K. (1973). The stages of mania: A new longitudinal analysis of the manic episode. *Archives of General Psychiatry, 28*, 221–228.

Carlson, G., & Stober, M. (1979). Affective disorders in adolescence. *Psychiatric Clinics of North America, 2*, 511–526.

Casarjian, R. (1992). *Forgiveness: A bold choice for a peaceful heart.* New York: Bantam Books.

Casper, R. C. (1990). Personality features of women with good outcome from restricting anorexia nervosa. *Psychosomatic Medicine, 52*, 156–170.

Casper, R. C., Hedeker, D. D., & McClough, J. F. (1992). Personality dimensions in eating disorders and their reference for subtyping. *Journal of the American Academy of Child and Adolescent Psychiatry, 31*, 831–840.

Chapman, R. F., & Maier, G. J. (2000, January/February). Forgiveness as an intervention for abused patients. *World of Forgiveness, 3*(2), 6–12.

Chemtob, C. M., Novaco, R. W., Hamada, R. S., & Gross, D. M. (1997). Cognitive–behavioral treatment for severe anger in posttraumatic stress disorder. *Journal of Consulting and Clinical Psychology, 65,* 184–189.

Chemtob, C. M., Novaco, R. W., Hamada, R. S., Gross, D. M., & Smith, G. (1997). Anger regulation deficits in combat-related posttraumatic stress disorder. *Journal of Trauma and Stress, 10*(1), 17–36.

Childre, D. L. (1998). *HeartMath discovery program.* Boulder Creek, CA: Planetary Publications.

Christensen, A., & Jacobson, N. S. (1999). *Reconcilable differences.* New York: Guilford Press.

Clancy, J. (1997). *Anger and relapse: Breaking the cycle.* Madison, CT: Psychosocial Press/International Universities Press.

Clark, D. B., Moss, H. B., Kirisci, L., Mezzich, A. C., Miles, R., & Ott, P. (1997). Psychopathology in preadolescent sons of fathers with substance use disorders. *Journal of the American Academy of Child and Adolescent Psychiatry, 36,* 495–502.

Clayton, P., Pitts, F. N., & Winokur, G. (1965). Affective Disorder: IV Mania. *Comprehensive Psychiatry, 6,* 313–322.

Cloninger, R. C., Bohman, M., & Sigvardsson, S. (1981). Inheritance of alcohol abuse: Cross fostering analysis of adopted men. *Archives of General Psychiatry, 38,* 861–868.

Close, H. T. (1970). Forgiveness and responsibility: A case study. *Pastoral Psychology, 21,* 19–25.

Coccaro, E. F., Astill, J. L., Herbert, J., & Schut, S. C. (1990). Fluoxetine treatment of impulsive aggression in *DSM–III–R* personality disorders. *Journal of Clinical Psychopharmacology, 10,* 373–375.

Coccaro, E. F., & Kavoussi, R. J. (1997). Fluoxetine and impulsive aggressive behavior in personality-disordered subjects. *Archives of General Psychiatry, 54,* 1081–1088.

Coccaro, E. F., Siever, L. J., Klar, H. M., Maurer, G., Cochrane, K., Cooper, T. B., Mohs, R. C., & Davis, K. L. (1989). Serotonergic studies in patients with affective and personality disorders: Correlates with suicidal and impulsive aggressive behavior. *Archives of General Psychiatry, 46,* 587–599.

Cohen, P., Velez, C. N., Brook, J., & Smith, J. (1989). Mechanisms of the relation between perinatal problems, early childhood illness, and psychopathology in late childhood and adolescence. *Child Development, 60,* 701–709.

Cohen, S. (1985). Aggression: The role of drugs. In S. Cohen (Ed.), *The substance abuse problems.* New York: Haworth Press.

Coleman, P. (1989). *The forgiving marriage.* Chicago: Contemporary Books.

Coleman, P. (1998). The process of forgiveness in marriage and the family. In R. Enright & J. North (Eds.), *Exploring forgiveness* (pp. 75–94). Madison: University of Wisconsin Press.

Comings, D., & Comings, B. (1988). Tourette's syndrome and attention deficit disorder. In D. Cohen, R. Bruun, & J. Leckman (Eds.), *Tourette's syndrome and tic disorders: Clinical understanding and treatment* (pp. 119–135). New York: Wiley.

Coopersmith, S. (1981). *Self-esteem inventories*. Palo Alto, CA: Consulting Psychologists Press.

Coyle, C. T., & Enright, R. D. (1997). Forgiveness intervention with post-abortion men. *Journal of Consulting and Clinical Psychology, 65*, 1042–1046.

Crockford, D. N., & el-Guebaly, N. (1998). Psychiatric comorbidity in pathological gambling: A critical review. *Canadian Journal of Psychiatry, 43*, 43–50.

Crowne, D. P., & Marlowe, D. (1960). A new scale of social desirability independent of psychopathology. *Journal of Consulting Psychology, 24*, 349–354.

Cunningham, B. B. (1985). The will to forgive: A pastoral theological view of forgiving. *Journal of Pastoral Care, 39*, 141–149.

Daley, D. C., & Marlatt, G. A. (1992). Relapse prevention: Cognitive and behavioral interventions. In J. H. Lowinson, P. Ruiz, & R. B. Millman (Eds.), *Substance abuse: A comprehensive textbook* (pp. 533–542). Baltimore: Williams & Wilkins.

Davis, R. E. (1979). Manic depressive variant syndrome of childhood: A preliminary report. *American Journal of Psychiatry, 136*, 702–706.

DeMoja, C., & Spielberger, C. (1997). Anger and drug addiction. *Psychological Reports, 81*, 152–154.

Denton, R. T., & Martin, M. W. (1998). Defining forgiveness: An empirical exploration of process and role. *American Journal of Family Therapy, 26*, 281–292.

Derogatis, L. R., & Spencer, P. M. (1982). *Administration and scoring procedures: BSI manual I*. Baltimore: Clinical Psychometric Research.

DiBlasio, F. (1998). The use of decision-based forgiveness intervention within intergenerational family therapy. *Journal of Family Therapy, 20*, 77–95.

Dien, D. S. (1982). A Chinese perspective in Kohlberg's theory of moral development. *Developmental Review, 2*, 331–341.

Donnelly, D. (1982). *Putting forgiveness into practice*. Allen, TX: Argus Communications.

Downie, R. S. (1965). Forgiveness. *Philosophical Quarterly, 15*, 128–134.

Droll, D. M. (1985). Forgiveness: Theory and research (Doctoral dissertation, University of Nevada, Reno, 1984). *Dissertation Abstracts International B, 45*(08), 2732.

Duck, S. W. (1983). *Friends, for life: The psychology of close relationships*. New York: St. Martin's Press.

Eastin, D. L. (1988). *The treatment of adult female incest survivors by psychological forgiveness*. Unpublished doctoral dissertation proposal, University of Wisconsin–Madison.

Eiraldi, R. B., Power, T. J., & Nezu, C. M. (1997). Patterns of comorbidity associated with subtypes of attention-deficit/hyperactivity disorder among 6 to 12 year old children. *Journal of the American Academy of Child and Adolescent Psychiatry*, *36*, 503–514.

Elliot, F. (1984). The episodic dyscontrol syndrome and aggression. *Neurologic Clinics*, *2*, 113–125.

Ellis, A. (1976). Techniques for handling anger in marriage. *Journal of Marriage and Family Counseling*, *24*, 305–315.

Ellis, A. (1994). *Reason and emotion in psychotherapy*. New York: Carol.

Enright, R. D. (1994). *The Enright forgiveness inventory*. (Available from the International Forgiveness Institute, P.O. Box 6153, Madison, WI 53716 or at www. ForgivenessInstitute.org).

Enright, R. D. (1997, October). If someone is unfair to my child can I forgive the wrongdoer? *World of Forgiveness*, *1*(3), 1–3.

Enright, R. D. (1999). Interpersonal forgiving in close relationships: Correction to McCullough et al. (1997). *Journal of Personality and Social Psychology*, *77*, 218.

Enright, R. D. (in press). *Forgiveness is a choice*. Washington, DC: American Psychological Association.

Enright, R. D., Eastin, D. L., Golden, S., Sarinopoulos, I., & Freedman, S. (1992). Interpersonal forgiveness within the helping professions: An attempt to resolve differences of opinion. *Counseling and Values*, *36*, 84–103.

Enright, R. D., Freedman, S., & Rique, J. (1998). The psychology of interpersonal forgiveness. In R. D. Enright & J. North (Eds.), *Exploring forgiveness* (pp. 46–62). Madison: University of Wisconsin Press.

Enright, R. D., Gassin, E. A., Longinovic, T., & Loudon, D. (1994, December). *Forgiveness as a solution to social crisis*. Paper presented at the Morality and Social Crisis Conference at the Institute for Educational Research, Beograd, Serbia.

Enright, R. D., Gassin, E. A., & Wu, C. (1992). Forgiveness: A developmental view. *Journal of Moral Education*, *21*, 99–114.

Enright, R. D., & the Human Development Study Group. (1991). The moral development of forgiveness. In W. Kurtines & J. Gewirtz (Eds.), *Handbook of moral behavior and development* (Vol. 1, pp. 123–152). Hillsdale, NJ: Erlbaum.

Enright, R. D., & the Human Development Study Group. (1994). Piaget on the moral development of forgiveness: Reciprocity or identity? *Human Development*, *37*, 63–80.

Enright, R. D., Lapsley, D. K., & Levy, V. M. (1983). Moral education strategies. In M. J. Pressley & J. R. Levin (Eds.), *Cognitive strategy training: Educational applications* (pp. 43–83). New York: Springer.

Enright, R. D., & North, J. (Eds.). (1998). *Exploring forgiveness*. Madison: University of Wisconsin Press.

Enright, R. D., Santos, M. J. O., & Al-Mabuk, R. H. (1989). The adolescent as forgiver. *Journal of Adolescence*, *12*, 95–110.

Erikson, E. (1968). *Identity: Youth and crisis*. New York: Norton.

Faraone, S. V., Biederman, J., Keenan, K., & Tsuang, M. T. (1991). Separation of *DSM–III* attention deficit disorder and conduct disorder: Evidence from a family genetic study of American child psychiatry patients. *Psychological Medicine*, 21, 109–121.

Fava, M. (1997). Psychopharmacologic treatment of pathologic aggression. *Psychiatric Clinics of North America*, 20, 427–451.

Fava, M. (1998). Depression with anger attacks. *Journal of Clinical Psychiatry*, 59 (Suppl. 18), 18–22.

Fava, M., Alpert, J. E., Nierenberg, A. A., Ghaemi, N., O'Sullivan, R., Tedlow, J., Worthington, J., & Rosenbaum, J. F. (1996). Fluoxetine treatment of anger attacks: A replication study. *Annals of Clinical Psychiatry*, 8, 7–10.

Fava, M., Anderson, K., & Rosenbaum, J. F. (1990). "Anger attacks": Possible variants of panic and major depressive disorders. *American Journal of Psychiatry*, 147, 867–870.

Fava, M., Grandi, S., Rafanelli, C., Saviotti, F. M., Ballin, M., & Pesarin, F. (1993). Hostility and irritable mood in panic disorder with agoraphobia. *Journal of Affective Disorders* 29, 213–217.

Fava, M., Kellner, R., Munari, F., Pavan, L., & Pesarin, F. (1982). Losses, hostility, and depression. *Journal of Nervous and Mental Disorders*, 170, 474–478.

Fava, M., Nierenberg, A. A., Quitkin, F. M., Zisook, S., Pearlstein, T., Stone, A., & Rosenbaum, J. F. (1997). A preliminary study on the efficacy of sertraline and imipramine on anger attacks in depression. *Psychopharmacology Bulletin*, 33, 101–103.

Fava, M., Rappe, S. M., West, J., & Herzog, D. B. (1995). Anger attacks in eating disorders. *Psychiatry Research*, 56, 205–212.

Fava, M., & Rosenbaum, J. F. (1997). Anger attacks in depression. *Depression and Anxiety*, 6, 2–6.

Fava, M., Rosenbaum, J. F., McCarthy, M., Pava, J., Steingard, R., & Bless, E. (1991). Anger attacks in depressed outpatients and their response to fluoxetine. *Psychopharmacology Bulletin*, 27, 275–279.

Fava, M., Rosenbaum, J. F., Pava, J., McCarthy, M., Steingard, R., & Bouffides, E. (1993). Anger attacks in unipolar depression: Part 1. Clinical correlates and response to fluoxetine treatment. *American Journal of Psychiatry*, 150, 1158–1163.

Favazza, A. R., & Rosenthal, R. J. (1990). Varieties of pathological self-mutilation. *Behavioral Neurology*, 3, 77–85.

Federal Bureau of Investigation. (1998). *Crime in the United States: Uniform crime reports*. Washington, DC: U.S. Department of Justice.

Fergusson, D. M., Hoorwood, L. J., & Lloyd, M. (1991). Confirmatory factor models of attention deficit and conduct disorders. *Journal of Child Psychology and Psychiatry*, 32, 257–274.

Finkelhor, D. (1984). *Child sexual abuse: New theory and research*. New York: Free Press.

Fitzgibbons, R. P. (1986). The cognitive and emotional uses of forgiveness in the treatment of anger. *Psychotherapy*, 23, 629–633.

Fitzgibbons, R. P. (1998). Anger and the healing power of forgiveness: A psychiatrist's view. In R. Enright & J. North (Eds.), *Exploring forgiveness* (pp. 63–74). Madison: University of Wisconsin Press.

Flament, M. F., & Godard, N. (1995). Social phobia: A risk factor for eating disorders? *European Neuropsychopharmacology, 5,* 360.

Flanigan, B. (1987, September). *Forgiving.* Workshops conducted at the Mendota Mental Health Institute, Madison, WI.

Flanigan, B. (1992). *Forgiving the unforgivable.* New York: Macmillan.

Fombonne, E. (1998). Suicidal behaviors in vulnerable adolescents: Time and their correlates. *British Journal of Psychiatry, 173,* 154–159.

Frankl, V. (1959). *The will to meaning: Foundations and applications of logotherapy.* New York: World Publishing House.

Frankl, V. (1969). *Man's search for meaning: An introduction to logotherapy.* New York, Washington Square Press.

Franklin, K. M., Janoff-Bulman, R., & Roberts, J. E. (1990). Long term impact of parental divorce on optimism and trust. *Journal of Personal and Social Psychology, 59,* 743–755.

Freedman, S. R., & Enright, R. D. (1996). Forgiveness as an intervention goal with incest survivors. *Journal of Consulting and Clinical Psychology, 64,* 983–992.

Frick, P. J. (1993). Childhood conduct problems in a family context. *School Psychology Review, 22,* 376–385.

Frick, P. J. (1998). *Conduct disorders and severe antisocial behavior.* New York: Plenum Press.

Frick, P. J., Lahey, B., Loeber, R., Stouthamer-Loeber, M., Christ, M. A. G., & Hanson, K. (1992). Familial risk factors to oppositional defiant disorder and conduct disorder: Parental psychopathology and maternal parenting. *Journal of Consulting and Clinical Psychology, 60,* 49–55.

Friedrich, W. N. (1993). Sexual victimization and sexual behavior in children: A review of recent literature. *Child Abuse and Neglect, 17,* 59–66.

Frueh, B. C., Henning, K. R., Pellegrin, K. L., & Chobot, K. (1997). Relationship between scores on anger measures and posttraumatic stress disorder symptomatology, employment and compensation-seeking status in combat veterans. *Journal of Clinical Psychology, 53,* 871–878.

Galanter, M., & Castaneda, R. (1985). Self-destructive behavior in the substance abuser. *Psychiatric Clinics of North America, 8,* 251–261.

Gardner, G. E. (1971). Aggression and violence: The enemies of precision learning in children. *American Journal of Psychiatry, 128,* 77–82.

Garner, D. M., Garfinkel, P. E., & O'Shaughnessy, M. (1985). The validity of the distinction between bulimia with and without anorexia nervosa. *American Journal of Psychiatry, 142,* 581–587.

Gartner, A. F., Marcus, R. N., Halmi, K., & Loranger, A. W. (1989). *DSM–III–R* personality disorders in patients with eating disorders. *American Journal of Psychiatry, 146,* 1585–1591.

Gassin, E. A. (1995). *Social cognition and forgiveness in adolescent romance: An intervention study*. Unpublished doctoral dissertation, University of Wisconsin–Madison.

Geller, B., Chestnut, E. C., Miller, M. D., Price, T. D., & Yates, E. (1985). Preliminary data on *DSM–III* associated features of major depressive disorder in children and adolescents. *American Journal of Psychiatry, 142*, 643–644.

Geller, B., & Luby, J. (1997). Child and adolescent bipolar disorder: A review of the past 10 years. *Journal of the American Academy of Child and Adolescent Psychiatry, 36*, 1378–1387.

Geller, D., Biederman, J., Griffin, S., Jones, J., & Lefkowitz, T. R. (1996). Comorbidity of juvenile obsessive–compulsive disorder with disruptive behavior disorders. *Journal of the American Academy of Child and Adolescent Psychiatry, 35*, 1637–1646.

Geller, D., Biederman, J., Reed, E., Spencer, T., & Wilens, T. (1995). Similarities in response to fluoxetine in treatment of children and adolescents with obsessive–compulsive disorder. *Journal of the American Academy of Child and Adolescent Psychiatry, 34*, 36–44.

George, D. T., Anderson, P., Nutt, D. J., & Linnoila, M. (1989). Aggressive thoughts and behavior: Another symptom of panic disorder? *Acta Psychiatrica Scandanavica, 79*, 500–502.

Gilligan, C. (1993). *In a different voice: Psychological theory and women's development*. Cambridge, MA: Harvard University Press.

Gilmartin, B. G. (1987). Peer group antecedents of severe love-shyness in males. *Journal of Personality, 55*, 467–489.

Girard, M., & Mullet, E. (1997). Forgiveness in adolescents, young, middle-aged, and older adults. *Journal of Adult Development, 4*, 209–220.

Gittelman, R., Mannuzza, S., Shenker, R., & Bonagura, N. (1985). Hyperactive boys almost grown up: I. Psychiatric status. *Archives of General Psychiatry, 42*, 937–947.

Glenn, N. D., & Kramer, K. B. (1987). The marriages and divorces of the children of divorce. *Journal of Marriage and the Family, 49*, 811–825.

Goodman, W. K., Price, L. H., Rasmussen, S. A., Mazure, C., Delgado, P., Heninger, G. R., & Charney, D. S. (1989). The Yale-Brown Obsessive-Compulsive Checklist. *Archives of General Psychiatry, 46*, 1012–1016.

Goodwin, F. K., & Jamison, K. R. (1990). *Manic-depressive illness*. New York: Oxford University Press.

Gorski, T. (1983). *Relapse warning sign assessment*. Hazel Crest, IL: Cenaps Corporation.

Gottman, J. M., & Levenson, R. W. (1992). Marital processes predictive of later dissolution: Behavior, physiology, and health. *Journal of Personal and Social Psychology, 63*(2), 221–233.

Gould, R. A., Ball, R., Kaspi, S., Otto, M. W., Pollack, M. H., Shekhar, A., & Fava, M. (1996). Prevalence and correlates of anger attacks: A two site study. *Journal of Affective Disorders, 39,* 31–38.

Gouldner, A. W. (1973). *For sociology: Renewal and critique in sociology today.* London: Allen Lane.

Griest, J. H., & Jefferson, J. W. (1996). Obsessive–compulsive disorder. In G. Gabbard (Ed.), *Synopsis of treatments of psychiatric disorders* (pp. 627–635). Washington, DC: American Psychiatric Press.

Greist, J. H., & Jefferson, J. W. (1998). Pharmacotherapy for obsessive–compulsive disorder. *British Journal of Psychiatry Supplement, 35,* 64–70.

Guidubaldi, J. (1988). Differences in children's divorce adjustment across grade level and gender. In S. Wolchik & P. Karoly (Eds.), *Children of divorce* (pp. 185–231). Lexington, MA: Lexington Books.

Gunderson, J. G., & Singer, M. T. (1975). Defining borderline clients: An overview. *American Journal of Psychiatry, 132,* 1–10.

Haimes, A. K., & Katz, J. L. (1988). Sexual and social maturity versus social conformity in restricting anorectic, bulimic and borderline women. *International Journal of Eating Disorders, 7,* 331–341.

Hall, G. S. (1891). The moral and religious training of children and adolescents. *Pedagogical Seminary, 1,* 196–210.

Hargrave, T. D. (1994). *Families and forgiveness: Healing wounds in the intergenerational family.* New York: Brunner/Mazel.

Hargrave, T. D., & Bomba, A. K. (1993). Further validation of the relational ethics scale. *Journal of Marital and Family Therapy, 19,* 292–299.

Hargrave, T. D., & Sells, J. N. (1997). The development of a forgiveness scale. *Journal of Marital and Family Therapy, 23,* 41–62.

Hatsukami, D., Owen, P., Pyle, R., & Mitchell, J. (1982). Similarities and differences on the MMPI between women with bulimia and women with alcohol and drug abuse problems. *Addictive Behavior, 7,* 435–439.

Hawton, K., Kingsbury, S., Steinhardt, K., James, A., & Fagg, J. (1999). Repetition of deliberate self-harm by adolescents: The role of psychological factors. *Journal of Adolescence, 22,* 369–378.

Hawton, K., Osborn, M., O'Grady, J., & Cole, D. (1982). Classification of adolescents who take overdoses. *British Journal of Psychiatry, 140,* 124–131.

Hayworth, J., Little, C., Carter, S. B., Raptopoulos, P., Priest, R. G., & Sandler, N. (1980). A predictive study of postpartum depression: Some predisposing characteristics. *British Journal of Medical Psychology, 53,* 161–167.

Hebl, J. H., & Enright, R. D. (1993). Forgiveness as a psychotherapeutic goal with elderly females. *Psychotherapy, 30,* 658–667.

Hecht, A. M., Fichter, M., & Postpischil, P. (1990). Obsessive–compulsive neurosis and anorexia nervosa. *International Journal of Eating Disorders, 2,* 69–77.

Hechtman, L. (1991). Developmental, neurobiological, and psychological aspects of hyperactivity, impulsivity and inattention. In M. Lewis (Ed.), *Child and adolescent psychiatry* (pp. 324–328). Baltimore: Williams & Wilkins.

Helzer, J. E., & Pryzbeck, T. R. (1988). The co-occurrence of alcoholism with other psychiatric disorders in the general population and its impact in treatment. *Journal of Studies on Alcohol, 49,* 219–224.

Hepp-Dax, S. H. (1996). *Forgiveness as an educational goal with fifth-grade inner-city children.* Unpublished doctoral dissertation, Fordham University, New York.

Hertzberg, M. A., Feldman, M. E., Beckham, J. C., Moore, S. D., & Davidson, J. R. (1998). Open trial of anfazadone for combat-related posttraumatic stress disorder. *Journal of Clinical Psychiatry, 59,* 460–464.

Herzog, D. B. (1984). Are anorectics and bulimics depressed? *American Journal of Psychiatry, 141,* 1594–1597.

Herzog, D. B., Keller, M. B., Sacks, N. R., Yeh, C. J., & Lavori, P. W. (1992). Psychiatric comorbidity in treatment-seeking anorexics and bulimics. *Journal of the American Academy of Child and Adolescent Psychiatry, 31,* 810–818.

Hetherington, E. M. (1989). Coping with family transitions. *Child Development, 60,* 1–14.

Holeman, V. T. (1994). *Relationship between forgiveness of a perpetrator and current marital adjustment for female survivors of childhood sexual abuse.* Unpublished doctoral dissertation, Kent State University, Kent, OH.

Hollander, E., Greenwald, S., Neville, D., Johnson, J., Hornig, C. D., & Weissman, M. M. (1996–1997). Uncomplicated and comorbid obsessive–compulsive disorder in an epidemiologic sample. *Depression and Anxiety, 4,* 111–119.

Holmgren, M. R. (1993, October). Forgiveness and the intrinsic value of persons. *American Philosophical Quarterly, 30,* 341–352.

Holmgren, M. (1997, April/May). Forgiveness and self-respect. *World of Forgiveness, 1*(2), 5–8.

Hootman, M., & Perkins, P. (1982). *How to forgive your ex-husband (and get on with your life).* New York: Warner Books.

Hope, D. (1987). The healing paradox of forgiveness. *Psychotherapy, 24,* 240–244.

Horesh, N., Apter, A., Lepkifker, E., Ratzoni, G., Weizmann, R., & Tyano, S. (1995). Life events and severe anorexia nervosa in adolescence. *Acta Psychiatrica Scandinavica, 91,* 5–9.

Horesh, N., Gothelf, D., Ofek, H., Weizmann, T., & Apter, A. (1999). Impulsivity as a correlate of suicidal behavior in adolescent psychiatric inpatients. *Crisis, 20,* 8–14.

Horowitz, M. J. (1981). Self-righteous rage and the attribution of blame. *Archives of General Psychiatry, 38,* 1233–1238.

Huang, S. T. (1990). Cross-cultural and real-life validations of the theory of forgiveness in Taiwan, the Republic of China (Doctoral dissertation, University of Wisconsin–Madison, 1990). *Dissertation Abstracts International B, 51*(05), 2644.

Hudson, J., Pope, H., Jonas, J., & Yurgelun-Todd, D. (1983). Phenomenologic relationship of eating disorders to major affective disorder. *Journal of Psychiatric Research, 7,* 435–439.

Hughes, M. (1975). Forgiveness. *Analysis, 35,* 113–117.

Huizinga, D., Loeber, R., & Thornberry, T. (1991). Urban development and substance abuse In *Program of research on the causes and correlates of delinquency* (Technical reports, Vols. I, II, and Appendices). Washington, DC: Office of Juvenile Justice and Delinquency Prevention, U.S. Department of Justice.

Hunter, R. C. A. (1978). Forgiveness, retaliation, and paranoid reactions. *Canadian Psychiatric Association Journal, 23,* 167–173.

Jackson, H. J., Whiteside, H. L., Bates, G. W., Bell, R., Rudd, R. P., & Edwards, J. (1991). Diagnosing personality disorders in psychiatric inclients. *Acta Psychiatrica Scandinavica, 83,* 206–213.

Jaeger, M. (1998). The power and reality of forgiveness: Forgiving the murderer of one's child. In R. D. Enright & J. North (Eds.), *Exploring forgiveness* (pp. 9–14). Madison: University of Wisconsin Press.

Jain, U., Leslie, V. C., Keefe, B. R., Sachs, G. S., & Fava, M. (1997). *Anger attacks in bipolar depression versus unipolar depression.* Paper presented at the 150th Annual Meeting of the American Psychiatric Association, San Diego, CA.

Jenike, M. A., Baer, L., & Minichiello, W. E. (1990). *Obsessive–compulsive disorders: Theory and management.* St. Louis, MO: Mosby-Year Book.

Jensen, P. S., Martin D., & Cantwell, D. P. (1997). Comorbidity in ADHD: Implications for research, practice, and *DSM–IV. Journal of the American Academy of Child and Adolescent Psychiatry, 36,* 1065–1079.

Johnson, J. G., Cohen, P., Brown, J., Smailes, E. M., & Bernstein, D. P. (1999). Childhood maltreatment increases risk for personality disorders during early adulthood. *Archives of General Psychiatry, 56,* 600–606.

Johnson, J. G., Cohen, P., Skodal, A. E., Oldham, J. M., Kasen, S., & Brook, J. S. (1999). Personality disorders in adolescence and risk of major mental disorders and suicidality during adulthood. *Archives of General Psychiatry, 56,* 805–811.

Johnston, J. R., Kline, M., & Tschann, J. M. (1989). Ongoing post-divorce conflict. *American Journal of Orthopsychiatry, 59,* 576–592.

Judd, L. L., Kessler, R. C., Paulus, M. P., Zeller, P. V., Wittchen, H. U., & Kunovac, J. L. (1998). Comorbidity as a fundamental feature of generalized anxiety disorders: Results from the National Comorbidity Study (NCS). *Acta Psychiatrica Scandinavica* (Suppl. 393), 6–11.

Kahrhoff, R. E. (1988). *Forgiveness: Formula for peace of mind.* St. Charles, MO: Capital Planning Corporation.

Kalter, N. (1987). Long-term effects of divorce on children. *American Journal of Orthopsychiatry, 57,* 587–600.

Kasen, S., Cohen, P., Skodol, A. E., Johnson, J. G., & Brook, J. S. (1999). Influence of child and adolescent psychiatric disorders on young adult personality disorder. *American Journal of Psychiatry, 156,* 1529–1535.

Kashani, J. H., Dahlmeier, J. M., Borduin, C. M., Soltys, S., & Reid, J. C. (1995). Characteristics of anger expression in depressed children. *Journal of the American Academy of Adolescent Psychiatry, 34,* 322–326.

Kaufman, M. E. (1984). The courage to forgive. *Israeli Journal of Psychiatry and Related Sciences, 21,* 177–187.

Kavoussi, R. J., & Coccaro, E. F. (1998). Divalproex sodium for impulsive aggressive behavior in clients with personality disorders. *Journal of Clinical Psychiatry, 59,* 676–680.

Kavoussi, R. J., Liu, J., & Coccaro, E. F. (1994). An open trial of sertraline in personality disordered clients with impulsive aggression. *Journal of Clinical Psychiatry, 55,* 137–141.

Kazdin, A. E. (1995). *Conduct disorders in childhood and adolescence.* Thousand Oaks, CA: Sage.

Kazdin, A. E., Siegel, T. C., & Bass, D. (1990). Drawing upon clinical practice to inform research on child and adolescent psychotherapy: A survey of practitioners. *Professional Psychology: Research and Practice, 21,* 189–198.

Kernberg, O. F. (1992). *Aggression in personality disorders and perversions.* New Haven, CT: Yale University Press.

Kessler, R. C., McGonagle, K. A., Zhao, S., Nelson, C. B., Hughes, M., Eshleman, S., Wittchen, H. W., & Kendler, K. S. (1994). Lifetime and 12-month prevalence of DSM–III–R psychiatric disorders in the United States. *Archives of General Psychiatry, 51,* 8–19.

Kiel, D. V. (1986, February). I'm learning how to forgive. *Decisions,* 12–13.

King, M. L., Jr. (1963). *Strength to love.* Philadelphia: Fortress Press.

Klein, R. G., & Last, C. G. (1989). *Anxiety disorders in children.* Newbury Park, CA: Sage.

Klein, R. G., & Mannuzza, S. (1991). Long-term outcome of hyperactive children: A review. *Journal of the American Academy of Child and Adolescent Psychiatry, 30,* 383–387.

Koenigsberg, H. W., Kaplan, R. D., Gilmore, M. M., & Cooper, A. M. (1985). The relationship between syndrome and personality disorder in DSM–III: Experience with 2,462 clients. *American Journal of Psychiatry, 1422,* 207–212.

Kohlberg, L. A. (1969). Stage and sequence: The cognitive–developmental approach to socialization. In D. A. Goslin (Ed.), *Handbook of socialization theory and research* (pp. 347–480). Chicago: Rand McNally.

Kolnai, A. (1973–1974). Forgiveness. *Proceedings of the Aristotelian Society, 74,* 91–106.

Korn, M. L., Kotler, M., Molcho, A., Botsis, A. J., Grasz, D., Chen, C., Plutchik, R., Brown, S. L., & van Praag, H. M. (1992). Suicide and violence associated with panic attacks. *Biological Psychiatry, 31,* 607–612.

Korn, M. L., Plutchik, R., & van Praag, H. M. (1997). Panic-associated suicidal and aggressive ideation and behavior. *Journal of Psychiatric Research, 31,* 481–487.

Kotin, J., & Goodwin, F. K. (1972). Depression during mania: Clinical observations and theoretical implications. *American Journal of Psychiatry, 129,* 679–686.

Kovacs, M., Gatsonis, C., Paulauskas, S., & Richards, C. (1988). Depressive disorders in childhood: IV. A longitudinal study of comorbidity with and risk for conduct disorders. *Journal of Affective Disorders, 15,* 205–217.

Kovacs, M., Gatsonis, C., Paulauskas, S. L., & Richards, C. (1989). Depressive disorders in childhood: IV. A longitudinal study of comorbidity with and risk for anxiety disorders. *Archives of General Psychiatry, 16,* 776–782.

Kovacs, M., & Pollock, M. (1995). Bipolar disorder and comorbid conduct disorder in childhood and adolescence. *Journal of the American Academy of Child and Adolescent Psychiatry, 34,* 715–723.

Krauthammer, C., & Klerman, G. L. (1978). Secondary mania: Manic syndromes associated with antecedent physical illness or drugs. *Archives of General Psychiatry, 35,* 1333–1339.

Kubler-Ross, E. (1997). *On death and dying.* New York: Simon & Schuster.

Kumpfer, K. L., & Hopkins, R. (1993). Recent advances in addictive disorders: Prevention: Current research and trends. *Psychiatric Clinics of North America, 16*(1), 11–20.

Kumpfer, K. L., & Turner, C. (1990–1991). The social ecology model of adolescent substance abuse: Implications for prevention. *International Journal of Addictions, 25,* 435–462.

Kumpulainen, K., Rasanen, E., Henttonen, I., Almqvist, F., Kresanov, K., Linna, S. L., Moilanen, I., Piha, J., Puura, K., & Tamminen, T. (1998). Bullying and psychiatric symptoms among elementary school-age children. *Child Abuse and Neglect, 22,* 705–717.

Kushner, M. G., Sher, K. J., & Erickson, D. J. (1999). Prospective analysis of the relation between *DSM–III* anxiety disorders and alcohol use disorders. *American Journal of Psychiatry, 156,* 723–732.

Kutcher, S. P., Marton, P., & Korenblum, M. (1989). The relationships between psychiatric illness and conduct disorder in adolescents. *The Canadian Journal of Psychiatry, 34,* 526–529.

Lacey, J. H., & Evans, C. D. H. (1986). The impulsivist: A multi-impulsive personality disorder. *British Journal of Addictions, 81,* 641–649.

Lacks, H. E. (1988). Anger and recovering substance abuser. *Alcoholism Treatment Quarterly, 5*(3–4), 37–52.

Lahey, B. B., Loeber, R., Hart, E., Frick, P. J., Applegate, B., Zhang, Q., Green, S., & Russo, M. F. (1995). Four-year longitudinal study of conduct disorders in boys: Patterns and predictors of persistence. *Journal of Abnormal Psychology, 104,* 83–93.

Lahey, B. B., Piacentini, J. D., McBurnett, K., Stone, P., Hartdagen, S. E., & Hynd, G. W. (1988). Psychopathology and antisocial behavior in the parents of children with conduct disorders and hyperactivity. *Journal of the American Academy of Child and Adolescent Psychiatry, 27,* 163–170.

Lakatos, I. (1978). Falsification and the methodology of scientific research programs. In J. Worral & G. Currie (Eds.), *Imre Lakatos philosophical papers: Vol. 1. The methodology of scientific research programs* (pp. 8–101). Cambridge, England: Cambridge University Press.

Lambert, J. C. (1985). *The human action of forgiveness*. New York: University Press of America.

Landman, I. (Ed.). (1941). Forgiveness. *The universal Jewish encyclopedia: In ten volumes* (Vol. 4). New York: Universal Jewish Encyclopedia, Inc.

Lapsley, D. K. (1996). *Moral psychology*. Boulder, CO: Westview Press.

Lasko, N. B., Gurvits, T. V., Kuhne, A. A., Orr, S. P., & Pitman, R. K. (1994). Aggression and its correlates in Vietnam veterans with and without chronic posttraumatic stress disorder. *Comprehensive Psychiatry, 35*, 373–381.

Last, C. G., Francis, G., Hersen, M., Kazdin, A. E., & Strauss, C. C. (1987). Separation anxiety and school phobia: A comparison using *DSM–III* criteria. *American Journal of Psychiatry, 144*, 653–657.

Last, C. G., Hersen, M., Kazdin, A. E., Francis, G., & Grubb, H. J. (1987). Psychiatric illness in the mothers of anxious children. *American Journal of Psychiatry, 144*, 1580–1583.

Lauritzen, P. (1987). Forgiveness: Moral prerogative or religious duty? *Journal of Religious Ethics, 15*, 141–150.

Lazare, A. (1979). Manic behavior. In A. Lazare (Ed.). *Outpatient psychiatry: Diagnosis and treatment* (pp. 261–264). Baltimore: Williams and Wilkins.

Leckman, J. F., Grice, D. E., Boardman, J., Zhang, H., Vitale, A., Bondi, C., Alsobrook, J., Peterson, B. S., Cohen, D. J., Rasmussen, S. A., Goodman, W. K., McDougle, C. J., & Pauls, D. L. (1997). Symptoms of obsessive–compulsive disorder. *American Journal of Psychiatry, 154*, 911–917.

Leff, J. P., Fischer, M., & Bertelsen, A. C. (1976). A cross-national epidemiological study of mania. *British Journal of Psychiatry, 129*, 428–442.

Levin, A. P., & Hyler, S. E. (1986). *DSM–III* personality diagnosis in bulimia. *Comprehensive Psychiatry, 27*(1), 47–53.

Lewis, C. E., Rice, J. P., Andreason, N., Endicot, J., & Hartman, A. (1986). Clinical and familial correlates of alcoholism in men with unipolar major depression. *Alcoholism: Clinical and Experimental Research, 10*, 657–662.

Lewis, C. S. (1960). *The four loves*. New York: Harcourt Brace Jovanovich.

Lewis, M. (1980). On forgiveness. *Philosophical Quarterly, 30*, 236–245.

Linn, D., & Linn, M. (1978). *Healing life's hurts: Healing memories through the five stages of forgiveness*. New York: Paulist Press.

Lloyd, S. R. (1995). *Developing positive assertiveness*. Menlo Park, CA: Crisp Publications.

Loewen, J. A. (1970a). Four kinds of forgiveness. *Practical Anthropology, 11*, 153–168.

Loewen, J. A. (1970b). The social context of guilt and forgiveness. *Practical Anthropology, 17*, 80–96.

Loudon, J. B., Blackburn, I. M., & Ashworth, C. M. (1977). A study of the symptomatology and course of manic illness using a new scale. *Psychological Medicine, 7*, 723–729.

Luskin, F. (1998). *The effect of forgiveness training on psychosocial factors in college age adults*. Unpublished doctoral dissertation, Stanford University.

Mace, D. R. (1976). Marital intimacy and the deadly love–anger cycle. *Journal of Marriage and Family Counseling, 2*, 131–137.

MacIntyre, A. (1984). *After virtue*. Notre Dame, IN: University of Notre Dame Press.

Magee, W. J., Eaton, W. W., Wittchen, H., McGonagle, K. A., & Kessler, R. C. (1996). Agoraphobia, simple phobia, and social phobia in the national comorbidity survey. *Archives of General Psychiatry, 53*, 159–168.

Mammen, O., Shear, K., Greeno, C., Wheeler, S., & Hughes, C. (1997). Anger attacks and treatment nonadherence in a perinatal psychiatry clinic. *Psychopharmacology Bulletin, 33*, 105–108.

Mammen, O., Shear, K., Jennings, K., & Popper, S. (1997). Case study: Egodystonic anger attacks in mothers of young children. *Journal of the American Academy of Child and Adolescent Psychiatry, 36*, 1374–1377.

Mammen, O., Shear, K., Pilkonis, P., Kolko, D., Thase, M., & Greeno, C. (1999). Anger attacks: Correlates and significance of an underrecognized symptom. *Journal of Clinical Psychiatry, 60*(9), 633–642.

Mannuzza, S., Klein, R. G., Konig, P. H., & Giampino, T. L. (1989). Hyperactive boys almost grown up: IV. Criminality and its relationship to psychiatric status. *Archives of General Psychiatry, 46*, 1073–1079.

March, J. S., Biederman, J., Wolkow, R., Safferman, A., Mardekian, J., Cook, E. H., Cutler, N. R., Dominguez, R., Ferguson, J., Muller, B., Riesenberg, R., Rosenthal, M., Sallee, F. R., & Wagner, K. D. (1998). Sertraline in children and adolescents with obsessive–compulsive disorder. *Journal of the American Medical Association, 280*, 1752–1758.

March, J. S., & Leonard, H. (1996). Obsessive–compulsive disorder: A review of the past ten years. *Journal of the American Academy of Child and Adolescent Psychiatry, 35*, 1265–1273.

March, J. S., Leonard, H. L., & Swedo, S. E. (1995). Pharmacotherapy of obsessive–compulsive disorder. *Child and Adolescent Psychiatric Clinics of North America, 52*, 289–295.

March, J. S., & Mulle, K. (1998). *OCD in children and adolescents: A cognitive–behavioral treatment manual*. New York: Guilford Press.

Margolin, G. (1979). Conjoint marital therapy to enhance anger management and reduce spouse abuse. *American Journal of Family Therapy, 7*, 13–23.

Markovitz, P. J., Calabrese, J. R., Schulz, S. C., & Meltzer, H. Y. (1991). Fluoxetine in the treatment of borderline and schizotypal personality disorders. *American Journal of Psychiatry, 148*, 1064–1067.

Mauger, P. A., Freeman, T., McBride, A. G., Perry, J. E., Grove, D. C., & McKinney, K. E. (1992). The measurement of forgiveness: Preliminary research. *Journal of Psychology and Christianity, 11*, 170–180.

McCann, J. T., & Biaggio, M. K. (1989). Narcissistic personality features and self-reported anger. *Psychological Reports, 64*, 55–58.

McCormick, I. A., Hahn, M., Walkey, F. H. (1984). Reliability and normative data for the simple Rathus Assertiveness Schedule. *New Zealand Journal of Psychology, 13*, 69–70.

McCullough, M. E. (1995). Forgiveness as altruism: A social–psychological theory of interpersonal forgiveness and tests of its validity (Doctoral dissertation, Virginia Commonwealth University, Richmond, 1995). *Dissertation Abstracts International B, 56*(09), 5224.

McCullough, M. E., & Worthington, E. L., Jr. (1994). Encouraging clients to forgive people who have hurt them: Review, critique, and research prospectus. *Journal of Psychology and Theology, 22*, 3–20.

McCullough, M. E., & Worthington, E. L., Jr. (1995). Promoting forgiveness: The comparison of two brief psychoeducational interventions with a waiting-list control. *Counseling and Values, 40*, 55–68.

McCullough, M. E., Worthington, E. L., & Rachal, K. C. (1997). Interpersonal forgiving in close relationships. *Journal of Personality and Social Psychology, 73*, 321–336.

McElroy, S. L., Hudson, J. I., Pope, H. G., Keck, P. E., & Aizley, H. G. (1992). DSM–III–R impulse control disorders not elsewhere classified: Clinical characteristics in relationship to other psychiatric disorders. *American Journal of Psychiatry, 149*, 318–327.

McElroy, S. L., Soutullo, C. A., Beckman, D. A., Taylor, P., & Keck, P. (1998). DSM–IV intermittent explosive disorder: A report of 27 cases. *Journal of Clinical Psychiatry, 59*, 203–210.

McElroy, S. L., Strakowski, S., West, S., Keck, P., & McConville, B. (1997). Phenomenology of adolescent and adult mania in hospitalized clients with bipolar disorder. *American Journal of Psychiatry, 154*, 44–49.

McFarland, R. (1992). *Coping through assertiveness.* New York: Rosen Publishing Group.

McGary, H. (1989). Forgiveness. *American Philosophical Quarterly, 26*, 343–351.

McGee, R., & Williams, S. (1988). A longitudinal study of depression in nine-year-old children. *Journal of the American Academy of Child and Adolescent Psychiatry, 27*, 342–348.

McKeon, R. (Ed.). (1947). *Introduction to Aristotle.* New York: Random House.

Milberger, S., Biederman, J., Faraone, S. V., Murphy, J., & Tsuang, M. T. (1995). Attention deficit hyperactivity disorder and comorbid disorders: Issues of overlapping symptoms. *American Journal of Psychiatry, 152*, 1793–1799.

Miller, M. M., & Potter-Efron, R. T. (1989). Aggression and violence associated with substance abuse. *Journal of Chemical Dependency Treatment, 3*, 1–36.

Millon, T. (1996). *Disorders of personality: DSM–IV and beyond* (2nd ed.). New York: Wiley.

Mitchell, J. E., Hatsukami, D., Eckert, E. D., & Pyle, R. L. (1985). Characteristics of 275 patients with bulimia. *American Journal of Psychiatry, 142*, 482–485.

Moffitt, T. E. (1993). Adolescence-limited and life-course-persistent antisocial behavior: A developmental taxonomy. *Psychological Review, 100*, 674–701.

Montfort, J. C. (1995). The difficult elderly patient: Curable hostile depression or personality disorder? *International Psychogeriatrics, 7*, 95–111.

Morand, P., Thomas, G., Bungener, C., Ferreri, M., & Jouvent, R. (1998). Fava's Anger Attacks Questionnaire: Evaluation of the French version in depressed patients. *Journal of European Psychiatry, 13*, 41–45.

Murphy, D. L., & Beigel, A. (1974). Depression, elation, and lithium carbonate responses in manic patient subgroups. *Archives of General Psychiatry, 31*, 643–648.

Murphy, J. G. (1982). Forgiveness and resentment. *Midwest Studies in Philosophy, 7*, 503–516.

Murphy, J. G., & Hampton, J. (1988). *Forgiveness and mercy.* Cambridge, England: Cambridge University Press.

Neblett, W. R. (1974). Forgiveness and ideals. *Mind, 83*, 269–275.

Nelson, M. K. (1992). A new theory of forgiveness (Doctoral dissertation, Purdue University, 1992). *Dissertation Abstracts International B, 53*(08), 4381.

Newman, L. E. (1987). The quality of mercy: On the duty to forgive in the Judaic tradition. *Journal of Religious Ethics, 15*, 141–150.

Nietzsche, F. W. (1887). *The genealogy of morals* (P. Watson, Trans.). London: S.P.C.K.

North, J. (1987). Wrongdoing and forgiveness. *Philosophy, 62*, 499–508.

Nousse, V. E. (1997). *Forgiveness as related to post-abortion healing.* Unpublished master's thesis, University of Wisconsin, Madison.

Novaco, R. (1976). The functions and regulation of the arousal of anger. *American Journal of Psychiatry, 133*, 1124–1128.

Offord, D. R., Boyle, M. H., & Racine, Y. A. (1991). The epidemiology of antisocial behavior. In D. J. Pepler & K. H. Rubin (Eds.), *The development and treatment of childhood aggression* (pp. 9–23). Hillsdale, NJ: Erlbaum.

Oldham, J. M., Skodol, A. E., Kellman, H. D., Hyler, S. E., Doidge, N., Rosnick, L., & Gallagher, P. E. (1995). Comorbidity of Axis I and Axis II disorders. *American Journal of Psychiatry, 152*, 571–578.

O'Shaughnessy, R. J. (1967). Forgiveness. *Philosophy, 42*, 336–352.

Outka, G. (1972). *Agape: An ethical analysis.* New Haven, CT: Yale University Press.

Overall, J. E., Goldstein, B. J., & Brauzer, B. (1971). Symptomatic volunteers in psychiatric research. *Journal of Psychiatric Research, 9*, 31–43.

Overall, J. E., Hollister, L. E., Johnson, M., & Pennington, V. (1966). Nosology of depression and differential response to drugs. *Journal of the American Medical Association, 195,* 162–164.

Pan, H., Neidig, P., & O'Leary, D. (1994). Predicting mild and severe husband to wife physical aggression. *Journal of Consulting and Clinical Psychology, 62,* 975–981.

Park, Y., & Enright, R. D. (1997). The development of forgiveness in the context of adolescent friendship conflict in Korea. *Journal of Adolescence, 20,* 393–402.

Patton, J. (1985). *Is human forgiveness possible?* Nashville, TN: Abingdon.

Perry, J. C., Banon, E., & Ianni, F. (1999). Effectiveness of psychotherapy for personality disorders. *American Journal of Psychiatry, 156,* 1312–1321.

Peterson, B. S. (1996). Considerations of natural history and pathophysiology in the psychopharmacology of Tourette's syndrome. *Journal of Clinical Psychiatry, 57* (Suppl. 9), 24–34.

Piaget, J. (1932). *The moral judgement of the child.* New York: Free Press.

Piaget, J. (1952). *The child's conception of number.* New York: Humanities.

Pickens, R., Hatsukami, D., Spizer, J., & Suikis, D. (1985). Relapse by alcohol abusers. *Alcoholism: Clinical and Experimental Research, 9,* 244–247.

Pilowsky, D. J., Wu, L., & Anthony, J. C. (1999). Panic attacks and suicide attempts in mid-adolescence. *American Journal of Psychiatry, 156,* 1545–1549.

Pitt, B. (1968). "Atypical" depression following childbirth. *British Journal of Psychiatry, 122,* 1325–1335.

Poloma, M. M., & Gallup, G. H., Jr. (1991). *Varieties of prayer: A survey report.* Philadelphia: Trinity Press International.

Potter-Efron, P. S., & Potter-Efron, R. T. (1991a). Anger as a treatment concern with alcoholics and affected family members. *Alcoholism Treatment Quarterly, 8*(3), 31–46.

Potter-Efron, R. T., & Potter-Efron, P. S. (1991b). *Anger and alcoholism.* New York: Norton.

Potvin, L., Lasker, J., & Toedter, L. (1989). Measuring grief: A short version of the Perinatal Grief Scale. *Journal of Psychopathology and Behavioral Assessment, 11,* 29–45.

Powell, J. E., & Taylor, D. (1992). Anger, depression and anxiety following heroin withdrawal. *International Journal of Addictions, 27*(1), 25–35.

Prabhupāda, A. C. (1984). *Bhagavad-Gita as it is.* Los Angeles: Bhaktivedanta Book Trust.

Prager, D. (1997, December 15). The sin of forgiveness. *Wall Street Journal,* editorial page.

Prien, R. F., Himmelhoch, J. M., & Kupfer, D. J. (1988). Treatment of mixed mania. *Journal of Affective Disorders, 15,* 9–15.

Primeau, F., & Fontaine, R. (1987). Obsessive disorder with self-mutilation: A subgroup responsive to pharmacotherapy. *Canadian Journal of Psychiatry, 32,* 699–700.

Pugh, R. (1983). An association between hostility and poor adherence to treatment in patients suffering from depression. *British Journal of Medical Psychology*, *56*, 205–208.

Rasmussen, S. A., & Eisen, J. L. (1994). The epidemiology and differential diagnosis of obsessive–compulsive disorder. *Journal of Clinical Psychiatry*, *55*(Suppl.), 5–10.

Rasmussen, S. A., & Eisen, J. L. (1997). Treatment strategies for chronic and refractory obsessive–compulsive disorder. *Journal of Clinical Psychiatry*, *58*(Suppl.), 9–13.

Reason, P. (Ed.). (1988). *Human inquiry in action: Developments in new paradigm research*. Beverly Hills, CA: Sage.

Rebert, W. M., Stanton, A. L., & Schwarz, R. M. (1991). Influence of personality attributes and daily moods on bulimic eating patterns. *Addictive Behavior*, *16*, 497–505.

Reed, G. (1998). *Forgiveness as a function of moral agency in the context of infidelity and divorce*. Unpublished master's thesis, University of Wisconsin–Madison.

Reed, G., Ashleman, K., Nousse, V., Hansen, M., Marks, N., & Enright, R. (1999). *Forgiveness and families: Four correlational studies*. Paper presented at the meeting of the Association for Moral Education, Minneapolis, MN, November.

Regier, D. A., Boyd, J. H., & Burke, J. D., Jr. (1988). One month prevalence of mental disorders in the United States. *Archives of General Psychiatry*, *45*, 977–985.

Regier, D. M., Framer, M., Rae, D., Locke, B. Z., Keith, S. J., Judd, J. L., & Goodwin, F. K. (1990). Comorbidity of mental disorders with alcohol and other drug abuse: Results from the Epidemiologic Catchment Area (ECA) study. *Journal of the American Medical Association*, *264*, 2511–2518.

Reich, J. H., & Green, A. I. (1990). Effect of personality disorders on outcome of treatment. *Journal of Nervous and Mental Disorders*, *178*, 592–600.

Reich, J. H., & Vasile, R. G. (1993). Effect of personality disorders on the treatment outcome of Axis I conditions: An update. *Journal of Nervous and Mental Disorders*, *181*, 475–484.

Reilly, P. M., Clark, W. H., Shopshire, M. D., Lewis, E. W., & Sorensen, D. J. (1994). Anger management and temper control: Critical components of posttraumatic stress disorder and substance abuse treatment. *Journal of Psychoactive Drugs*, *26*, 401–407.

Rest, J. (1986). *Moral development: Advances in theory and research*. New York: Praeger.

Richards, N. (1988). Forgiveness. *Ethics*, *99*, 77–97.

Rigby, K., & Slee, P. (1991). Bullying among Australian school children: Reported behavior and attitudes toward victims. *Journal of Social Psychology*, *131*, 615–627.

Rigby, K., & Slee, P. (1999). Suicidal ideation among adolescent school children, involvement in bully-victim problems, and perceived social support. *Suicide and Life Threatening Behavior, 29,* 119–130.

Riley, W. T., Treiber, F. A., & Woods, M. G. (1989). Anger and hostility in depression. *Journal of Nervous and Mental Disorders, 177,* 668–674.

Roberts, H. R. (1971). Mercy. *Philosophy, 36,* 352–353.

Robins, L. (1978). Sturdy childhood predictors of adult antisocial behaviour: Replications from longitudinal studies. *Psychological Medicine, 8,* 611–622.

Robins, L., & McEvoy, L. (1990). Conduct problems as predictors of substance abuse. In L. Robins & M. Rutter (Eds.), *Straight and devious pathways from childhood to adulthood* (pp. 182–204). Cambridge, England: Cambridge University Press.

Robins, L. N. (1981). Epidemiological approaches to natural history research: Antisocial disorders in children. *Journal of the American Academy of Child Psychiatry, 20,* 566–680.

Rogers, C. R. (1951). *Client-centered therapy.* New York: Houghton Mifflin.

Rounsaville, B. J., Kranzler, H. R., Ball, S., Tennen, H., Poling, J., & Triffleman, E. (1998). Personality disorders in substance abusers: Relation to substance abuse. *Journal of Nervous Mental Disorders, 186,* 78–95.

Rounsaville, B. J., Weissman, M. M., Crits-Christoph, K., Wilber, C., & Kleber, H. (1982). Diagnosis and symptoms of depression in opiate addicts. *Archives of General Psychiatry, 39,* 151–156.

Ryan, N. D., Puig-Antich, J., Ambrosini, P., Rabinovich, H., Robinson, D., Nelson, B., Iyengar, S., & Twoney, J. (1987). The clinical picture of major depression in children and adolescents. *Archives of General Psychiatry, 44,* 854–861.

Rye, M. S. (1997). *Evaluation of a secular and a religiously-integrated forgiveness group therapy program for college students who have been wronged by a romantic partner.* Unpublished doctoral dissertation, Bowling Green State University.

Sabini, I., & Silver, M. (1987). Emotions, responsibility, and character. In F. Schoeman (Ed.), *Responsibility, character, and the emotions* (pp. 165–175). Cambridge, England: Cambridge University Press.

Safer, J. (1999). *Forgiving and not forgiving.* New York: Avon Books.

Salzman, C., Wolfson, A. N., Schatzberg, A., Looper, J., Henke, R., Albanese, M., Schwartz, J., & Miyawaki, E. (1995). Effect of fluoxetine on anger in symptomatic volunteers with borderline personality disorder. *Journal of Clinical Psychopharmacology, 15,* 23–29.

Sarinopoulos, I. (1996). *Forgiveness in adolescence and middle adulthood: Comparing the Enright Forgiveness Inventory with the Wade Forgiveness Scale.* Unpublished master's thesis, University of Wisconsin–Madison.

Satir, V. (1988). *The new peoplemaking.* Mountain View, CA: Science and Behavior Books.

Satterfield, J. H., Hoppe, C. M., & Schhell, A. M. (1982). A prospective study of delinquency in 110 adolescent boys with attention deficit disorder and 88 normal adolescent boys. *American Journal of Psychiatry, 139,* 795–798.

Scahill, L., Schwab-Stone, M., Merikangas, K. R., Leckman, J. F., Zhang, H., & Kasi, S. (1999). Psychosocial and clinical correlates of ADHD in a community sample of school-age children. *Journal of the American Academy of Child and Adolescent Psychiatry, 38,* 976–984.

Schlosser, S., Black, D. W., Blum, N., & Goldstein, R. B. (1994). The demography, phenomenology, and family history of 22 persons with compulsive hair pulling. *Annals of Clinical Psychiatry, 6,* 147–152.

Schuckit, M. A. (1986). Genetic and clinical implications of alcoholism and affective disorder. *American Journal of Psychiatry, 143,* 140–147.

Schutz, W. C. (1958). *FIRO: A three-dimensional theory of interpersonal behavior.* New York: Reinhart.

Shapiro, D. S. (1978). The doctrine of the image of God and imitatio Dei. In M. M. Kellner (Ed.), *Contemporary Jewish ethics* (pp. 127–151). New York: Sanhedrin Press.

Shear, M. K., Cooper, A. M., Klerman, G. L., Busch, F. N., & Shapiro, T. (1993). A psychodynamic model of panic disorder. *American Journal of Psychiatry, 150,* 859–866.

Sherman, N. (1990). The place of emotions in Kantian morality. In O. Flanagan & A. O. Rorty (Eds.), *Identity, character, and morality: Essays in moral psychology* (pp. 140–170). Cambridge, MA: MIT Press.

Shriver, D. W. (1995). *An ethic for enemies: Forgiveness in politics.* Oxford, England: Oxford University Press.

Siegal, J. M. (1986). The multidimensional anger inventory. *Journal of Personality and Social Psychology, 51,* 191–200.

Simon, Y. (1986). *The definition of moral virtue.* New York: Fordham University Press.

Simonds, J., McMahon, T., & Armstrong, D. (1991). Youth suicide attempters compared with a control group: Psychological, affective and attitudinal variables. *Suicide and Life Threatening Behavior, 221,* 134–151.

Singer, H., & Walkup, J. (1991). Tourette syndrome and other tic disorders: Diagnosis, pathophysiology, and treatment [Review]. *Medicine, 70,* 15.

Slater, E. J., & Calhoun, K. S. (1988). Familial conflict and marital dissolution. *Journal of Social and Clinical Psychology, 6,* 118–126.

Smart, A. (1968). Mercy. *Philosophy, 43,* 345–359.

Smedes, L. B. (1984). *Forgive and forget: Healing the hurts we don't deserve.* San Francisco: Harper & Row.

Smedes, L. B. (1996). *The art of forgiving: When you need to forgive and don't know how.* Nashville, TN: Moorings.

Smith, C., & Nylund, D. (Eds.). (1997). *Narrative therapies with children and adolescents.* New York: Guilford Press.

Smith, M. (1981). The psychology of forgiveness. *The Month, 14,* 301–307.

Snaith, R. P., & Taylor, C. M. (1985). Irritability: Definition, assessment and associated factors. *British Journal of Psychiatry, 14,* 127–136.

Snyder, J. (1994). *National report on juvenile offending and victimization.* Washington, DC: American Psychiatric Press.

Snyder, S., & Pitt, W. M. (1985). Characterizing anger in the *DSM–III* borderline personality disorder. *Acta Psychiatrica Scandinavica, 72,* 464–469.

Spalt, L. (1980). Hysteria and antisocial personality: A single disorder. *Journal of Nervous and Mental Disorders, 168,* 456–494.

Specker, S. M., Carlson, G. A., Christenson, G. A., & Marcotte, M. (1995). Impulse control disorders and attention deficit disorder in pathological gamblers. *Annals of Clinical Psychiatry, 7,* 175–179.

Spielberger, C. D., Gorsuch, R. L., Lushene, R., Vagg, P. R., & Jacobs, G. A. (1983). *State–Trait Anxiety Inventory (Form Y): Self evaluation questionnaire.* Palo Alto, CA: Consulting Psychologists Press.

Spielberger, C. D., Jacobs, G., Russell, S., & Crane, R. (1983). Assessment of anger: The State–Trait Anger Scale. In J. N. Butcher, & C. D. Spielberger (Eds.), *Advances in personality assessment* (Vol. 2, pp. 161–189). Hillsdale, NJ: Erlbaum.

Starcevic, V., Uhlenhuth, E. H., Kellner, R., & Pathak, D. (1993). Comparison of primary and secondary panic disorder: A preliminary report. *Journal of Affective Disorders, 27,* 81–86.

Stasiek, C., & Zetin, M. (1985). Organic manic disorders. *Psychosomatics, 26,* 394–402.

Stein, D., Apter, A., Ratzoni, G., Har-Even, D., & Avidan, G. (1998). Association between multiple suicide attempts and negative affects in adolescents. *Journal of the American Academy of Child and Adolescent Psychiatry, 37,* 488–494.

Stinson, F. S., & DeBakey, S. (1992). Alcohol-related morality in the United States, (1979–1988). *British Journal of Addictions, 87,* 232–240.

Straus, M. (1974). Leveling, civility, and violence in the family. *Journal of Marriage and Family, 36,* 13–29.

Strause, M. A., Gelles, R. J., & Steinmetz, S. K. (1980). *Behind closed doors.* Garden City, NY: Anchor/Doubleday.

Subkoviak, M. J., Enright, R. D., Wu, C., Gassin, E., Freedman, S., Olson, L., & Sarinopoulos, I. (1992, April). *Measuring interpersonal forgiveness.* Paper presented at the annual meeting of the American Educational Research Association, San Francisco.

Subkoviak, M. J., Enright, R. D., Wu, C., Gassin, E. A., Freedman, S., Olson, L. M., & Sarinopoulos, I. (1995). Measuring interpersonal forgiveness in late adolescence and middle adulthood. *Journal of Adolescence, 18,* 641–655.

Sugawara, M., Toda, M. A., Shima, S., Mukai, T., Sakakura, K., & Kitamura, T. (1997). Premenstrual mood changes and maternal mental health in pregnancy and the postpartum period. *Journal of Clinical Psychology, 53,* 225–232.

Szatmari, P., Offord, D. R., & Boyle, M. H. (1989). Ontario Child Health Study: Prevalence of attention deficit disorder with hyperactivity. *Journal of Child Psychology and Psychiatry, 30*, 219–230.

Tachibana, S. (1926). *The ethics of Buddhism*. London: Oxford University Press.

Tavris, C. (1984). *Anger: The misunderstood emotion*. New York: Simon & Schuster.

Tavris, C. (1989). *Anger: The misunderstood emotion* (Rev. ed.). New York: Touchstone.

Taylor, M. A., & Abrams, R. (1973). The phenomenology of mania: A new look at some old patients. *Archives of General Psychiatry, 29*, 520–522.

Taylor, M. A., & Abrams, R. (1977). Catatonia: Prevalence and importance in the manic phase of manic-depressive illness. *Archives of General Psychiatry, 34*, 1223–1225.

Tedlow, J. R., Leslike, V. C., Keefe, B. R., Nierenberg, A. A., Rosenbaum, J. F., & Fava, M. (1997, May). *Are anger attacks in unipolar depression a variant of panic disorder?* Paper presented at the 150th Annual Meeting of the American Psychiatric Association, San Diego, CA.

Ten Boom, C., Sherrill, J., & Sherrill, E. (1971). *The hiding place*. Old Tappan, NJ: Fleming H. Revell.

Thompson, K. M., Wonderlich, S. A., Crosby, R. D., & Mitchell, J. E. (1999). The neglected link between eating disturbances and aggressive behavior in girls. *Journal of the American Academy of Child and Adolescent Psychiatry, 38*, 1277–1284.

Tivis, L. J., Parsons, O. A., & Nixon, S. J. (1998). Anger in an inpatient treatment sample of chronic alcoholics. *Alcoholism: Clinical and Experimental Research, 22*, 902–907.

Trainer, M. F. (1984). Forgiveness: Intrinsic, role-expected, expedient, in the context of divorce (Doctoral dissertation, Boston University, 1981). *Dissertation Abstracts International B, 45*(04), 1325.

Twambley, P. (1976). Mercy and forgiveness. *Analysis, 36*, 84–90.

Valgum, S., & Valgum, P. (1985). Borderline and other mental disorders in female alcoholic psychiatric patients. *Psychopathology, 18*, 50–60.

Velez, C. N., Johnson, J., & Cohen, P. (1989). A longitudinal analysis of selected risk factors for childhood psychopathology. *Journal of the American Academy of Child and Adolescent Psychiatry, 28*, 861–864.

Vine, W. E. (1985). *An expository dictionary of biblical words*. Nashville, TN: Thomas Nelson.

von Knorring, L., von Knorring, A. L., Smigan, L., Lindberg, U., & Edholm, M. (1987). Personality traits in subtypes of alcoholics. *Journal of Studies on Alcoholism, 48*, 521–527.

Wade, S. H. (1990). The development of a scale to measure forgiveness (Doctoral dissertation, Fuller Theological Seminary, School of Psychology, 1989). *Dissertation Abstracts International B, 50*(11), 5338.

Walfish, S., Messey, R., & Krone, A. (1990). Anxiety and anger among abusers of different substances. *Drug and Alcohol Dependence, 25*, 253–256.

Wallerstein, J. (1983). Children of divorce: The psychological tasks of the child. *American Journal of Orthopsychiatry, 53,* 230–243.

Wallerstein, J. (1985). Children of divorce: Preliminary report of a ten-year follow-up of older children and adolescents. *Journal of the American Academy of Child Psychiatry, 24,* 545–553.

Wallerstein, J. (1991). The long-term effects of divorce on children: A review. *Journal of the American Academy of Child and Adolescent Psychiatry, 30,* 349–360.

Wallerstein, J., & Blakeslee, S. (1989). *Second chances.* New York: Ticknor & Fields.

Wallerstein, J., & Blakeslee, S. (1996). *Second chances* (2nd ed.). New York: Houghton Mifflin.

Walrond-Skinner, S. (1998). The function and role of forgiveness in working with couples and families clearing the ground. *Journal of Family Therapy, 20,* 3–20.

Wampold, B. E., Mondon, G. W., Moody, M., Stich, F., Benson, K., & Ahu, H. (1997). A meta-analysis of outcome studies comparing bona fide psychotherapies, "all must have prizes." *Psychological Bulletin, 122,* 203–215.

Wand, R., Matazow, G., & Shady, G. (1993). Tourette syndrome: Associated behaviors and most disabling features. *Neuroscience and Biobehavioral Reviews, 17,* 217–275.

Washton, A. M. (Ed.). (1995). *Psychotherapy and substance abuse.* New York: Guilford Press.

Webster's new collegiate dictionary. (1979). Springfield, MA: Merriam.

Weil, B. E., & Winter, R. (1994). *Adultery, the forgivable sin.* Mamaroneck, NY: Hastings House.

Weinberg, W. A., & Brumback, R. A. (1976). Mania in childhood. *American Journal of Diseases of Children, 130,* 380–385.

Weiss, G., Milroy, T., & Perlman, T. (1985). Psychiatric status of hyperactives as adults: A controlled prospective 15-year follow-up of 63 hyperactive children. *Journal of the American Academy of Child Psychiatry, 24,* 211–220.

Weissman, M., Fox, K., & Klerman, G. L. (1973). Hostility and depression associated with suicide attempts. *American Journal of Psychiatry, 130,* 450–455.

Weissman, M. M., Wolk, S., Wickramaratne, P., Goldstein, R. B., Adams, P., Greenwald, S., Ryan, N. D., Dahl, R. E., & Steinberg, D. (1999). Children with prepubertal-onset major depressive disorder and anxiety grown up. *Archives of General Psychiatry, 56,* 794–801.

Wicki, W., & Angst, J. (1991). The Zurich study. X. Hypomania in a 28- to 30-year-old cohort. *European Archives of Psychiatry and Clinical Neuroscience, 240,* 339–348.

Williams, B. (1973). *Problems of the self.* Cambridge, England: Cambridge University Press.

Williams, J. A. (Ed.). (1961). *Islam.* New York: Braziller.

Wilson, H. P. (1994). Forgiveness and survivors of sexual abuse: Relationships among forgiveness of the perpetrator, spiritual well-being, depression, and anxiety. *Dissertation Abstracts International, 55* (03), 616.

Winokur, G., Clayton, P. J., & Reich, T. (1969). *Manic depressive illness*. St. Louis: CV Mosby.

Winokur, G., & Tsuang, M. T. (1975). Elation versus irritability in mania. *Comprehensive Psychiatry, 16*, 435–436.

Wisner, K. L., Peindl, K. S., Gigliotti, T., & Hanusa, B. H. (1999). Obsessions and compulsions in women with postpartum depression. *Journal of Clinical Psychiatry, 60*, 176–180.

Wolberg, A. R. (1973). *The borderline client*. New York: Intercontinental Medical Book.

Wolraich, M. L., Hannah, J. N., Pinnock, T. Y., Baumgaertel, A., & Brown, J. (1996). Comparison of diagnostic criteria for attention deficit hyperactivity disorder in a country-wide sample. *Journal of the American Academy of Child and Adolescent Psychiatry, 35*, 319–324.

Wolter, D. L. (1989). *Forgiving our parents: For adult children from dysfunctional families*. Minneapolis, MN: CompCare.

Wonderlich, S. A., Swift, W. J., Slotnick, H. B., & Goodman, S. (1990). DSM–III–R personality disorders in eating-disorder subtypes. *International Journal of Eating Disorders, 9*, 607–616.

Woody, G. E., O'Brien, C. P., & Rickels, K. (1983). Depression and anxiety in heroin addicts: A placebo controlled study of doxepin in combination with methadone. *American Journal of Psychiatry, 40*, 649–653.

Worthington, E. (1998). An empathy–humility–commitment model of forgiveness applied within family dyads. *Journal of Family Therapy, 20*, 59–76.

Worthington, E., & DiBlasio, F. (1990). Promoting mutual forgiveness within the fractured relationship. *Psychotherapy, 27*, 219–223.

Wozniak, J., Biederman, J., Kiely, K., Ablon, J. S., Faraone, S. V., Mundy, E., & Mennin, D. (1995). Mania-like symptoms suggestive of childhood onset bipolar disorder in clinically referred children. *Journal of the American Academy of Child and Adolescent Psychiatry, 34*, 867–876.

Yandell, K. (1998). The metaphysics and morality of forgiveness. In R. D. Enright & J. North (Eds.), *Exploring forgiveness* (pp. 35–45). Madison: University of Wisconsin Press.

Zanarini, M. C., Frankenburg, F. R., Dubo, E. D., Sickel, A. E., Trikha, A., Levin, A., & Reynolds, V. (1998). Axis I comorbidity of borderline personality disorder. *American Journal of Psychiatry, 155*, 1733–1739.

Zanarini, M. C., Gunderson, J. G., Marino, M. F., Schwartz, E. O., & Frankenburg, F. R. (1989). Childhood experiences of borderline clients. *Comprehensive Psychiatry, 30*(1), 18–25.

Zanarini, M. C., Williams, A. A., Lewis, R. E., Reich, R. B., Vera, S. C., Marino, M. F., Levin, A., Yong, L., & Frankenburg, F. R. (1997). Reported childhood experiences associated with the development of borderline personality disorder. *American Journal of Psychiatry, 154*, 1101–1106.

AUTHOR INDEX

MacIntyre, A., 253
Magee, W. J., 148
Magen, J., 182
Maier, G. J., 249
Maloney, M. J., 216
Mammen, O., 8, 117, 131
Mannuza, S., 174
Mannuzza, S., 174
March, J. S., 184
Marcotte, M., 232
Marcus, R. N., 216
Margolin, G., 194
Marino, M. F., 245
Markovitz, P. J., 240
Marlatt, G. A., 156, 157
Marrs, A., 183
Martin, D., 174
Martin, M. W., 66
Matazow, G., 234
Mauger, P. A., 319, 320
Mays, W., 216
McCann, J. T., 243
McClough, J. F., 216
McConville, B., 227
McCormick, I. A., 137
McCullough, M. E., 43, 288–292, 303
McElroy, S. L., 227, 231, 233, 236
McEvoy, L., 166
McFarland, R., 194
McGary, H., 47, 48, 303
McGee, R., 115, 173
McGinnis, C., 3
McGonagle, K. A., 148
McKeon, R., 31
McMahon, T., 115
Meltzer, H. Y., 240
Mendelsohn, S., 115
Mendelson, M., 90
Merry, J., 216
Messey, R., 156
Mick, E., 114
Milberger, S., 174
Miller, M. D., 115
Miller, M. M., 156
Millon, T., 240, 242
Milroy, T., 174
Milton, K., 292
Minichiello, W. E., 150
Mitchell, J. E., 216, 217
Mock, J., 90
Moffitt, T. E., 177

Montfort, J. C., 114
Moore, P., 183
Moore, S. D., 136
Morand, P., 114, 116
Morino, J. K., 216
Mulle, K., 184
Mullet, E., 63, 283, 284
Munari, F., 114
Murphy, D., 226, 227
Murphy, J., 174
Murphy, J. G., 34, 39, 258, 269

Neblett, W. R., 68
Neiding, P., 195
Nelson, M. K., 32
Newcorn, J., 174
Newman, L. E., 35, 259
Newman, S. C., 232
Nezu, C. M., 174
Nietzsche, F. W., 268, 270
Nixon, S. J., 156
North, J., 24, 31, 68, 76, 261, 262, 273
Novaco, R. W., 123, 136, 152
Novoca, R., 123
Nugent, S. M., 174
Nutt, D. J., 145
Nylund, D., 326

O'Brien, C. P., 161
Ofek, H., 115
Offord, D. R., 173, 174
O'Grady, J., 115
Oldham, J. M., 240
O'Leary, D., 195
Olson, M. E., 235
Orn, H., 232
Orr, S. P., 136
Osborn, M., 115
O'Shaughnessy, M., 217
O'Shaughnessy, R. J., 40, 258, 269
Outka, G., 31
Overall, J. E., 114, 119
Owen, P., 217

Pan, H., 195
Park, K. S., 235
Park, Y., 281
Parsons, O. A., 156
Pathak, D., 136
Patton, J., 68, 71
Paulauskas, S. L., 114, 181

Williams, B., 264
Williams, J. A., 259
Williams, S., 115, 173
Winokur, G., 114, 226
Winter, R., 3
Wisner, K. L., 131, 149
Wittchen, H., 148
Wolberg, A. R., 245
Wolraich, M. L., 174
Wolter, D. L., 3
Wonderlich, S. A., 216, 241
Woods, M. G., 114
Woody, G. E., 160

Worthington, E. L., Jr., 43, 49, 194, 288–290
Wozniak, J., 227
Wu, C., 54
Wu, L., 183

Yandell, K., 7, 77, 80, 81, 87, 261, 262, 272
Yates, E., 115
Yeh, C. J., 216
Yergelun-Todd, D., 216
Young, J., 279

Zanarini, M. C., 216, 241, 245, 246

SUBJECT INDEX

Apology, need for, 258
Aretaic judgment, 256
Aristotle, 31, 253, 265
Attention deficit hyperactivity disorder
  (ADHD), 173–177
  and bipolar disorders, 227
  checklist for identifying, 191–192
  as future focus area, 328–329
  and obsessive—compulsive disorder,
    184
  obstacles to treatment of, 180
  and Tourette's syndrome, 235
Attitude Toward Mother/Father Scale, 94
Avoidant personality disorder, 240, 241,
  244–245

Beck Depression Inventory, 90, 99, 115
Beneficence, 30, 84–85, 263–264
Bhagavad Gita, 259
Bipolar disorders, 225–231
  forgiveness in clients with, 229–231
  origins of anger in, 228–229
Borderline personality disorder (BPD),
  236, 240, 241, 243, 245–249
BPD. See Borderline personality disorder
Brief forgiveness therapy, 287–304, 302–
  303
Buddhism, 259
Bulimia nervosa, 216–219, 222–223
Bullying
  and adjustment disorder, 185–186
  and anorexia, 219
  and panic disorder, 147
  and social phobia, 162
  and substance abuse disorder, 162
Burns Depression Checklist, 318

Case examples
  adjustment disorder, 186
  adopted child, anger in, 188–189
  angry spouse, 204–207
  attention deficit hyperactivity disor-
    der, 174–177
  bipolar disorder, 229–231
  borderline personality disorder, 247–
    249
  conduct disorders, 177–179
  controlling spouse, 201–204
  decision to use forgiveness therapy,
    13–14

defenses, examination of psychological, 69–70
divorce, anxiety disorder in adult
  children of, 143–144
eating disorders, 221–223
emotionally distant spouse, 197–200
family conflicts, anxiety disorder resulting from, 141–143
major depressive episode, 127–129
major recurrent depression, 129–130
narcissistic spouse, 210
obsessive—compulsive disorder,
  150–152, 184–185
oppositional defiant disorder, 179
panic disorder, 145–148, 183
postpartum depression, 131–132
posttraumatic stress disorder, 152–
  154
process model of forgiveness therapy,
  20–22
separation and divorce anger, 213
separation anxiety disorder, 181–182
sexual abuse, depression in victim
  of, 125–127
social phobia, 148–149
stepchild, anger in, 186–187
substance abuse disorders, people
  with, 161–166
work conflicts, anxiety disorder resulting from, 140–141
Catholicism, 35
CD. See Conduct disorder
Charity, 255
Child forgiveness, 204
Children, 169–189. See also Adolescents
  adjustment disorder in, 185–186
  adopted, 187–189
  antisocial behavior in, 115
  attention deficit hyperactivity disor-
    der in, 173–177
  with bipolar disorder, 227
  bullying of, 185–186
  conduct disorders in, 177–179
  denial in, 170–171
  divorce, adult children of, 143–144
  inner-city 5th graders, intervention
    with, 299–302
  learning about forgiveness by, 172,
    329
  obsessive—compulsive disorders in,
    184–185

oppositional defiant disorder in, 179–180
origins of anger in, 172–173
panic disorder in, 182–183
passive—aggressive expression in, 171–172
personality disorders in, 241, 242
separation anxiety disorder in, 181–182
stepchildren, 186–187
Tourette's syndrome in, 234–236
Christ, 23, 31
Christianity, 23, 31, 35, 42, 58, 257–261, 263, 323
Clients, 9
Cluster A personality disorders, 242–243
Cluster B personality disorders, 243–244
Cluster C personality disorders, 244–245
Cocaine, 156
Cognitive-behavioral therapy, 5
Cognitive forgiveness, 35, 121–122, 222
Cognitive rehearsal, awareness of, 73
College students
    interventions with, 292–297
    parents, hurt by, 93–99
Colloquialisms often confused with forgiveness, 38, 50–51
Commitment, forgiveness as, 36, 78
Community right, 272
Compassion, 30–31, 81–83
Compensational forgiveness, 56–57
Conciliation, forgiveness vs., 43
Condonation, forgiveness vs., 40–41
Conduct disorder (CD), 177–179, 236
    and bipolar disorders, 227
    obstacles to treatment of, 180
Confucianism, 281
Continuum, forgiveness as, 32
Controlling spouse, 200–204
    husband, 201–203
    wife, 203–204
Coopersmith Self-Esteem Inventory, 90, 94–96, 99
Coping strategy(-ies)
    forgiveness as, 36
    recognizing ineffectiveness of previous, 76–79
Cosmic perspective, 7
Crowne—Marlowe Social Desirability Scale, 309

Dalai Lama, 259
Decision Phase (process model of forgiveness therapy), 18, 76–79
    anxiety disorders, patients with, 137–138
    depression, patients with, 118–120
    forgiveness as option, consideration of, 77–78
    ineffective coping strategies, recognition of, 76–77
    offender, commitment to forgiveness of, 78
    substance abuse disorders, people with, 159
    use of journaling/homework exercises in, 78–79
Decision to forgive, 49
Deepening Phase (process model of forgiveness therapy), 19, 85–88
    affective transformation, awareness of, 88
    anxiety disorders, patients with, 139
    depression, patients with, 124–125
    meaning, discovery of, 85–86
    new purpose, realization of, 87–88
    others' forgiveness, awareness of, 86–87
    substance abuse disorders, people with, 160
    support, awareness of, 87
    use of journaling/homework exercises in, 88
Deep forgiveness, 34
Defenses, examination of psychological, 69–71
Defining Issues Test, 279
Definitional drift, 265–266, 320
Denial, in children, 170–171
Dependent personality disorder, 240, 241
Depleted emotional energy, awareness of, 72
Depressive disorders, 113–133
    anger in, 16, 113–118
    Decision Phase in patients with, 118–120
    Deepening Phase in patients with, 124–125
    major depressive episode, 127–129
    major recurrent depression, 129–131
    postpartum depression, 131–132
    in sexual abuse, victim of, 125–127

ABOUT THE AUTHORS

Robert D. Enright, PhD, received his doctorate in educational psychology from the University of Minnesota in 1976. He is a licensed psychologist and professor of educational psychology at the University of Wisconsin, Madison, a position he has held since 1978. The author of over 80 publications, Professor Enright has specialized in the social scientific study of forgiveness since 1985. He has pioneered the study of how people forgive others who hurt them deeply and the study of psychological outcomes when people forgive. Currently, he is supervising 12 graduate students in their own studies of forgiveness. Professor Enright is the recipient of numerous awards for both his teaching and his forgiveness studies. His forgiveness work has appeared in such publications as *Time*, *McCall's*, *the Wall Street Journal*, *the Washington Post*, *the Chicago Tribune*, and *the Los Angeles Times*. He has appeared on ABC's "20/20," NBC's "Nightly News," and many other television and radio shows.

Richard P. Fitzgibbons, MD, received his medical degree from Temple University School of Medicine in 1969 and completed his training in psychiatry at the Hospital of the University of Pennsylvania and the Philadelphia Child Guidance Center in 1976. He participated in cognitive therapy research in his training with Aaron T. Beck. Currently, he is the director of a private practice outside Philadelphia. Since 1976 he has used forgiveness in psychotherapy, and in 1986 he wrote a seminal paper on the use of forgiveness. Dr. Fitzgibbons has given over 40 seminars to mental health professionals, educators, and business and church leaders on forgiveness therapy in the resolution of excessive anger. He has made numerous appearances on radio and television discussing the prevalence and treatment of excessive anger through forgiveness.